o-founded the Reuters Institute for the Study of Journalism
rsity of Oxford, where he is a Senior Research Fellow. Lloyd
several books, including *What the Media Are Doing to Our*
urnalism in an Age of Terror. He is also a contributing editor at
Times and a columnist for both Reuters.com and *La Repubblica* of

oyd has an eye for both detail and the bigger picture and his
and analysis reflect the complex and dynamic recent histories
n and politics.' Charlie Beckett, *Literary Review*

ner for those interested in questions of who decides and writes
e are permitted to read... Masterly' Santiago Gamboa, *Tribune*

l... Nuanced and compelling' Anthony Giddens, Former
ondon School of Economics

d is a master journalist with serious insights into the changing
of his field.' Graham Allison, Douglas Dillon Professor of
ent and Director, Belfer Center for Science and International

Ren
by nating and enlightening... For anyone concerned about the future
in n, freedom and information, this makes for fascinating and
by nsable reading.' Sylvie Kauffmann, Editorial Director, *Le Monde*

THE POWER AND THE STORY

The Global Battle for News and Information

John Lloyd

Atlantic Books
London

First published in Great Britain in 2017 by Atlantic Books,
an imprint of Atlantic Books Ltd.

This paperback edition first published in Great Britain in 2018
by Atlantic Books.

10 9 8 7 6 5 4 3 2 1

A CIP catalogue record for this book is available from the British
Library.

E-book ISBN: 978-1-78239-361-0
Paperback ISBN: 978-1-78239-362-7

Printed in Great Britain by
Clays Ltd, Elcograf S.p.A.

Atlantic Books
An Imprint of Atlantic Books Ltd
Ormond House
26–27 Boswell Street
London
WC1N 3JZ
www.atlantic-books.co.uk

For Jacob Fortune-Lloyd

Contents

Preface

We have understood, or misunderstood, the world beyond our immediate ken mainly through journalism for the last two centuries. The circles of those who read news and commentary widened progressively as time passed, as did the number of countries developing some form of journalism; men, and later women, became increasingly literate, and public life more and more depended on some knowledge of current events. Fact and the pursuit of truth have, in that time, been unevenly served – though it was only during that period, and in particular in the latter half of the twentieth century, when the pursuit was elevated to a public duty and trust.

Yet however serious a journalist's dedication to discovering facts, which can amount to a skeletal truth, the call of the alluring fiction is often stronger than the hard (hard to understand) fact. The creative writer and the factual journalist share the word 'story' to describe their output: the narrative form common to both invites the author to import themes from current events – and the journalist to evoke, through invention, stronger and more compelling interest and passions than the complexities of a purely factual account would allow.

The public pleasure in fantasy was always amply accommodated in the development of journalism. Before newspapers and magazines began to widen their very limited circulation in the nineteenth century, the literate elites were served, from the invention of printing, by newsletters in which gossip, invention, propaganda and fact were mixed, with the non-factual often commanding a higher market value. In mid-sixteenth-century Venice, where newsletters were early established, the Duke of Modena's representative wrote that those written by a priest, Padre Sciro, 'which everyone likes, are mostly full of lies'. Three decades later, the Turin historian Pier Giovanni Capriata wrote that newsletter writers can 'bring true disaster on themselves just to please others by the publication of falsehood [my italics]'.[1] 'Liking' lies has long been the dirty secret of journalism. Readers of newspapers which care little for establishing truthful accounts, usually the most numerous, separate affection from trust.

Rulers and states sought and got increasing control over journalism as its power became more evident – though it remained, precariously and at times fatally for the journalists, a place where radicals could flourish for a time. Thomas Paine, among the most fertile of radical journalists of the eighteenth century, was convicted (in absentia) of seditious libel in England and imprisoned in France. He was the most consequential journalist of his age: his pamphlet, Common Sense (1776), arguing for American independence from the United Kingdom, remains the bestselling book in the US (in terms of ratio of sales to population). By the nineteenth century, in the United States first and in the United Kingdom later, journalists increasingly broke away from political patronage and control, aided, in the latter half of the century, by the growing role of advertising in giving the ever-larger newspaper companies financial independence. It brought the temptation to pander to moneyed interests, but also turned a restricted circle of readers, treated as a politically active elite, into a much wider audience, who were envisaged as consumers as well (or instead), and which provided 'an economic basis for press autonomy and power that the early printers and editors never enjoyed'.[2]

Reporting by reporters, rather than opinionating by editors, became the developing form of journalism in the US from the early 1800s, taking on a 'brash character',[3] which fitfully spread to the more deferential British press. From the 1830s on, in both America and Britain, 'beats' developed, in which reporters specialized in covering areas of interest, increasingly through established institutions and bureaucracies – 'the story of early journalism, in short, is the story of an emergent institution seeking out more established institutions in order to feed the nineteenth-century "hamster wheel".'[4] The 'Anglo Saxons' thus became, in different but allied ways, distinct from the continental Europeans and others in producing a 'journalism of information',[5] which bit by bit came to see accuracy as a main selling point for a largely upper- and middle-class male readership, relying on fact and informed opinion for their business, governmental, institutional and conversational roles.

The lower classes, increasingly literate, were enrolled in newspaper readership by the US city papers owned by the new media oligarchs active in the late nineteenth and early twentieth centuries – James Gordon Bennett, William Randolph Hearst and Joseph Pulitzer – and later in the UK by their transatlantic counterparts, Harold Harmsworth (Lord Rothermere), his brother Alfred Harmsworth (Lord Northcliffe) and Max Aitken (Lord Beaverbrook). Common to all was a style brasher than brash, with crime, scandal and sex as main selling points – an approach first pioneered from the 1840s in the UK's *News of the World*.

In most countries now ruled by autocratic regimes, journalism didn't develop through centuries-long struggles for independence – the history which most buttresses the news media's claim that they are a pillar of democracy. In Russia, China, Egypt and the rest of the Muslim world, Japan, Africa, India and South East Asia, it didn't develop at all until the mid nineteenth century: before that, news and analysis, such as that done by Chinese scholar-officials, charged with making accurate reports on the state of the nation, was for the elite only. A newspaper culture was often brought in by colonialists and missionaries – as in India, Egypt and Africa. It was thus identified less with freedom than with subordination, and had to be 'nationalized' as a pro-independence press before spreading among and beyond the educated classes.

The influences of their origins and the fact that they are produced for the market renders newspapers, everywhere in the democratic world, unstable entities, constantly tugged between the mission to report and explain well-grounded facts and the desire to please and flatter the readership. The 'serious' journalist's view of what constitutes the most important news differs from their readerships' view, even in upmarket papers produced for a highly educated middle class. The ability to track 'most viewed' stories shows that they are often quite different from the papers' editors' own hierarchy. As an example: on 6 March 2017, the editors' top stories in the *Guardian* concerned, first, the FBI director's demand that President Donald Trump provide proof that former President Barack Obama had ordered a wiretap on Trump's phone calls; second, a piece on the UK budget due later in the week; and third, a story on sexual harassment in British universities. By contrast, the most viewed article was a piece on the failure of a new team at the BBC car show *Top Gear* to match the success of the previous team, led by Jeremy Clarkson; a satirical story on Trump's unannounced destruction of ISIS; and the news that a popular Arsenal player, Alexis Sanchez, had been dropped for a match against Liverpool and had later sparked an altercation with his teammates.

This isn't just the case in democratic states. Media in authoritarian states, with few exceptions, keep and build audiences with a mixture of news that pleases the regime and news that pleases the audience; though the two have now come together, in many cases, more successfully than in liberal democratic states. A nationalist, anti-Western stance is popular and emotionally satisfying for many, especially if the news features such triumphs as the peaceful seizure of Crimea by Russia, or the defiance – reaching 'stratospheric levels'[6] – by China's leadership of the US when, in the summer of 2016, the Permanent Court of Arbitration in The Hague invalidated China's 'historic' claims to stretches of the ocean and territories in the South China Sea. Dramatically presented, these passages can make compelling viewing and reading – and underpin the legitimacy of the regime at the same time.

There is no neat dividing line between authoritarian and democratic, especially in the later reaches of the 2010s. The former Communist states of East and Central Europe and the Soviet Union are for the most part authoritarian, or tending in that direction. But though the election of a president or a parliament may in many cases have been corrupted, in very few cases was it likely that the winner would not have won on the strictest electoral criteria:[7] the elections, though often corrupt, were not a farce. President Putin in Russia, the Law and Justice Party dominated by Jarosław Kaczyński in Poland, the Fidesz Party led by Prime Minister Viktor Orbán in Hungary and others pointed to results and polls which underscore their popularity – and the unpopularity of the still-existing competitors. In Hungary, for example, the ruling party, Fidesz, is revealed in the polls as being thought of as corrupt,[8] but in April 2018, it won a crushing victory over all other rivals. A system of elective democracy remains in these states, but it has detached itself from the word 'liberal'.

Yet if there is no absolute distinction between the despot and the democrat, the basic institutions and processes by which each must live differ fundamentally. Democrats still believe that elections are – and are seen to be – free, fair and uncorrupted; that elected power is under the law; that judges and the courts are independent; that civil society, with a plethora of institutions, charities, religious organizations, policy institutes, clubs, associations and advocacy groups, should be free to act under the law; and that the freedom of news media and speech are protected by law and precedent. None of these are true in authoritarian states.

Journalists' independence in states proclaiming themselves as fully democratic cannot be absolute, but its borders are set much wider and they are always negotiable. The power which has been given to and taken by journalists can be large – even decisive, as in the choice of an elected leader.

In early 2017, the leading contender for the French presidency was François Fillon of the centre-right Republican Party, an experienced politician (a former prime minister), professing a strong Catholic faith and with a plan for economic reforms deep enough to jolt the country out of its stagnation. In February, the investigative–satirical weekly *Le Canard Enchaîné* revealed that Fillon's wife Penelope and two of his adult children had been paid around one million euros in all as his assistants – but appeared to have done little or nothing to earn it;[9] Penelope Fillon later denied this, as did her husband.[10] Fillon had been the favourite to win against Marine Le Pen in the second round of the presidency: he rapidly lost support, allowing the centrist Emmanuel Macron to take the place of favourite, and to win.

One of the world's great political prizes – the French presidency housed in the magnificence of the Elysée Palace – had been, in the view of most pollsters, Fillon's. Then the near certainty was snatched from him by a hundred-year-old (in 2016) muckraking, mocking weekly. Authoritarian leaders cannot allow this to happen, hence the need to ensure the enthusiastic loyalty of the leading journalists, especially broadcasters, and the reduction of all mass journalism to obedience, leaving at best only a fringe of upmarket publications and websites in opposition, struggling to have any leverage on politics or policies.

Journalists in authoritarian societies usually know something of how democratic journalism works, and sometimes want to import it into their practice (though it's wrong to assume, as can be the case, that all want to exchange a servile, low-energy, low-risk place for an independent, risky, pressured one). The attraction of a 'journalism of information' is that it gives them the chance of a useful, rather than a subservient, working life, and the opportunity of revelation in societies which take a hard line in stopping that which they don't want exposed. It also puts them in potential conflict with the authorities and with most of their fellow citizens, who will tend to favour security over confrontation; and in some countries – such as Mexico, Pakistan and Russia – makes violent death more likely.

A journalist who follows that road must imagine a situation in which the ills and corruptions of the society are susceptible to change through investigation and publication; that is, a state of affairs which does not exist.

The journalistic culture which usually most inspires them is that of the US. Because it has been the most explicit and ambitious in expressing its aims and its ethics, because it projects itself with most force, because film and television have routinely endowed their journalist characters with a heroic status and because it uses the language closest to being a global lingua franca, it is the American journalistic culture which beckons journalists round the globe to emulate it. Not just American journalism: it is post-Watergate journalism – sure of its power, brooking no denials and few defences of privacy, with higher bars than in most states against being successfully sued for libel or slander, wedded to hard, concentrated reporting that reveals governmental and corporate misdemeanour – which has become the model. The high position which the US news media assume themselves to occupy naturally produces arrogance and an assumption that all criticism of them, especially from politicians, is self-interested and false. But the devotion to a constant concern for accuracy is shown in the open debates about how that is attained, such as on whether or not to call President Trump a 'liar' – a step taken by the *New York Times* in a news story in January 2017, soon after he assumed office;[11] it was one which the editor of the *Wall Street Journal* thought overly moralistic.[12]

The 'Anglo Saxons' (in the US at least, the tag wouldn't fit most of the population, though many Europeans cling to its use) had produced an institution which had the nerve and confidence, backed by constitutions and legislation, to set up as a judge of the state and politicians, the corporations and the leading figures, the institutions of civil society and foreign governments, and in being so, was attractive to would-be journalists and feared by autocratic regimes across the world. It was and remains an audacious claim – for unlike professions such as law, medicine, engineering, accounting or academia, the trade of journalism requires no specialized knowledge beyond learning how to report and broadcast clearly and the technicalities of Net-based working. Journalists in democracies are militant in defence of their independence and freedom, but don't often care to reflect on what their real influence is on politics, and what their practice does to the societies in which they operate. Michael Schudson writes that 'Journalists' reflections on their own business are not tested in the discipline of actually having to influence institutional policy. In contrast, even a rube [novice] academic, working out the freshman general education course or revising admissions requirements or preparing a report for an accreditation committee has more firsthand experience in policymaking than many experienced journalists who write about it.'[13]

This does not mean that commentary, much less well-based reportage, is necessarily jejune: much of it is sharply perceptive. But its wisdom is Platonic, its gloss untouched by the compromises, evasions and errors of practice.

This emptiness where expertise and experience might be is amply compensated by the fact that journalism, vigorously practised, really is a necessary concomitant to democratic, civil societies – because it is or should be there to gather audiences to attend to those who are the victims of injustice, neglect and injury, to the digging up of illegal or asocial practices, to the strong expression of opinion on issues both timeless and of the day and to the humbling of the arrogance power usually accrues about it. This is what journalists like to say they do, and some actually do. And the less proclaimed duty of making a record of events, speeches, policies, debates and initiatives, which require attendance, a recording or shorthand note and the ability to write an accurate and readable narrative, remains an understated glory of the trade.

'Free' journalism has many constraints, as is emphasized throughout this book, but though the adjective deserves to be between quotation marks, it is still free enough to be serviceable, and to be the envy of those wishing to attempt truthful reporting or strong opinionating in states where 'free' cannot be used at all, with or without quotation marks.

In the democratic world, the largest issue troubling liberals, and many conservatives, from late 2016 onwards was the election of Donald Trump as US president on a programme which, as his presidency rolled out in 2017, became ever more confusing and contradictory. It appeared to be a mixture of strong nationalism ('America First'), protectionism, opposition to immigration of (especially) Mexicans and Muslims, contempt for the European Union and an approach to NATO so insouciant and contradictory that it was simply unknowable whether or not he would maintain the promise that an attack on one member was an attack on all.

In Europe, strong populist parties of the right grew quickly in France, Italy, the Netherlands and Sweden, often displacing much older parties that had dominated post- (and sometimes pre-) war politics; in March 2018, populist parties were the victors in the Italian parliamentary elections. Only in Germany and the UK did established parties continue to be confident of beating new nationalist groupings, such as the Alternativ für Deutschland party and the UK Independence Party (though not, in the latter, the Scottish National Party in its own part of the Union).

The belief that the post-war liberal order is now over was widely shared. Even commentators who had vigorously opposed many liberals' desire to spread or defend democracy up to and including by force of arms – 'realists', who accepted that some states and regions had political cultures antithetical to liberal democracy and that orderly international relations depended on taking no action which aggressively challenged that culture – were shocked by the success of the authoritarian regimes and by anti-liberal movements within democracies. As the realist-inclined Harvard scholar Stephen M. Walt put it, 'it turns out that many people in many places care more about national identities, historic enmities, territorial symbols, and traditional cultural values than they care about "freedom" as liberals define it'.[14]

Trump did not seem to care much about freedom as liberals define it. Any person or organization – the courts, the intelligence services, Muslims, Mexico – which crossed or displeased him was violently called out on Twitter, his preferred way of expressing the frustrations that swept across him day and night, and which demanded an outlet. The tweets and phrases he tossed out indicated one who did not care whether 'America First' was the slogan of the US far right in the 1930s, including fascist sympathizers, such as the aviator Charles Linbergh and the car manufacturer Henry Ford, among many others, nor if 'enemies of the American people' was a lift from the Stalinist phrase book, usually the prelude to a death sentence.[15] His mind seemed to know none of the boundaries that public men and women are careful to place on their voiced views – a care often, to be sure, resulting in a maddening blandness. Like a Kong unbound, he roared and beat his chest when he felt hunted or cornered. His anger waxed and waned. He loved the CIA when he addressed some of its staff the day after his inauguration; he hated it, and the FBI, when they insisted on investigating Russian links to his campaign and the FBI demanded that the Justice Department deny his charge that a wiretap was ordered to be put on his phones by former President Obama. He thought Obama and his wife Michelle were wonderful, gracious people when they received him in the White House, days before he took over. Later, he called Obama bad and sick. His attention skidded from accusations of presidential misconduct of enormous constitutional consequence to gloating over Arnold Schwarzenegger's early departure from his old TV show, *The Apprentice*, because of poor ratings. The actor, straight-faced, told a radio talk show host: 'I think he's in love with me.'[16]

In one thing he was almost constant: he hated mainstream journalism. He called reporters 'dishonest', 'disgusting' and 'scum'. In a press conference a few days before he became president, he refused to take a question from CNN's senior White House correspondent, Jim Acosta, shouting him down – apparently enraged that CNN had been the first to report that former President Obama had been briefed on lurid allegations about him in an intelligence dossier.[17]

The reason why his constancy on this has 'almost' before it is because, on a visit to the New York Times as president-elect in November 2016, he said he 'had great respect for the New York Times'[18] – a paper he had consistently called 'failing', 'a joke', 'really disgusting' and much more, all of which the Times printed together, after he was president for a month, with long lists of insults he had levelled at other institutions and public figures.[19] As soon as he cleared the Times' offices, he again began a string of insults, levelled also at other mainstream media (though CNN, the Washington Post and the Times featured most).

On 24 February 2017, Trump made a speech at the Conservative Political Action Conference, and said the news media 'make up stories and make up sources'.[20] In his sights was a Washington Post story, based on nine unnamed sources, which claimed that conversations that Mike Flynn, who had been appointed National Security Adviser, had had with the Russian ambassador, Sergey Kislyak, had been misrepresented and the stories 'made up'. Trump said that journalists should not be allowed to use unnamed sources, and that they hid behind the First Amendment on freedom of speech and the press to publish lies about him. More ominously, he continued: 'Many of these groups are part of the large media corporations and they have their own agenda – and it's not your agenda. It doesn't represent the people, it will never represent the people, and we're going to do something about it.'

Trump came to office at a fortuitous time. The main institution of journalism for more than two centuries, the newspaper, had been gravely weakened by the Net – which pushed out huge quantities of journalism and information for free, hosted new start-ups like Craigslist that leeched away classified advertising and which funnelled most other advertising to Google and Facebook. He was responsible for a sharp spike upwards in TV and cable news viewing, and in subscriptions to the upmarket newspapers – he was the hottest piece of political news since Watergate – but, welcome as this was, it didn't address the lack of a new business model for newspapers, and the question over what they would become. At the same time, social media energized his supporters, whom he fed (along with everyone else) a constant stream of tweets, often pandering to the view many of them held that the liberal establishment had betrayed them, lied to them, denied them a decent living and were ruining America by opening its borders to terrorists and scroungers. The writer Paul Berman wrote that 'whole sectors of the population float on tides of electronic rumor and mischief, where ... panic is promoted. In Donald Trump, those people have elected one of their own.'[21]

In his plot against American journalism – and by extension all journalism which strives for independence – Trump was deliberately destroying an ideal which, however much it inflated itself and was inflated by others, proposed a practice of robust enquiry based on checkable truth, and which was a large part of the international belief in America's greatness. He attacked the media for the same reason as he attacked the secret services: 'to destroy trust in two of the institutions most requiring it as the basis for their existence. In doing so, he has both implicitly and explicitly demanded that trust be placed only, or at least mainly, in him. The truth begins, and ends, in him.'[22]

This behaviour from one who glories in his office's power and disdains to observe many of its constraints is dangerous to a law-governed, pluralist state. In one thing President Trump is right: the mainstream media are, nearly all, against him; a state of affairs that the *Washington Post* editor, Marty Baron, said at a seminar at the Reuters Institute he regretted.[23] Yet it was inevitable. The mainstream news media, with exceptions, based their journalism on observable, checkable fact: the president, in his speeches, interviews, tweets and off-hand comments, did not. It was a breach, not confined to America, which widens everywhere.

Acknowledgements

This is a book about journalism in the world. It necessarily contains some historical background, but it's meant mainly to assist the understanding of that which claims to assist us to understand the world as it now is: journalism.

It's not comprehensive. I have separate chapters on big countries and regions, smaller pieces on countries and themes which may stand as examples in a larger whole, such as Africa, Central Europe, Latin America; and particular forms of journalism, such as public service broadcasting, leaking and tabloids. Much has been left out, but this approach at least avoids being a list.

The debts owed to those who assisted *my* understanding are very many. I want to mention first the Atkin family, Edward and Celia, who for years supported my work both on this book and at the Reuters Institute. Similar thanks are due to David Ure: like the Atkins, he gave generously to fund work which he believed would be valuable.

Toby Mundy, first at Atlantic then as my agent, has been a large inspiration for the book. At Atlantic now, James Nightingale and Alison Tulett put great effort into editing, checking and shaping.

The Reuters Institute for the Study of Journalism, now part of the University of Oxford, has been a necessary background to work on the book, and I have picked the brains of and asked for help from many of the former

Reuters Fellows, who include some of the most thoughtful and experienced journalists from every part of the globe. The Institute was fortunate to find, soon after its creation, a director in David Levy; its creation was due to the hard work of Tim Gardam, as well as Tim Garton Ash, Stephen Coleman, Geert Linnebank, Neil MacFarlane and Monique Villa. It is now established as a major centre of research and discussion on journalism, as well as of a fellowship programme.

Of special help in working out the themes of the book have been, in first place, Arkady Ostrovsky, followed by Barry Cox, Ferdinando Giugliano, Abdallah Hassan, Cristina Marconi, Lena Nernirovskaya, Yuri Senokosov, Janice Winter and a Chinese journalist who asks to remain anonymous. Ilaria Poggiolini, though increasingly immersed in preserving her ancient university of Pavia, gave me tremendous support.

Others, in differing capacities, include Ramy Aly, Lucia Annunziata, Scott Anthony, Andrei Babitsky, Iradj Bagherzade, Lionel Barber, David Bell, Carlo De Benedetti, Aluf Benn, Ian Benson, Inna Berezkina, Luca De Biase, Nigel Biggar, James Blitz, Graham Bowley, Pierre Brochand, Neil Buckley, Hugo de Burgh, Ian Buruma, Alastair Campbell, Duncan Campbell, Adriana Carranca, Shubhranshu Choudhary, Jon Cohen, Stephen Coleman, Mandy Cormack, Paddy Coulter, James Crabtree, Wenming Dai, Mark Damazer, Caroline Daniel, Rima Dapous, Sunday Daré, James Dawson, Sonia Delesalle-Stolper, Jeremy Drucker, David Elstein, Alexei Eremenko, Steven Erlanger, Harold Evans, Giuliano Ferrara, Lara Fielden, Jason Fields, James Fishkin, Mikhail Fishman, Enrico Franceschini, Nick Fraser, Chrystia Freeland, Sean French, Tim Gardam, Paolo Garimberti, Timothy Garton Ash, Agnès Gaudu, Philip Gawith, Nicci Gerard, Gabriela Giacomella, Anthony Giddens, Jo Godfrey, David Goodhart, Arnab Goswami, Roy Greenslade, Anton Harber, Luke Harding, James Harkin, John Harris, Jim Haynes, Peter Hennessy, Tamar Herman, Julia Hobsbawm, Jeremy Isaacs, Andrew Jack, Ian Jack, Alan Johnson, Chaitanya Kalbag, Jan Kasl, Terezie Kaslová,

Markandey Katju, Sylvie Kauffmann, Lucy Kellaway, Bill Keller, Lorien Kite, Ivan Krastev, Kimiko Kuga, Richard Lambert, Noa Landau, Joseph Lelyveld, Leonardo Maisano, Mark Malloch-Brown, Ezio Mauro, John McLaughlin, Enrico Mentana, Elhanan Miller, Mikhail Minakov, Augusto Minzolini, Martin Moore, William Moy, Marco Niada, Rasmus Kleis Nielsen, Richard Norton-Taylor, Natalie Nougayrède, Daniel Ockrent, Onora O'Neill, Neil O'Sullivan, Geoff Owen, James Painter, Ella Panfilova, Peter Pomerantsev, Dick Pountain, Manar Rachwani, Alex Reid, Thomas Rid, Max Rodenbeck, Jay Rosen, Prannoy Roy, Alan Rusbridger, Alec Russell, Naomi Sakr, John Scarlett, Michael Schudson, Jean Seaton, Hend Selim, Arijit Sen, Scott Shane, Anuradha Sharma, Supriya Sharma, Hu Shuli, Anthony Smith, Kate Hanneford Smith, Al Stepan, Stefan Stern, Václav Štětka, Frederick Studemann, Asher Susser, Tim Suter, Celia Szusterman, Abiye Megenta Teklemarian, Gillian Tett, Karan Thapar, John Thornhill, Daya Thussu, Laura Toogood, Howard Tumber, Marco Varvello, Gudrun Vickery, Monique Villa, Alessio Vinci, Graham Watts.

PART I

THE AUTHORITY OF THE STATE

INTRODUCTION

'I hate your scary truth'

Journalism is controlled and suppressed in authoritarian societies because their rulers believe they have a better grasp of the truth than journalists could ever have. Theirs is not the truth of mere facts. It is the alternative truth of what keeps social peace, promotes development, preserves necessary power and serves faith.

Authoritarian societies often have the form of democratic systems, including news media which can at times report accurately and express mildly dissenting views. But the rulers and the journalists know that such licence can be revoked at any time. The Russian oligarch Mikhail Prokhorov, who had, in the early 2010s, sharpened his RBC news media group to do investigative reporting – including of the Kremlin – enjoyed a year or two of high-profile existence. However, in May 2016, after pieces on allegedly corrupt activities in President Vladimir Putin's family, including links to the tax-dodging revelations in the Panama Papers, the group found itself the subject of a criminal investigation. Three top editors were offered as sacrifices, but by early June, Prokhorov was reported to be on the lookout for a buyer:[1] he later sold most of his largest Russian assets including RBC, and shifted investments to the US where he already owned the Brooklyn Nets basketball team.[2]

The higher truth of Putin's Russia – a truth that talented 'political technologists' employed by the Kremlin have developed for many years

– is that the president is a powerful, determined but compassionate ruler, dedicated to the welfare of Russians and to reviving the glory of an abused nation. Political technologists, a very Russian term, are different from public relations people who, everywhere, give policies an inspiring gloss. The technologists construct framework narratives for the exercise of power, with the aim both to legitimize power and to show that society has no alternative but to accept it. This version of the truth is necessary for the project of patriotic recovery, Putin's main task in his third term as president, and is based on the belief that the threat to Russia from the West is unsleeping, and criticism assists the enemy. In April 2016, the most proactive media supporter of the president, the TV presenter Dmitry Kiselev, accused the RBC group's coverage of the Panama Papers' revelations as assisting the United States; a few weeks later the state moved against it.[3]

Russia, in common with most countries in the world, has no centuries-long tradition of striving for, and gradually increasing, press freedom. Its newspapers, as its politics, had a brief and fevered period of licence at the turn of the nineteenth and twentieth centuries, but with the Bolshevik victory, an increasingly tight censorship choked off all criticism until, by the late twenties, none could exist.[4] The Leninist party believed truth was under its control; to call its main newspaper 'Truth' (*Pravda*) was confirmation. The system's decay under Leonid Brezhnev and his two short-lived successors, and the progressively rapid opening of the Mikhail Gorbachev years (1985–91), slithered into the post-Soviet wonderland of media, disciplined not by the state but by the market and the oligarchic lords of television who, facing an election, tuned their channels to Boris Yeltsin's wandering star, fearful of returning Communists. Putin, stricken by the collapse of a Soviet Union that had raised and nourished him, and understanding that to consolidate his power he needed compliant media, made it a priority to wrest ownership from over-mighty (as he saw it) private hands and bring the channels, and most print, under Kremlin-state control once more.

China had little exposure to press pluralism. Newspaper and journals came first through Western missionaries in the early nineteenth century; indigenous periodicals appeared in mid century, witness to growing nationalist sentiment sparked by French and British military humiliation. 'Journalism became the ideal career for the patriot … and the only political journalism was patriotic, change-oriented journalism.'[5] When, from the 1920s, the Nationalists and the Communists began a fight to the death, the press – which had shown signs of independent development – was mobilized into political order, an approach that 'established the absolute dominance of politics over facts: a dominance which remains in authoritarian states'.[6] Under Maoism, journalism had no more freedom than in Stalin's Soviet Union, but after the successive liberalizations of Deng Xiaoping in the 1990s (Deng died in 1997), a degree of pluralism was permitted, and there was a closely observed flourishing of investigative journalism. These openings were narrowing in the 2000s, and largely closed down after Xi Jinping's assumption of power, as general secretary of the Communist Party from 2012 and president from 2013. In double-digit-growth times, a certain laxity flourished, in harder times, not. 'Working in the Chinese media,' an anonymous editor told a *Guardian* correspondent in February 2016, 'feels like you are wasting your life.'[7]

Journalism has meaning for those who practise it if it allows the free pursuit and publication of facts seen as important, and if it is permitted to operate in a society ready to host a competition of ideas and political positions – a readiness that has waxed and waned through the centuries. A meaningful life for a journalist in that sense had been possible for centuries in the West, where freedom to propose and oppose had begun to take a grip on the nascent civil societies of England, France, Italy, the Netherlands, Scandinavia and others from the sixteenth century onwards. By the seventeenth came the first periodical publication of news and opinion. The professionalization of journalism in the nineteenth century created markets for sensation, scandal and *schadenfreude*, but rested on a steadily plumper bed of belief that this was indivisible from societies of law and political choice.

A journalist in a democracy can aspire to a sometimes harried, sometimes easy life that can be democratically constructive because of their autonomous activities in recording, criticizing and investigating the powers that be. But journalists cannot see themselves thus in an authoritarian society. There, most journalists have little independent agency, recording statements, speeches and interviews or reflecting the regime's priorities and guidance through stories designed to underpin its wisdom and success, or opinion calibrated to its policies.

States like Eritrea, which had a lively political press,[8] and North Korea, which never did,[9] take care to reduce their journalists to clerks taking dictation, and succeed in jailing or killing those journalists who attempt rebellion. Populations that are cowed and constrained by long labour for subsistence living under the ceaseless gaze of secret services and informer networks struggle to produce revolts, and would mostly be uninterested in press freedom. But such complete tyrannies are now few. Umberto Eco wrote that a true totalitarian state is one where 'a regime ... subordinates every act of the individual to the state and to its ideology'.[10] Italy under Fascism was not that, neither is Putin's Russia, Xi's China, el-Sisi's Egypt nor Erdoğan's Turkey. Journalism exists, or is suppressed, according to the will of the ruler; but it seems presently that ideologically guided societies, such as China and Saudi Arabia, are more inclined to suppress journalism than a post-ideological authoritarian state like Russia.

The states that have been and remain least given to develop a firm basis for journalism, independent of state and ideology, are the Middle Eastern Muslim countries, where the curbing of journalistic attention to its activities suits the state, and the disqualification of journalism to say anything of real value to the people is often an aim of the state-religion, Islam.

The strength of a community of faith and law derived from Islam's precepts varies widely in these states – from weak in a many-faiths state like Lebanon to strong in the Wahabi-inspired kingdom of Saudi Arabia, or the Ayatollah-guided theocracy of Iran. Where secularism has penetrated widely enough in society, observation of the religion is reduced to a milder series of rituals and pieties, as in Egypt – where, during the brief period in power of an ineffective Muslim Brotherhood-led government (June 2012–July 2013), the fear of a more strictly imposed observance caused public support for a military intervention, returning the country to the military rule which has been the 'normal' since the officers' revolt of 1952 brought Gamal Abdel Nasser to power.

Ernest Gellner noticed that Islamic societies, which are more observant than other faiths, run practical politics by networks of clientelism: 'the formal institutional arrangements matter far less than do the informal connections of mutual trust based on past personal services, on exchange of protection from above for support from below'.[11] Many Muslim journalists in Islamic societies do challenge the state, and grasp freedom where possible, but they have not succeeded in establishing a stable order where free speech is protected. In 2014, a senior member of Saudi Arabia's Commission for the Promotion of Virtue and the Prevention of Vice, or religious police, Ahmed Qassim al-Ghamdi, read the Koran and discovered that habits in the Prophet's time were markedly more relaxed than they had become in the Kingdom. He publicized his views on television, his wife with face uncovered sitting beside him, and was deluged with hatred; the family of his eldest son's fiancée called off their wedding. Much worse happened to journalists who crossed the red line of extreme public sexual puritanism or showed disrespect to the sprawling oligarchic monarchy.[12]

The Islamic faith in the mutually hostile states of Saudi Arabia (Sunni) and Iran (Shia) shows little distinction between the secular and the religious. Christianity now leaves Caesarean matters to fallen politicians; Judaism and Hinduism, in their home states, seek to increase their influence on political conduct, but a secular core remains in both their homelands, fiercely defended by non-believers and many moderate believers alike (though the Indian prime minister from May 2014, Narendra Modi, rose in politics through a powerful organization dedicated to the promotion of Hinduism and the submission of Islam). Only in Islam, of the major religions with real social weight, do the precepts of the founding Prophet act as a practical and normative guide, usually enforced. The religion is seen as a higher truth than anything journalism could produce. Alexis de Tocqueville wrote that 'Islam is the religion which has most completely confounded and intermixed the two powers ... so that all the acts of civil and political life are regulated more or less by religious law'.[13] The satellite TV 'revolution' of the 2000s shakes that, but still far from to destruction.

Journalism had little or no indigenous tradition which could be used as inspiration, while the example of the Western media is routinely condemned as mere propaganda. The coming of Al Jazeera, funded by the Qatari monarchy, followed by other Arabic-language satellite stations has made large waves – though the autocrats retain as strong a grip as they can on their power, their politics and their societies, with Islam as their handmaiden.

The trade of the reporter, the essential act of journalism, is a Western invention. From the mid nineteenth century, the Americans were the drivers of reporting as a regular employment, progressively distancing the trade from the political parties and other institutions that controlled it, to become an institution in itself, a centre of judgement, policy development and power that could match itself against other large powers, including that of the state. This Western tradition has penetrated authoritarian societies, but has not been allowed to take strong root. The first decades of the 2010s have been testimony to the weakness of independent journalism in authoritarian states, compared to the resilience of authoritarianism itself.

Journalists can make a name for themselves in such states. In Egypt, under President Nasser, Mohamed Heikal did, in his editorship of the main state organ, Al-Ahram, and in his closeness, as adviser, speechwriter and friend, to the president. In the Soviet Union, Yevgeny Primakov made a name for himself, and indeed became prime minister in (post-Soviet) Russia, securing the post because President Boris Yeltsin needed someone with Primakov's (abiding) Communist loyalties at a time of political weakness. But though he had been well trained in Arabic and Middle Eastern politics and knew many of the leaders, his more important job was not as a *Pravda* correspondent, but as a KGB agent who reported directly to the Central Committee's international department.

Making a name for oneself, or at least a good living, in authoritarian systems means serving the system not the trade; it means cleaving to the agreed line (though you may have had a hand in making it); it means jostling most fiercely for the ear and favour of the rulers, over and above the eyeballs of the readers. There were a few, besides Primakov, in the Soviet Union who were permitted some licence in commentary – Alexander Bovin, mainly in *Izvestia*, took a relatively independent line on international issues, especially the Middle East; and Otto Latsis, an accomplished economic and political journalist, was an advocate for reform in lean years for such proposals, and when circumstances changed, he turned the monthly *Kommunist* review into a forum for debate on the meaning and limits of perestroika and glasnost in Gorbachev's period of rule. But they were few.

Reporters in unfree societies have few role models from the past. Chinese journalists have little desire to pick out Scots Christian missionaries as the founders of their trade. If and when they do look back, they might see such figures as Yu Youren, active in Shanghai in the early years of the twentieth century, as a passionate advocate for an end to the empire and a spread of democracy. In his *People's Appeal*, which lasted two years, he wrote that 'if the government is unable to protect its people, the government will lose its right to rule; if the people are unable to supervise the government, the rights of the people will be lost'. But in Xi's China, a public embrace of Yu would be risky to one's career.[14]

———

In Ethiopia, in the mid 2000s, Prime Minister Meles Zenawi, with a contested parliamentary victory behind him, a rapidly growing economy and foreign donors voicing concerns about the lack of civil and human rights, relaxed the controls on the press, sufficient to allow the publication of a remarkably liberal and enquiring newspaper, *Addis Neger*. After a few years of freedom, there was a darkening of the political (though not economic) space, and warnings began that the paper was going too far. When the editors continued, the clamps came down, and, faced with treason and other charges that could have meant death or certainly long imprisonment, they fled the country.

Such windows of relative openness have occurred, and continue to occur, regularly. Czechoslovakia in the late 1960s, China in the 1990s and 2000s, Egypt in the late 2000s to early 2010s, all allowed a spurt of opinionating and reporting, which gave journalists and their publics a glimpse of the possibilities – and limitations – of a little independence of published thought and a few revelations of the way in which power operated in these societies. None could survive renewed disciplining, and, of that group, only in Czechoslovakia, which benefited from the collapse of Communism and had a tradition of some journalistic independence before the Nazi invasion and the Communist rule, could independent journalism establish itself. Yet at the same time it discovered how necessary it was and how hard it is to grapple with the forces released by regime and ideological collapse – when the structures of both still permeate society, and there has been little preparation for the complexity of independence.

In sub-Saharan Africa, as Ethiopia and still more brutally Eritrea demonstrate, the state is more often an enemy than a protector. African states vary very widely, and there's a broadly optimistic story to be told that the journalists are better equipped and more confident, and that the powers that be have to take more notice of them. In some states, such as Kenya, Ghana and Nigeria, that seems to be true, if patchily so.

The journalism of South Africa is among the freest and best resourced on the continent, where, after apartheid ended in 1994 with the first democratic elections on a full franchise, the press retained both a combative spirit and a public commitment to independence of comment and of reportage. It's a commitment which the government, albeit with significant public reservations and larger private withdrawals, feels obliged to endorse, and which many in positions of authority really do support.

But the first decades of a democratic society witnessed a growing impatience on the part of successive governments and presidents with the cussed awkwardness of the press. The papers continue to reveal private deals, print leaks of policies, play up on the front page corruption and cronyism in politics and in the economy, and claim that, in a country where the African National Congress seemed set to dominate parliament and the presidency for many years, the press is the only effective opposition.

Many of the men and women who fought, died, were tortured, imprisoned, forced into exile and finally caused the downfall of apartheid didn't like this barrage, especially when it came – as it often does – from white journalists owned by white proprietors (though they were more hurt when it came, as it also often does, from black journalists in black-owned newspapers). The to-and-fro between the press and the ruling party continues, as does the multi-party democracy: in August 2016, the Democratic Alliance made large gains in countrywide elections, including in the municipality of Nelson Mandela Bay[15] – an outcome that would seem to assist the continued existence of a pluralist journalism. The danger to press independence is much less in South Africa than in Turkey, but it's worth understanding the strains independence necessarily produces with politics, everywhere.

Autocratic rule isn't usually a matter of a mass forcibly held down by a malignant but powerful tyranny. More often, the autocrat takes pains to give the majority of people something of what they want: territorial gain, in Russia; rapid development, in China and Ethiopia; the rehabilitation of religious observance, in Turkey; the promise of security with military rule, in Egypt. The journalist or dissident who makes clear the absence of political and intellectual freedom pits individual judgement against that of the regime, and usually of the majority of fellow citizens who will often see the dissident journalist as the regime wishes: a defamer of the nation and the people.

In Recep Tayyip Erdoğan's Turkey, the press, which had been diverse in its views, came under sustained attack. The country became the world's main jailer of journalists. Erdoğan, both as prime minister (2003–14) and as president (2014–), a previously ceremonial role he strove, sucessfully, to make executive, intervenes constantly and directly in the output of the news media. Neuralgic issues – the Armenian massacres of 1915–17 is certainly one – cannot be broached, except to deny the genocide label. When the journalist and novelist Ece Temelkuran did so, moved by the murder of her friend Hrant Dink, an Armenian-Turk, in 2007, she was fired from her newspaper. Temelkuran wrote that 'the silent fear among journalists is impossible to put into numbers; consider the 3,500 Kurdish and Turkish politicians, the 500 students and the 100 journalists who are now in jail'.[16] The failed coup of July 2016 put many more journalists – and army officers, judges and civil servants – into jail, a tide of suspects whose guilt or innocence, if properly judged, will take years to settle.

Those who command unfree societies find life harder now, in one large respect. The Net and social media give some power to their citizens, and more power to their journalists. It is true, as Evgeny Morozov writes, that the liberating potential of the new communication technologies has been over-hyped; that blogs, Facebook and Twitter are allies of regimes' secret police as much as they are rallying cries to protest, since they locate with increasing precision who the protestors are.[17] But it needs ever-larger armies of watchers and listeners to adequately invigilate the millions of messages whizzing to and fro, and the portability and ubiquity of smartphones in the hands of millions make the task either entirely stifling at huge cost and labour or necessarily more permissive, cutting off the heads of only the most uppity poppies, thereby allowing the citizens to win a few victories, as long as these do not amount to too many.

President and former army chief Abdel Fattah el-Sisi has ensured that most of the Egyptian media follow his orders. He has been ruthless with those he has designated his enemies – hundreds of supporters of the Muslim Brotherhood have been killed, thousands imprisoned, including the former president, Mohamed Morsi. The heads of the media companies, and their editors, have sworn allegiance and obedience. He remains, in the latter half of the 2010s, popular, but the social media are not as biddable as the media companies who have much to lose, and they sometimes win the campaigns they run.[18]

In October 2015, one such campaign attracted hundreds of thousands to use social media to criticize the pro-regime host Riham Saed for blaming a rape victim for the assault upon her. As a result, the sponsors pulled out and her show was taken off air. The state and pro-regime commercial media keep the faith with the ruler, yet for younger Egyptians, the taste of diverse and critical media in 2011–13, and the spread of computing and social media to more than 50 per cent of the population, make that faith shakier. Another consequence is that the subordination of women does not pass unchallenged. The image of the young woman being dragged away by the military during protests in Tahrir Square in December 2011, her black abaya torn away revealing a blue bra, mobilized thousands of women to protest.[19]

The social media in authoritarian societies are, as everywhere, carriers of every kind of message – but they can also function as the samizdat of today. In the high period of Soviet samizdat (*sam* = self, *izdat* = publish), forbidden works, protests and manifestoes were typed and retyped, with many carbon copies growing ever fainter the further from the keys they lay. A few thousand in a state of nearly 300 million read them. People *will* express themselves, will want to know the truth and dissenting opinions; journalists – and now a legion of netizens who see themselves as partaking, even a little, of the trade – will wish to proclaim and to publish: I don't care what you say, I think this, or, this happened.

But to insist on discovering the truth, to set oneself against the narrative of authoritarian power, isn't usually to be popular. When the Belarusian Nobel Prize winner Svetlana Alexievich published her book about the demoralization of young Soviet soldiers in Afghanistan, Boys in Zinc, she was sued by some of the subjects of the book, and by an organization of soldiers' mothers. One, giving evidence against her, cried: 'I loved the USSR, the country we used to live by. And I hate you! I hate your scary truth!'[20]

ONE

'We must unwaveringly persist in ... politicians running newspapers'

For about a decade until the mid 2000s, journalism in China was, compared to past decades under Communism, relatively lightly constrained. Newspapers and even television carried out investigative journalism – most of it sanctioned, but some not. At the same time, the exploding social media told a usually youthful audience about demonstrations, strikes and elite scandals. Even the core Party papers, such as the *People's Daily* and *People's Youth Daily*, were caught up in the euphoria of openness.

Then it was, bit by bit, narrowed. Hu Jintao, president from 2003 to 2013, disliked what he saw as anarchy in the media. Unsanctioned reporting on the 2008 Sichuan earthquake (nearly 70,000 dead), some of which pointed to the shoddiness of the collapsed buildings suggesting corruption in their construction, was thought intolerable. So was the reporting of a train crash in Wenzhou in 2011: the official response to the crash had been to do a hasty rescue, then literally to bury the derailed carriages. Even Party papers had ignored the call for their reporting to run the official line 'great love in the face of great disaster'. Journalism was getting too uppity.

In August 2013, the leader of 1.36 billion people and of eighty-eight million communists, Party leader and president delivered a speech to the National Propaganda and Ideology Work Conference, convened in Beijing, designed to remind the Party and the people that journalism's priorities and tropes were far too important to be decided on by journalists.[1]

Change, Xi noted, was as rapid and large in propaganda and ideology as in every other sphere of his country's fevered progress, but at root, its fundamental task had not changed – '*and cannot change*' (my italics). Its central effort must remain directed to the consolidation of 'the guiding spirit of Marxism', and 'a common ideological basis for the united struggle of the entire Party and the entire people'.

Workers in propaganda and ideology – that is, in the media – had become lax, even somewhat treacherous: 'they speak without restraint, they are completely unscrupulous, they are cheered on by hostile forces'. No one should think, he said, that there exists some realm, which could call itself 'independent', or 'objective', above politics, even above national interest. 'Western countries flaunt "press freedom", but in fact, they also have ideological baselines, they are under the control of interest groups and the inclinations of political parties, there are no completely independent media': in principle a correct, if highly limited, observation – but one which neglected to say that independence from the state and the ruling group was the indispensable 'baseline' for a journalism which could claim autonomy and rights.

The media had become celebrity obsessed, he argued. TV channels and magazines 'seek novelty, pursue pretty women, chase them like ducks!' Attacks on socialism, on the nation, rumours and lies must have no space on any medium – not on 'newspapers, periodicals and magazines, platforms and forums, meetings and conferences, films, television and radio stations, theatres ... digital newspapers, mobile television, mobile media, mobile text messaging, WeChat, Weibo, blogs, microblogs, forums and other such new media' – a list so comprehensive it seemed Xi was afraid of not listing one in case it was seized on as a permitted deviation.

The Net was a particular threat – for 'Western anti-China forces continue to vainly attempt to use the Internet to "topple China"'. Xi was again on the right track. Bill Clinton, in August 2000, asked his audience to 'imagine how much [the Net] could change China ... [the Beijing regime] has been trying to crack down on the Internet – good luck. That's sort of like trying to nail Jell-O to the wall.' In 2010, when Hillary Clinton was Secretary of State, she said that 'countries that restrict free access to information or violate the basic rights of Internet users risk walling themselves off from the progress of the next century'. Xi *did* want to nail Jell-O (a gelatin-based dessert) to the wall, and had already partly succeeded when he gave the speech.

One phrase in his speech was particularly telling. Xi said that 'we must unwaveringly persist in the principle that the Party manages the media, persist in *politicians running newspapers* [my italics], periodicals, TV stations and news websites'. 'Politicians running newspapers' is a Maoist phrase, and a vitally important one.

In February 1957, Mao's report to a Party Congress included a reflection on the Soviet invasion of Hungary the previous year. *People's Daily*, the Party paper, covered this conference with a banner photograph and a news story of several hundred words. The paper published nothing more on the report.

After some weeks, Mao summoned all the members of *People's Daily*'s editorial board to his office in the government enclave of Zhongnanhai. He charged them with being aloof and indifferent, and claimed the paper was run by 'scholars and dead persons'. Editor Deng Tuo – who had, in 1944, compiled the first edition of the *Selected Works of Mao Zedong* – was demoted to Secretary of Culture and Education for the Beijing Municipal Party Committee. In May 1966, *People's Daily* published a series of articles charging Deng as an anti-party, anti-socialist, reactionary gang member. He committed suicide.

In 1959, Mao repeated his orders to Wu Lengxi, Deng's successor: the paper should not be run by intellectuals, dead or alive, but by politicians. Wu tried his best to follow Mao's advice, but was fired in May 1966. On 1 June 1966, the paper published an editorial with the title 'Sweep Away All Monsters and Demons'.

In later writing, Mao made clearer his view: 'Some people are intellectuals, and their greatest weakness is that they are devoid of decisions
yet full of ... pointless ideas. The key points should be grasped at once ...
Newspapers must be run by politicians.'[2] It was this which Xi invoked.

This time, *People's Daily* got it. In October 2013, the Party's flagship paper
eagerly parsed the speech, writing that 'it clarified the basis, preconditions,
methods and objectives for us to better persist in politicians running the
media in the new period and under new technological conditions' – which
meant that the 'bigger picture of reform, development and stability' would
take precedence over the mere phenomena of news.

Xi had interpreted the situation facing the Party as dangerous.
Corruption was rampant, inequalities in wealth had grown more rapidly
than the economy and with it arrogance born of a sense of entitlement,
recently acquired. In October 2010, Li Qiming, the son of a senior police
officer in Baoding in the Hebei province, drunk and driving his girlfriend
back to her dormitory in Hebei University, knocked over two students, one
of whom died.

When security guards detained him, he shouted, 'Sue me if you dare,
my father is Li Gang!' The phrase went China-wide, was set to music and
was trotted out as a joke, and a warning. The authorities prevaricated – but
some months after the incident, Li Qiming was arrested and sentenced
to six years' imprisonment and a fine of nearly 70,000 dollars. Xi said
he wanted to change the culture which produced that behaviour, but he
also wanted to suppress the media which reported it.

In the China of the 2010s, stability was difficult to maintain, as
commercialism, corruption and great disparities of wealth (with the
emergence of a widely disliked and arrogant class of wealthy families)
embedded themselves into a social structure, which, a mere two decades
before, had been much more egalitarian and statist. Evan Osnos wrote
that Xi Jinping was repelled 'by the all-encompassing commercialization
of Chinese society, with its attendant nouveaux riches, official corruption,

loss of values, dignity and self-respect, and such "moral evils" as drugs and prostitution'.[3] David Shambaugh, an influential US scholar and China watcher, characterized the path Xi had chosen as one of 'hard authoritarianism', which, if continued, is likely to have the result that 'economic development will stagnate and even stall, exacerbating already acute social problems and producing the protracted political decline of the ruling Chinese Communist Party'.[4] His harder line most constrains journalists and civil society activists in the more liberal regions of the country – in the south, and along the eastern seaboard, such as the cities of Shanghai and Beijing (Hong Kong is a special case) and provinces such as Guangdong and Jiangsu – where journalists have worked most freely. These are also the richer parts of China.

Osnos comments that the drive had a separate, perhaps more important aim beyond punishing corruption, since it was 'also a proven instrument for political consolidation, and at the highest level Xi has deployed it largely against his opponents'. As the campaign proceeds, stability remains the central value – of the society, but also of the leadership. It is hostile to experiments with democracy, and to a freer press. The prominent commentator Eric X. Li believes that Xi's coming to power in 2012 'might one day be seen as marking the end of the idea that electoral democracy is the only legitimate and effective system of political governance'. Unlike the system in the US, the Chinese form of rule is dedicated to producing the most skilled administrators: 'a person with Barack Obama's pre-presidential professional experience would not even be the manager of a small county in China's system'.[5]

In February 2016, Xi tightened the ropes further. On the nineteenth of that month, he told a gathering of officials who dealt with the media that 'All news media run by the Party must work to speak for the Party's will and its propositions, and protect the Party's authority and unity.'[6] On the same day, a well-known property entrepreneur, Ren Zhiqiang, was attacked on the Beijing's Party committee website for having 'lost his party spirit' and 'opposing the party' when he wrote on his microblog, in reaction to Xi's announcement, that the media should serve the people not the Party; his posts were deleted.[7] David Bandurski, the editor of the China Media Project at the University of Hong Kong, wrote: 'I think the sense is, "We own you, we run you, we tell you how things work. The party is the centre, and you serve our agenda".'[8]

Xi's vision is that journalism should learn again its place – not as servile as in Mao's day, but certainly not in pursuit of the powers of revelation and criticism for which it was grasping in the 1990s and 2000s. At the same time, his rule does not appear to be unpopular. Tough on corruption, he is also tough on what he defines as China's interests beyond its borders and shores – especially in the South China Sea. When, in July of 2016, the UN's Law of the Sea Tribunal in The Hague found China guilty of illegal acts in that region, the media were instructed to ignore the finding, or to represent it as part of a US-inspired attack on China. And ordinary Chinese, deprived of any alternative narrative about other countries' claims, seemed happy to go along with the Party's stance, posting aggressive threats, some of which called for war against the US.[9]

In the years since Xi's assumption of power, he has taken under his control the Party leadership, the state leadership and – through chairmanship of the Central Military Commission – leadership of the armed forces, as well as of several key committees. The power he has accumulated derives its mandate from his leadership of the Communist Party, which in turn rests on the success with which it has, since the 1980s, presided over a steadily rising standard of living, the maintenance of peace and national unity and an ever-more widely recognized position as a major world power. Wise one-party rule has brought success, and Xi is adamant that Western-style democracy cannot be tolerated.[10]

China's leader came to the view that Western democracy is failing, and with it, its hysterical media; at the same time, he also seems to believe that the Chinese media, especially the Net and social media, infected by Western viruses, are straws waiting for a spark. He has a sophisticated and subtle apparatus for putting out threatened fires, which concentrates on narrowing the political space open to the over-indulged media of the two years before his assumption of power, while retaining and expanding, as far as possible, consumer choice and Party-sanctioned entertainment.

'Youwei' (a pseudonym) writes that 'people smart enough to avoid politics entirely will not even feel it ... but it has reduced the chances of any mature civil society developing in contemporary China, let alone a political one'.[11] China's new generation of journalists had seen themselves as developing civil society, and thus were knocked back, hard.

The easing of Party control in the 1980s led to a more negotiable relationship with political and ideological dictates and had given the trade a taste of what it was to make independent journalistic judgements. Editors now had leverage over the Party, of which they would be members, for in order to fulfil their commercial task, they had to interpret the political line more loosely. They now had two masters – the Party (which kept at least 51 per cent of the ownership of media outlets) and the market – and many editors and producers became adept at playing the first off against the second, within limits which the Party controlled.

The number of newspapers, magazines and TV channels, swollen with advertising, grew rapidly. The new journalists, magazine writers, editors and producers were often born in Mao's time, but were young during the last great deadly spasm, the Great Proletarian Cultural Revolution (Mao ended it in 1969, seven years before his death, years after the death of many millions from its effects). They found their professional feet in the rapid liberalization of the eighties – liberalization that allowed, even encouraged, new forms of writing and broadcasting explicitly designed to attract larger and more satisfied audiences. Many in this new audience liked revelatory journalism, since they knew of the system's defects and lies but had never seen them publicly examined.

Entertainment was, of course, more popular. Entertainment in the form of blockbuster films, soap operas, detective series, situation comedies, game shows and celebrity programmes were developed, copied from Hong Kong, Taiwan and the West, which quite soon equalled or surpassed the models in imagination and enthusiasm – the celebrity obsession that Xi grumbled about in his speech on propaganda could be as fevered as anywhere in the West. As his complaint showed, he had Victorian values: under his rule, the deeply unpopular State Administration of Press, Publication, Radio, Film and Television – a censorship body – deepened its reputation as 'a group of joyless, humourless government minders standing between Chinese citizens and the prospect of better movies and television'.[12]

The new freedoms made semi-dissident figures popular. One such was Han Han, born, in 1982, a few years after the Mao era ended, with a novel published when still an adolescent, which excoriated tedious, learn-by-rote school education. He was disapproved of by elders, but 'his visibility reflected how much wider the realm of Chinese intellectual life had become over the past decade. For every writer still barred from travelling abroad, and every novel prevented from publication, another popped up unmolested in a third- or fourth-tier city that was once a cultural desert.'[13] His blog attracted an audience of many millions; he continued to turn out novels and became an 'ambassador' for the smartphone company OnePlus. He developed a line in criticism of the authorities which put him on the side of greater democratic freedoms, while never quite embracing a wholesale democratic revolution, and sometimes appearing to pooh-pooh its possibility. In regretful mode, he wrote, 'In China, influence belongs only to those with power ... They own the theatre, and they can always bring down the curtain, turn off the lights, close the door, and turn the dogs loose.'

—

In democratic societies, journalists often have close ties with civil rights organizations and lawyers, free-speech institutes and NGOs that major on issues like inequality. It's mutually advantageous (if often mildly corrupting), since journalists want the kind of survey and policy information these organizations have, and they in turn want publicity. In China, the Party often judges such links as extremely dangerous, and has moved still more strongly against those involved in legal and civil rights, rather than against the journalists.

As in other authoritarian societies, the different registers of dissidence bleed into each other: art, writing, legal challenges to the political order, civil society activism and journalism have no precise boundaries since they inhabit a common space, which attracts at its mildest disapproval, often suppression and imprisonment. Rosie Blau writes that 'Since Xi Jinping took office, the crackdown on civil society has intensified. Tolerance of the more sensitive groups has declined, and previously accepted groups have been subjected to greater scrutiny.'[14] Xi's Mao-like strictness means that the punishment of dissidence is increasingly focused on the limitations of speech, and novelists are drawn to protest, often taking to journalism to do so.

Murong Xuecun (the pen name of Hao Qun) writes both fiction and reportage. In 2010, he published *China: In the Absence of a Remedy*, a book that revealed the workings of a pyramid scheme in which he had embedded himself as one of its promoters. It was acclaimed in China and won him the annual prize given by *People's Literature* magazine (founded by Mao), which had serialized the book.[15] He had prepared a 4,000-word acceptance speech for the ceremony in Beijing; however, the organizers, aware of its content, banned him from delivering it. On stage, he made a zipping motion with his hand across his lips, and left. He put the speech on the Net, where it became quickly popular;[16] and it was read at the Foreign Correspondents' club in Hong Kong in February 2011.

The speech described working with an editor from the Henan publishing house, who had insisted that the phrase 'an Indian-flavoured fart' should be cut, to avoid any diplomatic problems between the world's two largest countries. 'On this point,' said Murong, '[the editor-cum-censor] was unyielding: I wondered whether China and India would really start a war over a solitary fart.' The speech ended: 'The only truth is that we cannot speak the truth ... Sometimes I can't help wondering: Is the Cultural Revolution really over?'

Since the 1990s, the writer Yu Hua, who is older than Murong and better known in China and abroad, has in a series of novels and short stories been grimly critical of his society, and the ruthless way in which the powerful, revolutionary or capitalist treat the powerless. His reflections on contemporary China, *China in Ten Words*[17] – published in the West in 2010, but unpublished in China – paints a picture of a society where, 'in the short space of thirty years, a China ruled by politics has transformed itself into a China where money is king'. The last word of the ten that he chose was 'bamboozle' – for Yu, the word's popularity 'demonstrates to me the breakdown of social morality and a confusion in the value system in China today ... we live in a frivolous society, one that doesn't set much store by matters of principle'.

Some, clandestinely, do set some store. In 2008, a small group of historians began to gather periodically in a dark, badly fabricated flat in a township near Beijing to put out an occasional PDF to no more than 200 subscribers. It's called *Remembrance*, and it's one of several publications that seek to research and preserve the 'unofficial memory' of the country, especially in the Communist period.[18] Its projects have included cajoling a female Red Guard, who was the daughter of a high Party functionary, into admitting her role in torturing to death, with other girls, a vice principal of their school during the Cultural Revolution. Remarkably, *Remembrance* has survived and flourished. From ten issues in 2008, it published no less than thirty in 2016, each issue over sixty pages. An early review of the then fledgling magazine in 2009 by Michael Schoenhals in *China Quarterly* asked how the review, available only in web form, jumped the Great Firewall

– and speculated that 'it is a tiny mouse that darts through the cracks in the wall's foundation, noticed but left alone by the cybercensor's black and white felines'.[19] In a later extended evocation of the journal's extraordinary existence, the journalist and scholar of China Ian Johnson gives another explanation – that though 'the government still controls official history through textbooks, museums, movies and the media ... memory is more private, and setting it down on paper can be presented as a personal enterprise, even when the outcome is highly political'.[20]

Johnson, who has spent much of his professional life in China, is remarkably active in searching for the realities of China's recent past. In December 2016, he set out to find 'a garrulous, stubborn, and emotional editor', Tan Hecheng, who had made it his business to research and write about one of the worst massacres of the Mao era, the Dao County killing in 1967 (Dao County is in Hunan, in South-Central China). In 1986 Tan, and a reporter on a magazine, had been sent to write about the massacre – following a government report on the killings, in which some 9,000 people had died. He travelled and interviewed extensively, then wrote an article – only to have it rejected as too pessimistic, not the kind of upbeat story which stressed that the Party had efficiently and justly dealt with the massacre.

But he had heard too many stories of horror – killings, torture and infanticide – to be able to accept that justice had been served with a few minor imprisonments, and wrote his own book. It included the story of Mrs Zhou and her family, deemed 'bad elements' because her father had been a traffic policeman under the nationalist government. All the family, including the children, had been flung, still living, into a pit; only Mrs Zhou survived. Tan told the American writer: 'I can tell people what they want to hear, and I can write an article in the way you want it. But I have a minimum moral standard: I can't turn black into white. Somehow I just can't do that.'[21]

The Chinese dissidents are often put, or put themselves, in the same position in relation to the Party as Galileo vis-à-vis the Catholic Church.

Galileo had developed a heliocentric view of the universe against the Catholic dogma that the earth was at its centre, round which the sun moved (a greater 'truth', since it underpinned the Christian view of the centrality of God and his relationship with humanity). He was condemned by the Inquisition in 1533, and confined to house arrest for the rest of his life. Over centuries, the Church caught up; so, some dissidents believe, will Chinese politicians have to acknowledge that their authoritarian view of China is a dogma based on a falsehood. In their view, the current system is unsustainable in a world where the opinions of hundreds of millions of Chinese *are* attended to – closely – but only for reasons of control.

Journalists usually follow rather than lead. Most journalists in authoritarian societies more or less follow officially approved paths; it's a living, sometimes a good one, and in any case the paths are sometimes wider than they were. But even to follow properly means to exercise a certain freedom to discover and tell a story which makes sense in a pragmatic, factual sense. Some journalists would not or could not simply follow: one was Gao Yu.

Born in 1944, Gao Yu had a career in journalism which, from the early eighties, was marked by independence of thought. Freelancing for papers in China and Hong Kong, she published a piece in Hong Kong's *Mirror Monthly* magazine strongly attacking the Beijing government, which branded her an open dissident. She was later arrested for her participation in the Tiananmen Square protests and sentenced to six years in prison, but was released after fifteen months because of poor health. Arrested again in 1993 for 'publishing state secrets', she served five years before being released on health grounds for a second time. In April 2015, she was found guilty of 'leaking state secrets' and sentenced to seven years (the charge could have meant the death penalty). She had admitted to the charge, which was televised and broadcast widely; however, in court, she denied her admission, saying it had been given to protect her son, arrested with her and later released.[22]

The document she was accused of leaking was 'Document Number 9', titled 'On the Current State of the Ideological Sphere', which was circulated amongst the Party in April 2013 by the general office of the Central Committee, claiming endorsement from the leadership.[23] It describes the state/Party's main enemies as being the concept of civil society, neoliberal economic ideas (e.g. complete privatization and a market for everything, such as health care and pensions) and the universal applicability of liberal democratic values, which could allow a Western form of democracy underpinned by a constitution 'to undermine the Party's leadership, abolish the People's Democracy, negate our country's constitution as well as our established system and principles, and bring about a change of allegiance by bringing Western political systems to China'. Other threats that were identified included the call for complete freedom of the press and the Net, the opposition to the Party's leadership in the media and the challenge to the Party's view of its history. It concludes with an exhortation to the Party members to 'reinforce our management of all types and levels of propaganda on the cultural front … and allow absolutely no opportunity or outlets for incorrect thinking or viewpoints to spread'.

'Document Number 9' makes vividly clear the way in which the upper reaches of the Communist Party of China see liberal democracy, and draws a sharp line between the Chinese system and the West. This was a leak of real importance. Gao had shown that her state was determined to expunge all 'incorrect thinking', giving flesh to Shambaugh's description of 'hard authoritarianism'. Gao, displaying extraordinary courage in pursuing a vision of a more open society, was faced with a long jail sentence in her seventies, with health problems that made survival doubtful. Her brother, taking her supplies into prison during her trial, said that her clothes were too large for her, so thin had she become. In November 2015, she was released on health grounds, to serve out her sentence at home.[24]

—

For dissidents, the Net has been seen as a huge addition to their armoury: Liu Xiaobo, the literary critic imprisoned several times for calling for an end to Party rule and awarded the Nobel Prize in 2010, said that 'the Net is surely God's gift to the Chinese people'. But for most Chinese people, as it is for most people around the world, much of the Net is for entertainment and distraction, and although YouTube (owned by Google since 2006) is banned, Chinese services such as Youku Tudou, Sohu and QQ TV grew quickly and now host over 300 million unique views each month. They need a licence to operate, but otherwise have been left largely free to regulate themselves. In contrast, the 3,000 broadcast stations in China are all under the Central Chinese TV umbrella, which means that the state controls them and imposes a host of regulations. However, it is different for online video. Vincent Tao, head of one of the services, PPTV, says, 'In principle it's the same, but in reality it's very difficult to say what the standards are for the online-video content players.'[25] Since entertainment is by far the most popular online activity, the mildly transgressive nature of viewing some of the material opens the space in which private enjoyment can play unhindered.

For the Party, this is occasionally irritating, but minor. The real concern, after the hard-core dissidents, is what the news media are doing, and even there, even after Xi's speech, much that would have been unthinkable in Mao's time is now left alone. A relatively optimistic Western view held that 'for the Party as a whole the Internet holds much less terror than it does for local officials. The online mob can gorge itself on corrupt low-level officials because the party leaders allow it ... Allowing a distinctly Chinese Internet to flourish has been an important part of building a better cage. But it is constantly watched over and manipulated.'[26] And watched over more closely, now.

As Xi was approaching full power, the social network Weibo was also displaying its potential in leading the way for a freer Net. Launched by the SINA corporation in August 2009, Weibo is a close cousin of Twitter (banned in China), but allows longer messages. It quickly acquired a huge following and by December 2012, it had half a billion registered users. One Chinese journalist, preferring to be anonymous, told me via email that, assisted by Weibo,

> both the Chinese grassroots and the social elites have broken through traditional media's discourse monopoly and the government's strict surveillance, sharing information instantly, setting the agenda for public opinion actively, discussing sensitive topics implicitly, exposing injustice cases publicly, and even calling on the public to put pressure on the authorities directly. It is no exaggeration to say that Weibo has changed the Chinese media ecology.

Jiao Bei, a reporter for the *South China Morning Post*, isn't so sanguine.[27] She thinks it's constantly controlled, and now ever more closely, but identified a series of incidents in which Weibo had, in her experience, helped. One, the high-profile Wenzhou train crash in July 2011, where the hasty and secretive rescue operation – which reportedly included the attempted burial of a carriage with a live child in it –

> generated a seething outrage among media and online communities. The accident prompted passionate questioning of official hubris and safety standards by otherwise tightly-controlled Chinese media ... Fifty-four officials were held responsible for the accident and botched rescue effort. In August, the government also announced suspension of approvals for any new high-speed rail lines pending the outcome of the investigation.

Weibo and other social media elevated another local episode to nationwide attention. This was the Wukan incident, where a town of some 12,000 people protested against local corruption and saw representatives – who were elected to negotiate with the authorities over real estate sales which included the confiscation of land – imprisoned and in one case killed. The provincial and central authorities issued directives to play down, then to ban, all coverage. Bei writes that the incident was 'more political and sensitive from the Communist Party point of view, and ... if journalists had broadcast anything about it on Weibo, they would be recalled or punished by their employers. In other words, when a real instance of real democratization occurred, mainland journalists and their Weibo accounts fell silent.' Weibo had been the main medium of information before the ban – and was again when a deal was struck. The land in Wukan that had been confiscated was redistributed; two local officials were held responsible for the confrontation and a new town committee was elected.

Another reporter, who also preferred to remain anonymous, told me of the 'Smiling Head' incident – a large-scale accident in Yanan City in which thirty-six people were killed, where a photograph that was taken and put on Weibo showed a man who looked like a local official standing by the grisly scene, smiling. The picture went viral, and the man was quickly identified as Yang Dacai, head of the local Work Safety Administration, detailed to superintend the relief work. Such was the indignation whipped up that Weibo users found other images of Yang wearing different watches at different functions – eleven in total, five of them costly – and he soon acquired a second name: Uncle Watch. The Shanxi provincial government promised an inquiry, but the promise didn't stop the flood. Finally, the government accelerated the investigation, found evidence of corruption, expelled Smiling Head Uncle Watch from his job and from the Party and turned him over to the court, which sentenced him to fourteen years' imprisonment. Trial by Weibo.

Every year, the Centre for Civil Society Studies at Beijing University selects ten incidents which it considers to be the most influential from the preceding year. Over the three years from 2011 to 2013, the thirty incidents were, according to the centre, the hottest of topics on Weibo, and most were influenced by the message service. They include – the headlines tell the story – 'Guo Meimei flaunting wealth in 2011', 'Mother of a rape victim sent to a labour camp in 2012', 'Uncle Watch and Uncle House: corrupt officials revealed in 2012' and 'Chen Xiaolu apologizes for torture of teachers in 2013'. There were more, and in some cases – as in Uncle Watch – the Weibo torrents clearly swayed the government towards a corrective course of action which, left to itself, it would probably never have embarked upon.

But Bei's conclusions are downbeat. Weibo, even with the greater length of posts than Twitter allows, isn't investigative journalism and it doesn't allow for an examination of the facts. She quotes Shi Feike, one of the most prominent investigative reporters in China, who worked on the *Southern Weekend* (also known as the *Southern Weekly*) in Guangzhou and then on the magazine *Caixin*, as saying: 'My observation is that those journalists who are very active and high-profile on Weibo usually don't produce better investigative reports. They made their names on Weibo, but that didn't add any credit to their stories.'[28] Feike, often on the sharp end of the censors' and officials' efforts to stop him publishing, believes that much of the hope vested in Weibo is 'ludicrously overoptimistic', since however rapidly it allows information to be broadcast, in the end it falls into the hands of the authorities.

Weibo, hit by official disapproval and acquiring something of a danger-ous reputation, lost ground in the mid 2010s to a new, approved medium: WeChat. By 2016, WeChat had nearly three times as many users as Weibo.

A weight of institutions is dedicated to controlling the Net and social media. These authorities quickly come to understand the technology, then spread the word on how to monitor and confine it. The Party's Propaganda Department is generally thought to be the most powerful, since it is a Party institution, but there are many others that are responsible for protecting citizens from the Net, such as the State Council Information Office; the State Administration of Press, Publications, Radio, Film and Television;

the Ministry of Industry and Information Technology; the Ministry of Public Security; the State Administration for Industry and Commerce; the Chinese Academy of Sciences; and the National Administration for the Protection of State Secrets.

In 2011, the State Internet Information Office was established, nominally the dominant force, crossing as it does both Party and state lines, but it too was trumped, in February 2014, by the creation of the Central Leading Group for Internet Security and Informization, chaired by Xi, which includes twenty-two other Party chiefs, including the ministers of Foreign Affairs, of Public Security, of Education, of Industry and Information Technology and of Culture, the Governor of the Central Bank and the head of the Central Secretariat.

The efficiency of the various bodies in keeping journalism in general and Net journalism in particular in line is formidable. Drawing on the work of Xiao Qiang, who runs the invaluable China Digital Times site at the School of Information at Berkeley, Perry Link writes that the armoury of inhibitions open to the censors include: 'mention without hyping', 'publish but only under small headlines', 'put only on back pages', 'close the comment boxes' and 'downplay as time passes'.[29] A leaked summary of directives sent to censors in Hunan province in June 2011 reads:

> All websites should conscientiously grasp the relevant principles and use them to purge any material that: 1) blackens the image of Party and state leaders or obfuscates the great historical achievements of the Party; 2) attacks our system or advocates the Western democratic system; 3) incites illegal assembly, petitioning, or 'rights support' activity that harms social stability; 4) uses price rises, corruption cases, or other controversial events to spread rumours and incite hatred of officials, of police, or of the wealthy that could lead to activity offline; 5) incites ethnic hatred [of Han Chinese] that harms national unity.

And best of all, an entrant for the Orwell Prize in Newspeak: '6) attacks the Party's systems of managing the media and the Internet by using the slanderous claim that we limit free speech'.

The Party's investment in censorship and propaganda is huge, and – at least internally – subtle. Haifeng Huang, studying the latter, found that those who were trained in creating and disseminating didn't necessarily believe the content, but 'were more likely to believe that the government is strong'.[30] Other research has found that much criticism, even strongly put, does not provoke the censor; what does is 'the probability of collective action', such as the possible spreading of 'protests in Inner Mongolia after a coal truck driver killed a herder'.[31]

The energy, resources and time dedicated to media management is testimony to its central importance, especially in Xi's reign. A major element of that is the projection of 'soft power'. In a special plenary session which the Party Central Committee dedicated to endorsing this much-prized form of national projection in 2011, as Xi was preparing for the highest office, billions of dollars were set aside to be spent on China Central Television (CCTV) International broadcasting twenty-four hours in six languages round the world. Funding was also approved for dozens of cultural centres called Confucius Institutes, the Xinhua news agency with 3,000 journalists, 400 of them in 170 bureaus round the world and for promoting the teaching of Chinese in schools in the West. Yet, according to David Shambaugh, this vast expenditure has borne small fruit. 'It has yet to see any demonstrable improvement in its global image, as measured by public opinion surveys. In fact, the country's reputation has steadily deteriorated.'[32]

And censors can rebel. One, using his Weibo account in January 2013, disclosed how the company for which he worked, SINA, had to make compromises to continue its business: though a 'private' company, it is like all media corporations part-controlled by the Party and must employ a number of censors – 'If we don't delete your post, the alternative is that your account will be banned. This platform belongs to the public. It has changed our life and can exercise influence on the society and government through the spread of opinion. On the one hand, we have millions of netizens, on the other hand, we have ... a special group of people have the authority to decide on the criteria for giving out alert signals, and can make [SINA] Weibo go "game-over" as simply as treading on some ants without giving a damn about people's needs. When they issue urgent orders (like the Emperor's 18 golden orders in ancient time), you have to execute them.'[33]

The decisions of the censors are often detailed and precise, displaying a keen news sense as well as providing a valuable illumination of the worries, large and small, of the governing elite. China Digital Times collected some of the censors' decrees and published them in March 2014 – 'March 8: without official authorization, not to interpret and comment on the incident of the missing Malaysian plane' (this was in reference to the Malaysia Airlines plane that had been shot down over Ukraine); 'March 17: not to hype the Crimea referendum, not to correlate Crimea with China's Taiwan, Tibet and Xinjiang and not to comment on the Foreign Ministry's actions'; 'March 25: not to hype details of Michelle Obama's China trip, like her meal orders and the government's clearance preparation on the Great Wall before she visited it'; 'without official authorization, not to report the Deputy Director of the State Council Information Office Li Wufeng's accidental death, and delete all hypothetical and aggressive comments'.[34]

In 2016, the China Digital Times and the Washington-based Freedom House found that many directives were aimed at encouraging positive coverage of Xi, including: ordering all websites to credit Xi with eliciting a 'strong response' among his listeners for his speech on the Party's ninety-fifth anniversary; forbidding reprinting or referring to an article in a new website, The Paper, on dangerous, unrefrigerated vaccines; banning any reference to high-placed officials' control of foreign assets, as revealed in the Panama Papers, and restricting coverage of police misconduct, including a suspicious death in custody and a wrongful execution.

Away from the most sensitive points, Weibo and now the more popular WeChat do much to open up what had previously been hidden, or at any rate limited as to access. For example, the China Earthquake Administration's network centre, through its official Weibo@CENCExpress, pumps out large amounts of clear information on earthquakes – predictions, warnings, facts on the (moving) ground – both ending the government's previous obsessive secrecy about these (not infrequent, often deadly) incidents, and greatly assisting rescue and relief.

The Paper, which had offended the censors by its investigation into unsafe vaccines, is one of the slickest of the new Chinese publications: its very title is a joke, since it's a website. Started in the mid 2010s in Shanghai, it soon spun off an English-language sister publication, Sixth Tone – the title chosen, the editors explained,[35] to be an addition to the five tones in Mandarin Chinese, one which 'tells the uncommon stories of common people'. It's a hybrid, a Party publication carrying respectful stories mixed with investigations that seem to disturb officials. It attracts the young with entertainment and celebrity stories – but keeps up a diet of exposés of miscarriages of justice, health scandals and bribery. Liberals grumble that it's still hobbled, conservatives that it does little to promote the central role of ideology, which Xi had promised to renew.

A piece in Sixth Tone revealed that migrant construction workers, who often live in primitive conditions, had taken to poetry, spurred by a Shanghai social work centre which started a festival of poetry for the migrants. One poem concluded: 'To achieve equality, first we must struggle;/To achieve liberation, first we must fight./We will never allow the return of exploitation.'[36] The article, by the founder of a migrant centre in Beijing, Li Adun, ends by saying that for the workers, 'the only way out is to re-establish a socialist approach that acknowledges and respects labour and labourers as key pillars of Chinese society'. Is that a criticism of the Party and the state? Or does it chime with Xi's call for a refocusing on socialist values?

The famous answer of the former Chinese prime minister, Zhou Enlai, to a question on the effects of the 1789 French Revolution – 'it's too early to say' – may be applied more accurately to the effects of the Net and social media.[37]

Qian Gang is, under Western eyes, a strange figure to be a radically minded journalist. He joined the People's Liberation Army, became an officer and went to work on the army's newspaper, the *People's Liberation Army Daily*. Founded in 1956, the paper serves the 2.3 million members of the PLA (all military, including ground forces, air force, navy and rocket force) with stories and features on military life, cleaving closely to the Party line, leaving high military strategy to commentary in the *People's Daily* or specialized journals.

But Qian, who had an enquiring mind and a liberal bent, found that on the staff of the paper were several 'rightists', followers of the former military commander and vice-premier Lin Biao, who – designated by Mao as his successor – was accused of planning a coup against the Great Helmsman. He died in a plane crash in Mongolia, while apparently fleeing to the Soviet Union (there is much dispute about his flight); he was rehabilitated after the death of Mao in 1976.

In a talk at the offices of the China Media Project at the University of Hong Kong, co-founded with the Chinese–American journalist Yuen-Ying Chan, he told me that the 'rightists' had a concept of 'an idealistic journalism', which strongly influenced him. Taking advantage of a more liberal atmosphere in the eighties, they were able to get critical stories into the paper. One concerned a high-ranking general who had ordered a military kindergarten to be closed. A junior officer wrote a poem about the closure, entitled 'You Can't Do That!', which was published across an entire page. Predictably, the editor – 'my role model' – was fired.

Liberalism had its limits: Qian, by 1989 promoted to news editor, was also fired for his pro-student sympathies in the Tiananmen Square attacks. He left to work for the China Earthquake Bureau, researching a book on the Zhaotong earthquake of 1974 in Yunnan province, in which up to 20,000 people had died: 'This was investigative journalism, but we didn't call it that then. In fact, it was easier to research in the atmosphere of the time than it became later.' While he was there, Deng Xiaoping made a speech proclaiming that the reforms he had championed, halted by the Tiananmen Square incident, would continue – and by the mid nineties, the atmosphere of experimentation with new forms of journalism had penetrated into institutions that were once the most conservative and tightly controlled. CCTV, the country-wide TV monopoly, had perforce to hire creative and adventurous spirits to develop programming that had been given a mandate to attract rather than simply preach or exhort. A producer at CCTV had seen episodes of the CBS investigative programme *60 Minutes* in Chinese subtitled videos brought in from Hong Kong: these, with subsequent viewings of British and Australian programmes, formed one inspiration of a programme named *News Probe*, launched in 1996, with Qian initially hired as an adviser, later taking up a senior editorial position. Qian said that

We did some good things – as on river pollution, and on World War II. But we couldn't do much about one of the biggest problems, which was corruption among the higher-ups. We did do a story about an official who had been found guilty of corruption, but this was only allowed because he had already been punished. In that sense, we were investigating, not his corruption, but his feelings.

During my three years at *News Probe* I could feel the space for investigations getting smaller and smaller. The death of Deng in 1997 affected this too. So I was dissatisfied there. The paper in Guangzhou, *Southern Weekend*, was becoming well known for its stories, publishing a lot of good investigations. They had asked me several times to join them – and so in 1998, I went, as executive editor.

Guangzhou, in China's deep south – a short train journey over the border to Hong Kong – was one of the cities visited by Deng in his 1992 southern tour in which he reassured his followers that reforms were alive and well. The speed and tempo of the city's switch from controlled metropolis to production hub for the wakening tiger imparted excitement and elan into its journalistic community. Qian's qualities of curiosity, his desire to exhume the dark spots of the past as well as of the present, his forthrightness and cheerful character – he was an inspirational interviewee – as well as the authority he had acquired both in detailed reporting and in supervising the work of others made him an obvious choice. At *News Probe*, he had seen how Western models worked and realized the need for a journalism that broke free as much as it could from the suffocating 'guidance' of the Party, and he grasped the moral as well as the practical base for the journalism he helped to develop. 'The task now for us,' he said, 'is to make the news media more independent and also more responsible. Freedom and responsibility should be the slogan. Reform can happen in and out of the system. There are more and more journalists who are interested in this. We have been cheated for a long time, during our childhood and after. We don't want to go back.'

Qian went to *Southern Weekend* during a bleak period. As he noted in our talk, 'a time when there are big, negative cases are bad for the wider space the news media had been granted'. One of these cases was a huge demonstration by members of the Falun Gong spiritual cult, an offshoot of Buddhism, in April 1999, and the harsh crackdown on the group in the following October, which included a massive propaganda campaign and a strict prohibition against mentioning the cult's name. In May of the same year, the Chinese embassy in Belgrade was bombed during the Yugoslavian conflict and three visiting Chinese reporters were killed. The government called it a barbaric act, while a contrite US apologized and claimed it was accidental. Finally, 1999 was the tenth anniversary of Tiananmen Square. 'All of these were connected,' said Qian. All tended to narrow the 'wider spaces' within which journalists were learning to roam.

Two newspapers – the *Southern Metropolitan Daily* and the *Southern Weekly* – have, more than any other publications in China, placed themselves at the forefront of the investigative journalism movement, which gathered force through the 1990s. The new economic zone in Guangdong province, of which Guangzhou and the neighbouring city of Shenzhen were the hubs, had developed more rapidly than any other part of the country, except Shanghai, as they sucked in millions of labourers from the countryside. These new citizens lived in squalid hostels, while the rich built themselves luxury flats overlooking the Pearl River, and the expanding middle class moved into more modest apartments. There was a great deal to write about, to discover, to probe.

It was fitting that the craft took off in this raucous city, because journalism needed a market and the modicum of freedom that the southern cities were developing. Deng, in his second southern tour in 1992, had issued a general exhortation to the press to become more interesting, and to pay for itself – cease, that is, to be a burden on the state budget because it couldn't get enough people to buy, and latterly to advertise in, publications that printed verbatim empty speeches and lauded heroes of this labour or that meritorious action. The provincial and Guangzhou City Party bureaucracies, tasked with reforming the news media they ultimately controlled in Deng's spirit, had to modify the habits of a Party lifetime and permit journalistic experimentation.

The main news group in the area, the Southern Media Group, had a certain tradition for independence; it had been, even in Maoist times, a place for the Party's cautiously liberal wing. In 1957, during the 'Hundred Flowers' movement, the group launched a paper called the *Yangchen Evening News*: one of whose founders put it about that, even if they couldn't always tell the truth, they shouldn't tell lies. This was repeated, forty years and many horrors later, by the secretary of the provincial Propaganda Committee, Huang Wenyu, who told the journalists in the mid nineties that the key to breaking with the Party press model was to tell the truth.

Only when a newspaper tells the truth could it establish credibility. Asked by sceptical journalists if this was an absolute rule in all cases, he glossed his statement, saying, 'You do not tell some truths that you cannot tell for the time being, but you cannot in any circumstances tell lies.'[38] This was, of course, over-optimistic.

When, in the early 1990s, the ideological constraints eased and the editors were told to be interesting, they reached for investigative journalism – the uncovering of scandals and hidden issues – as one of the ways to make their papers popular. The group had a weekly, the *Southern Weekend*, which was already breaking old reportorial taboos, and they founded a new paper, the *Southern Metropolitan Daily*, to be the flagship of the new approach. A young reporter, Cheng Yizhong, was hired, even though he had taken part in local protests inspired by the students in Beijing's Tiananmen Square. When the group founded *Southern Metropolitan Daily* in 1997, he was made deputy, then chief, editor, at the age of thirty-seven. Philip Pan writes of Cheng that though he filled the pages of the paper with sports, celebrities and entertainment (he took a quarter of the tabloid's pages to cover the death of Diana, Princess of Wales, in August 1997, while other papers gave it a paragraph), he 'also saw to it that he provided the readers with another scarce commodity they craved – journalism that challenged the government ... he wanted reporters who would push the limits, not censor themselves'.[39]

Both the Party and the journalists – the senior ones were generally Party members, subject to its discipline – were pushing, with differing degrees of enthusiasm and courage, at the limits. The former editor of *Southern Weekly*, Zuo Fang, told me the story of a crisis in 1993, when a policeman turned rogue, threatened those he was supposed to protect and was murdered. The story was printed – and it was then discovered that the reporter had made it up. The conservative faction in the provincial Party, alarmed by the relative boisterousness of the paper, even before it spawned the more adventurous *Southern Metropolitan Daily*, demanded its closure.

Xie Fei, the Guangdong provincial Party secretary (no connection to the well-known film director of the same name), used his membership of the Party's politburo to argue it should not be closed because of one mistake: 'If the problem is the problem of the specific article, we can punish the editorial department but cannot close the whole newspaper.'

In Guangzhou I talked with Fan Yijing, who had been a director of the Southern Daily Press Group, then became a professor of journalism at Jinan University. He was regarded as something of a patron and protector of the new style; his walls are hung with affectionately jokey caricatures of him.

Speaking in his spacious, untidy office, he told me:

The *Southern Metropolitan Daily* and the *Southern Weekly* were started to deal with the new competition – for readers and advertisers. We wanted them to be bought on their own account – not, as the Party members did, subscribe to the Party papers because they must. So you had to be sure you were in tune with the thoughts and needs of the citizens. As, for example, with *Farmers' Daily*; it was closed during the Cultural Revolution and we restarted it, with tips on education and learning about farming work, and stories about the loss of land, which was worrying the farmers at the time. The central government wanted the farmers to get compensation; but the local Party wasn't keen. So we kept on writing about their worries, and kind of supervised the process [of their getting compensation]. At that time the central party wanted to be more liberal than the provincial party.

Fan is most proud of a story the *Southern Metropolitan Daily* published in 2003, which centred on the death of a student in police custody; indeed, it remains a source of pride for journalists in the entire group. Rather like the Watergate story, it depended on dogged, and unpopular, reporting and courage on the part of the reporters and the editors, with a 'happy' result for the society (though less so for the leading journalists). Fan says:

This was the best story this group has done. The whole press group supported us doing this story. And the central government in Beijing, then, supported this kind of reporting, though they've now revised their philosophy and don't allow this any more. But the local Party committee of the time hated it, and they demanded a price. In this province still there are people who hate us, and people who support us; and they fight a lot. The people who hate us are in power now [2011].

The student who died in police custody was named Sun Zhigang, son of a peasant family in Hubei province north of Guangdong, who had come to Guangzhou to find work as a designer with a clothing company. Picked up one night and lacking documents – though they were quickly produced by the friend with whom he was staying – he was taken to a police station, detained, then sent on to a shourong facility. Shourong stations had a bad reputation: these were the places police dumped beggars, out-of-towners without papers and others they didn't like, and they were often beaten. After a few days there, during which Sun's friends were unable to contact or get news of him, they were told he was dead. The *Southern Metropolitan Daily* reporters, one of whom, Chen Feng, had learned the story from a friend of a friend of Sun's, couldn't get most officials to speak, but the forensic pathologist said the marks on Sun's body were consistent with his having been badly beaten within seventy-two hours of his death.

The story was delicate. Discovered in a classic (to Western eyes) way, it was reported as fully as possible, given the official silence. But the reporters had no permission, the police were usually untouchable and the shourong system was a national policy. Cheng Yizhong, the bold editor, was aware of the risks he was running, but firmly gave the go-ahead, after telling his reporters – like every editor faced with a tough call – that they had better be sure of their facts. It ran with an uncompromising deck of headlines: 'Death of Shourong Detainee Sun Zhigang', and below it: 'University Graduate, 27, Dies Three Days after Being Detained on Guangzhou Street, Autopsy

Shows Violent Beating Before Death'. Cheng knew the story was going to be big, but he was not prepared for the tens of thousands of messages that flooded into the offices, testament to the hatred with which the shourong system and the police were seen by many.

The torrent of anger unleashed by the story – nationwide, not 'just' the 100-million-plus citizens of Guangdong province – put pressure on the government to change the system. Chen and his colleagues kept up the heat: they had been banned from writing further on the Sun case, so they wrote more about the victims of shourong. The resulting investigation into the incident showed that Sun had been covered in a blanket and beaten violently by a gang of men. A mere two months after the *Southern Metropolitan Daily* splash, Wen Jiabao, recently appointed prime minister, got his government to abolish the system.

Victory couldn't be allowed to be that sweet. Those who already hated the *Southern Metropolitan Daily* now had even more reason to hate it; and those who had protected the group were losing the argument. First one, then two of Cheng's colleagues, both senior editors, were arrested; one was tortured. Then they came for him, and though he avoided the worst, he was interrogated through the night, his hair pulled when he fell asleep, cold water thrown over him. But thousands of journalists, lawyers and others were petitioning for his release, which came after a few months. One of his colleagues was also released soon after; only one ended up serving a four-year sentence, reduced from eleven.

Cheng wasn't allowed back to his previous post, soon left Guangzhou and took the job of editing the Chinese edition of *Sports Illustrated*. He's spoken out a few times since; in one ironic microblog he wrote:

China's great ... as long as you feel it's no big deal if politics aren't civilized, the system isn't mature, there's no balance of power, and the future is uncertain; if you turn a blind eye to the rule of law not being set out, the lack of justice, unfairness in society, and the disparity between rich

and poor don't need freedom of expression, freedom of religion, freedom
from poverty, or freedom from terror; and if you don't care about resource
depletion, environmental collapse, and the pollution of the air, water, and
soil – well, this is your paradise.[40]

The Sun Zhigang story was the high-water mark; its effect reached
across the vast population. The documentary maker Ai Xiaoming, who has
made harshly realistic accounts of Chinese life, says that 'the Sun Zhigang
case awoke a lot of expectations – that slow, step-by-step qualitative
change was possible'.[41] But, she continues, the journalistic possibilities
that the story seemed to help open had closed, leaving a country in which:
'power has changed Chinese people's psychological make-up ... I just think
we shouldn't underestimate this barbaric totalitarianism. We shouldn't
underestimate how it has corroded people's hearts. Because this people's
character, having lived under this system for so long, has become weak,
and become powerless.'

The Southern Metropolitan Daily continued to do hard-hitting journalism,
but it compromised more. As the paper became richer, it became more
conservative: a new slogan, 'the mainstream is power', signalled a
reversion to a more moderate style. By 2009, the investigative reporting
team lost its autonomy and was incorporated into the general newsroom;
investigations appeared less frequently. In June 2011, a new editor, Cao Ke,
was appointed and he gave a speech to the staff, in which he said:

I know in the outside society, people praise SMD, say that you dare
confront the government, how great you are! But we shall not be affected
by this kind of comment. They are pushing SMD to the trap. They are
baking SMD on the fire. We do not want this kind of honour. We want
sustainable development. Do not think it is a violation of your journalistic
standard to cooperate with the government.[42]

The crisis in investigative journalism deepened. At the SMD, Chang Ping, a sharp critic of the political scene, was purged. Elsewhere, many who had made waves were reassigned to calmer duties, or were fired. Most noted was the sacking of the veteran reporter Wang Keqin, known as 'the Chinese Lincoln Steffens' (among the most famed of the early twentieth-century 'muckraking' journalists)'. Wang had exposed the taxi monopoly in Beijing, where taxi companies subjected their drivers to a range of illegal taxes for the right to continue to drive; fraud in the stock market; the seizure of farmers' land for property development; and – most famously – the exposure of an unsafe vaccine which had been administered to children in Shanxi province. Wang was fired from the Beijing-based *Economic Times*, along with his team and the editor who had tried to protect him.

The firing of some of the Guangzhou Group's bolder spirits, from both the SMD and the *Southern Weekend*, did not excise the tensions. In December 2012, a senior editor at the *Southern Weekend*, Dai Zhiyong, drafted the traditional New Year's greeting to its readers, calling it 'China's dream: the dream of constitutionalism' – coupling Xi Jinping's slogan 'China Dream' (an aping of 'the American Dream') with a call for a constitutional government that would defend human rights, would limit and divide power, 'so that people can voice their criticism towards public authority, so that all of us can live a free life according to our beliefs'. Dai said that 'we must learn from British and American constitutionalism and catch up with modern technology and civilization'. The chief editor, Huang Can, didn't like it, ordered it redrafted and cut it from 2,000 to 1,000 words. Submitted to the propaganda authorities on 31 December, it came back with major changes. The draft was signed off, but overnight the senior editors were called back and further changes made – probably (it remains unclear) by the propaganda officials.

Nothing of the former spirit remained save a vague reference to constitutional government, in no way recommended. Xi Jinping's evocation of a dream of the 'rejuvenation of the Chinese nation' is at the centre of the message; he dreams the dreams for all. Xiao Shu, a former editorial writer on the *Southern Weekend*, wrote that the tension was ratcheted up from May 2012, when

> Tuo Zhen became head of party propaganda in Guangdong ... Major topics of news coverage had to be approved by him, as did important articles, especially opinion essays ... Under Mr Tuo, the press in Guangdong retreated into its darkest period since the start of Deng Xiaoping's 'reform and opening up' policies in the late 1970s. *Southern Weekend*, a symbol of news professionalism because of its relative independence, bore the brunt of Mr Tuo's attacks.[43]

Many of the staff threatened to strike, which was an unprecedented step. After a few days in which the web and Weibo hummed with commentary, much of it supportive of the would-be strikers, a compromise was reached: the government banned pre-publication censorship, the strike threat was withdrawn. Xiao Shu was wary: 'The deep-seated question has not been resolved: is there, in fact, room for professional journalism to survive and develop within the system?'[44]

Speaking anonymously, a former staffer told me that investigative journalism is two-sided:

> One side of it is progressive, in the sense that in many cases investigative journalism is able to bring social change – even if usually confined to low levels and on a local scale. For instance, in an investigation of AIDS in a village, media reporting indeed led to better living conditions of the villagers, better medical treatment of the AIDS patients, better social order in the village, and better performance of the local government.
>
> But on the other hand, it has also demonstrated the conservative side of Chinese investigative journalism. It places the criteria for judging 'good journalism' in the hands of the party-state. It wields the power of the

social, moral and political establishment, and it punishes the relatively powerless (i.e. the blood dealers in the AIDS village case) while excusing the powerful government from any serious responsibility ... What is done in this limited space of 'critical reporting' is often, as a Chinese saying goes, to 'swat flies' but not to 'beat tigers'.

The logic of the position of the reporters who wish to continue investigative work leads them out of journalism into activism: or into activism mixed with journalism. Xiao Shu commented:

> There are two levels of things journalists can do. One is to intervene through writing in the public media. 'Make a change through writing' is what our predecessors, and the traditional Chinese intellectuals, believed. But there is another level. To penetrate into reality you have to get down from the level of abstract speeches and ideas. You need to take direct action. From 'making a change through writing' to 'making a change through action' is an important shift in the thinking of a journalist's role in civil society.[45]

Xiao Shu was at the head of a movement. The former *Southern Weekend* reporter Shi Feike endorsed his call, defining activist journalists as reporters usually working for mainstream media, but ambitious both to participate in and to influence society. Many of those most drawn to activism were from peasant backgrounds, the first generation to be university trained. Journalists in the SMD and the *Southern Weekend* had, in the early days, my anonymous interviewee told me:

> claimed that they are citizens first and journalists second, by which they meant that they remained strongly attached to the development and contradictions of Chinese society, while working as media professionals, by speaking for the marginalized people, exposing social injustice

and promoting democracy ... These reports won the *Southern Weekly* journalists a high reputation in the Chinese society, as being dubbed as 'the conscience of Chinese media'. But the golden period proved to be short.

Chinese leaders define responsibility as subservience to the wisdom of the Party, but responsibility that makes journalism effective and underpins its freedom is responsibility to a truth-seeking discipline, as a medium through which some measure of reality can be narrated and opinions allowed to flourish. Chinese journalism, for all that it has changed greatly in the decades since the late seventies, has been allowed to see what freer journalism can do, in some cases – as in Guangzhou – to practise it. The skill and determination of the journalists is evident to all who meet and speak with them; their journalism could change their world. But not yet.

TWO

'Egyptians will not again tolerate dictatorship'

Journalism in the Middle East is strongly controlled by a mix of state–party power and Islamic doctrine. A so-far stable – if increasingly polarized – competitive democratic system produces political leaderships only in Israel. Turkey, which had a measure of democratic electoral practice, had that sharply diminished after the failure of the July 2016 coup, a trend encouraged by the narrow victory for increased presidential power in an April 2017 referendum. The aftermath of the coup saw arrest warrants issued for thousands of suspected opponents of the ruling Justice and Development Party (AKP in the Turkish acronym), including over a hundred journalists and 131 media outlets suspected of links to Fethullah Gülen, the cleric formerly allied to President Recep Tayyip Erdoğan. Since 2013, Gülen has been a bitter foe, albeit from self-imposed exile in Pennsylvania.

In Tunisia and much more violently in Libya, neither parliaments nor new authoritarian leaders have yet securely held the power taken from dictators during the 'Arab Spring'. In Egypt, save a short period in 2012–13, the military has been in power since the officers' coup in 1952, which made Gamal Abdel Nasser president.

In nearly all, the passivity – amounting to servitude – of journalists has been the norm. Throughout the Middle East, the enquiring, enterprising journalist native to the area and working for a Middle Eastern news group, who seeks the truth with an open mind, is a rare figure. There are 'good' reasons for this: the uselessness of enterprising journalism when only officially sanctioned material will be published; the lack of a tradition of independent journalism; and the sceptical, at times hostile, view Islamic authorities take of journalism. Together, state, party and mosque have rendered the journalists' trade largely servile.

In September 2007, a senior cleric of the authoritative Al Azhar Islamic academy in Cairo, Sheikh Mohammed Sayed Tantawi, gave a speech before President Mubarak in which he called – with Allah as his authority – for eighty lashes for all those who slander others.[1] The Egyptian journalists' union protested against this, but Sheikh Tantawi said he hadn't singled out journalists in his comments, this was Allah's law, and it wasn't his fault if it applied to journalists.

Journalists have been lashed in Middle Eastern states, and are still being so. The Saudi journalist Rozanna al-Yami, who worked in Saudi Arabia on a show broadcast in Lebanon in which a man – also Saudi – showed sex toys and discussed his sex life, was sentenced to sixty lashes (the man was sentenced to 1,000 lashes and five years in prison).[2] In July 2014, the Iranian journalist Marzieh Rasouli, who covers arts and culture and also blogs, was sentenced to fifty lashes and two years in prison for anti-state propaganda – in her case, contributing to the BBC Persian service. Lubna Ahmed al-Hussein, a journalist working in the media department of the UN mission in Sudan, was prosecuted with twelve other women, not for any journalistic misdemeanour, but for wearing trousers, a crime of indecent dressing in public which carries a sentence of forty lashes and a fine.[3] The other women pleaded guilty and received ten lashes each. Offered a pardon because of UN immunity, al-Hussein refused the offer, arguing that the charge was 'not about religion, but about men treating women badly'. Pressure came on Sudan to change the law, and the case was dropped.

In 1993, the US journalist Lawrence Wright, who later wrote a gripping narrative account of the rise of terrorist Islamism,[4] spent three months training journalists at the English-language *Saudi Gazette* in Jeddah. When he arrived he was hopeful of change: 'I suspected that behind the closed gates of Saudi society there was a social revolution in the making. With some guidance, I thought, these journalists could help inspire change.'[5] But his time at the *Gazette* was deeply disheartening: women reporters were segregated, or segregated themselves, from their male colleagues and did few stories of any importance; relatives of the sprawling royal family and of course the members of the inner family itself were immune from criticism and the law; and much of the journalism, and the conversation, turned on the development of conspiracy theories in which Jews and Americans played the major evil roles. The journalism was more a matter of providing contemporary scripts for a morality play than a description of events.

One of the main causes of his frustration was the response of his colleagues on the *Gazette* to a fire at a girls' school in Mecca, only 40 miles away, where fifteen girls had died and many more were injured. The doors had been locked and, according to local accounts, the religious police stopped people prepared to put out the fire because the girls were not wearing their abayas, the long loose gown that covers all of the body. The public outrage was such that the government allowed angry commentary, then abruptly shut it down. Wright prodded his reporters to discover the facts of the story on the first anniversary of the deaths, but was blocked in his efforts. He assigned a woman reporter to dig into the story; though initially keen, she returned to say that she found the story depressing, largely because much was being covered up, and didn't wish to continue. 'Things are getting better,' she told Wright.

That which would spur on a Western reporter – suspicion of an official cover-up – had the opposite effect. Many of the male reporters did little or no work and when they did, wrote formulaic stories that conformed to the assumed limits. While Wright was there, the US–UK invasion of Iraq was taking place and the press had a 'relentless theme ... that the twin objects of American power were oil and murder'. Then a government edict went out to all editors-in-chief that the anti-American line be dropped. All conformed, instantly. A friend of Wright's, one of the editors, told him the editors had been ordered: 'No more pictures of dead babies. Also don't call it an invasion.'

The threat of the state has bred a culture of caution, indifference and self-censorship. 'The Middle East has had a dismal record in press freedom,' *The Economist* reported in March 2011, as the 'Arab Spring' gathered force, '... during recent protests, reporters have been attacked and locked up by security forces in Algeria, Egypt, Iraq, Yemen and beyond.'[6] A large-scale, cross-border survey of a sample of 601 Arab journalists quoted an unnamed journalist who had been arrested as saying: 'It was a very simple local news story [that caused him to be charged]. What if I wrote about some politics, or some political problems or what if I give some ideas about terrorism or about military or about security; the matters that really put journalists in serious cases?'[7]

Yet the survey found that many respondents saw themselves as committed to driving social and political change and standing up for human rights, were ready to strongly defend their nation and culture, were inclined to be secular, and believed that objectivity can be combined with strong support for political and economic reform policies. The desire to defend country and culture, which would generally be approved by the rulers, seemed to take precedence. Ibrahim Hamidi, a Syrian based in London, writing for the pan-Arab newspaper *Al-Hayat*, was quoted as saying: 'I do not run after scoops because I know a lot of scoops that may harm the country. I might be not objective, but it is the country that you live in that really matters more than your job. *The priority is the safety of your country* [my italics].'

The comparison constantly made, to the Arab media's disadvantage, is between the Israeli news media (see p. 288) and that of the surrounding states: it is made most insistently by Israeli politicians and officials, seeking to underscore the cultural and political differences between the Arab states and the Jewish one. The man who has most rubbed this in over the past decade is an Israeli Arab named Khaled Abu Toameh, who began his career in the mid 1980s, working for a PLO newspaper named *Al Fajr* (The Dawn) in Jerusalem, a paper whose line was dictated by Yasser Arafat, then still in exile in Tunisia: 'I was not able to write a word of my own free will.'[8]

Toameh crossed over, finding a place at the Israeli *Jerusalem Post*, as well as producing for the US channel NBC and contributing to the work of the US-based Gatestone Institute. 'Arab dictators', he wrote, '... see the role of the media as subservient to – and a mouthpiece for – their regimes. In the Arab world, if you are an independent journalist or you criticize the regime, then you are branded a traitor.'[9]

In October 2011, he wrote of the pressure exerted on the popular satirical Palestinian TV show *Watan al Watar* (Homeland on a String) by the Palestinian Authority security services, the police union and the PA's civil servants, all of whom the programme had mocked – in the case of the police, by doing a sketch showing drunken policemen inspecting a motorist for drunkenness.[10] A spokesman for the police said that 'we support criticism and freedom of expression but only in a positive way'.[11]

In 2010 I talked to the Syrian-born Jordanian journalist Manar Rachwani, who was then the culture editor of the *Al Ghad* daily, which he described as the country's 'most liberal' newspaper. He painted a bleak picture:

We don't have a civil society. So the problem in most Arab journalism is self-censorship: because there will be little support from civil society if you go over a line which the authorities don't want you to cross. You have to say you support some policies to show you are on the right side – even if you don't believe in them.

The situation improved, at least here, in 2003: President Bush decided to support democracy. Since then it's become narrower again. There are red lines round the things we can't write about except to praise them – as royalty; the army; the intelligence services. For us, if Israel disappeared, what would we write about? We had a story about a prominent public figure being corrupt. The person called the chairman of the newspaper and said: you shouldn't publish that story. If you do we will hit you with the taxes you should pay but don't. So we didn't.

Lebanon, for long the most tolerant of the Arab Middle Eastern states, has in the years of the Syrian conflict suffered an influx of over one million refugees, a huge increase in a country of five million.[12] The country, says the journalist Sahar Mandour, is 'going through a very scary time on all levels', yet a 'bargain with the moral order is still happening in the media'.

What Mandour means is illustrated by a remarkable event in 2012, in which she was both participant and chronicler.[13] The post-civil-war government of Rafik Hariri, a wealthy Sunni politician (assassinated by Hezbollah in 2005), liberalized both the economy and the society, including sexual relations. All but uniquely in the Arab world, same-sex relations were tolerated (though the toleration was fragile). The media, especially TV chat shows, began to discuss such topics as homosexuality, premarital sex and marital rape, though they were often condemned, or defended, by a religious or conservative secular figure in the conclusion to the show.

In July 2012, a reporter for the MTV channel secretly filmed young men having sex with each other in the Cinema Plaza in Beirut. The videos, including some shots of men being lured into the toilets by the reporter, were aired on the channel in a show called *Enta Horr* (You are Free). The show's presenter, Joe Maalouf, showed disgust at what the videos revealed, and appealed to Muslim and Christian leaders to condemn them, and police officers to make arrests. Later in the month, thirty-six men were arrested and charged with indulging in 'unnatural sex'.

So far, so apparently normal for the region. But in this case, the plurality of Lebanese television – the many channels owe allegiance to differing confessional and political groups – came to the men's aid. LBCI (Lebanese

Broadcasting Corporation International), the first privately owned network in the country and consistently the most popular, broadcast a commentary critical of the MTV entrapment. The station's lead was strongly supported on social media, and by a number of newspapers; MTV, caught in the spotlight of an anti-homophobic reaction, protested that it has always had a liberal policy.

This liberal victory wasn't final. A raid in April 2013 on a gay night club in Dekwaneh, a suburb of Beirut, included brutal interventions by the mayor of Dekwaneh, who supervised the stripping of those arrested and forced simulation of sexual acts. The social media outburst was strong, but in this case, the government supported the mayor, affirming that Lebanon opposed homosexuality. A powerful and well-connected mayor could not be publicly countered.

Two years after the Cinema Plaza case, I asked Mandour if she had been over-optimistic in seeing it as a breakthrough. She admitted a little of that: 'Of course the upper hand is still that of the conservative sectarian ownership and viewership, but there are still progressive events: the law protecting women from domestic violence was somehow "imposed" on the parliament earlier this year, due to an alliance between the feminist activists, progressive journalists and social pressure. So, yes, somehow the media is still preserving a delicate balance between its progressive and conservative discourses.'

The use of Facebook and Twitter to organize demonstrations, as in Iran, and to spread images of martyred youth in, for example, Tunisia and Egypt where young men immolated themselves in protests – coining the media-bequeathed phrase 'the Facebook Revolution'; and the relative ease with which the young in the Middle East took to the new technologies and the distrust or hatred with which their elders – and especially religious elders – greeted them, all contributed to a euphoric sense that digital communication was replacing conventional political struggle.

The founder of WikiLeaks, Julian Assange, linking together the uprisings in the Arab world with the anti-austerity protests in the West, wrote that 'the Internet was rapidly transitioning from an apathetic communications medium into a demos – a people with a shared culture, shared values and shared aspirations. It had become a place where history happens, a place people identified with and even felt they came from.'[14]

Assange, the social–technological revolutionary, shared that utopianism with the technological masters of the universe, whom he otherwise scorned: in their book *The New Digital Age*, the founder of Google, Eric Schmidt, and the former US administration adviser, then head of Google Ideas, Jared Cohen, wrote that 'on the world stage, the most significant impact of the spread of communication technologies will be the way they help reallocate the concentration of power away from institutions and transfer it to individuals'.[15] Cohen has avoided noting that the technologies have put huge concentrations of power and wealth into the hands of the communication corporations of Silicon Valley.

A reaction against the idealizing of social media has been given most coherence by Evgeny Morozov, who scolded the techno-optimists both in corporations and in politics as 'seasoned and sophisticated decision makers who should really know better'.[16] These decision makers, Morozov believes, were distraught that other authoritarian states did not follow the Soviet Union into history: 'The idea that the Internet favours the oppressed rather than the oppressor is marred by what I call cyber-utopianism: a naive belief in the emancipatory nature of online communication that rests on a stubborn refusal to recognize its downside.'

The British writer James Harkin, who wrote many brave reports on the Syrian conflict, did recognize the downside, but spoke also to the upside, based on his experience. He does believe that techno-optimism can be absurdly hopeful: in a critical blast during a speech in September 2011 against the techno-optimism of media commentator Clay Shirky, Harkin said that Shirky was 'equat[ing] the freedom to write things on Facebook with real and substantial freedoms like freedom of speech and freedom of association'.[17] He repeated these criticisms in an essay written in 2013, but at the same time reported that Syrian oppositionists relied heavily on Facebook and Twitter to organize demonstrations and rapidly uploaded videos taken on mobile phones on to YouTube – while 'there's also no doubt that the phenomenon of new media activism has been a huge boon for foreign journalists like me. In the last few years, in between trips to the region, I've conducted many hundreds of interviews with Syrian contacts, sources and activists via Facebook and Skype and other platforms for new media communication.'[18]

Social media organize and connect; they reveal waves of approval or disapproval; they give a sense of belonging to a like-minded community; and they expose. In December 2012, a Tunisian blogger, Olfa Riahi, published a blog which revealed bills that had been run up at the Sheraton Hotel in Tunis by the foreign minister, Rafik Abdessalem. They showed he had stayed in a luxury suite at government expense and suggested that he was conducting an extramarital affair, revelations which prompted massive tensions within the governing coalition.[19] Riahi was no militant; she had set herself up as an investigative journalist, mainly looking into the business practices of supporters of the deposed President Zine el-Abidine Ben Ali. This time, however, she trod on too many powerful toes and was denounced by her victim, the foreign minister, banned from travelling and charged with slander – but she was taken up by institutes and universities in the US, which afforded protection. Riahi sees her mission as an attempt, through revelatory journalism, to prevent 'new crooks taking over from the old ones'.[20]

Many Tunisians, without being told so by over-eager US politicians or Internet wonks, believe that the social media has been important in their overthrow of Ben Ali. The spreading of images via Facebook of the immolation of Mohamed Bouazizi – the young street vendor in a provincial town who burned himself to death as a protest against an official's confiscation of his cart and produce – was an electrifying charge. Facebook usage went up by several hundred thousand in the week after the Bouazizi video was shared;[21] and a life-size, photo-shopped picture of Mark Zuckerberg, Facebook's creator, was propped up outside the Saudi Arabian embassy.

In Saudi Arabia, where established power still seems secure enough, the dull journalism of submission by the apathetic journalists whom Lawrence Wright encountered are now here and there being circumvented. The greyness of state-approved media has impelled Saudis on to YouTube, Twitter and Facebook. YouTube, on which Saudis watch on average seven videos a day, has provided a platform for new media companies, such as UTURN Entertainment, which runs the gamut through religious programmes to romantic fiction. Twitter has penetrated more deeply into Saudi society than any other in which it operates and eight million people (from a population of thirty-one million) use Facebook.[22] The most popular Twitter accounts are religious; 87 per cent of the (generally young) social media users are men, while jihadists use the media to attract recruits to their bloody causes.

The Saudi authorities remain vigilant: in June 2014, Fawzan al-Harbi was sentenced to seven years under a law against cyber crime for passing out information 'harmful to public order ... including equating Saudi Arabia with a police state' (another Ministry of Truth last clause).[23] Al-Harbi is the co-founder of the Saudi Civil and Political Rights Association, harassed by the police for over a year before being convicted, vindicating Morozov's warning that social media empower the powers that be. But that al-Harbi was passing out his messages, even if drowned out by YouTube romances and Facebook trivia, shows that the princes jostling for power in their gilded palaces must contend with a new force that is capturing the attention of their youth, in competition with the jihadists.

—

The Arab world's best-known paper, Cairo's *Al-Ahram* (The Pyramids), was deeply loyal to Egyptian President Hosni Mubarak and it was prepared to lie for him. As criticism from the increasingly unbuttoned press and satellite channels mounted in the last years of his rule, and his presidency trembled in 2010, it doctored a photograph taken at the Middle East peace talks in Sharm el-Sheikh, which took place in September of that year.

The picture, on the front page, showed Mubarak heading a group of leaders, including US President Barack Obama; Israeli Prime Minister Benjamin Netanyahu; Mahmoud Abbas, head of the Palestinian Authority; and King Abdullah II of Jordan. In fact, in the un-doctored photograph, he was a couple of steps behind all the others, looking like an afterthought. The paper was still in a Soviet airbrushing mindset, but the president's younger subjects, who lived on social media, uncovered the deception, which caused widespread disdain.

On 4 May that same year, the paper's editor, Osama Saraya, had hailed the president's eighty-second birthday as 'the day Egypt was born'. The paper stayed with Mubarak as ever-larger numbers of people filled the streets of Cairo and other Egyptian cities ... right up to 11 February 2011, when the president resigned. *Al-Ahram*'s main front-page headline on the next day was 'The People Toppled the Regime'. Other headlines announced that 'The Youth of Egypt Forced Mubarak to Leave', and even, on a special supplement, 'We Won' in red lettering beside a young man waving an Egyptian flag. It was a vivid example of the flexibility an Egyptian newspaper must practise in order to remain on the right side of state power. It was also a demonstration of how deeply integrated with the state this, its most famous newspaper, had always been, as it remains so today, with a different president.[24]

Egyptian newspapers flourished from the latter half of the nineteenth century, mostly with a nationalist flavour that the British overlords tolerated, thinking it was unimportant.[25] Several European press agencies set up shop in a city that gave foreigners privileges and exemptions – including from censorship laws. Egyptian journalism was the freest and liveliest in the Middle East, though at best 'partly free'; it was freer, certainly, than it became after the cycle of military-dominated governments that began in 1952. When the military coup came in July of that year, led by General Mohammed Naguib, it was welcomed by a population with no experience of stable and clean government, who saw 'the youthful officers surrounding Naguib – earnest articulate soldiers, untainted with foreign affectation' as 'the ideal of a new kind of Egyptian man'.[26]

Thus began the modern period of Egyptian politics: a drear one. The military officers who have governed Egypt almost continuously since the early fifties have all seen themselves and the state they ruled as the only criterion against which journalism should be judged. At times they granted journalists limited freedoms as a tactic to keep the intelligentsia on their side or to impress those foreigners – the Americans, from the seventies onwards – with their liberal attitudes. But the news media were privileged slaves, echoes, not voices, dedicated to glorifying the leader and his policies – and to lying, where directed to do so.

These regimes owed most to Soviet Communism, in style and methods if not in substance; independent papers were suppressed, new pro-regime papers were launched and soon all media were made part of the state, with 'a single soft voice pour[ing] from the radio, drowning the old cacophony of debate'.[27]

Gamal Abdel Nasser, emerging as the president from the 1952 officers' revolt, was the most serious and politically ambitious – he aimed to establish a socialist society in Egypt and unity among the Arabs. For these goals, there had to be one voice, that of the leader; a plurality of views, as there had been before the military revolution, would leave the impression that there were legitimate arguments to be had about the nature of the truth in governance.

Nasser proved adept at the use of the darker arts of public relations. The first president, General Naguib, was a respected military commander whose plan was to depose a vacillating government, stabilize the country, then return it to a constitutional democracy within a few years. Nasser and his more radical colleagues opposed that, withdrawing after an over-hasty effort to depose Naguib, then regrouping to build up Nasser, who soon displaced him as president. The journalist Rania Saleh, who studied how photographs and cartoons were used in Nasser's time, told me that 'because Nasser [when prime minister under Naguib, who was president until deposed in 1954] had overall control of the Ministry of Information, he ensured that photographs showed him bigger than Naguib. For a country where many people couldn't read well, it was a powerful message.' Rania, like many young and liberal Egyptians, rejoiced in the coup – under way as we spoke, in the summer of 2013 – which deposed the elected Muslim Brotherhood president, Mohamed Morsi. But she said she had laughed when she saw demonstrators' signs reading 'Down with military rule' jostling amicably with portraits of Nasser.

Naguib Mahfouz – with Alaa Al Aswany, one of the two most distin-guished Egyptian novelists of the twentieth century – finished his *Cairo Trilogy* just before the 1952 revolution: it was published in serial form in *Al-Ahram* in 1959. He wrote *Children of the Alley* six years after it, only to be denied publication for nearly fifty years, in large part because of a charge of blasphemy brought against it (a 1994 knife attack by an Islamist extremist severed nerves in Mahfouz' neck, reducing his work routine to short bursts). His popularity and fame protected him, allowing him to be critical of the Nasser regime – though he praised him for his nationalization of the Suez Canal, seeing this as the mark of a great leader. By contrast, Sonallah Ibrahim, who wrote *The Smell of It*, based on his five-year stretch in prison for Communist Party activism, saw his book banned because of its frankness about filthy prison conditions and torture.

Samia Mehrez, professor of Modern Arabic Literature at the American University of Cairo, said in an interview she gave to Abdallah Hassan, the Egyptian journalist with whom I worked when in Egypt, that true independence of thought at that period was rare: 'we cannot begin to speak about an autonomous literary field because most, if not all of our writers ... worked within the state cultural apparatus'.[28] Nasser used radio and the new medium of television, as well as mass rallies, to amplify his message of unity and equity across the Arab nations, as well as his own. 'He was Rob Roy and Robin Hood,' writes the *Economist* correspondent Max Rodenbeck. 'See the rayyis [or rais: a leader, president] in the newsreels ... biting the tail of the British lion, nationalizing the Suez Canal. See him champion the cause of the little man, opening schools, granting diplomas, working for Arab independence and unity ...'[29] His grab for the media had worked: one voice did command, and reassured the masses with strong, stable military rule – as they were to be reassured once again, sixty years later.

The Six Day War of 1967, in which the Arab armies were defeated by a smaller Israeli force fighting for its national life, was an effective end to plans for Arab unity. The Egyptian media, in these early days of June, had poured out a stream of fiction – of Israeli armies surrounded, Israeli war planes shot down and airports bombed, an Israeli battleship sunk, Tel Aviv the next stop for the victorious Egyptian army. Quite suddenly, it stopped, and the president took to the airwaves to say, 'We cannot hide from ourselves [the hiding was a huge fabrication perpetrated not by 'ourselves' but by him, on a credulous population] that we've faced a devastating setback during the past few days.' He took responsibility, offered to resign, and was rewarded with a popular outcry calling for him to stay.

It was only after he rescinded his decision that another outpouring, that of anger, began – dangerous, and staunched. One of the most prominent victims was the singer–poet Ahmed Fouad Negm, 'poet of the people'.[30] Negm wrote a poem after the 1967 defeat called 'Slapping Ourselves in

Grief', which ends: 'So what, if in Aqaba we ran/Or in Sinai?/Can this defeat make us forget/That we are "free"?' Irony of that kind earned him a total of eighteen years in jail, under Nasser and his successor, Anwar Sadat. If a penitent President Nasser was to stay, he would show how tight the limits to his penitence were.

In the brief period of rage over the 1967 defeat, one of the slogans that students wrote on walls was 'Stop the lies of Heikal's Lying Press!', bringing into the public sphere one who casts as long a shadow over the subsequent decades of Egyptian politics and journalism as did his master, Nasser. Mohamad Heikal – Nasser's confidant, chief scribe and editor of the Al-Ahram, the paper that became the dominant source of news, opinion and the presidential line – had worked closely with Nasser on the wartime fabrications of victory, while Egyptian troops were captured or killed by the many thousands. He did not go to prison, but instead lived in comfort well into the regime of a fourth military autocrat, el-Sisi, whose coming he welcomed. His 'lying press' dominated in the Nasser period, in part through his own skill and intelligence, but more importantly (since there were many skilled and intelligent journalists rotting in jail) through his relationship with Nasser.

He was sometimes credited as being the Nasser period's co-ruler because he wrote so much of the script. He rose to be head of the most important newspaper in the Arab world, while almost every other editor in the previously relatively outspoken press was sacked and/or jailed. His span of influence was huge and lasted deep into the 2010s. He wrote Nasser's speech of resignation after the defeat of the Egyptian armies by Israel in the 1967 war and is credited – there is no proof, and he has been ambiguous about the issue – with writing the speech with which el-Sisi re-established military power in 2013, a little less than half a century later. From Nasser's time on, he has been called on to have long sessions of conversation with the ruling figure. He is the defining figure of Middle

East journalism: he viewed success as service to the supreme power. Very few journalists could hope to reach the heights he did with his service, but it told them: your trade is to obey.

In his memoir, *Year of Conflict*,[31] Heikal writes of a ten-hour session with Nasser on 9 June 1967, when the president received a report by phone from the commander of his armed forces, Field Marshal Abdel Hakim Amer: Israeli forces were crossing the Suez Canal and moving into Egypt. This was a final confirmation that the war was irremediably lost. The two men, alone at a time of calamitous defeat, spent some time on a journalistic quest: to find the right word with which to present the defeat to the people – as a tabloid editor might agonize over the handful of words in a front-page splash to seize attention on a newsstand.

It was a matter to which, Heikal says, Nasser attached huge weight, since he claimed to wish to leave his successor the ability to reconstruct the armed forces ready for another war with the Israelis, and did not wish to upset the Soviets, with whose weaponry the Egyptian forces were supplied. They went through a list: *Hazimah* (defeat), *Sadmah* (shock), *Karithah* (catastrophe) as well as the dialect word *Nakbah* (also catastrophe), used still by the Palestinians to describe the result of the 1948 war, which resulted in the expulsion of some 700,000 Arabs from Israel. Heikal's suggestion was a masterly understatement: *Naksah* – a setback, the word that Nasser used in his broadcast.

Journalists in democratic countries, where the journalistic and political trades are thought best to be kept separate, do – usually discreetly – write drafts of speeches for politicians whom they support or admire, though typically on issues on which the journalists feel strongly, or have some expertise, or which announce a course of action they favour. In Heikal's case, however, the relationship was not just open, but proclaimed, seen generally as a source of power and high status, not of embarrassment: this was what a top journalist should do, as a sign both of his skill and of his patriotism.

An interview he gave in July 2012 saw him willing to see the new Brotherhood government tested in power.[32] He said President Mohamed Morsi should be 'given a chance' – but added, again prophetically, that 'the problems of the modern world are too complicated to be solved by religious thinking that only sees black or white, heaven or hell, so I don't think it will succeed, but it is the choice of the majority – for now'. When Morsi was overthrown, he thought Field Marshal el-Sisi a good choice, since his military background was suitable for Egypt, but, in his interview, he denied he was an adviser: 'I'm not the man of all times'.

On his death in February 2016, he was widely regarded in Egypt, the Middle East and in many parts of the world as a wise figure. But Heikal has been a bad example to successive generations of Egyptian journalists. He took his power and authority from his closeness to the president, and his journalism, with some permitted exceptions, stuck rigidly to the Nasserite line; and because Nasser remained a largely untouchable guiding spirit in spite of the sharp change of policies after his death, Heikal retained his position as a sage, adviser and distributor of benisons. His journalism in articles and books was, though at times compellingly told, an amalgam of unsourced and unverifiable claims and – as Claire Talon put it in *Le Monde* – is 'full of plots, conspiracies, *éminences grises*, reversals, empires, alliances and failed plans'.[33] He started the rumour, on his Al Jazeera TV show in 2010, that Nasser was murdered by Anwar Sadat with a cup of poisoned coffee, and that Sadat planned an essentially fake war in 1973 with the aid of the US, in order to bring the Israelis to peace negotiations. No other credible chronicler has confirmed these stories.

The present generation of Egyptians have mixed views on Heikal. The anti-Mubarak stance he took became fashionable in the 2000s – especially his opposition to a presidential succession to Gamal Mubarak – and won him a new audience for his series of lectures on Al Jazeera. For others he was, as the academic and writer Ramy Aly told me, 'really the Goebbels of Egypt, deriving all of his power from his worship of Nasser'. Yet he was the model journalist of the Middle East – where, even less than in China or Russia, journalism has not managed to lay a solid basis for its own authority.

Al Aswany thought that 'Egyptians will not again tolerate dictatorship', but he was proven quite wrong. In the reign of el-Sisi, it was more plausible to believe that the Egyptian electorate had made a choice between two kinds of authoritarian government – one religious, one military – and chosen the latter, concluding that no democratic option was available, or when it came, with President Morsi, was not desired. Al Aswany wanted democracy, but the anti-Brotherhood revolution that he welcomed, and which he helped to further, could not deliver it.

He was deluded, but so were many ardent for reform, who thought that the period of freedom, initially borne in on the shoulders of radical youth, betokened a new psychology, a denial of the judgement of Al Aswany's corrupt politician in his 2002 novel, *The Yacoubian Building* – that 'Our Lord created the Egyptians to accept government authority'. Meeting journalists in Cairo as the Brotherhood rule crumbled, I found the refusal to submit to that fatalistic resignation – really, a wish as father to the belief – among the most creative and determined of the new journalists.

The relatively free period for Egyptian journalism lasted little less than a decade, from 2003 – when President Mubarak, under pressure from US President George W. Bush, loosed the bonds on journalism – to 2013, when they were tied tightly again. In that brief window, it was never free, as that is defined in settled democracies: there was no habit of seeing the news media as necessary pillars of civil society, were no binding constitutional guarantees of independence and, more importantly, no implicit assumption that journalism should be independent from state tutelage and have some autonomous existence.

But in that time there appeared and were developed signs of what journalism, underpinned by a thickening of civil society, could become. These included the development of a serious and mildly investigative news culture, which was heralded by the creation of the first daily newspaper that could claim some real independence: *Al-Masry Al-Youm* (The Egyptian Today). Founded in 2003, with the explicit mission of giving the facts, together with a secular, liberal editorial line, it began publishing in 2004 – very much the product of the Cairene liberal intelligentsia – and quickly grew an audience attracted both by its criticisms of the Mubarak government and by the detail it gave on issues and events that the state media ignored or downgraded.

In Cairo, I talked to one of the paper's founders and, for many years, its publisher, Hisham Kassem, a strongly liberal figure in the Egyptian political landscape, a founder of the Egyptian Organization for Human Rights. A burly, brusque man, we spoke in his cluttered central-Cairo apartment in the summer of 2013, just as the Morsi presidency and the Muslim Brotherhood government were careering towards their end. Kassem saw the Brotherhood as narrow, messianic, determined to enforce their brand of Islamism on a culture which, while largely Muslim, was resistant to Islamism as a governing ideology, and had a large (some fifteen million strong) Christian minority. He said in a debate on Al Jazeera a few days after the election of el-Sisi in June 2014 that the Brotherhood was 'a supremacist extremist cult'. When, on 22 November 2013, Morsi effectively suspended the constitution and took all effective power to himself, Kassem said it became obvious to all that here was a religious dictatorship in the making:

> The 2011 revolution ousted the political class who could run the country. The amateurs came in. The Brotherhood had electoral superiority but the secularists had political superiority – and the media, and the justice system. After the constitutional declaration, it was obvious – the Brotherhood is not capable of running a democratic state.
>
> Morsi now got out of prison during the revolution because there was a raid, probably by Hamas or Hezbollah, to get him out. Well, that's a raid by a foreign terrorist group on an Egyptian prison. That's a big crime.

Forced from power by the demonstrators and the army in July 2013, Morsi was imprisoned, and later that summer charged with a variety of crimes: inciting deadly violence against protestors; espionage for foreign militant groups, including Hamas and Hezbollah; and breaking out of jail after conspiring with these groups to create chaos in the country. He was sentenced to death in May 2015, but the sentence was commuted to life imprisonment in June 2016.

Kassem, both by choice and probably from caution, did not place his paper as a voice of the diverse but weak opposition groups. Instead, he tried to make it – in some ways more subversively – a paper of record, based not on what the state wished the people to know, but on what were the ascertainably important facts on the ground. He claims he had a brusque way with state security officers, if they came to complain about the facts he put into the public sphere – 'I would tell them that if the facts are treacherous then we are in a very bad way.'

Aware that Egyptians were tired of a self-censored state media and of 'opposition shouting', he drove his staff to get the facts on stories of weight, especially those that showed the way in which the government governed. When one of the government's acts was to erect a wall round the resort of Sharm el-Sheikh to keep the locals away from the holidaymakers, other papers led with opinion on the rightness or otherwise of the policy. Kassem said: 'What we want are the facts: how big? Why? What does it do? Interview the people who are upset. What's the opinion of the tourists? We were the first to do this. We led with the facts.'

It was a lesson he was required to teach again and again: insisting on the primacy of facts over opinion, the so-called 'Anglo-Saxon' approach to the news, with its separation of the fact-based narrative from the expression of opinion. When his editor came to him to express his disapproval of a government edict forcing all mosques to call for prayers at the same hour, Kassem again knocked him back, saying what he, or a columnist, thought of it was less important than the grittiness of the order: 'which mosques are affected? All? Some? What do the imams think? If we were doing something on poverty – get the reporter to go to a poor area – tell him: "Go with one big idea in mind, like the lack of education. But take notes of everything. Keep the main thing in mind but remember the rest for later coverage."'

In Egypt, even more than elsewhere, television is by far the prime source of news and views. The satellite station revolution happened under Mubarak's rule, and resulted in a host of stations vying for the eyeballs, and the consumption choices, of the country's eighty-three million people. It brought more immediate, less stodgy (though still loyal) news – and many talk shows, some of which, taking their cue from Al Jazeera, broached subjects rarely debated publicly. Kassem, however, thought they did little for a journalism which informs rather than titillates:

> The level of journalism is still bad. Not so much now because of the state – but because of commercial pressures. The advertising agencies now command TV; an agency will call up the director of a show and say, 'If you get X and Y on and they will have a good fight, I can sell a lot of advertising round that.' We are closer to India in our style of journalism than to the West. On the other hand – there are now thirty million users of the net ...

His optimism, as often in such societies, depends on the next generation:

> I anticipate a revolution in the media. A lot of young journalists have been well trained and have good ideas but they can't do anything in the papers they work on because they are told not to bring their fancy ideas into the newsroom. An example of our problem – 25 per cent of Egyptians have hepatitis C. It's not written about properly. You have to do something big on that, because at the moment it's written about in terms of conspiracies, like so much here – it's the fault of the Americans, the Israelis.

The difference in the new generation is simple. This generation has got social media.

Kassem was voicing a strongly held faith in the period of relative freedom after Mubarak's fall – faith that a new generation of journalists, allied to social media users, would break the grip of the state and begin to lay the foundations for a journalism that gave Egyptians both the facts and some context within which to place them, and the means to develop stronger conventions for the reporting of the issues that affect most people, except the rich. The biggest problem for an Egyptian audience – true throughout most of the Middle East – is the small circulation of the informative newspapers, the formulaic and uninformative news on television, and the confining of 'analysis' to chat shows that put a premium on drama, confrontation and polemic.

When well conducted, chat shows are valuable; when they feature dilemmas and problems little discussed in the society but needing to be aired, they can be revelatory, as the early Al Jazeera chat shows were and can still be. But when they feature a polemicist/presenter shouting at the camera, or a free-for-all among public figures who have been chosen because they will disagree histrionically, they can be entertaining but little more, as the experience of chat – really, shout – shows in the United States, Italy and elsewhere demonstrates.

Kassem saw the need in Egyptian society for reliable, neutral information, and sought to address it. Ramy Aly, in his early thirties when I interviewed him in 2013, with an associate professor's job at Cairo's American University, is more politically radical – he is of the left, where Kassem is a liberal – but also laments the fact that the varied and opinionated (though never popular) press that jostled for the attention of the elites and middle class before the 1950s was abruptly closed down by Nasser's military government – 'zeroed out by sixty years of military rule', as he put it.

He paid tribute to *Al-Masry Al-Youm*: 'the first private paper and the first to try to represent events squarely'. By contrast, the state media were 'platforms which should have represented society, but were wholly without legitimacy. The media were part of the reason for the downfall of the regime. The state TV played the role of control, and propaganda. So it became one of the first targets of the revolution.'

We spoke in the Café Riche, off Tahrir Square, a few days before President Morsi was forced from his post. Aly saw the Brotherhood government as little different from the previous military administrations:

> The constitution proclaims freedom of the press but the penal code is harsh, penalizing journalists for insulting the president. Morsi did cancel pre-trial detention for journalists, but that's all. The Shura Council [the upper house of parliament, then packed with Brotherhood members] still appoints editors of the papers and the heads of the channels. The state still controls.

The night before, Morsi had given a long and rambling speech in front of an audience of his ministers and invited notables. Attempting the pose of a man who could take a joke but had reached the limits of decency, he said that 'one year of lampooning and satire is enough', and reminded the audience that military rules should apply to those who defame the commander in chief – the president. It was evident that he and his fellows in the Brotherhood were angered not just by the lack of respect on which they believed leaders should count, but also that they – people mainly from provinces and villages, as was Morsi himself – were being humiliated by the highly educated city intellectuals and media folk, who sat in TV studios and sneered at them. 'The Brotherhood really dislikes the upper middle class and the urban sophisticates,' said Aly. 'They are a product of Nasser's reforms – he created a new petty bourgeoisie, educated in the state schools and universities, and sometimes abroad. They see them as godless: but it's a class hatred, too.'

Aly, like Kassem, saw in his country what he called 'an absence of narrative'. There was neither the ability nor the will to devote resources to describing the world, at home and abroad, in detail-rich stories that could give a sketch of an event, an issue, a problem or a threat. Nor was there any attempt to give background information, or context to the flow of news:

They don't have science or medical programmes. There is no commissioning system for current affairs. The channels spend money on soap operas. There isn't a shared public media space. It's all chat shows. People think that the best way to impart information is via discussion. There has been no journalism which seeks to establish the facts. I've been working with others to try to shine a light in areas which have been left as mysteries. For example: 544 hospitals were planned to be built in this country in the last twenty years. Only forty-four of these are in operation. That is, 500 were closed or were never opened. We are trying to make people understand why the medical services are so bad. The problem is journalistic standards. They are so low. The training of journalists is usually very bad but even if it is good there is nowhere to exercise the skills. There is no space given to journalism which is analytical.

Aly went on to cite an incident that had occurred a few days before we talked, in which four Muslims from the tiny Shia community in Egypt (an overwhelmingly Sunni state) were killed in a village near Cairo by a mob, while, reportedly, the police did nothing, and the reporting was brief, uninterested in details. Roused to anger by such ineffective journalism, Aly said that

The reportage of such an incident needs to be complex but also full of human interest. Where were the families in this? What was the nature of the relationship between the Shia and the rest of their society before?

What animated the killers? All these details are lacking. It is as if a tweet about the incident – it happened here, so-and-so were killed – is enough. The straight reporting on TV is terrible. If you didn't have the visuals it would be like bad radio.

Like Kassem, Aly believed in a future carried by 'a new generation of journalists':

Satire and criticism is now very popular. Bassem Youssef [the satirist, see below] is popular at all levels of society – but if they took him off it wouldn't matter – because the habit is now ingrained and the contempt with which the Brotherhood is viewed is very deep. The instinct to be a lackey is fading. People know this country is in a mess, not because of the Brotherhood but because of sixty years of authoritarian rule.

But Aly, too, was over-sanguine about the mood of the Egyptian people, at least in the short term. However much of the Egyptian 'mess' is due to six decades of authoritarian rule, a period of instability with constant demonstrations, shortages and an ineffective and vaguely menacing Muslim Brotherhood government pointed most in one direction. For more authoritarian rule.

President el-Sisi's view of the media is strictly practical. He feels they should support the government, which he, the elected president, led. In a meeting with editors and TV anchors in May 2014 – just before he was elected – he 'urged the media to play its part in protecting the state', according to Al-Ahram.[34] He had neither Nasser's charisma nor his goals to bring unity to the Arab world and socialism to Egypt. Instead, he had the threat of terrorism with which to demand unity in the face of attacks.

These threats were not fiction. The Sinai Peninsula – the 23,000-square-mile space in Egypt's north-east between the Suez Canal and the border with Israel – became in the second decade of this century increasingly prone to attacks by both Islamist and radicalized Bedouin groups. The attacks on Egyptian police and military rose sharply after Mohamed Morsi was forced from the presidency – allowing the new regime to blame the Brotherhood for initiating the attacks, charges that the leaders (by then mainly underground) denied. In October 2014, two separate atrocities killed over thirty police and soldiers. El-Sisi, who blamed unnamed foreign forces for the attacks, declared a state of emergency and a daily curfew from 5 p.m. to 7 a.m. in the area.[35] There were also signs that the terrorists, some of whom – in particular the Army of Islam, suspected of bombing a Coptic church in Alexandria in 2011, resulting in twenty-three deaths – had strong links to Hamas in the neighbouring Gaza Strip. The terror continued in spite of el-Sisi's security state: in separate bombings in April 2017, in the cities of Tanta and Alexandria, around fifty Copts were killed while worshipping. ISIS claimed responsibility.

A few days after the October attacks, a group of editors and TV presenters gathered to condemn them – and to oppose a 'hostile culture toward the national project and the foundations of the Egyptian state'.[36] In a statement, they supported 'all measures taken by the state in combating terrorists and protecting national security'. The meeting had been called by the TV host Mohamed Sherry, who was quoted as telling his colleagues that it was the media's role to become 'tools of the state' in a war against terrorism. Al-Ahram, as obedient as ever to the ruling power, was there – but so were the editors of the previously feisty Al-Masry Al-Youm and Al-Watan, as were the heads of the Journalists' Syndicate. The Egyptian Radio and TV Union, representing the privately owned channels – including CUBIC, Not and Dream TV, which had run programmes highly critical of the Mubarak and Brotherhood administrations – also pledged their fealty to the armed forces.

The wheel came full circle. Al-Ahram reverted to pre-Spring, falsifying type. A speech the Egyptian president gave to the UN General Assembly in late September 2014 received a sceptical report from the *New York Times'* Cairo correspondent David Kirkpatrick, who noted that, in his country's news media, el-Sisi's performance was hailed as 'a transformational moment',[37] and by the chat show host Arm Adobe as 'a thing of genius', while viewers in Egypt saw the speech receive 'raucous applause'. The editorial continued, however, to say that the event demonstrated not genius but 'the strength of the cult of personality' being built round him; and that 'what the viewers back in Egypt could not see was during the General Assembly, almost all of the diplomats present watched in amused silence as Mr Sisi's small entourage did the clapping'.

Al-*Ahram's* version of this report read, in part:

> [Kirkpatrick] described the unique scene at the headquarters of the United Nations, when el-Sisi received warm applause from the assembled world leaders after he shouted 'Long Live Egypt'. In Kirkpatrick's view, el-Sisi was able to erase the image that was in the minds of some people, that what happened in Egypt in June 2013 was a 'coup', not a revolution. He wrote that el-Sisi's rule has come to rely on the strength of his personality and his tremendous popularity in an unprecedented way ... [He] pointed out that all the diplomats were in a state of hushed enjoyment throughout el-Sisi's speech.

The last sentence of the Al-*Ahram* report is poignant.

Yet to merely note that the news media have become captive to the administration's agenda once more is only part of the story. In the first two years after el-Sisi's election in May 2016, there was little evidence that the supportive stance taken by nearly all is unpopular, and, even after some years, the support for el-Sisi remains high – though it dropped from over 80 to 68 per cent in October 2016 in the wake of price increases for basic commodities, prompting an effort to reach out to the young, whose support was most reduced.[38]

Mohamed Anwar, a young cartoonist, did a cartoon gently mocking el-Sisi's habit of asking Egyptians to 'share the burden in the economic crisis' by showing a father responding to his young son's plea to be taken to the toilet with, 'Why do you want to go right now? We must all share the burden at this critical moment!' The cartoon stopped well short of satirizing el-Sisi personally – the paper would never have carried it – but a reader, in tears, called Anwar to ask, 'Why are you doing this to el-Sisi? Why are you always fighting him?'[39]

By the year's end, there were few independent or critical voices left. Al Jazeera, which had established an Egypt Channel, was worst affected. Its bias towards the Brotherhood had become increasingly clear, and increasingly resented. Pressure on the channel grew during the mass anti-Morsi protests, and after his ousting six of its staff resigned, citing bias in its coverage.

In July 2013, during a military press conference, a journalist from the Egyptian news agency demanded that the Al Jazeera journalists be excluded. They left, followed by chants of 'Out, out, out!' from their colleagues, who then repeatedly applauded during the spokesman's presentation: the channel was barred from further press conferences.[40] In a statement, Al Jazeera said, 'We've always given all sides of opinion airtime, it's our mantra … [but] large sections of the Egyptian media object to this open-minded ethos.'

Three Al Jazeera staffers in Egypt were arrested in December 2013 and charged with aiding terrorists and making false statements. In July 2014, the Egyptian producer Baher Mohamed, the Egyptian–Canadian bureau chief Mohamed Fahmy and the Australian Peter Greste were sentenced to between seven and ten years, having been found by Judge Mohamed Nagy Shehata to have been in league with the devil, who had 'encouraged them to use journalism and direct it towards action against this nation'.[41] A fifty-seven-page document drawn up by the judge referred to a secret investigation by the security services, but gave no details. El-Sisi, in later comments, said he regretted the severity of the sentences – which drew worldwide condemnation – and that he wished the journalists had been deported. But he made no intervention. Fahmy, apparently dissatisfied with the lawyers provided by his employer, enlisted the English barrister Amal Clooney, recently married to the actor George Clooney and thus with the highest of profiles, to argue that a dose of hepatitis merited his release for medical treatment. She added that his trial was 'fundamentally unfair … and a travesty of justice'.[42] All three were released in February 2015; Fahmy, while saying they were jailed unjustly, said that Al Jazeera had had a strongly pro-Brotherhood agenda, and had waged 'a media war against Egypt'.

The Egyptian media purged their ranks of most of the thorns in the military's sides. These included Alaa Abd el-Fattah, a blogger with a wide readership and a years-long history of dissidence, who received a fifteen-year sentence for violating a ban on unofficial protests; the day after his court appearance, his sister, Sanaa Seif, was jailed for three years with twenty-two others for protesting her brother's original sentence. Abd el-Fattah had a huge Twitter following, and had been arrested and sometimes jailed several times over the years – one time, for attending a protest against military trials for civilians, organized by another of his sisters, Mona Seif. The Seif family is the outstanding example of dissidence in the cause of freedom in Egypt.

The broadcasters quickly made good their pledge to el-Sisi. When Dream TV's chat show host Wael El Ebrashy criticized corruption in two government ministries – education and housing – he was fired mid show. The Al-Nahar station banned Mahmoud Saad, another critic, before he got to his studio – replacing him with the editor of the newspaper *Youm7*, Khaled Salah, who had attended the editors' meeting. The channel later released a statement saying that it could not tolerate 'those who mock the blood of our martyrs and practise verbal terrorism live on air'.[43]

Bassem Youssef had connected most strongly with both an Egyptian audience and those who had heard of him abroad. A cardiac surgeon in his late thirties when the Egyptian revolt began, he, along with some collaborators, developed the 'B+' (his blood type) show in his laundry room, filming it on a video camera and uploading it to YouTube. The show was an unashamed tribute to Jon Stewart's satirical *Daily Show*, which Youssef had watched while studying in the US, but Youssef had a richer, and more dangerous, field in which to romp. The YouTube videos quickly attracted an audience of some three million and he was hired by the private channel ONTV. The show was renamed *Al Bermaneg* (The Programme), with a licence to skewer the new president, Mohamed Morsi, which it did with gusto. At the summit of his power and popularity, Jon Stewart appeared on the show in June 2013, a little before Morsi was deposed.

The CBC channel had picked up the programme late in 2012, moved it from a small studio to a big theatre with a live audience, and added guests, interviews and glitz; the show got forty million viewers. Youssef took a break of several months after Morsi's deposition, then returned in October 2013 with an episode that poked fun at el-Sisi, effectively the ruler of Egypt even before his election, and at the personality cult which enveloped him. At the end of the show, when Youssef was declaiming passionately to the camera that he would not be silenced, a film clip was shown of an interview with el-Sisi in which he says that 'a strong arm' is needed to guide Egypt – then a muscular arm appears from a hole on the desk, substitutes another script for the one from which Youssef is reading, smacks him on the head when he refuses to read it, then grabs his crotch when he says he will not be silenced – thus silencing him. CBC cited violations of the contract, and took him off air.

He came back briefly in early 2014 on the Saudi-based channel MBC, where he continued to satirize the cult of el-Sisi, and made the prohibition on mentioning him a running gag. But – as protests grew – he realized the joke had turned potentially deadly. In June 2014, he called a press conference and said he was ending the show, since it had become too dangerous to continue. He settled in the US, and developed a new programme – *Democracy Handbook with Bassem Youssef* – which poked fun at a more genial target: US politics. He did some shows elsewhere in the West; in April 2016 he appeared at one of London's Curzon Cinemas, joking that the nearby Egyptian embassy was still not owned by the Saudi embassy, pointing up the dependence of Egypt's budget on Saudi subsidies. More sourly, he noted that 'we came back to the exact same spot where we started, with the same lies. The textbook of bullshit is very slim.'[44]

In tune with his country when the majority turned against Morsi, Youssef was out of tune when it turned to el-Sisi for protection. He made the Western assumption that the politicians had to take it. But they didn't, and anyway Youssef's public wasn't like that: he was unacceptable to the majority when he guyed el-Sisi. The field marshal, at the helm when Egypt faced a jihadist onslaught, was their protector.

Private owners do not, in themselves, solve the problem of state control. Fatima el-Issawi, among the most insightful of commentators on the contemporary Arab news media, writes:

> The nature of this private sector, largely owned by business tycoons linked to the regime, defies the notion of an 'independent' media. The ability of the regime to apply different pressure tools on these media outlets – such as behind-the-scenes control of advertising revenues – further limited the ability of these media outlets to provide counter narratives.[45]

The harsh turn against the press which el-Sisi introduced had a certain inevitability, but also a certain irony. In his period in 2005–6 at the US Army War College in Pennsylvania, when a brigadier general and chief of staff of the 2nd Mechanized Infantry Division, el-Sisi wrote an essay on 'Democracy in the Middle East', in which he argued that the state must 'be willing to let go of media control ... one of the key first steps may be to initiate this approach with the help of international news organizations and pressure from democracies with a free press'.[46]

Egypt's situation is a long way from Pennsylvania. In his autocracy, el-Sisi has enrolled Islam on the side of oppression. In February 2016, a court sentenced the novelist Ahmed Naji to two years for 'outraging modesty' because his novel, *The Guide for Using Life*, featuring scenes of sexual relations and drug taking, had made a reader, Hani Salah Tawfiq, seriously ill. He wasn't alone. In January 2016, the poet Fatima Naoot got three years for writing to condemn the killing of animals during the Eid holiday. In December 2015, the court of appeal upheld a year's sentence on Islam Al-Beheiry, who had in a TV show he presented questioned the foundations of some Islamic doctrine, and the credibility of sayings attributed to Muhammad – angering the leading imams at the supreme centre of Sunni Islam theology, Al-Azhar, who had demanded the programme be closed down. Bravely, the journalist Ibrahim Eissa addressed the president directly in his daily newspaper *Al-Tahrir*: 'Your state is a theocracy, Mr President, even if you never cease to talk of a state which is modern and civil'.[47]

If overt opposition is rare, and when practised, usually punished, there came to be stirrings of conscience among the Egyptian press as the el-Sisi rule continued. As the presidential press corps waited for a briefing during the president's November 2015 visit to the UK to meet then Prime Minister David Cameron, one of its number, Fathia Eldakhakhny of *Al-Masry Al-Youm*, told the US reporter Peter Hessler that el-Sisi had held only one press conference in Egypt since taking office, and for that three reporters were given scripted questions to ask (the three reporters confirmed this to Hessler). 'They chose three Egyptian journalists and told them that these are the questions you will ask.' Laughing, Eldakhakhny told him: 'I wrote an article about it. They didn't allow me to enter the presidential palace for three months!' Yet at the London briefing, there were tentative signs of a change. A few days before the visit, a jet carrying Russian tourists had crashed on take-off from the resort of Sharm el-Sheikh in Sinai, killing all 224 on board. Though both British and Russian investigators quickly believed a bomb had been planted, the Egyptian authorities, desperate not to damage tourism, insisted it was a technical malfunction (they admitted it was a terrorist act three months later: an affiliate of ISIS claimed credit). Eldakhakhny asked about the flight at the briefing, and was told, 'We don't want to focus on this issue.' She said she would at least print the denial – and told Hessler the other journalists said they would, too. Yet at the same time, her paper, once a liberal institution, emphasized the pro-presidential demonstrators while mentioning the anti-el-Sisi protests, and wrote that the antis were connected to the Muslim Brotherhood.[48]

To date, Ibrahim Eissa is correct. El-Sisi has failed in his first years of office to modernize or protect, let alone expand, civil society – and has presided over a stagnant economy, dependent on Saudi and IMF loans to avoid collapse. The central purpose of his presidency has been the attempted extirpation of the Muslim Brotherhood – which has deep roots in Egypt – and of other allied and independent terrorist groups, a purpose that appears to have left all other concerns to one side. His popularity derived in large part from his identification of and a campaign against real or alleged terrorism which threatens Egyptian society. In a strongly critical essay published late in 2016, the Middle Eastern scholar Steven Cook notes that the other large factor buoying up the president is a 'compliant media'[49] – whose diversity, commercial ownership and short period of radicalism in the early years of the 2010s have not saved them from again coming to heel. Yet popularity so supported can be evanescent: as Egypt's recent history has shown.

And, in mid-2017, is shown again. The deterioration of the economy, constant price rises and continuing high levels of terrorism combined to force a sharp drop in his popularity levels, and a rise in voiced opposition; an anti-presidential rant by a tuk-tuk (motorised rickshaw) driver garnered 10 million hits on a TV station website before diappearing.[50] In the Middle East's most important state, the popular voice is now harder to still – and journalism, and social media, more apt to make it heard.

THREE

'You saw it on television?
That means they are lying!'

Journalism can only assist the creation and maintenance of a civil society if it itself is assisted by the active attention of the citizens for whom it is written or broadcast. It must also be recognized by the various elites in society – political, corporate, civic – that any journalistic revelations should be acted upon where they point to real dangers and uncover real scandals. There must be trust from citizens that journalism is some part of the real state of affairs, and not produced only for diversion. The American journalism scholar Michael Schudson proposed that journalists assume 'a small, interested body of readers' who pay attention to the results of investigations and analyses, so that 'the news media can be viewed not as communicators to the public but as guardians of the public, stand-ins for public scrutiny, gatekeepers who monitor the political process on the part of the public'.[1]

When journalism was yearning to breathe freer in the late-1980s and early-'90s USSR, there was no history of mutual trust. One who expressed the dilemma well was the Georgian philosopher Merab Mamardashvili, one of the few who prefigured the liberalization and thus collapse of the Soviet Union. Mamardashvili saw the Soviet people as individuals who were in no condition to receive and act upon the messages a newly independent journalism would send them – even where it was responsibly done.

Born, like Joseph Stalin, in the small city of Gori, he thought little of official Soviet philosophy, believing it to be a waste of his time – circling, as it did, endlessly round the works of Karl Marx. In a 1989 interview with an American colleague while a fellow at Kettering College in Dayton, Ohio, Mamardashvili said that an ideal state, though easy to imagine, could not be attained, and certainly not by a revolution: 'We can't jump out of history. Gradually it occurred to me that it was what Russia did: she jumped out of history and committed the metaphysical suicide of trying to bypass reality for the ideal.'[2]

Russia, since Ivan IV (the 'Terrible') in the sixteenth century, had been under a despotic rule in which all property, all power, ultimately resided in the tsar. Mamardashvili had come to believe that 'all of society became an elongated shadow of the tsar. But shadows aren't real. From that time forward *unreality became the condition of social life in Russia* [my italics]. Russia became a shadow society.' He saw the Revolution of 1917 as 'unreality built on unreality. As a consequence, Soviet citizens are still always shadow boxing ... *finding every attempt at a rational action thwarted by the shadows* [my italics].'

The resulting gulf in Soviet citizens' minds enforced an attitude of confused cynicism, in which nothing was, or need be, real: 'They are people without consequence, that is people who cannot understand social processes, who are unable to make social judgements and who lack the ability every citizen must have to relate external events to their internal convictions. In Marxian language they are alienated', Mamardashvili concluded. In contemporary conditions, as the decades of the 2000s and 2010s were to find, they were ideal subjects for the reception of propaganda. In conversation, the writer and journalist Arkady Ostrovsky puts it differently:

I think the mechanisms of reception and internalizing propaganda were very different – and happened for different reasons – in different periods. In Stalin's period it worked like a mythology – the only way of explaining the world and pointless cruelty. In the 1970s it bred deep cynicism. In the

2010s it was a craving for status. In the 1970s few people wanted to believe propaganda. In the 2010s – a lot of people chose to do so.

The decade after Mamardashvili's death in 1990 cannot be summed up either as a disaster or as a triumph. On the one hand, there was impoverishment; wars, most of all in the Caucasus and worst of all in Chechnya; the cornering of resources by a handful of savvy and ruthless men, the oligarchs, who created corporate capitalism; and the flourishing of crime, especially organized crime; while on the other hand there was the growth of market mechanisms; the encouragement of liberal initiatives and attitudes; the retention of a rackety but functioning democracy; the opening to Europe and to the US; the gathering of the nuclear weapons stockpiles back into Russia and the deep cuts in warheads; the beginnings of serious examination of the crimes of Stalinism and after; and the freedom for speech, publication, debate and religious belief, which allowed the faithful to worship openly and restored the Orthodox Church. Light and dark were integrally linked.

Journalism covered, in the political press, a huge ideological spectrum, much larger than in any settled democratic state, from stoutly liberal to bitterly communist to militantly patriotic (the last two tended to merge). Circulations shrank rapidly from the Soviet times, from the many millions to the hundreds, even tens, of thousands. News and current affairs on television was freed from party, though not from all state control, and became more diverse and informative. However, much of the news was over-hyped and its veracity could not be trusted. There was no overall guiding hand; instead, there was a quite unaccustomed swirl of different political and polemical currents, vying for primacy. As the 1990s went on and poverty deepened, nostalgia for the Soviet period grew and tolerance of liberal, pro-Western attitudes declined.

—

'Openness' (one of the translations of 'glasnost', the policy of making public much of what had been previously suppressed) was adopted – largely from ideas supplied by Alexander Yakovlev, older than Gorbachev and with a lifetime of reformist frustrations in the senior ranks of the Soviet Communist Party – by a relatively young (fifty-four in 1985, when he became general secretary) Soviet leader. He believed that his fellow Soviets had internalized the 'socialist choice' and could thus be trusted with more freedom within it. Mikhail Gorbachev spoke at times in Mamardashvili's vein, saying (as he put it in an interview in 2000) that 'it isn't so easy to give up the inheritance we received from Stalinism and Neo-Stalinism, when people were turned into cogs in the wheel, and those in power made all the decisions for them'.[3] He sought to oppose that condition 'through democracy, through glasnost, [to] compel people, rouse people to speak for themselves, analyse, and decide for themselves what is to be done ...' His economic initiatives, including giving more control to enterprise through a restructuring of the rules governing them (perestroika), failed. Given more freedom from state control, those in charge tended to loot their enterprises rather than reform them.

Glasnost was a success. The first to be freed were literary works, which meant much to the intellectuals. 'Freedom of speech', says Arkady Ostrovsky, 'was not meant to be all-embracing, but had to be dished out in small doses and mostly to the intelligentsia.'[4] They came out at first in a trickle, then in a flood of publication: long-forbidden poems, plays and novels. These caused real joy in the ranks of the intelligentsia – but indifference among the majority of people for whom the daily struggle was tougher, as staples became harder to afford.

The first to be declassified were the works of poets, such as Nikolai Gumilev, Anna Akhmatova and Osip Mandelstam. The works of Alexander Solzhenitsyn, and the Great Patriotic War (Second World War) novel of Vasily Grossman, *Life and Fate*, followed. These were incendiary works: Akhmatova's *Requiem*, written when her son Lev had been imprisoned and condemned to death (a sentence later commuted to hard labour), invokes the experience of seventeen months queuing outside the prison in Leningrad to which he had been taken, waiting for news or taking in food, with other haggard women. *Life and Fate*, written by one who traded the position of an acclaimed war correspondent for that of a dissident writer, puts on the same moral level the horrors of Nazism and those of Stalinism – an insight voiced by a Nazi SS officer. Neither Akhmatova nor Grossman were executed, but they did not live to see their greatest works published in Russia: *Requiem* came out in the USSR in 1987, *Life and Fate* in 1988. Both authors died in the mid sixties – Grossman in obscurity, Akhmatova famed but still censored, an inspiration for other dissident writers, such as Joseph Brodsky.

These publications signalled to the intellectuals that they had a space for freedom; but it had to be *responsible* freedom, which adhered to the socialist choice of the Soviet peoples. The main papers, such as *Pravda* (Truth), published by the Central Committee of the Communist Party, and *Izvestia*, published by the Soviet government, remained subordinate and official. The glasnost action, from the late 1980s, was in journals like *Ogonyok* (Little Flame), a glossy magazine edited by the adventurous Vitaly Korotich, and *Moskovskiye Novosti* (Moscow News), founded in 1980 and edited by Yegor Yakovlev, a weekly paper which became a leader in breaking taboos.

Television, in the last years of the Soviet Union, had played a subaltern role to the press – unable to carry the vital messages for or against reform, at best allowed only to discuss some of the themes in the talk shows, which became a much more central, and much more interesting, feature of the schedules. This soon changed: in the late eighties and beginning of the nineties, TV began its ascent into the central position in the nation's media menu that it had already achieved in the West. New programmes included *Fifth Wheel*, *Vzglyad* (View), *Before and After Midnight* and *120 Minutes* – which for the politically engaged were supremely exciting. These shows featured long, uninterrupted discussions on the nature of Communism, socialism, the global market and relations with the US and Europe; debates on politics could go on for three hours or more.

In April 1987, one of the most spirited programmes featured Prime Minister Margaret Thatcher, on a visit to see Gorbachev, with whom she had close relations. Confronted with three senior and courteous Soviet commentators, she – to their evident confusion – pressed home arguments on the need for freedom of speech and of the market, and on the importance of nuclear weapons as deterrents to aggression. The leap, from the ritual demonization of the pre-glasnost years to a respectful conversation in which the most enthusiastically free-market politician of the age was given space to make her points, was huge.

Vzglyad mixed Western rock music videos with interviews and panels on the issues of the day. Many, especially among the young, found Soviet TV tedious and shows like this were a way to win them back. The programme started out quite sedately, but soon became more radical. In 1990, it aired an interview with Eduard Shevardnadze, the foreign minister, who had walked out of a politburo meeting as a protest against what he saw as a reactionary turn by Gorbachev, then at a low point in his leadership, to give a dramatic speech, made for TV, in which, addressing his allies, he cried: 'I'll put it bluntly, comrade democrats. You have scattered. The reformers have slunk into the bushes. Dictatorship is coming.'[5] There was no hesitation about broadcasting this; the young producers of *Vzglyad* had quickly adopted the values and practices of Western current affairs, but it was taken off the air soon after, and remained so until 1994, when it came back as a Russian, no longer Soviet, programme. Their insubordination caught on, as it became more obvious that the state-party could no longer command obedience since it was ceasing to command the country. In January 1991, the beginning of the last year of the Soviet Union, a newsreader, Tatyana Mitkova, with tears in her eyes, refused to read the official version of an attack on demonstrators in the Lithuanian capital of Vilnius, which ended in thirteen of those taking part being killed.

The standout programme, launched from Leningrad (now St Petersburg), was *600 Seconds*, a pure child of television.[6] Every night after the still-staid nine o'clock news programme *Vremya* (Time), Alexander Nevzorov – a dashing, leather-jacketed thirty-something stuntman and attention seeker – would be shown charging into the back storerooms of shops to film the goods that were being hoarded to sell on the black market, or winkling out prostitutes from their hiding places in red-light districts, or reporting on radioactive courgettes in a food market. Nevzorov said the programme allowed Soviet citizens 'to feel that there are still forces of light and people of courage in Russia'. It turned increasingly nationalistic and anti-liberal in the Yeltsin period, after 1990, but when the Russian president tried to shut it down in 1991, the protests were so large that he backed away: it ended in 1993. Charged by his critics for copying American-style reality TV, Nevzorov was, mostly, ahead of Western shows of the time in his willingness to report, dispassionately but vividly, on horrors like child rape, or on other sensationalist stories, such as the gravediggers who were taking the shoes and gold fillings of the dead before burial or cremation.[7]

In the late-Soviet glasnost period and the first years after the collapse of Communism, a 'perestroika' of journalism began. Much of it was confused and confusing, self-indulgent and patronizing. But the first institutions of a freer press appeared, including a concern for establishing a reliable record, investigating abuses with a degree of transparency about sources and analysing events soberly and neutrally. With these practices came reporters and commentators of independent standing, in newspapers, magazines and think tanks. A business press appeared which, like business journalism everywhere, had greater pressures on it to be accurate, since the readership might base financial decisions on it. The most successful of these was *Kommersant*, founded in 1989, covering both business and political news with a sharp, often ironic style.

Revelations and scandals poured out of the press. At first, these were mainly about past repressions and betrayals, then the focus shifted to the manoeuvres of the new oligarchs. It was impossible to tell what was true and what false in the reportage; and in many cases, nothing came of the revelations, since the new government and parliament (the Duma) were not geared to pursue allegations of criminality and corruption – being, in many cases, corrupt themselves, bought by the new rich to be their lobbies within parliament or simply too burdened with work. But when the reporting struck a nerve, it could be powerful: the highly critical coverage of the first Chechen war by NTV, for example, pushed the administration towards a peace agreement.

Glasnost allowed some experimentation in TV and the development of new formats – though its efforts to remain within the framework of a reformed Communism were futile. The young guard brought contempt for what their state had become (a contempt that would be repaid in full in the 2000s, as patriotic Russian programming, the president's taste, displaced chic anti-Sovietism and took over the studios). In the 1990s, however, the leading figures rubbed in the consequences of the Soviet collapse and the debased state of Russia. Yevgeny Kiselev, a tall and imposing man in his early thirties during the glasnost period, developed a current affairs show, *Itogi* (Results), for the main state channel, which ran reports from Russia and from abroad and broke the Soviet habit of journalistic deference to political figures. He once asked Andrei Kozyrev, the Russian foreign minister, if it were 'not the case that the rest of the world thinks Russia to be a decrepit nuisance?' A few years earlier – or later – that remark would have resulted in the destruction of his career.

In 1994, Kiselev offered to sell *Itogi* to one of the bounciest of the new oligarchs, the former stage director Vladimir Gusinsky. Instead of buying the programme, Gusinsky created his own TV company called NTV. The 'N' was left vague, and could stand for *Nezavisimoe* (Independent), *Novoe* (New), *Nashe* (Our) or *Negosudarstvenoye* (Non-governmental). Kiselev took

Itogi to Gusinsky's channel and made it more radical. He was scathing about the progress of the Chechen war, which he and his reporters represented as a piece of bloody stupidity on the part of the Russian state.

Gusinsky disclaimed any pretences to be a fighter for free speech or human rights. He said he fought for personal rights, for the right of him and his family to live in a 'normal' country (one other possible use for the 'N' was '*normalnoe*' – Normal TV). NTV's first managing director, Igor Malashenko, a graduate from both the Communist Party's Central Committee bureaucracy and Soviet central TV, encouraged an atmosphere of experimentation and debate, shrewdly hanging the station's output between the two pillars of Kiselev's current affairs output and a selection of recent, mainly Hollywood, films. His staff included the satirist Victor Shenderovich, who adapted the British satirical show *Spitting Image* into a show simply called *Kukly* (Puppets). Shenderovich loved to pull the tail of the government, and pulled hard – hard enough to shock many, and delight many other, Russians.

The puppet representing the president, Boris Yeltsin, had the drunkard's purple nose and slurred speech; one episode showed Yeltsin and his prime minister, Viktor Chernomyrdin, lolling drunkenly on a park bench. The prosecutor general, Alexei Ilyushenko, held that to be insulting to the president and moved to prosecute. Chernomyrdin, whose PR team arranged for the prime minister to be photographed next to his puppet, smiling indulgently, stopped him in his tracks. Corruption in government, brutality in the Chechen wars, chaos in public services – all were grist to the *Kukly* mills. The satire was more bitter, more serious, sometimes more absurdly funny than the British original. The stakes were much higher.

From 1994, another fabulously rich man, Boris Berezovsky, the oligarch who was closest to the Kremlin and to the Yeltsin family, controlled the main state channel, ORT. Prodded by NTV, ORT sharpened up its act and developed new shows – though it was much more loyal to the leadership. It was also one of many new zones of corruption that had sprung up, more or less openly, in the post-Soviet era: in this case, the rake-offs obtained by middlemen who negotiated between the channel's programmes and advertisers, with all sides taking a cut from the large sums spent on advertisements on the most popular programmes. A new channel director, the popular TV host and producer Vladislav Listyev, tried to put a stop to the black market by having all ad sales handled by the channel itself: within a few weeks, he was assassinated in the entrance to his flat by a killer(s) who left his valuables and a large cash sum untouched: no arrests were made.

Konstantin Ernst, in his early thirties in 1995, was appointed programme director of ORT: cool, fluent in English, from an academic family and with a Ph.D. in molecular biology, he wanted the channel not to reflect life – which could be nasty in the nineties – but to improve on it. Though he had been an academic – a researcher in an institute before joining the *Vzglyad* team – he had little of the Soviet intelligentsia's disdain for mass tastes. Ernst was as sure-footed a player in the Russian media world as any – and was to rise, in the 2000s, to be one of the most important in the land.

The Yeltsin presidency dealt with the oligarchs through a series of bargains, driven both by the huge bribes paid by the suddenly rich businessmen and by the conviction that passing Russia's assets into private hands was the best insurance against a Communist comeback. The grandest bargain was with Mikhail Khodorkovsky, Vladimir Potanin, Boris Berezovsky and the other new plutocrats – they were granted shares in energy and other assets in return for financing a campaign to have Yeltsin re-elected for a second term in 1996. This meant that the channels they commanded became propaganda outlets for Yeltsin. Kiselev did not try to hide his preferences and prejudices: the coverage helped save tattered, corrupt liberal politics from a reactionary Communist Party, at the price of compromising the media which had promoted themselves as an antidote to reaction and corruption. Kiselev, though uncomfortable with the shift to propaganda, defended it as necessary to save the country from a return to Communism. Others, less involved, emphasized the price: the TV critic

Irina Petrovskaya lamented – 'What happened to its [NTV's] European correctness? ... if they manage to [get Yeltsin elected] will television be able to return to its democratic principles? ... Or will it turn a temporary love affair with the media into a compulsory admiration?'[8]

With others, I covered the collapse of the Soviet Union and the first years of the Boris Yeltsin presidency for the *Financial Times*, both as East Europe editor from 1988 and as Moscow bureau chief from 1990 to 1995. The *FT* was strongly in favour of the radical reformers led by Yegor Gaidar: I shared its view. I have thought since that many of us – not all – who were Western correspondents missed some of the immiseration of Russians in these years, and much of the regret for the loss of the modest certainties of Communism. In May 2003, I wrote a review of David Remnick's *Lenin's Tomb*: Remnick, editor of the *New Yorker*, was then a *Washington Post* reporter in Moscow, who left at about the time I came to live there. I thought, and still think, it is a finely crafted and insightful book, but in rereading my admiring review, and the excerpts from the book I quote, I recognize a common mindset among Western reporters: that of privileging radical reforms because they were part of an attack on the tyranny of the Communist period and in particular the suppression of freedoms of speech, the press and travel. 'It's as if', Remnick wrote, 'the regime were guilty of two crimes on a massive scale: murder and the unending assault against memory. In making a secret of history, the Kremlin made its subjects just a little more insane, a little more desperate.'[9]

That was right, but many of us were too little alive to the personal gratifications post-Stalinist Communism had offered – security, pride in empire (something even a post-imperial Brit should know about), comradeship in a rough material equality (except for the highest officials), and satisfaction that the rich and titled, who had treated the peasant masses and the new industrial workers abominably even after the end to serfdom in 1861, had been dispossessed – something insistently drummed in by Soviet propaganda.

Recognizing that Communism had popular features doesn't dictate approval: often the contrary. But it would have made us less surprised by the popularity of Putin's authoritarianism. Journalism, including that which strives for objectivity, can't help but work within unconscious mental boundaries. The lack of freedom, the twisted history, the low living standards in Soviet society were all outrages to Westerners with middle-class living standards: less so for most Soviets.

The recoil from Soviet-era obedience to the state and the development, in the media, of a critical and sarcastic commentary on government and the leading figures of the land appealed most of all to the educated young and to the intelligentsia; it shocked and disgusted many more. The Jewishness of most of the first oligarchs – of the seven most prominent, only one, Vladimir Potanin, had no Jewish ancestry – was a constant theme of complaint and prejudice. The loss of global influence and reach, and the erratic, at times drunken, behaviour of Yeltsin, provoked national shame. A wave of nostalgia for the Soviet Union swept over the land, which was to grow stronger and find a militant champion in the new president.

The media picked up on this and both reflected and furthered it. In 1995, Ernst at ORT joined with the stylish, ironic presenter Leonid Parfenov to develop a programme called *Old Songs about Important Things* – the old songs being from the Soviet era, still remembered by most of the adult population. It was presented in an ironic way – but not so drenched in irony that it couldn't be enjoyed for its content. Soviet films were exhumed and shown – reminding those who needed the jog of memory that many were technically accomplished, finely acted and often witty.[10]

At the same time, TV was becoming more 'Western': the schedules were filled with game shows, consumer programmes, soap operas (Russian and imported), chat shows and comedy.

Throughout the nineties, defying attempted coups both public and semi-hidden, defying the eccentric rule of Boris Yeltsin, defying the impoverishment of millions of Russians, defying the flood of foreign goods and influences, defying the conspicuous enrichment of a very few, defying the suddenly revealed corruption which had always been part of the Soviet system and the large new opportunities for corruption in the market economy – defying all these, the central power of the Kremlin remained. It survived, very largely, because the suddenly enriched and powerful wished it so – seeing Yeltsin, for all his waywardness, as the best guarantee of continued freedom from Communism. Boris Yeltsin was able to pass the reins of power to Vladimir Putin, who had in a few years rocketed up through the Russian administrative system from middle-ranking – lieutenant colonel – KGB officer, through deputy mayor of St Petersburg, to high posts in the presidential administration in Moscow, to head of the FSB security service, to deputy prime minister, to become, in the autumn of 1999, prime minister (the fifth in eighteen months), then acting president at the end of the year when Yeltsin resigned, then president. He was elected in the spring of 2000, in the first round, with 53 per cent of the votes cast. The beginning of the Putin era neatly coincided with the beginning of the millennium and, more importantly, with the restarting of economic growth. It was a new era, too, for Russian journalism, one that now stands, as the Soviet system had done before, as a model for authoritarian rulers everywhere.

Journalism in the age of Vladimir Putin has been termed as a reversion to Soviet norms – even, to Stalinist times. That isn't the case. There is a substantial part of the press – in Moscow, always more liberal, but also in Russia beyond Moscow – which is critical, in some cases nothing but critical, of the Putin presidency. Even on broadcast channels, where uniformity is most evident and most strongly enforced, some critics get air time now and again, and the news will occasionally cite criticism of the president and of Russia in a way Soviet news never would. Most importantly of all, there is the Internet, which now hosts critical websites and blogs – though some important sites, such as Lenta.ru, have been pressured into dropping their critical content, usually after a radical change of editorial leadership.

This was not the Soviet Union; it was a quite different kind of authoritarianism, preferring to marginalize dissent, while at the same time brandishing it as proof of a robust civil society, rather than to murder or imprison those responsible (though both murder and imprisonment were options). The Soviet system was at once massive and fragile: massive in the construction of institutions and systems designed to support the embedding of Communism in its vast landmass, and in the Central and East European states brought into the Soviet ambit; fragile, in that it could not tolerate any public challenge to its practice or ideology. Post-Soviet authoritarianism proved more flexible.

Most of the criticism and hostile reporting now possible in Russia would have been suppressed and punished in the Soviet Union right up to the Gorbachev leadership in 1985. The historian Arseny Roginsky, who co-founded Memorial in 1988, a non-governmental organisation – a revolutionary thing for the time – dedicated to exhuming the millions swept up into the Gulag, was imprisoned in the early 1980s for his reinterpretation of the Stalin period, about which there had to be only one, official, line.[11]

Putin came to power claiming to believe in a free press. As prime minister, he said – at the ninety-fifth anniversary of ITAR TASS news agency – that 'the Russian government ... will continue to support freedom of speech in every way'. When acting president in December 1999, he released a statement to the effect that 'free speech and free access to information, right for the accurate coverage of what is really happening in the country, will remain an immutable law for the Russian authorities'. A year later, a presidential decree commended forty-eight Russian journalists 'for their coverage of the Caucasus events': Putin said then that 'free press and mass media remain the most important condition for the society and state development'. Yet at the same time, he was taking over the main TV channels.[12]

And there was a thorn in the bouquets. It was in the phrase '[a] right for the *accurate* coverage of what is *really* [my italics] happening in the country'. Freedom of speech and of the press doesn't rest on accuracy, but on the right to speak and publish, including inaccuracies. Good journalism seeks to avoid these, but in a free society, bad, inaccurate journalism isn't banned for not doing so: and the state doesn't define what bad journalism is. The problem of 'accurate' reporting, as against free journalism, was to remain and grow as a theme of the Putin presidency. In September 2000, Putin signed a document named the 'Doctrine of Information Security', which listed as 'the greatest dangers in the sphere of spiritual life' threats that included:

> deformation of mass information system through mass media monopolization or through uncontrolled expansion of foreign mass media within the national information space; use by foreign Special Branches of mass media on the Russian territory, with the purpose to damage Russian National Defence and Security and to disseminate false information.

The Doctrine reflected the new president's already settled conviction: that foreign forces, spearheaded by the intelligence agencies, would work to destabilize the government. In his third term as president, this conviction led to the effective banning of a range of NGOs working in the broadly defined political sphere that were funded from abroad, together with mainly foreign institutes that were classed as 'undesirable organizations'. The insistence that journalism must be accurate, information not false, would allow the regime to argue that the media approved by it were truthful, not 'deformed'.

In the late summer of 2000, the nuclear submarine *Kursk* – the most advanced and largest attack submarine in the Russian fleet – suffered an internal explosion and sank in a relatively shallow 100 metres of water in the Barents Sea. Putin, who had been criticized in the media for continuing his vacation some days into the incident, went to Murmansk and met the victims' families. Even though journalists were barred, his remarks were recorded unofficially and a transcript obtained by the main state Channel One in a programme presented by the channel's news presenter Sergei Dorenko, who a year earlier had been one of the journalists most to the fore in promoting the new young president. Dorenko referred to Putin's response to relatives who were shouting at him for not accepting offered Western aid, which they had seen reported on TV. The president had said:

> You saw it on television? That means they are lying. They are lying! They are lying! There are people on television who have been working to destroy the army and the navy for ten years ... All they really want to do is to finish it off! They've stolen all the money and now they are buying everyone off and making whatever laws they want to make![13]

Dorenko was removed from his post as senior news presenter soon after.

When Putin came into the presidency he revealed a belief that he had more or less disguised for the previous decade. He thought that 'the demise of the Soviet Union was the greatest geopolitical catastrophe of the century ... as for the Russian people, it became a genuine tragedy. Tens of millions of our fellow citizens and countrymen found themselves beyond the fringes of Russian territory.'[14] It was a tragedy he later sought at least partially to remedy: he did not want to reconstitute the Soviet Union – in the same 'geopolitical catastrophe' speech, he said that anyone who tried that lacked a brain – but he used the loss and the popular need for a restoration of greatness to bolster nationalism and suspicion of, even enmity to, the West.

From a working-class Leningrad family, he had gained status, education and a foreign posting from the Soviet KGB, and he had felt the withdrawal of Soviet power in East Germany as a piece of rank cowardice and weakness on the part of his political masters. His chief complaint was that the US and its European allies had promised that NATO would not move east, to take in the former Warsaw Pact states, but it did, starting with East Germany, which was quickly reunited with the West.

The complaint has some substance: initial conversations between Gorbachev, the US Secretary of State, James Baker, and the German foreign minister, Hans-Dietrich Genscher, saw the two Western politicians agree to some form of pledge that NATO would not expand. But in a careful reconstruction of the negotiations Mary Elise Sarotte writes that 'Gorbachev ultimately gave his assent to a united Germany in NATO in exchange for face-saving measures ... he also received twelve billion Deutschmarks to construct housing for the withdrawing Soviet troops and another three billion in interest-free credit. What he did not receive were any formal guarantees against NATO expansion.'[15] She adds that 'a young KGB officer serving in East Germany in 1989 offered his own recollection of the era in an interview a decade later, in which he remembered returning to Moscow full of bitterness at how "the Soviet Union had lost its position in Europe". His name was Vladimir Putin, and he would one day have the power to act on that bitterness.' The bitterness was not confined to loss of power in the Soviet bloc: it was stimulated at least as painfully by the loss of power in Russia itself.

To be able to give concrete form to that bitterness, the president had to do more than merely nurse his wrath to keep it warm. He had to dominate his own country, best done by cutting other sources of power down to size. The oligarchs, whom he had seen commanding easy access to the presidential suite and who flaunted both their wealth and their power, were brought into the Kremlin in the summer of 2000 and told the facts of life, with Putin reportedly saying: 'You built this state yourselves, to a great degree, through the political or semi-political structures under your control, so there is no point in blaming the reflection in the mirror.'[16] In this, Putin was right: to function, the state had to be more powerful than any private centres of power – and it had not been. The oligarchs who had seen themselves as the true rulers of the state were tamed, in exile or imprisoned: a new class of oligarchs, created by the Kremlin, took their places.

The attack was the verbal equivalent of *deashi harai* – a judo move designed to throw the opponent instantly by sweeping him off his feet – which Putin, a black belt, has said is his favourite gambit. They were, in truth, already off balance. The oligarchic period had made them all very rich and some politically powerful. But it was an unstable, robber-baron kind of wealth that could be snatched away at any time. Not far from the gilded hall in which they met, they knew, Putin was keeping *kompromat* on them: piles of material gathered by the security agencies on their rise to wealth, piles that were, a Putin adviser said, 'metres high'.[17]

Before the meeting, Putin had already moved against those oligarchs whose power he disliked most. In June, Vladimir Gusinsky was arrested and jailed briefly on charges of embezzlement. The charges were dropped, but not before the heavily indebted Gusinsky had signed a deal transferring Media-Most, his conglomerate of newspaper and broadcasting properties, to Gazprom, the government-dominated energy company, for 300 million dollars. By the time of the meeting, he was complaining that he had agreed to the transaction in jail, under duress; the government had threatened new investigations. At the same time, Putin tried to get Berezovsky to agree to be bought out from his control, through a 49 per cent stake, of the main broadcaster, ORT. Berezovsky took the opportunity to do some grandstanding, saying he would transfer his shares to journalists and members of the intelligentsia: 'I will not do anything under pressure. I am prepared to go to jail if necessary.'

But they were both dispossessed – with large compensation – of the media corporations that they had only just built, and which they had hoped would save them from any action, legal or otherwise, against them, because the state would be too much in the thrall of favourable coverage. Both went abroad: Berezovsky to the UK, with a heart full of bitterness, since he had spotted Putin, thought he would be both efficient and pliable, boosted him through his media and assumed he would remain a close consigliere to the untested president, even something of a controller.

Taking back power to the Kremlin meant more, for Putin, than displacing oligarchs. His sense of humour – a caustic one – did not stretch to an appreciation of the NTV programme *Kukly* (Puppets), which often featured a sinister Vladimir Putin. The show's main writer, Victor Shenderovich, told me that Putin had told the *Kukly* team they could continue if they did not criticise the government or him. 'In that case,' Shenderovich said, 'we would have nothing to say.'

Shenderovich told me that political satire is no longer possible in the mass media. He is not explicitly banned from TV, but, he says, the producers of the programmes that might use him understand the dangers of having him on: 'Kultura [an arts and culture channel] asked me to appear recently. I said, fine, but it will be forbidden. The producer said, let's try. So he did try and it was forbidden: I didn't get on.

'We must recognize that they do this very cleverly. The intelligentsia – one to two million people at most – have their papers and Ekho Moskvy [a critical Moscow radio station: since that talk, TV Dozhd (Rain), a shoestring operation of mainly critical talk shows, has started and managed to continue], they have books and the Internet. The administration isn't worried by that.' But Shenderovich believes that Russian satire's time will come again. 'It will get harder for them with the economic crisis. Their rule has depended on strong growth and on success. When that stops the opposition voices will become more attractive. The paradox is that when satire becomes popular again, it will get dangerous again: and then we might lose what freedom we have.'

The canning of Kukly was one sign among many that Putin was clearing the media ground – though NTV, for a few years after its owner was dispossessed, continued to report proactively, including on the sinking of the Kursk in 2000 and the seizing of the Dubrovka Theatre and its audience by Chechen gunmen in October 2002. The other oligarchs had not experienced the heady sense of power which ownership of a TV channel gives: and Mikhail Khodorkovsky, the richest of them, had yet to make the moves which consigned him to the twenty-first-century gulag for a decade. Some even saw the sense in being limited to making huge sums of money: Petr Aven, chairman of the banking division of Alpha Group, the largest private bank in Russia, and a former minister in Boris Yeltsin's first government, told me: 'Those who were closest to Yeltsin behaved as if they were running the government. Put yourself in Putin's shoes. You can't have that kind of relationship!'

Khodorkovsky did not feel so constrained, and in a gathering of oligarchs in the Kremlin in February 2003, he, unasked, gave a presentation on Russian corruption, pointedly instancing a recent merger between the state oil corporation Rosneft and a smaller private company. Khodorkovsky said the deal had 'a second layer' – an allusion to the widespread suspicion that the high price was meant to give cuts to the main players. Putin, angered, hit back, asking where Khodorkovsky's company Yukos got its 'extraordinary [financial] reserves'. In the course of the year, several of Khodorkovsky's senior colleagues were arrested, followed in October by Khodorkovsky himself. He spent the next ten years in prison camps.

The arrest and sentence was a demonstration that a figure like Khodorkovsky, who had decided to live as if he were in a free, law-governed country, would not be tolerated. Most of his assets were seized. At the same time, Putin's closest colleagues were enriched – and became the new generation of oligarchs.

The state Putin built is a corporate one, which is arguably the dominant system (in differing forms) both of political control and of capitalism in the twenty-first century. Putin inherited a state in which the corporate barons called many of the shots: but, writes the British historian Perry Anderson, he had 'turned the tables on them. Under his system, a more organic symbiosis between [political control and capitalism] has been achieved, this time under the dominance of politics.'[18]

This fusion of politics with business, says Shenderovich, is welded together by Putin's most striking achievement: the creation of a 'virtual space'. As in the trilogy of Matrix films released in 1999, Putin's virtual space is one in which the population is kept quiescent in a world they take for real, but which is actually a simulation created by machines. 'Putin's own experience convinced him of the immense power wielded by the media, so it was logical that now, in power, he should be the one to control the matrix and create the virtual space that, thanks to TV, millions of Russians take for reality.'[19] In this space, TV reigns; most people don't read much, but they watch TV and support the Kremlin: the minority of people who read a lot and don't watch TV don't support the Kremlin. Yet more significant for the majority or Russians than the virtual space was the rapid rise of incomes; and within the 'virtual' space, often acting as content for the TV, were wars in the Caucasus and the annexation of Crimea.

Holding centre stage also demands that he has the trappings of power, which in Russia today brings, to those at the top, great wealth. In the late summer of 2012, a number of leaders of the shrunken opposition presented a report ironically titled 'The Life of a Galley Slave', written by Boris Nemtsov and Leonid Martynyuk (Putin had complained he had such a life, chained to the remorseless rhythm of running Russia), which revealed that Putin had ensured that as president, he had access to 'four yachts ... palaces, fifty-eight planes and helicopters and twenty homes with opulent fittings worthy of the tsars, not to mention eleven watches which alone are worth several times Putin's annual salary'.[20] In a 2014 book, Putin's Kleptocracy, the Russologist Karen Dawisha builds up details on Putin's fabulous riches and those of his closest circle, whom he has enriched, writing that

Putin does not 'own' any of these, except his St Petersburg properties and perhaps his first yacht, the *Olympia*, which was presented to him as a gift by a group of oligarchs headed by Roman Abramovich just prior to Putin's becoming president, and delivered in 2002. Without the presidency, Putin would theoretically not be allowed to keep any of these accoutrements of power, except perhaps for the $700,000 in watches that he routinely sports – six times his declared income ... thus his motivation to leave power is reduced to zero.[21]

The work of the British–Russian sociologist Alena Ledeneva unveils a system in which influence peddling, connections, bribery, skimming of state funds, dispossession of property and blackmail are part of everyday government and business life.[22]

Dawisha quotes Lennart Dahlgren, who had been the head of IKEA in Russia till 2006, as saying that he asked to see Putin to complain of the pressure on the company to pay bribes, which it always refused to do: a 'high-ranking official told [him] that a meeting with Putin would cost five to ten million dollars'.[23] Putin had cowed the oligarchs, who were marshalled into a system in which he became one of them, and the greatest of them, at that. His readiness to attack also cowed Dawisha's British publisher, Cambridge University Press: it declined to publish *Putin's Kleptocracy*, citing a 'significant risk' that the English courts would uphold a libel complaint against the book. With some asperity, Dawisha wrote to her editor that

these Kremlin-connected oligarchs feel free to buy Belgravia, kill dissidents in Piccadilly with Polonium 210, fight each other in the High Court, and hide their children in British boarding schools. And as a result of their growing knowledge about and influence in the UK, even the most significant British institutions ... cower and engage in pre-emptive book-burnings as a result of fear of legal action.[24]

The oligarchs were contained, the most important newspapers passed into friendly, nominally private, hands, and the two most important channels brought close to the state: NTV was taken over by Gazprom Media, as, in 2005, was *Izvestia*, the most authoritative, very pro-regime daily, then sold on to the National Media Group in 2008. Putin did, however, require more than simply control: he wanted to project himself across his vast land – and the world. For that, he needed savvy and proactive public relations people (called political technologists): Putin, who successfully presents himself as a man of the people, is the object of very sophisticated public relations, and has taken care to have constant access to some of the most creative image-makers in Russia.

The first public example of such a figure working for the presidency pre-dates Putin's era by some years. Gleb Pavlovsky, a mildly dissident figure in the late Soviet years, founded the Foundation for Effective Policy in the 1990s and assisted Putin to win his first election in 2000. His comrade in the Foundation was Marat Gelman, son of the well-known Soviet playwright and scriptwriter Alexander Gelman. Their influence on Yeltsin and later Putin is a matter of some dispute, but Pavlovsky was credited with much power within the Kremlin in the early years, and happily spoke for it.

The determination to take power back into Putin's Kremlin – it came to be called 'sovereign', later 'managed' democracy – was the organizing principle for the technologists. Pavlovsky and Gelman were both, as they said of themselves, 'post-modernist' figures, flitting between the worlds of the moderately liberal intelligentsia (Gelman opened a smart art gallery) and the Kremlin. Pavlovsky worked in or near the Kremlin; Gelman was deputy head of Channel One Russia.

Gelman left first, in 2004, when Putin was triumphantly re-elected. In a 2012 interview, he said that the experience of the election taught him that the new elite didn't just want to win, they wanted to make sure no one else could win. He said:

This so-called 'sovereign democracy' lost all sense of shame. What happened was against my views – not only mine, but others' as well. We thought society could develop differently … in Soviet times the concept of truth was important. Even if they were lying they took care to prove what they were doing was the truth. Now no one even tries proving 'the truth' you can say anything. Create realities.[25]

Pavlovsky stayed on, though he became increasingly restive. In 2008, he wrote an essay in which he said that Russian TV was 'a drama with only one character [Putin]', and called for a wider choice of voices, including oppositionists. He got a rocket from Putin for that, and was dismissed three years later – even joining, or at least observing, the series of demonstrations and protests that flared in that year.

The most inventive of these artists of narratives, and with steadier nerves, was Vladislav Surkov, half Chechen, half Russian, who in the late 1980s joined Mikhail Khodorkovsky's Menatep banking group. He rose to head of advertising, before moving to Mikhail Fridman's Alpha Group, briefly to fill the post of director of public relations for Channel One, then becoming deputy chief of staff in the presidential administration in 1999 at the young age of thirty-five, just as Putin was moving in. He gathered golden opinions from Khodorkovsky and his colleagues, who pointed to his ' non-standard mindset … every new step taken by this man is a sensation!'[26]

A claimed admirer of Allen Ginsberg and the US beat poets, Surkov developed a strong belief that 'there is no democracy in this country and the bureaucracy is ineradicable'. He argued that liberal reforms would lead to a collapse into chaos and in an article published in 2009, he wrote: 'even now when power is rather consolidated and ordered, many projects are very slow and difficult. If we add any sort of political instability to that then our development would simply be paralysed … authority that is unconsolidated and unbalanced [and] weak democratic institutions are unable to ensure an economic revival.'[27]

Surkov used his high position to lay down the lines to be followed in a weekly meeting with the heads of the TV channels. He told them that he believed that TV should be 'bread and circuses', the formula for keeping the mobs both amused and satiated.[28] 'Surkov's philosophy from the first was that there is no real freedom in the world, and that all democracies are managed democracies, so the key to success is to influence people, to give them the illusion that they are free whereas in fact they are managed. The only freedom in his view is "artistic freedom".'[29] He had framed photographs of John Lennon, Che Guevara, President Obama and the rapper Tupac Shakur in his office; he has written songs for the rock group Agata Kristi, and has written a novel, Almost Zero. He has also been likened to a 'Confucian official': one who serenely carries on with his mission – in his case preserving the existing system – smiling at insults and unfazed by attacks.[30] He was among the first seven officials put under executive sanction by President Obama in March 2014, after the Russian annexation of Crimea.

In an interview in February 2010 with the economic daily Vedomosti, Surkov scorned the 1990s, with the 'squabbling of the liberals ... under the noise and chatter about freedom, they'll carry away everything ... it is crucially important to preserve political stability. Stability does not mean stagnation, it does not mean petrification. It is a tool of development. Modernization cannot result from chaos.'[31] Admitting that 'the system' had to adapt to change, he added that 'the system is inseparable from the people – it is deeply rooted in the social fabric. Anyone who wants to destroy it is a social danger.'

The Bulgarian political scientist Ivan Krastev has argued that the technologists trade merely in 'a meaningless melange of Kremlin-produced sound bites'.[32] It's a melange, certainly, but it isn't meaningless to many Russians. It relies for its considerable success on a core Russian idea, which had underpinned Tsarism, Communism and then Putinism: the indissolubility of the paternalistic relationship between the rulers and the ruled – and the need to see any critics radical enough to demand a different 'system' as alien, a 'social danger'. Those Russian NGOs that accepted support from abroad and concerned themselves – even marginally – with politics were, under a 2013 law, branded 'foreign agents', which limited their activities in Russia, or even made them impossible – since few Russian sponsors would support institutions of which the Kremlin disapproved. When, in December 2014, Putin was asked about the political opposition to him, he said he was happy to have it, except where it was a 'fifth column'. Later, posters went up with caricatures of opposition politicians – including Boris Nemtsov, murdered on 27 February 2014 – labelled 'Fifth Column'.

One of the ideological sources for the Kremlin worldview has been Ivan Ilyin, a prolific writer who, expelled from the Soviet Union in the 1920s, took up the powerful current of fascism and recommended a supreme leader as a model of leadership. He saw bourgeois societies as both effete and corrupt because they fostered individuality, against the need for total unity in a state ruled by a dictator. 'Through Ilyin,' wrote Anton Barbashin and Hannah Thoburn, 'the Kremlin transmits what it sees as a proper ideology for today: a strong cocktail of uncompromising hatred for the West, denial of the European nature of Russian civilization, favour of dictatorial methods of governing, rabid nationalism, and a dash of conspiracy theory.'[33] According to the historian Timothy Snyder, Ilyin has been 'rehabilitated as Russia's leading ideologue', enthusiastically taken up by both Surkov and Putin – the latter having been seen to lay flowers on the philosopher's grave. Linking the new cult of Ilyin to the 2016 US presidential election, Snyder writes that

> Russia's interventions in our presidential elections are not only the opportunistic support of a preferred candidate, Donald J. Trump, who backs Russian foreign policy. They are also the logical projection of the new ideology: democracy is not a means of changing leadership at

home, but a means of weakening enemies abroad. If we see politics as Ilyin did, Russia's ritualization of elections becomes a virtue rather than a vice. Degrading democracy around the world would be a service to mankind.[34]

Surkov prepared the ground for the journalism of the Putin period's greatest task: becoming propaganda media. That meant accepting that truth was secondary to effect: that which worked on the emotions of the audience could be true, partly true or wholly false – the only measure was the degree of the required emotion stirred up. Above all, there is no such thing as objective reporting; everything is relative: you have your truth, I have mine. The difference being Surkov's power made Surkov's truth – and thus the president's truth – true, because it had the larger effect.

Propaganda was a positive trade, even a sacred one, before the nineteenth century. It was used first by the Vatican in the seventeenth century when the Sacra Congregatio de Propaganda Fide (the Sacred Congregation for the Propagation of the Faith) was established both to proselytize for the Catholic faith and to train missionaries. The office was renamed in 1982, since the word, after two world wars and especially the activities of the Nazi ideologist Joseph Goebbels, had given the practice a bad name. It is now the Congregation for the Evangelization of Peoples.

Russian propaganda in the twenty-first century does what propaganda has done everywhere: it 'canalizes an already existing dream'.[35] But it adds certain features, many of which derive from Surkov's approach. And it owes much to the Soviet/Communist cast of mind: 'the Communists, who do not believe in human nature but only in the human condition, believe that propaganda is all-powerful, legitimate and instrumental in creating a new type of man'.[36]

The British–Russian writer Peter Pomerantsev worked as a TV producer in Russia, and came to grasp its political heft. He writes that the output 'reaches deep into the nation's emotional traumas. Politicians and presenters feed the audience non-stop reminders of the difficult 1990s when, they argue, the West cheered at the sight of a weakened Russia ... [then] lifting them up with tales of glorious victories achieved by national leaders from Joseph Stalin to Putin.'[37] At the same time, it's revived past practice: Maria Lipman observes that Russia 'has resumed its traditional pattern: the overwhelming dominance of the state over the public and an aversion to Western liberalism'.[38] State dominance means that the news media operate only on the condition that they are loyal to the state and its leader; and its leader, aided by the technologists, has inserted himself into narrative after narrative – political, of course, but also economic, social, ideological, military and sports.

That last is particularly important. Effective control of the media, as well as political and economic life, could not be enough: the technologists, and Putin himself, were aware of the dangers of stagnation. He had to give the roused national spirit some tangible, popular achievements. 'The general state of society is one of dejection and pessimism,' Putin remarked. 'We need to cheer up.'[39] The chosen medium for national cheer was the Winter Olympics in 2014, an event that was staged in the subtropical resort of Sochi, on the Black Sea, and cost fifty-one billion dollars, significantly more than China spent on the 2008 Summer Olympics – which had three times the number of events. The Chinese spent 132 million dollars per event: the Russians, 520 million dollars.[40]

Sochi was a huge success, reasserting the country's primacy after its disastrous sixth place in the previous Winter Olympics, in Vancouver, Canada. Feared problems with the infrastructure, or with terrorist violence, did not emerge, and Russian athletes topped the medal table – in part, as subsequent revelations and admissions have made clear, because performance-boosting drugs were pumped into Russian athletes in a systematic, state-approved fashion.[41] The opening ceremony – now, in Olympic events, a vast display of the host nation's image of itself – was choreographed by the head of the main state TV company, Konstantin Ernst, by then the leading creator of the national geist. He put on a show of Russian history, its epochs signalled by excerpts from widely known and loved historical events, or fictional renderings – the Imperial period was presented as a ballet, named for a central character in Tolstoy's *War and Peace*, 'Natasha Rostova's First Ball'. The Soviet period, shorn of purges, gulags and even Stalin, was alluded to by a Bolshevik agitprop train surrounded by early Soviet avant-gardist, supremacist and constructivist images.

Ernst's show conformed to Putin's view of the healthy version of Russian–Soviet history, which was demonstrated in 2007 at a televised meeting between the president and history teachers, at which Putin said that Russia had 'nothing to be ashamed of', and that 'no one must be allowed to impose the feeling of guilt upon us'. Like much else developed by the technologists, with the leader and his circle, the historical idea is to emphasize those respects in which Russia is not like the rest of Europe. The unity of people with their rulers is stressed continually; the achievements of historical, pre-democratic figures are played up (such as Peter the Great, starring in Ernst's Sochi show) and a sense of national uniqueness is put at the centre of both the government's and the media's policies.

Ernst, the new man in television at the beginning of the Yeltsin era, was a big man when the Putin era came. As Putin acceded to the presidency, Ernst became director general of the main state channel, ORT (he renamed it 'First Channel' in September 2002). In 2000, the Soviet anthem came back in adapted form as the Russian anthem and Ernst brought back the Soviet musical jingle for the news programme *Vremya*. It had no commercials, followed Soviet practice in foregrounding the leader, Putin, and kept bad news, mainly, for foreign events. Ernst believed that the news should be a calming experience – 'Stabilization makes the news calmer. If news works like a nervy irritant – as it did in Russia in the 1990s – it is a sign of instability.'[42]

Through the first decade of the 2000s, Ernst produced 'nearly forty films or serials ... some of the most popular and historically interesting films from the era ...'[43] He and his First Channel continued to mine the past – it proved to be fertile territory – serving up historical remembrances for hungry audiences, and using Channel One to advertise his productions. His productions retrofitted Soviet classics for post-Soviets, explored the historical collapse of empires as tragic events, featured past and present-day detectives that could solve crimes and explored Soviet history from Stalin to Brezhnev as 'our national past'.

His films included two about the Russian special forces, the Spetsnaz, echoing Hollywood productions featuring special service groups. He did a four-part series named simply *Brezhnev*, which portrayed the former general secretary as a basically decent figure. His productions were not all simple patriotic boilerplate stuff: he produced a sixteen-part serial, *Children of the Arbat*, shown in 2004, based on the novel by Anatoly Rybakov, which was banned until the glasnost period because of its 'anti-Soviet' tendencies and its harsh portrayal of Stalin as a paranoid conspiratorial figure.

Two films by the director Timur Bekmambetov, *Night Watch* (2004) and *Day Watch* (2006), depicted a fantasy world in which the Light and Dark Forces face off against each other. The critic Thomas Campbell saw it as of a piece with the 'post-modernist' project of the technologists, where the finale to *Day Watch* 'falsifies history by making it utterly unreadable; a utopian pot-pourri of post-imperial melancholy, revanchism, imperial restorationism, castrated sixties-ness and anti-American cinematic Americanism'.[44]

Two other figures were crucial to this re-creation of popular Russian history. One is the film director and entrepreneur whose prominence has spanned the late Soviet, Yeltsin and Putin periods: Nikita Mikhalkov, whose filmography includes lyrical recreations of Chekhov plays through to (in the Putin period) patriotic blockbusters. He was elected president of the Russian Cinematographers' Union in December 1997, and called –

at the most turbulent of the fevered Yeltsin years – for 'new heroes' in the Russian cinema, to build a revived Russian patriotism. In April the following year, the director Karen Shakhnazarov became head of Mosfilm, and said that the cinemas needed 'audience friendly' films. In a keynote address in April 1998, Mikhalkov argued that Russian directors in the 1990s only portrayed anti-heroes, prostitutes, murderers – quite the opposite of the American heroes and superheroes who embodied strong patriotic values. After showing a selection of scenes from these films, Mikhalkov asked: 'What will become of our children? What will they know of their own country? What should keep them in this land? What can help them survive in such harsh conditions?' Mikhalkov wanted – and helped create – a patriotic film culture, with Russian heroes.[45]

'Dissident' works are produced, but with increasing reluctance. The most notable is the deeply pessimistic film *Leviathan*, which received 35 per cent of its budget from the state and was entered in the 2014 Cannes Film Festival, where it won best screenplay for its director, Andrei Zvyagintsev, and writer, Oleg Negin. However, it was not at first shown widely in its home country, and was harshly criticized by the culture minister, who told *Izvestia*: 'I did not recognize myself, my colleagues, acquaintances or even acquaintances of acquaintances in *Leviathan*'s characters. Strange, but among the movie's characters there is not a single positive one.'[46] The minister later published guidelines banning films that 'defiled' the national culture: yet *Leviathan* was subsequently released, and was a hit at the box office.

Remaking the Russian idea through history is intimately linked to facts on the ground – the mid 2010s has seen Russia project its force to secure more territory: the seizure of the Ukrainian province of Crimea, which had a Russian majority, in the late winter of 2014; the support shown, barely disguised domestically, for the separatist rebels in the Donbass region in Eastern Ukraine; and the backing given to President Bashar al-Assad's Syrian army in wiping out large tracts of armed resistance, and, with that resistance, thousands of civilians.

The political commentator Maria Lipman told me that the hardening of Russian attitudes towards foreign influences had much to do with events in Ukraine in 2013–14, and the Western sanctions that followed. She recalled how, following the election that clinched a third term as president for Putin in 2012, there were widespread anti-government demonstrations that reflected 'every kind of civic activism'. But the annexation of Crimea followed soon after the crackdown on the activists, which unleashed a flood of patriotism that identified those liberals who opposed it as 'fifth columnists'. 'Crimea was a trump card,' said Lipman. 'It made the vast majority of people into patriots and to oppose it, you are made to feel a national traitor.' Lev Gudkov, director of Levada Centre, an independent polling agency, showed me a graph tracing the sharp decline in the president's popularity before March 2014, when the occupation of Crimea began. At this point the Putin line shot up, to attain the 80+ level.[47]

Crimea needed little propaganda; it was taken easily, and the majority, ethnic Russians, were glad to be 'home'. Eastern Ukraine, in which Russian soldiers were soon dying in combat, was another matter. It needed harder-edge material, something that would test the limits of propaganda's method of working; giving the people some of the 'truth' they need to know with that which they want to know. It needed Dmitry Kiselev.

Kiselev (no relation to the liberal presenter Yevgeny Kiselev, who moved to pursue his TV career in Ukraine in 2008, saying freedom had ended in Russia) was an up-and-coming broadcast journalist in the late nineties, as Putin was shooting rapidly up the Kremlin steps. In 1999, when Putin was voicing boilerplate liberal views on the freedom of the news media, Kiselev did the same in a talk on television – now a video much shown to mockery in liberal circles. 'A journalist', he says, 'cannot be separated from his or her ethics. But people who appear on TV – you cannot often call them journalists. Because very often they're just agitators.'[48] Where the fading Communist power repelled him, the growing power of the national idea attracted him. In 2013, already deputy head and a presenter of *News of the Week* (*Vesti Nedeli*) on the state Russia Channel, he was appointed head of Russia Today – the new group taking in the agency RIA Novosti and the Voice of Russia radio station (but not the TV channel now broadcast round the world, now to be known as simply RT).

Oleg Dobrodeyev, one of Russian TV's most talented figures, came to direct the Russia Channel, and was Kiselev's boss. Both men had had liberal pasts: Dobrodeyev had, as a young TV producer in the mid nineties, joined in the anathemas levelled at the Soviet system, where journalists were 'no more than transmission belts of the ideological system'.[49]

As a reporter in 1991, Kiselev had refused on moral grounds to broadcast false information on the deadly attack by Soviet special forces on demonstrators in Vilnius, in the last months of the USSR. In 1999, he still espoused democratic views, saying in a video commissioned by the NGO Internews and paid for by the UK's Department for International Development that 'If we [journalists] talk crap, there will be a constant decline in standards ... then one sunny day we'll find ourselves swimming in the dirt like pigs'.[50]

They were part of a group of journalists who had been enthusiastic liberals, but who – probably sincerely as much as opportunistically – grew more and more distant from what they saw as their fellows' excessive pro-Westernism and lack of Russian patriotism. They include Vladimir Kulistikov, director general of the NTV channel, owned by the state-controlled energy behemoth Gazprom since being wrested away, early in Putin's presidency, from its co-creator, Vladimir Gusinsky, who fled into exile; Arkady Mamontov, ex-NTV, who harshly criticizes dissident figures and gay activists in TV shows, calling the latter 'perverts'; and Mikhail Leontev, head of communication at the state oil company Rosneft and presenter of a TV commentary programme *Odnako* (However), which goes out after Channel One's news and is ultra patriotic.[51]

The new boss, Kiselev, gave a speech to his RIA Novosti staff soon after the announcement of his appointment.[52] He argued that a state news agency had to steer away from an 'objectivity' that 'distort[ed] the picture [so that we] look at our own country as if it were foreign ... objectivity often flows into estrangement, contempt, rubbing one's hands, a position of "the worse the better"', adding that 'I think this period of distilled, estranged journalism is over'. He devoted much of his speech to that commodity which the technologists had sought to destroy – 'objectivity' – 'I believe there isn't a single publication in the world which would be objective. Is CNN objective? No. Is BBC objective? No.'

In a concluding passage, he said that 'the creation of values – it seems to me that this is such a worthy mission ... to take part in the general process of reflection and self-identification of Russia, this seems to me to be a noble task'. The journalists' job, as their new boss saw it, was to both develop and express Russian values, to allow a greater 'self-identification' with Russia. This becomes clearer when, in answer to one of the few questions asked by the staff after he had finished, he said that 'there are always a lot of complaints against the government, but not against a fatherland – no, because you are part of the fatherland ... the fatherland – that's sacred'.

Much of the commentary on Kiselev has picked out his comments on homosexuality, among the most extreme of which stated that gays should be prohibited from donating blood or sperm – and that 'their hearts, in case they die in a car accident, should be buried or burned as unfit for extending anyone's life'. Still more threateningly, he had pointed out – with an animated chart by his side – that 'Russia is the only country in the world that is capable of turning the US into radioactive ash. Even if all our command posts go dead silent after an enemy nuclear attack, an invulnerable system will automatically send our strategic missiles out of silos and submarines in the right direction.'

Kiselev has been a leader in the multi-pronged project of representing the war in Ukraine as one begun by the leaders of the coup against former

President Viktor Yanukovych, and as a fascist uprising; a fascist-supported junta then being put in place. That junta immediately turned against the peaceful Russian-speaking citizens of the Donbass, the industrial area in the east of Ukraine on the Russian border; Crimea was voluntarily reunited with Russia; Russia sent these citizens some supplies to help protect them against the fascist troops; while a few Russian volunteers joined the noble struggle on the separatists' side.

The poles on which these stories are hung are slim and few. It is the case that Yanukovych fled over 21–22 February 2014, after prolonged and bloody struggles on the Maidan, now Independence Square, in which around 100 protestors were killed. The police and the security services, it seemed, advised him they could no longer ensure protection, as their troops were melting away or refusing to fight. It is true that, in the immediate aftermath of Yanukovych's flight, a law was proposed to the interim parliament that the status of Russian as an official language be rescinded, but the law, though passed, was not implemented. It is true that some participants in the Maidan were in far-right groups, but these groups had tiny electoral support.

On these bases of largely ersatz repression, a raft of reports was built. One, broadcast by Channel One and told by a refugee woman, was of a four-year-old child crucified in the city of Slavyansk, which had been occupied by Ukrainian soldiers and then by separatists. No confirmation, pictures or any other witness to this was produced; even RT, the international service of Russian TV, refused to carry it. Asked to comment on a story that would be horrific if true, the Russian deputy communications minister, Alexei Volin, sidestepped a direct answer, instead stating that 'the public likes how our main TV channels present material, the tone of our programmes'. Volin's view of journalism had been made clear in a 2013 talk to journalism students at Moscow State University: 'We should give students a clear understanding: they are going to work for The Man, and The Man will tell them what to write, what not to write, and how this or that thing should be written. And The Man has the right to do it, because he pays them.'[53]

In this spirit, the Russian media broadcast a series of differing explanations for the downing of a Malaysian plane, routed over the eastern border of Ukraine in July 2014. These included a US-prompted attack on the plane by Ukrainian fighter jets, as well as a NATO attack on a plane they thought contained Vladimir Putin – sourcing the story to an unnamed Spanish air traffic controller. The Donbass republic's minister of defence, Igor Girkin (known as Igor Strelkov), told Russian TV viewers that the plane was full of dead bodies when it fell from the sky, claiming that they had been 'drained of blood' and 'stank of decomposition because they had been dead for days'. Any explanation was offered apart from the most likely (though not yet conclusively proven): that it had been shot down by separatists, who had recently taken delivery of anti-aircraft rocket batteries and who mistook it for a Ukrainian aircraft.

The scope of the international Russian broadcaster RT grew greatly in the 2000s. With an initial 300 staff, it numbered 2,000 by 2015; it is available to eight-five million viewers on cable in the US, though only a tiny number watch it regularly. Its director, Margarita Simonyan, only twenty-five when appointed, had spent a year in the US on a Future Leaders' programme: she has responded to criticism of the channel by insisting its purpose is not to broadcast propaganda for the government, merely to balance news with the Western media's relentlessly negative picture. In an interview with *Spiegel Online* in 2013, she said, 'There is no objectivity – only approximations of the truth by as many different voices as possible.'[54]

Simonyan featured prominently in the unclassified version of a US intelligence report on Russian hacking during the presidential campaign.[55] She was quoted as claiming on the arts programme *Afisha* that,

> in some sense, not having our own foreign broadcasting is the same as not having a ministry of defence. When there is no war, it looks like

we don't need it. However, when there is a war, it is critical ... the word 'propaganda' has a very negative connotation, but indeed, there is not a single international foreign TV channel that is doing something other than promotion of the values of the country that it is broadcasting from ... when Russia is at war, we are, of course, on Russia's side.

Simonyan's channel has a large audience worldwide, especially on YouTube, where it claims a higher number of hits than Fox News. It garnered support on the US left for its sympathetic coverage of the Occupy Wall Street protests, where thousands of protestors occupied Zuccotti Park in New York's financial district in the autumn of 2011, with slogans like 'we are the 99 per cent' – highlighting the huge gulf between the very richest in society and those on middling or low incomes. It even attracted a complimentary comment from President Obama – 'I think it expresses the frustrations the American people feel, that ... you're still seeing some of the same folks who acted irresponsibly trying to fight efforts to crack down on the abusive practices that got us into this in the first place.' RT won an Emmy award for its coverage.

It employed established stars, such as (the late) David Frost and Larry King, as well as Western political radicals, such as the head of the Respect Party and former British MP George Galloway and WikiLeaks' Julian Assange – whose first interview, in April 2012, was with Sayyid Nasrallah, leader of the Lebanese Hezbollah group, which, like the Russian government, supports Syrian President Bashar al-Assad. Galloway, who continues to appear regularly, mounts fierce defences of Russian policy and congratulates the British Labour Party for electing a new leader, Jeremy Corbyn, from its far left. It's often deceptively mild and balanced – but becomes aggressive when the Russian state interest is in play, as in August 2008, during the Russian–Georgian war when it took Putin's line that the Georgians' ham-fisted effort to retake the enclave of South Ossetia – formally part of Georgia – was 'genocide', that the then Georgian president, Mikheil Saakashvili, was a 'psychopath' and that Russia intervened for purely humanitarian reasons.

RT's bias caused at least one of its reporters to leave it. The British reporter Sara Firth, employed by the RT London bureau, resigned from the channel in July 2014 in protest against its coverage of the Malaysian airliner crash. She told the *Guardian*:

> It was the most shockingly obvious misinformation and it got to the point where I couldn't defend it any more. I walked into the newsroom and there was an eyewitness account making allegations [against Ukraine] and analysis, if you can call it, from our correspondent in the studio. It was just appalling, in a situation like that where there are families waiting to be informed and a devastating loss of life.[56]

RT has not pushed any of the more outré theories. But it did air a documentary – *MH-17: The Untold Story* – which argued that no one had proven anything about what downed the plane.

Oliver Bullough writes that the channel does not tell flat lies, but that

> it is selective about what facts it uses. Indeed, from its coverage of US politics, you might gain the impression that the only thing saving the Obama administration from collapse is police oppression of dissidents. 'Several well-respected individuals have recently warned on the possibility of a severe social crisis erupting in the United States,' RT warned on 21 January, basing its conclusion on quotes sometimes more than six years old. Its relentless focus on Washington's opponents has, however, won the channel their gratitude.[57]

It partakes of the view that objectivity is in the eye of the beholder. It is objective as far as the Occupy Wall Street protestors are concerned, or the fans of Julian Assange, or the supporters of al-Assad. Those who don't hold these positions can find their brand of objectivity elsewhere.

Naturally, that destroys any useful definition of objectivity. But that has been the idea, and the practice, of the Russian news media in the 2000s. The downing of MH17 stands as the largest illumination of the regime mindset: four days after it happened, the Ministry of Defence gave a briefing in which various scenarios were proposed – most of which were clearly bogus. 'But this was not a Russian concern: the scenarios' instant rejection by foreign and Russian experts did not prevent them from being reported in the West.'[58] Furthermore, a poll by the Levada Centre showed that 37 per cent of those polled believed that the Russian authorities were telling the truth about there being no Russian troops in Ukraine; and while 38 per cent said they didn't believe it, they thought that 'in the current international situation it was correct for Russia to deny this'.

The independent and oppositionist media are corralled into ever-tighter spaces; fear being one of the organizing principles. Some twenty journalists have been killed since 2000, usually in murky circumstances. One such death occurred in March 2007, when Ivan Safronov,[59] who had recently revealed that the Russian military's prized new Bulava intercontinental missile didn't work, fell from a fifth-floor window. Prosecutors quickly labelled it suicide: his friends said he had no reason to kill himself.

But opposition, though small and regarded with hostility – prompted by constant insistence from the propagandists of a popular president that these are 'foreign agents' and a 'fifth column' – continues to function, and to oppose. Since 1990, the radio station Ekho Moskvy has worked against the tide of broadcasters supporting the Kremlin line by digging deep into the news, the past and the (often subterranean) intellectual trends. It is, wrote David Remnick, 'one of the last of an endangered species, a dodo that still roams the earth'.[60] That was in September 2008, and it roams still, though it does so by a dispensation from the Kremlin, a decision by Putin – to whom the editor-in-chief of the station, Alexei Venediktov, has occasional access – to retain a non-propagandist outlet, an act which may, ironically, be undertaken for propagandist effect.

A project called Last Address, developed by the journalist Sergei Parkhomenko in 2015, has a different kind of purpose, one at least frowned on by the Putin administration. That is, to remember the Stalinist past and honour its victims. He and a few others put up plaques on buildings to commemorate the arrest of people for whom it usually was a last address. Parkhomenko told me it was a way both of salvaging small shards of history and of puncturing the miasma of hyper-patriotism that had settled on the state. For all that, writes Maria Lipman, the most mordant of Russia's liberal commentators, 'the media are reduced to being a political tool of the state or marginalized to the point of making no difference to policy making'.[61]

Russians, especially the young, have taken to the Net – and it's still a rich field of relatively free opinionating. But it is, of course, monitored, and a law against 'unsanctioned public gatherings' or 'extremism' can be brought in at will. The editor of the website Lenta.ru, Galina Timchenko, was fired in March 2014 by the owner, the oligarch Alexander Mamut, and replaced by Kremlin loyalist Alexei Goreslavsky, who had edited the pro-administration website Vz.ru. Most of the newsroom resigned from Lenta.ru after the sacking, and went to Latvia, to found the oppositionist Meduza.io.[62]

Putin and his technologists have sought to achieve a Russian dream: the absolute unity of leader and people. They've come close. Yet, extraordinarily, one of the most innovative and enlightening journalists in the world learned her trade within the Soviet Union, and after its collapse has fashioned – using the most common of reportorial tools, the interview – a record of Soviet and post-Soviet life which stands as an intimate account of what it was to be Soviet, and what it is to live in the aftermath.

Svetlana Alexievich – a Belorussian, writing in Russian – has produced a handful of books, including *Zinky Boys* (better translated as 'Boys in Zinc'), which was about the young soldiers fighting a losing war in Afghanistan (the dead were shipped back to the Soviet Union in zinc coffins, hence the title); *Voices from Chernobyl*, on the survivors and rescuers of the nuclear explosion in 1986; and *Second-Hand Time*, mainly on Russians living in the post-Soviet period.[63] In more than three decades of patiently chronicling the stories of those caught up in the massive dislocations of the 1980s, 1990s and 2000s, Alexievich, a modest, friendly woman, has stripped away layers of defensiveness and protestations of victimhood to reach accounts of the ways in which people see their lives.

Alexievich came to similar conclusions on the dilemma of the post-Soviet people as the Georgian Mamardashvili. In an interview in the summer of 2016, given when on a visit to the UK, she said she had studied 'Red Man' – Soviet citizens, men and women – for decades and found that they mostly still lived in the mould into which they had been pressed by Communism. They were small people, who 'when asked, what did you think when they told you to fight in a war, they didn't know – what should I think? They thought they had no right to think anything about it.'

She said that it had been a common view among the intelligentsia immediately after Communism's collapse that a new generation would be free of the Soviet impress:

> but in fact the new generation was more servile than we were. Even someone with an iPhone in every pocket, able to speak English, thinks: Putin is our leader. When I asked them if they would rather live in a strong country or a normal country, they all said: a strong country! They still think their life doesn't belong to them, and they have no importance.[64]

Inclined to pessimism, Alexievich may underrate the new generation of the intelligentsia, born at or soon after the Soviet collapse. The times in which they passed their childhood were chaotic, but imbued with themes of freedom and self-reliance – not all of which were cancelled in the Putin years. As chairman of the Russian NGO, the School of Civic Education (named as a 'foreign agent' in 2014 and thus unable to work in Russia) I meet many of the post-Soviet generations, and see in them men and women of informed and forthright opinions.

Alexievich received the Nobel Prize for literature in 2015, the first journalist to do so. With no Western models, she saw into the heart of the people among whom she lived and conjured up a kind of revelation from empathy and endless patience. She was of the people about whom she wrote, and recognized, she said – quoting Dostoevsky – that 'we are people from the same madness'.

FOUR

Three degrees of despotism

Every authoritarian state is despotic in its own way. In the twenty-first-century world, most states have some sort of parliamentary system, for which elections are organized – as in Egypt and Russia. These forums exist in a suspension between having some power and none, between present façade and future potency.

In Ethiopia, economic growth in the 2000s has been one of the highest in the world, underpinning the political force of the Ethiopian People's Revolutionary Democratic Front and the authority of its leaders, Meles Zenawi (1995–2012) and Hailemariam Desalegn (from 2012). A brief period of relative relaxing of curbs on journalism and on opposition politics allowed the flourishing of a daily newspaper that was both liberal and strongly analytical, and was prepared to bring an informed, sceptical but objective eye to a society unused to such reporting. In its brief span it showed how pervasive the ideas of independent and sceptical journalism are, and how much these ideas are feared by despotic states.

In Turkey, the news media had flourished in the early years of rule by the Muslim-based Adalet ve Kalkınma Partisi (AKP: in English, the Justice and Development Party) of Recep Tayyip Erdoğan. In the 2010s, that's ceased to be the case. The party, dominant politically and in thrall to the commanding figure of Erdoğan, has ceased to regard journalism as an independent institution, but as a threat, with those news media which express opposition seen as treacherous, or potentially so. Turkey, after an April 2017 referendum which gave President Erdoğan much more power, seems on its way to a regime as closed as that of Ethiopia.

The case of South Africa is a contrast with stable and developing authoritarianism, but also contains a possible early warning. Since the ending of apartheid and of harshly authoritarian white-minority rule with the election of Nelson Mandela as president in 1994, successive administrations formed by the African National Congress have grumbled ferociously about the effects of the free press – alleging racism on the part of white journalists and owners, a servile (to whites) mentality among black reporters and editors critical of the ANC, and a lack of understanding of the difficulties under which post-apartheid governments must work. Yet they have broadly allowed independent journalism, and have not – as in Ethiopia and Turkey – closed newspapers and broadcasters and imprisoned journalists. The pressures on a barely growing economy, factional struggles within the ruling ANC and the continuing poverty and unemployment among the majority black population will be a test for the maintenance of some of the freest journalism in Africa.

i The New Thing

In 2003, a few young graduates from Addis Ababa University in Ethiopia began talking about starting a newspaper.

They had grown up in a country marked by terror, crisis and civil war. In 1974, a group of officers and soldiers had deposed the emperor, Haile Selassie, and executed his senior officials and some members of his family; Selassie himself died in custody. In 1991, a coalition of various forces defeated the regime's army, and a new government, formed by the Ethiopian People's Revolutionary Democratic Front (EPRDF) and headed by Prime

Minister Meles Zenawi, was elected. It has remained a stable, if despotic, administration.

The young graduates believed in independent journalism, thought that reportage should be as objective as possible, and also strongly analytical. The government and ruling figures should be reported on, but with neither automatic obeisance nor enmity. They were inspired not so much by partisan politics as by a desire to found a medium for a portrayal, as accurate as it could be made, of the actions and policies of the government and the main trends in Ethiopian society. They believed that such an act, though not party-political, was a political act in itself, the announcement of a space in which something of the truth of events could be transmitted, so that an audience – inevitably more educated than the majority – would have a public record. They began modestly, with a weekly paper called *Meznagna*, which started as a cultural journal but strayed into politics, and was closed for its cautious support of the main opposition force, the Coalition for Unity and Democracy.

In 2007, five of the *Meznagna* journalists, whose leading members were Mesfin Negash, who had worked for an NGO as well as writing a column, and Abiye Teklemariam, who worked in a law firm, founded a daily paper, *Addis Neger* (New Thing). The EPRDF had won the 2005 election, albeit attended by disputes about its fairness, and after a year or two in which opposition leaders were imprisoned, a more relaxed atmosphere emerged, of which the founders of *Addis Neger* took advantage. The country, the second largest after Nigeria but also one of the poorest in Africa, was achieving high growth – and foreign donors, necessary for investment and expertise, pushed for more openness. The paper's founders judged that the government could tolerate a non-subservient voice, though they took the precaution of hiring and featuring two pro-government columnists.

The paper was a near-instant success among the capital's educated classes. The founders and staff were determined to raise journalism out of the ill-paid, semi-skilled, come-to-heel trade it had been. In a country where circulations were measured in the few thousands, *Addis Neger* leapt ahead of the pack, selling at its peak 50–60,000 copies a day; the Addis Ababa newsboys, who defied death and injury by selling in the traffic, and whose approval of a paper was essential in order to get it distributed, clamoured for copies.

Ministers and officials would take calls from the paper; the editors were regular guests in foreign embassies and they took part in debates on TV. But about a year after the paper was launched, they picked up tips that a debate about it had started within the ruling group. 'We had become,' says Teklemariam, 'too popular.' As the political weather worsened, the government published three laws – on anti-terrorism, on civil society and on the media. *Addis Neger* opposed all three, viewing the first as an over-reaction to a relatively minor threat; the second an attack on the many NGOs, both Ethiopian and foreign, in the capital, which Zenawi believed were 'a state within a state'; and the third, a statement of intent to rein in criticism, aimed particularly at the print media.

Under its provisions, a critical piece about the country's economy could be construed as 'economic terrorism'. The information minister, who had been relatively friendly before, told them that the paper 'was walking on a razor's edge'. A source within the government, who kept them up to date, told them that charges were being prepared.

Preparing charges took almost a year: and when they were finally laid, in 2011 – against Teklemariam and Negash – they included one of 'moral support for terrorist groups', based on articles about a group that was strongly opposed to the regime, but had not gone over to terrorism. The articles were analytical and, in one case, critical of the group. The charges carried a penalty of at least eight years' imprisonment.

They were not the first. Eskinder Nega, a journalist and member of an opposition party, had been in jail in 2005;[1] his subsequent release had helped convince Negash and Teklemariam that there was a more permissive mood. Nega had returned to Ethiopia from the US, where he had been educated, in 1991; he started his first paper, *Ethiopia*, as early as 1993. After its closure, he founded another, *Satenaw*, a popular tabloid modelled on the *New York Post* – which led to his first spell in jail, where he was joined by his wife, who gave birth to their child in prison. Released in 2007, he was imprisoned again in 2011, where he remains at the time of writing, with many Western NGOs' freedom awards for his determination and courage – and a long sentence.

In a 'Letter from Ethiopia's Gulag' written in July 2013, Nega wrote:

> I am jailed, with around 200 other inmates, in a wide hall that looks like a warehouse. For all of us, there are only three toilets. About 1,000 prisoners share the small open space here at Kaliti Prison. One can guess our fate if a communicable disease breaks out.

Noting that US Secretary of State John Kerry had visited the country in May and praised the economic growth, he wrote that

> Sanctions tipped the balance against apartheid in South Africa, minority rule in Zimbabwe, and military dictatorship in Myanmar. Without the hope of peaceful resolution embedded in the sanctions, a descent to violence would have been inevitable. Now that large swathes of Africa have become safely democratic, ancient and fragile Ethiopia, where a precarious dictatorship holds sway, is dangerously out of sync with the times ... Ethiopia must not be allowed to implode. And it would be irresponsible for the world's lone superpower to stand by and do nothing.[2]

All of the defendants in the *Addis Neger* case left the country before their trial, and remain abroad, part of the large Ethiopian diaspora, many of whom are in opposition to the current regime. Zenawi died in 2012 and was succeeded by his deputy, Hailemariam Desalegn, who rules more erratically than his predecessor.

The country – the second most populous in Africa at near 100 million – presents a familiar dual picture: its growth puts it among the five fastest-growing economies in the world, raising millions out of poverty and creating an ever-larger middle class. An IMF note of September 2015 put 2014/15 growth at 8.7 per cent, and forecasts only a slight drop to 7.5–8 per cent in succeeding years – commending a tight monetary stance by the Central Bank, 'appropriate' pro-poor policies and a strong export sector.[3] The country of poor farmers is becoming a manufacturing hub, the 'Germany of Africa', as its leaders like to say. But human rights haven't improved. According to the US Department of State's Human Rights report, the problems include:

> restrictions on freedom of expression, including continued restrictions on print media and on the Internet, and restrictions on freedom of association, including through arrests; politically motivated trials; and harassment and intimidation of opposition members and journalists. The government continued restrictions on activities of civil society and nongovernmental organizations (NGOs) imposed by the Charities and Societies Proclamation (the CSO law).[4]

It was this report, which his own department had issued, to which Nega was asking Kerry to respond.

Teklemariam, Negash and others started a website in 2015, named Sebat Kilo (Kilo Seven) – a name that places it in the intellectual camp, since Kilos 1–6 are campuses of the University of Addis Ababa – thus Kilo Seven is the seventh faculty to which educated Ethiopians should attend. The site has correspondents in Ethiopia, working at some risk, and it has, says Teklemariam, a high take-up in the country, mainly on Facebook. When asked about the new publication, Getachew Reda, the senior adviser to Prime Minister Desalegn, sarcastically replied: 'I know the guys. I hope they will be balanced and fair. I am willing to write for them.'

Serious riots gathered force from the end of 2015, in the Oromia region in the south. In August 2016, they spread to Amhara to the north of Addis, with reports of hundreds of deaths at the hands of riot police – which were denied. The government claims that Facebook activist journalists and two opposition satellite TV channels beamed in from the US instigated the riots, and arrested and imprisoned two Facebook journalists. Some former *Addis Neger* reporters work for one of these channels (ESAT, Ethiopian Satellite Television).

Freedom House, in its 2016 survey of press freedom, sees Ethiopia's media environment as

one of the most restrictive in Sub-Saharan Africa. The government of Prime Minister Hailemariam Desalegn continues to use the country's draconian antiterrorism law and other legal measures to silence critical journalists and bloggers ... the government employs a variety of strategies to maintain a stranglehold on the flow of information; these include outright censorship of newspapers and the Internet; arbitrary detention and intimidation of journalists and bloggers; and heavy taxation on the publishing process.[5]

Paris-based Reporters sans Frontieres, in its survey of the same year, wrote that

Ever since the 2009 anti-terrorism law took effect, terrorism charges have been systematically used against journalists. The charges carry long jail sentences and allow the authorities to hold journalists without trial for extended periods. There has been little improvement since the purges that led to the closure of six newspapers in 2014 and drove around thirty journalists into exile. Physical and verbal threats, arbitrary trials and convictions are all used to silence the media.[6]

In a December 2011 essay, Teklemariam stated that 'the tactics of divide and rule, co-option and repression have eviscerated Ethiopia's social trust, destroyed political institutions and decimated independent voices'.[7] Economic success and a reduction of poverty have, he believes, blinded the Western political and intellectual world to the reality of the country: that of a ruling party determined to marginalize and suppress not just dissent, but also those who seek to understand, by speaking and publishing the facts.

ii 'I am having it cut off right away, sir!'

Among the monarchies and military-authoritarian states of the Muslim Middle East, Turkey has long stood out. It had, at least sometimes, genuinely competitive elections, diverse media, an ambition to join the European Union and a secular tradition hammered into place by Kemal Atatürk (in presidential office 1923–38). But in the second decade of the 2000s, things are changing.

When challenged, Recep Tayyip Erdoğan, the country's leader in both prime ministerial and presidential roles since 2003, exerts greater control, first of all on the news media. In July 2013, widespread protests, which were quashed, left the country in a volatile political state, with debates and calls for the resignation of Prime Minister Erdoğan. On 14 July, Devlet Bahçeli, leader of the Nationalist Movement Party (MHP in the Turkish acronym), was giving a press conference, which was being broadcast live on the popular (private) Haberturk channel. As Bahçeli ramped up the rhetoric, Erdoğan watched with increasing anger. He had already protested in June to Fatih Saraç, the chief executive of the channel, that Bahçeli was getting too much airtime. And here he was again. The Nationalist leader, a practised polemicist who challenged Erdoğan on his home turf of national pride, was in full flow. The prime minister called the channel's CEO once more; from a translation of the transcript of the call, which was recorded and leaked, this was part of the conversation:

Erdoğan: Look, Fatih, are you all out of your mind? This bugger appears there, issuing a manifesto, as if Turkey was finished, collapsed, entirely out of control. And you are airing this LIVE?

Fatih: Oh, sir, I am having it cut off right away, sir. Immediately, as you tell me, sir!

Erdoğan: What is this? It's been on a while.

Fatih: Yes, but sir—

Erdoğan: It has been twenty to twenty-five minutes already! Bloody twenty-five minutes!

Fatih: Just, just give me three minutes, sir; I'll have it cut.

Erdoğan: What the heck is going on there?

Fatih: Right away, sir! I'll tell them immediately!

Erdoğan: This is a disgrace! How can you let it go on like this?

Fatih: With all due respect, sir, it's for having statements aired by all the parties in parliament, for the record ...

Erdoğan: What for? Why on earth would you do that? For the record? Why should you be under any obligation?

Fatih: Yes, Prime Minister!

Erdoğan: He talks as if traitors have taken over the country, as if we are in cooperation with them. This press conference is unacceptable ...

Fatih: Yes, sir, fully understood, sir!

Erdoğan: Bloody hell!

Fatih: Right away, sir! My deepest apologies, dear sir!

The excerpt appears in an essay by the former ombudsman – a government post, from which he was fired – Yavuz Baydar.[8] Baydar writes that 'the top manager, in sheer panic, called the news editor and made it very clear, that "our honourable elder is very sad". The editor tried to resist, but the press conference was soon taken off air.'

The craven behaviour had a compelling reason behind it. The Haberturk (Turkish News) channel is part of the Ciner Group, which has large interests in mining, energy and hydroelectric power, among others. It owns not only the Haberturk TV channel but also the *Haberturk* newspaper, with twenty-two columnists. One of these, Balçiçek İlter, was heavily criticized for writing that a woman in Muslim dress was beaten and urinated on by protestors during the Gezi Park protests in 2013 – a charge later shown by video footage to have been false and for which she apologized.

This close presidential attention to the media does not stop at Turkish papers and channels. Shortly before winning an election to become president of Turkey in August 2014, Erdoğan harshly condemned Amberin Zaman, *The Economist*'s Turkey correspondent: 'A militant in the guise of a journalist – a shameless woman. Know your place!'[9] Shortly before the June 2015 election, which reduced the AKP's share of the vote, Erdoğan told the *New York Times* and the *Guardian* to know their 'limits', adding that 'Jewish capital is behind the *New York Times*, unfortunately'.[10]

The pressure on Turkish journalism from the country's most powerful leader since Atatürk has grown steadily through Erdoğan's rule (prime minister from 2003 to 2014, president from August 2014). The AKP rule has been, in many ways, a success: Turkey's economy has grown faster than that of any other major state except China through the 2000s and into the 2010s; pensions, health services and housing have all improved markedly; the rigidities which the secular and military rulers inherited from the Atatürk era – prescribing all Muslim dress and many ceremonies – have been relaxed.

The journalist Aslı Aydıntaşbaş, a columnist for the *Akşam* newspaper, wrote in 2009 that 'Mr Erdoğan is a man who can both spearhead revolutionary reforms – like pushing for Kurdish and minority rights and opening the border with Turkey's historic enemy Armenia – and rebuke journalists for "disrespecting" him'. The two have gone together: the growing authoritarianism did not seem to damage his standing with his core vote, the conservative, Muslim masses in small towns and villages in Anatolia, as well as the urban poor – 'few of whom read newspapers or follow the news closely'.[11]

Aydıntaşbaş also noted that the 'barons' of the news media, almost all owners of big conglomerates, were 'particularly susceptible to political pressure' because of the importance of state contracts – and that they had 'never made freedom of expression a priority. But soon there may be no independent media left.' Foreign observers believe much the same: the clamps on media are 'the most glaring example of the AK party's creeping annexation of the public sphere ... the party has come to exercise control over all but a handful of broadcasters and news publishers'.[12] In 2016, only three of the country's main forty news channels were in any way critical (that is, allow criticism of) Erdoğan. One of the few remaining independent daily newspapers, Hürriyet, was attacked by a mob after the president criticized its editors on TV.

Before the failed coup against him in July 2016, there were still some centres of overt opposition. The Doğan Group (energy, hydroelectric, wind power, oil, finance, real estate, tourism, various manufacturing), which publishes Hürriyet and broadcasts the popular CNN Türk, suffers constant blasts of criticism from Erdoğan. The president ordered criminal charges to be levelled against Hürriyet over a headline – 'World in shock: Death sentence for president who won 52 per cent of the vote' – a headline which Erdoğan claimed was directed at him, since in his last election he secured 52 per cent of the vote, but which the newspaper protested, not entirely convincingly, had nothing to do with the Turkish leader, but instead referred to the former Egyptian president, Mohamed Morsi, who was under a death sentence.[13]

On the stump in February 2015, Erdoğan addressed himself personally to the head of the Doğan Media Group, Aydın Doğan:

Why did you feel uneasy, Doğan? Wasn't it you who ran a story with the headline '411 hands were raised for chaos'? [A reference to a parliamentary vote in 2008 that aimed to remove a ban on headscarves for students entering Turkish universities.] Wasn't it you who ran a story with another headline claiming that I should not even be elected as a muhtar [head of a village]?[14]

The paper that ran the story on Erdoğan's blast against Doğan, the daily *Zaman*, is also in the oppositionist camp: it is part of the Feza group, a rare example of a publications-only company, close to the Hizmet movement of Fethullah Gülen, the one-time ally of Erdoğan who broke with him and now lives in the US, charged with being the inspiration and paymaster for the attempted coup in 2016.

In December 2014, police arrested Ekrem Dumanlı, editor of *Zaman*, along with twenty others, charging them with 'forming, leading and membership of an armed terrorist group' – a move that roused protests from the EU and the US. Dumanlı was released for lack of evidence. He later wrote in the *Washington Post*: 'All it takes to be called a terrorist under Erdoğan's regime is speaking out against government corruption and abuses of power. Verbal attacks, smear campaigns by pro-government media and legal harassment soon follow.'[15]

Zaman was to suffer worse than smear campaigns. After months of investigation into its links with the Gülen organization, a vaguely worded court order allowed the paper to be seized by the government – to reappear after a few days' closure as an Erdoğan-supporting daily. The seizure came while Donald Tusk, president of the European Council, was in Istanbul, and two days before a visit by Angela Merkel, the German chancellor, both seeking Turkey's assistance in stopping the flow of migrants into the EU. It seemed that Erdoğan was making a point: he would deal with his opponents as he liked, whatever the EU thought of it.[16]

Turkish companies have bargained with, or been frequently reminded of their subservience to, the state before Erdoğan dominated it. From Atatürk's time, newspapers, even when nominally independent, were closed, and/or editors and reporters jailed for criticism, or for running too strongly against national policy.[17] Since the news media are mainly owned by companies that have large industrial interests strongly dependent on state favour, the deal – supportive, even slavish coverage in return for contracts – has been commonplace, at least from the 1980s:

> For those huge holdings, owning media outlets became vitally important to preserving and growing their investments in other sectors; being in the media sector provided them with a competitive advantage in benefiting from privatization of government assets and public tenders. Their Ankara bureau chiefs often acted as 'lobbyists' for their companies' financial interests.[18]

Erdoğan had attacked the media, putting as many as fifty journalists in jail in 2012 and 2013 (precise figures vary: the Committee to Protect Journalists' figures for the two years are forty-nine in each year, nine more than the next most enthusiastic jailer, China). By 2014, however, most were let out and only seven remained imprisoned in that year. But jail was replaced with unemployment as the pace of firings stepped up: nearly 200 journalists were let go in 2014. Most owners, like the wretched Fatih, were simply too cowed, too determined to flatter Erdoğan, to stand up to the pressure. The editor of the independent website T24, Doğan Akın, wrote that 'this country has always had a media ready to buy suppression ... Without a doubt, the influence [proprietors] gain through the media outlets convert somehow into profits that overwhelm the losses. This is the very architecture of the media order.'[19]

The Net and social media, here as elsewhere, are a recourse. Aslı Tunç, a professor and head of the department of communication at Istanbul Bilgi

University, told me that 'the mainstream media don't allow journalists to work so they turn to the Net. The Gezi Park protests brought many young people together, and they organized themselves through Twitter, and have used it since to put out news and comments.' Indeed, most broadcast channels and newspapers were wholly silent about the mass protests of Gezi Park in May 2013, though many had studios a few minutes' walk from the park. CNN Türk broadcast a long documentary about penguins through much of the protests; thereafter, the penguin became a symbol of journalism's silencing.

The government followed its critics on to the Net and social media. Smear campaigns against independent journalists and government critics became frequent on Twitter, which then spread to the pro-government newspapers. In May 2014, the German weekly *Der Spiegel* withdrew its Turkey correspondent, Hasnain Kazim, after he received more than 10,000 aggressive messages, including death threats, about his coverage of a mining accident.[20]

When corruption allegations reached the senior officials of the AKP, the government moved to close down the investigations. When wiretaps were leaked, the mainstream media mostly didn't pick them up, although they appeared on Twitter and YouTube, which were then closed down, as Erdoğan fumed: 'We'll eradicate Twitter. I don't care what the international community says. Everyone will witness the power of the Turkish Republic.'[21] Both services were restored by order of the Constitutional Court – which also overturned a law designed to give the government the power to block a website at will, before obtaining a court order, while service providers had to keep a record of their activities.

In July 2015, Twitter was temporarily shut down after it carried images from a suicide bombing, killing thirty-two, in Suruç, a largely Kurdish city near the Syrian border. Yet social media proved to be Erdoğan's saviour – of his post if not his life – during the failed 2016 coup. The US reporter Dexter Filkins wrote:

Over the past decade, Erdoğan has silenced, marginalized, or crushed nearly anyone in the country who might oppose him, including newspaper editors, university professors, aid workers, and dissident politicians. (What an irony that Erdoğan, who has imprisoned so many journalists, and gone to great lengths to censor Twitter, Facebook and YouTube, may have saved his presidency by using FaceTime to make an early Saturday appearance on a Turkish television news channel.)[22]

The attempted coup on 15 July 2016 was blamed, probably correctly, on elements in the army loyal to Gülen as well as wider forces associated with them. In Erdoğan's eyes, it legitimated sweeping arrests and imprisonment – of some 60,000 civil servants, 10,000 military, many hundreds of academics and teachers. The government closed over 130 media outlets within two weeks of the coup and jailed around 140 journalists – making it the leading jailer of journalists in the world. The arbitrariness of the sweep was dramatized by the journalist Bülent Mumay, who had been fired from *Hürriyet* in 2015 – 'I was out in the streets protesting against these people [the Gülenists]. Now the government accuses me of being one of them. That is bullshit.'[23] He was released after a few days – as were some others. *Cumhuriyet*, the daily of the secular left, was closed: its editor-in-chief, Murat Sabuncu and its literary editor, Turhan Günay, were jailed.

Turkey is the victim of repeated internal attacks – some by ISIS, some by Kurdish separatists. But the response has been indiscriminate: of the hundreds of thousands arrested, jailed, sacked or suspended, most seem to have no connection to terrorism (and many have since been released). In an ISIS-claimed attack on a night club on New Year's Eve 2016, a lone gunman killed thirty-nine, wounding many more. One foreign observer wrote that 'if the shooting were an isolated event, the effect on Turkish society would probably be minimal. But it was the latest in a series of violent attacks against the Turkish state, which has prompted sweeping retaliatory measures that have seriously undermined Turkish democracy.'[24]

While Erdoğan is at the summit of his country's political heap, he is likely to remain, or become more, intolerant towards any opposing views – indeed, even neutral reporting – being expressed by the news media, seeing it as close to treachery. At the same time, the structural and personal weaknesses of the journalistic community have meant that the major part of the output has been partial, mute on many subjects and enslaved to a government line. This has been brought into effect – more so as the years passed – less by direct intervention of the state than by pressure on the owners, usually conglomerates who had taken on media divisions in order to show loyalty to the government by bolstering it.

The deal was perfectly plain – the destruction of good journalism, the cowing of the bosses, enabling the continued flow of contracts.

iii 'We can't criticize our own'

Rhoda Kadalie has a distinguished forebear. Her grandfather, Clements Kadalie (1896–1951), born in Nyasaland (now Malawi), moved to South Africa for work and created the first successful African trade union, the Industrial and Commercial Union of Africa, which was founded in protest against harsh labour laws. Later, he became a regional organizer of the ANC. His granddaughter followed him into the ANC and she was appointed by President Nelson Mandela as a Human Rights Commissioner (1995–7). It was a good appointment. Kadalie was no placewoman, putting party loyalty before the demands of her responsibility. What she saw, as she wrote in reflections on her period in office four years later, was that 'self-censorship [had] become the order of the day' in much of the South African media:

> there are the whites who feel guilty about the past and don't want to be
> seen to be criticizing a black government. Others are too busy ingratiating

themselves with government ... ANC people will talk behind closed
doors, but believe it is disloyal to speak out ... What it demonstrates is
that apartheid worked: we have internalized the notion of victimhood so
deeply that we can't criticize our own ... unfortunately *it is true that those
who have been oppressed make the worst democrats* [my italics].[25]

Timidity and self-censorship are more marked in television; the South
African Broadcasting Corporation (SABC) is under constant threat of
becoming a mere mouthpiece of the ANC, as it had been for the apartheid regime. In an essay, the South African journalist Janice Winter writes
that a TV service was only founded in the country in January 1976, delayed
past those of most other countries because of religious fears that TV was
'the devil's own box' – but more to the political point, because of a fear of
'the impact television might have on its minority political rule by
uniting the nation that it was systematically trying neatly to divide
through official apartheid policies'.[26] More, since the new channel lacked
resources to put on a full choice of programmes, it might have to import
dangerous fare – like *The Cosby Show* from the US, in which the incendiary
spectacle of a middle-class African American family would be piped into
the majority's homes.

That it can at times show itself as relatively independent, and employ
journalists and editors who have insisted on fulfilling the role of a public
rather than a state broadcaster, attests to the still-feisty subsoil of South
African journalism, in large part nurtured in opposition during the
apartheid years and expanded and embedded in the soil of a democratic
South Africa. Past oppression in the SABC, supposedly the national
broadcaster, was brought to light in evidence given to the Truth and Reconciliation Commission – a restorative justice body set up in 1996 under the
chairmanship of Archbishop Desmond Tutu. It revealed a corporation that
systematically discriminated against, and humiliated, its black staff – and
through them, its audience. The Commission report showed that:

- Legislation (passed between 1950 and 1990) 'did not eliminate the production of information and statements of opposition [but] it severely restricted them'.

- The Broadcast Act of 1976 required the SABC to 'disseminate information' to 'all the national communities ... unambiguously, factually, impartially and without distortion'. But it prevented the SABC from broadcasting anything that would cause, amongst other things, 'unrest or panic ... threaten state security ... [or] damage the Republic's image abroad'.

- An analysis by Professor John van Zyl over a period of sixteen years revealed that 'news bulletins maintained and cultivated a mindset amongst white viewers that apartheid was natural and inevitable'.

- Many of the middle-ranking and top managers, and the Board, were members of the Broederbond, an organization founded in 1918 to further the interests of the Dutch community, strongly opposed to black emancipation and equality – 'a look at management positions over the years shows that career possibilities for English speakers were extremely limited'.

- 'Bantu' – black community – programmes began in an organized way from 1960: the five-member control board was entirely white, while 'the officials in charge of SABC programmes for black listeners and viewers comprised eighty-five senior employees: six black and the rest white and almost exclusively Afrikaans-speaking.

- Treatment of black staff was extraordinarily oppressive. A former SABC employee, Jakes Nene, said that 'No black person, however well qualified, could reach supervisory level. Any white person in the employ of the SABC was an automatic superior.' Under Section 14 of the Staff Code, a member of staff could be fired without being given a reason or explanation, as long as the manager suspected that his or her ideological convictions were not in line with the government of the day. Nene said that 'any white person at the SABC had the right to fire any black person who was *hardegat* (intransigent). Workers received severe reprimands for looking at white women and had to give way in the passages.' Nene revealed that, between 1975 and 1985, if people were fortunate enough to be called to a disciplinary hearing, they could choose to be sjambokked (whipped) rather than fired. Those who refused to be sjambokked were dismissed without a proper disciplinary hearing. This startling revelation about sjambokking at the old SABC was confirmed after the hearing, when the media trade union MWASA produced a list of those who had been punished in this way.[27]

That all changed.[28] The transmission of the investiture of the new executive president, Nelson Mandela – already a world-historical figure who was seen as an example of endurance, wisdom and nobility, and whose hem all world leaders and media celebrities wished to touch – was in epic vein. The SABC framed the inauguration as a matter of destiny, the fitting, even pre-ordained, end to a long and bitter struggle, light conquering darkness. But in 1999, the inauguration of Thabo Mbeki – previously Mandela's deputy, he ran the administration behind the scenes while Mandela took centre stage – was framed slightly disrespectfully. The absence of all of the G8 leaders – they were meeting in Cologne – was contrasted with the stellar turn-out five years earlier. When a noisy fly-past interrupted Mbeki's eighteen-minute speech, the clip of his brief discomfort was the only one shown on the news. Mbeki's second inauguration in 2004, however, was more of a loyalist show – indeed, there was much more emphasis on the military hardware that was prominently displayed, the TV commentator pointing up the allegiance shown by the military to the 'commander in chief'.

Journalists found it hard to orient themselves. Jimi Matthews, head of TV news since 2002, left after the 2004 inauguration, complaining that distance and scepticism were absent. He was replaced by Snuki Zikalala, who compiled a blacklist of nine public figures, whose common feature was their willingness to criticize the government ministers and their policies and who were never to be asked on SABC. Karima Brown, the political editor of the *Business Day* newspaper, found out about the list when, having been asked on to the *SAfm Live* radio show, her appearance was cancelled – a friend, John Perlman, producer of the show, told her why: 'We've been told not to use you.'[29]

The SABC's board, hearing of the blacklist, formed a commission to probe into the affair and wrote a lengthy report – but then didn't release it; inevitably, it was leaked. Commission members Gilbert Marcus and Zwelakhe Sisulu wrote that the head of news 'appears to intervene at a micro-level inappropriate to his level of management in a seemingly ad hoc and inconsistent manner'. They learned, from conversations they held with SABC staff, that 'the prevailing climate resulted in decisions being taken to avoid the censure, real or perceived, of Dr Zikalala. We do not find these views exaggerated or implausible.'[30]

Pippa Green, head of Radio News, had objected strongly to Zikalala that she was not allowed to use a range of spokesmen and -women, writing in a letter to her superior that 'if your instruction was not to use Moeletsi Mbeki, Archbishop Pius Ncube, Trevor Ncube or Elinor Sisulu, all legitimate public figures, then I submit that it is so unreasonable to be un-implementable. It would be morally wrong, professionally wrong and ethically wrong, and violate not only our editorial code but the spirit of our Constitution.' Zikalala replied: 'I don't think that I will have the time and energy to be involved in such arguments.'

Yet, though the report was scathing and seemed to call for at least a reprimand, the board and the broadcaster's CEO, Dali Mpofu, expressed their full confidence in Zikalala, saying in a statement that he and his staff 'operate under very difficult circumstances ... [where critics are] always challenging the integrity of the public broadcaster'. The row attracted a lot of coverage, much of it critical of Zikalala and the board – a criticism that increased when the Corporation announced that it would take action against Zikalala but would also discipline the producer, John Perlman, who had contradicted, on air, the broadcaster's previous position that there was no blacklist.

This angered Mpofu, who played the trump card by arguing that the issue was really about race. Writing in City Press in October 2006, he claimed that a 'right-wing lobby and its fellow travellers in the mass media' were attacking the SABC for 'not feeding into their gluttonous, greedy smell of black blood which must be sacrificed at every whim'.[31] In publishing the report of the internal inquiry into the matter, the Mail & Guardian was, among other things, motivated by 'pervasive anti-establishment hatred of anything connected to the democratically elected black-dominated government of the day'. The Mail & Guardian responded that, since it was black-owned and -run, the charges were absurd.

Controversy dogged Mpofu – including rumours he had an affair with Winnie Mandela in the early nineties; the affair was widely believed to be the reason for the divorce between Mandela and his wife. He packed the SABC board with former or present ANC senior officials, allowed the finances to slide into debt – requiring yearly government bail-outs – and paid 123,000 rand for a glossy advertorial about himself in Leadership magazine. He was fired in 2009.

That polemics should fly between black ANC leaders and white journalists is natural enough, though dispiriting. In one passage of arms involving Jacob Zuma in 2008 – when Zuma, twice elected president in 2009 and 2014, was the heir apparent of Mbeki – the (South African) Sunday Times cartoonist Zapiro (whose real name in Jonathan Shapiro, and who is white) showed the figure of Justice held down on the ground by leading ANC officials while Zuma, towering over her, unbuckled his belt. One of the officials says, 'Go for it, boss.' The cartoon appeared soon after Zuma had been accused, then acquitted, of rape.

The ANC called it 'an abuse of press freedom', disgusting and racist, and demanded an apology, which Zapiro refused to give. He had already enraged the ruling party by drawing Zuma with a shower sprouting from his head, reminding readers that the president-to-be had remarked, during his trial for rape, that he always showered after sex to avoid catching AIDS. The Sunday Times is owned by the Times Media Group (formerly Johnnic Communications, then Avusa), in turn a division of the Mvelaphanda Group, founded by Mosima 'Tokyo' Sexwale, a former anti-apartheid activist convicted of terrorism in 1977 and imprisoned, with Mandela, on Robben Island, serving thirteen years. The editor of the Sunday Times, Mondli Makhanya (later editor-in-chief of the Times Media Group), strongly defended Zapiro; Makhanya, as a columnist, had been highly critical of the ANC, especially the 1999 five-billion-dollar arms purchases, after which Zuma had been accused of receiving bribes – but was again acquitted, in 2006. Zuma dropped the case in 2012, the two sides sharing the legal costs.[32]

The Times Media Group includes the popular daily Sowetan, which was also embroiled in a race controversy in 2011, when the columnist Eric Miyeni – a writer and film-maker close to Julius Malema, former head of the ANC's Youth League – wrote a column excoriating the editor of City Press, Ferial Haffajee, for the investigation her paper had mounted on Malema's finances, when still the Youth League leader. Miyeni's column – headlined 'Haffajee does it for white masters' – said that the editor, who belongs to the country's Indian, or coloured, minority, was 'deployed by white capitalists to sow discord among blacks', that she harboured an 'utter hatred of ANC politicians' and that in the 1980s she would 'probably have had a burning tyre around her neck' – a reference to a once-used unofficial capital punishment for those considered traitors to the anti-apartheid cause.[33] Miyeni was fired from his column – and the acting editor of the paper, Len Maseko, was later also fired. Malema left the ANC to found a new party of the left, the Economic Freedom Fighters – of which Dali Mpofu, who also left the ANC, is the chairman.

Part of the context into which these eruptions should be fitted is provided by the Truth and Reconciliation Commission, whose members noted that many of those who gave evidence to it expressed anger at the lack of understanding of the position of the black community by white colleagues. The prominent journalist and editor Moegsien Williams, from the coloured (Asian-descended) community, said the English press was an opposition press in the sense of white sectarian politics only:

> They did not support the ANC, never articulated ANC policies, never wrote about the aspirations of the vast majority of South Africans, about their views, what they wanted, their need for a vote. Nothing happened outside white parameters. They were under a delusion – their real opposition sat on Robben Island [the ANC prisoners, including Mandela].[34]

Other black figures, however, commended the role of the white press. Cyril Ramaphosa, for decades a large figure in the trade union movement and in the ANC, a minister and since 2014 deputy president to Jacob Zuma, said that English newspapers 'in the main played a courageous role, imparting information when the government was trying to restrict it ... specific journalists [had] focused on the struggles of ordinary people'. Jon Qwelane, a severe critic of the mainstream media, acknowledged that 'it was the English-language newspapers whose journalists demonstrated "periodic flashes of courage and brilliance" by exposing the gross injustices perpetrated by the system of apartheid ... [citing] examples such as reporting on the inhumane conditions in South Africa's prisons'.[35]

Janice Winter writes:

> The ANC sees itself as unifying the nation, resting on the mandate it has been given by over 65 per cent of voters and on its heritage as liberator of 'the people' ... [it argues that] the liberation government needs to

ensure that the media are adequately held to account to protect the national interest and to advance social transformation ... [and] that the overtly critical stance characteristic of the print press is unpatriotic as it undermines the young democracy and the government's project of nation building and development, in which they believe the media have a responsibility to play a key role. President Zuma, for example ... has told the media that they have 'a leading responsibility to ensure the deepening of our democracy by being constructive, developmental, educational, transformative and generally positive about our future'.[36]

The South African constitution commits its fifty-three million citizens to build a non-racial society – in a state which for much of its history was the most racially defined, in its laws, practices and media, in the twentieth-century world. That will be a long haul: Guy Berger, a former anti-apartheid activist, says that race can't be approached by being artificially colour blind; instead, the journalist 'has to be sensitive to correcting the remaining historical imbalances wherein those people defined as black are neglected'.[37]

'Sensitivity' shouldn't become collusion. But journalism in South Africa, for black and white journalists, is more of a minefield than in other democracies – because democracy is new and the memories of oppression fresh. The former editor Anton Harber asks, 'Does one hold the new authorities to higher standards than their [apartheid era] predecessors who after all were authoritarian and corrupt, or does one accept lower standards because they [the ANC governments] are new and inexperienced? Does one serve democracy better by putting the government under unrelenting pressure or by allowing it a honeymoon period?'[38]

Apartheid, which Harber strongly fought from an editorial chair at the *Weekly Mail* (now *Mail & Guardian*), was 'relatively easy' to oppose, since the moral position was clear. Deciding on whether to write about the flaws of those whom the apartheid state oppressed was much harder, as Harber found when he had to decide whether or not to write about charges that Winnie Mandela had, in 1989, abducted four boys in Soweto. Conscious that the stories were 'so horrific', he decided to publish (though unsensationally) – and was followed by the rest of the anti-apartheid papers. Mandela, who changed her name to Madikizela-Mandela, was found guilty on a number of counts of kidnapping, fraud and theft, and was accused, but not found guilty, of collaboration in murder. After a period when she gave up her leadership positions following the finding of fraud against her, she resumed her seat on the ANC National Executive Committee. She remained a divisive force, prone to denigrate her former husband, Nelson Mandela, as over-accommodating to the whites; in one interview, she called Archbishop Desmond Tutu 'a cretin'.

When, in 2009, the woman athlete Caster Semenya became embroiled in a widely reported controversy over her sex (it was later found she was a woman, with a very high testosterone count), Madikizela-Mandela warned the media, 'We know your responsibility is to inform us, but do so patriotically without insulting one of our own. Use the freedom of press we gave you properly, because we can take it from you.'[39] Semenya later won gold in the 2016 Rio Olympics.

Mzilikaza Wa Africa, a much-decorated investigative journalist, was arrested in August 2010 on charges of fraud and defeating the ends of justice a day after his story, on a dubious 500,000-rand lease on a new police station that had been taken out by Bheki Cele, a police chief, appeared in the *Sunday Times*. Wa Africa was released, and Cele later fired. Wa Africa subsequently won another case taken against him, for publishing a story, based on leaked documents, that prosecutors were sure that corruption charges against President Zuma could be pressed successfully – but were overruled by the acting head of public prosecutions, Mokotedi Mpshe. In an essay on his craft, Wa Africa wrote that, when he contacted Albert Mokean, director general of the Home Affairs department, to comment on a story on officials selling ID cards, he was asked by the high official,

'Why are you doing this to your own brothers just to please your white bosses?'[40]

Ferial Haffajee took one of the four International Press Freedom Awards of 2014. Presenting the award, Clarence Page, a commentator for the *Chicago Tribune*, said that the hope kindled by Mandela – when he proclaimed that a free press, with no links to the state, was 'the lifeblood of democracy' – had faded. Haffajee echoed that in her brief acceptance speech, pointing to laws now being discussed by the ANC (as well as old apartheid-era laws not repealed, but still used) that were crafted, it seemed, to neuter a press whose attentions the administration was finding more and more unwelcome. The government's initiatives included laws on secrecy, on criminal defamation, permitting or inciting harassment of photographers by the police, and the creation of a new Communications Ministry charged with branding the country abroad, which a new civil society group Right2Know claimed would 'be used to amplify government propaganda rather then to create a democratic communication system for all South Africans'.[41]

No workaday politics, or workaday journalism, can live up to the highest ideals sketched for them by figures with as strong an attachment to a politics of reason and grace as Nelson Mandela. The journalism of South Africa remains in much better shape than the authoritarian megaphones and disregarded protests of the apartheid era, and is in better shape than anywhere else on the continent.

But it is hobbled, and may become more so, if the politics of the country, already becoming toxic, worsen further. The September 2016 victories of the opposition Democratic Alliance, slicing off larger chunks of the ANC's majority in previously safely held areas, have made the struggles within the ruling party more deadly. The South African writer R. W. Johnson argues that we are now witnessing 'the virtual dissolution of the ANC leadership and its descent into squabbling factionalism'.[42] Corruption is reaching ever-higher levels.[43] Johnson concludes that 'the notion of the ANC as a party able to hold the country together is now just about gone. We have reached a point where simple continuity from what has gone before is no longer possible'. Journalism, however bold and independent, cannot get a sufficiently strong lever on such a process to influence it.

'Mandela's vision,' warns Ferial Haffajee, 'is being eroded.'

PART II

THE AUTHORITY
OF THE MARKET

INTRODUCTION

'Without reliability, one cannot be a journalist'

In societies where the market coexists with democracy, and where the state has relatively small media holdings, the general principle for journalism is that it should tell the truth. It should have an existence independent enough to proclaim that as its goal, and to be able to deliver at least some of the promise: that is, owners and controllers of the media should have the rights of ownership diluted by the responsibilities of the trustee. Ownership of the news media brings profits and/or power, influence and status. The trusteeship which comes with ownership of the news media enjoins a care that the journalism practised in the media owned informs the audience truthfully. That is the assumption behind the claim made for free news media: that their truth-telling, uncensored by state or owner, is a necessary prop for a democratic state.

It is everywhere proclaimed, and was so from the beginning. One of the earliest papers in England – and the first to publish daily from 1702 – the *Daily Courant*, promised to rely on 'the best and most certain intelligence'. The editor of the first paper in France – the state-owned *Gazette de France* – claimed that 'In one thing I will yield to nobody – I mean in my endeavour to get at the truth.'[1]

The rise of 'the fact' from the courtroom through other disciplines, including reporting, has been traced by Barbara J. Shapiro, who sees the use of the 'matters of fact' becoming dominant in the English courtrooms from the sixteenth century (replacing trial by royal or baronial pardon, or ordeal), and rising through other disciplines, such as history, travel writing and news.[2] The latter, she writes, strove to be 'discourses of fact', and sought to adopt from the disciplines of law and the writing of history 'norms of impartiality and fidelity and their emphasis on first-hand credible witnessing'.

It's still asserted. The *Washington Post* has long had as one of its principles telling 'the truth as nearly as the truth may be ascertained'. Hubert Beuve-Méry, tasked by General de Gaulle with founding *Le Monde* in Paris as the Second World War drew to a close, demanded that he be free to create 'an independent newspaper which owes nothing to the state, nor to the power of money, nor to the established powers, whether these be the church or the trade unions'.[3] Most importantly, he would not take orders from de Gaulle himself, whom he much admired. Anything less would compromise the search for the truth.

When becoming chief editor of the new daily *Gazeta Wyborcza* in May 1989, after the fall of Communism in Poland, Adam Michnik wrote, in florid style:

> Our God, who led us out from bondage, has two names: Freedom and Truth. To this God we subordinate ourselves completely. If we bow to other gods – the state, the nation, family, public security – at the expense of Freedom and Truth, we shall be punished with the loss of reliability. Without reliability, one cannot be a journalist.[4]

Truth, as often flouted or fumbled as found in journalism, is nevertheless the baseline of the space accorded to journalism in market democracies. It is part of the ideology of liberal democracy, injected into the practice of the market in news, information and opinion, and it has real force and consequence. This isn't everywhere accepted: indeed, it's accepted much less in the third millennium than it was in the nineteenth and twentieth centuries of the second. The linguist and radical activist Noam Chomsky, who remains, for many much younger than he, the truth teller about the 'lying press', believes that any claims to be truth-telling on the part of the liberal news media are a cynical 'game':

> If the media were honest, they would say, Look, here are the interests we represent and this is the framework within which we look at things. This is our set of beliefs and commitments. That's what they would say, very much as their critics say. For example, I don't try to hide my commitments, and the *Washington Post* and *New York Times* shouldn't do it either. However, they must do it, because this mask of balance and objectivity is a crucial part of the propaganda function. In fact, they actually go beyond that. They try to present themselves as adversarial to power, as subversive, digging away at powerful institutions and undermining them. The academic profession plays along with this game.[5]

Chomsky does not accept that those media which strive for accuracy in reporting and illumination of dark corners derive their disciplines from centuries of struggle for a press independent from state power. They are not free from the power of proprietors, but the fact of relative freedom from the state in democratic countries with a strong civil society has conferred on them a legitimacy, to report, investigate and comment, and to claim for journalism a realm separate from that of one wholly subservient to the commercial and other imperatives of the owners. It is a claim Chomsky wholly rejects, and in doing so he has received powerful support from his president, Donald Trump.

Trump's deliberate efforts to define the truth as that which he says it is and to extol the existence of – in the words of his counsellor, Kellyanne Conway – 'alternative facts', has been the largest threat to journalism in the democratic states since the war – coming as it does from the world's most powerful political office, in the country which has most proclaimed, practised and exported the rights and duties of an active and truthful journalism.

The explicit commitment to some form of popular democracy and some framework of market relations does impose constraints; far left, far right and populist (sometimes the same as popular) voices are heard rarely in the mainstream media, and then only as guest commentators. Commenting on the protests prompted by this lacuna, the former public editor of the *New York Times*, Daniel Okrent, wrote that

> if you are among the groups the *Times* treats as strange objects to be examined on a laboratory slide (devout Catholics, gun owners, Orthodox Jews, Texans); if your value system wouldn't wear well on a composite *New York Times* journalist, then a walk through this paper can make you feel you're traveling in a strange and forbidding world.[6]

With some differences, the same is roughly true across most of Europe and North America; in Germany, to be on the 'right', with echoes of Nazism, has been automatically suspect, yet a 2015 poll showed that 44 per cent of all Germans thought their news media biased to the left.[7]

The American scholar-journalist Walter Lippmann, the most influential voice on the responsibilities of the news media in the first part of the twentieth century, wrote that truth and news are not the same thing: 'the function of news is to signalize an event' or make people aware of it. 'The function of truth is to bring to light the hidden facts, or set them in relation with each other, and make a picture of reality upon which men can act.'[8] (Lippmann grew less and less optimistic that journalism could paint a 'picture of reality'.)

To follow a narrative based on facts, hidden or open, takes time and effort: most people don't give that time and effort to most news. A series of focus groups conducted by a group of scholars in Leeds to discover how much people trusted the news media shocked their organizers. The focus groups took place in 2008, during the series of primaries for the Democratic Party nomination for president, in which Hilary Clinton was matched against Barack Obama, the eventual winner. The primaries were in the news media, including the TV news, most days, yet not one of the forty to fifty people taking part in the groups knew that the contest was for the party nomination, not for the presidency itself. The scholars' group, led by Professor Stephen Coleman of Leeds University, wrote that they 'were completely surprised by the universal lack of understanding amongst members of all focus groups about how the primary elections worked ... in none of the focus groups did anyone know that both candidates were Democrats'.[9]

News should be accompanied by analysis and debate in order to make it fully comprehensible, but when television attempts such exercises, the audiences are always relatively small. So broadcast news-talk shows are often deliberately constructed to be aggressive shouting matches – a formula followed most faithfully and successfully by US, Italian and Indian television, where these programmes normally score more highly than analysis or sober debate. In 2015–16, Donald Trump, showed that he had grasped most fully the lesson that shock, controversy, evidence-free claims, insults and boasts were much more compelling, both for the audiences that loved him and for those that hated him. His haters in the media, transfixed and fascinated, provided vast amounts of useful derision, confirming to Trump supporters that the establishment feared him and they were right to support him.

Much of what follows in this part of the book is devoted to the problems of practising journalism that lives by one form or another of market rules, and the pressures market exerts on the creation of truthful accounts. Increasing numbers are willing to agree that truth isn't to be found in journalism, and sometimes they are right. But sometimes they are wrong. It's certainly the case that the search for truthful accounts is at least as lively as ever – probably livelier, since the destruction of the newspaper business model, based on advertising and circulation, has stimulated an anxious and at times successful search for other ways to put the facts of matters into comprehensible narrative form.

The year 2016, which saw a referendum vote in the UK to leave the European Union and the election of a strongly nationalist president, Donald Trump, in the US (quite diverse events), also saw a sudden and intense concern over fake news, which found fertile ground to grow in the American campaign, especially on the right. Its influence on the Trump victory is hard to gauge: its implications for journalism may be so disastrous that a separate chapter is devoted to it.

Among the most important developments credited with giving journalism a base for a more independent existence were those that gave rise to the figure of the reporter. These included the spread of printing and literacy, encouraged by the Protestant revolutions, and the need for commercial information in trading ports ('gazette' derives from a Florentine coin, the *gazeta*, the cost of a news sheet informing the merchants of Venice what cargoes were coming and going: 'What news on the Rialto?' – Venice's commercial heart – are the first words Shylock addresses to the merchant, Antonio, his tormentor and later debtor). David Zaret shows that media was used to construct a public sphere before the theorists of the enlightenment published their works.[10] There were practical developments during the English Civil War, when monarchic suppression of debate was lifted and political divisions were intense. The efforts to suppress the press throughout Europe and to bring the publication of news under the control of the state – as, in France, the *Gazette de France* was – gave way to the rise of democratic sentiment, of literacy and the political enfranchisement of the middle classes.

The US was different.[11] Its politicians encouraged its press, and subsidized its spread. Yet even there, the founders and the early Congresses barred their doors to newspapermen – going so far as to jail one for printing details of a debate he had gleaned from a participant – a state of affairs that only changed in the 1820s. Thereafter, as in the UK and in Europe, the reporting of public events bit by bit became routine and acquired a moral imperative of its own.

In an essay, Michael Schudson contrasts two prominent US reporters of different generations: Lincoln Steffens (1866–1936) and Harrison Salisbury (1908–93), portraying the first as a man of powerful, radical opinions which drove his reporting and the other one who presents the closely observable and carefully ascertainable facts.[12] In a letter to Schudson, Salisbury wrote: 'Stef was a crusader and quite a public figure. I am, as you note, basically a reporter, not an exhorter. I try to dig out what is what and present it and let the facts (as I see them) move people's minds.'

Steffens was a member of a famed group of reporters on *McClure's Magazine* in the first years of the twentieth century, who bid fair to be the inventors of investigative journalism. And investigate they surely did, especially the corruption of government and booming new corporate America, and they brought to it radical perspectives about which they made no secret. Salisbury was disciplined, in terms of both speed and factual accuracy, by twenty years of reporting for United Press International (by the mid 2010s, a tiny shadow of a once mighty foreign news service). His opinions – on Communism, and the conduct of the Vietnam War, for example – were, he argued, merely conclusions drawn from dispassionate observation of things as they were.

Schudson writes: 'Steffens is confronting politics; Salisbury is confronting a career in journalism and a name for himself. Steffens has an aim outside of reporting; Salisbury is the more consummate professional – whose only aim is defined within reporting itself, a passion to master the trade.'[13] Both the Steffens and the Salisbury ways of doing journalism are dangerous to authoritarian societies; Salisbury less obviously so than the openly committed liberal Steffens, but just because he wants to make 'a name for himself' within journalism, Salisbury cleaves the more resolutely to an independence from all political or state power: Steffens was close to President Theodore Roosevelt, who suggested corrupt subjects for his investigation.

French reporters may find inspiration in the figure of Albert Londres – a figure transmuted by the Belgian cartoonist Hergé into his character of Tintin – who developed a style of reporting on suffering, in a Guyanese penal colony, for example, or a mental asylum, with an immediacy and narrative flow rivalling that of a novel. Since the seventies, the investigative reporter who dives deep into murky water and comes up with proof of incompetence, venality or criminality is the trade's central figure. My own hero is the Belarusian writer Svetlana Alexievich (see Chapter Three), who raised interviewing into a means of gaining the deepest understanding of those who sought, often desperately, for some solid ground on which to lead a meaningful life.

On 3 April 2016, a site created by the International Consortium of Investigative Journalists (ICIJ), based in New York, went active. It contained a series of narratives of prominent people who had used, or whose close associates had used, various low- or no-tax jurisdictions to avoid paying tax in their own countries. These stories were based on a trove of 11.5 million documents – emails, documents and spreadsheets, dating back to 1977 – taken by a still-anonymous figure from the computer files of the Panamanian firm Mossack Fonseca, which specializes in assisting clients with their tax avoidance strategies.

Some of these, though interesting and important to get on the record, were in the 'what do you expect?' category. The footballer Lionel Messi, for example, already arraigned in Spain on tax fraud, was claimed to have set up a company in Panama just a day after Spanish tax authorities unveiled the charges for the alleged irregularities – and received a jail sentence (which he did not serve) as a consequence.[14] But others were shocking: few seemed more so than the case of the Ukrainian president, Petro Poroshenko, who had proclaimed himself strongly committed to fighting corruption, but was revealed to be the sole shareholder of a company set up in the British Virgin Islands, on the 'same day ... around 1,000 Ukrainian soldiers were reported killed after a pro-Russian offensive in east Ukraine'.[15] Poroshenko, a billionaire, was defended by two Western experts, Adrian Karatnycky and Alan Riley, both from the Atlantic Council, who argued that the president, whose fortune came largely from a confectionary business, was in good company: 'well-respected companies making legitimate use of offshores and of Mossack Fonseca's services includes the world's financial elite: Bank of America, Wells Fargo, JP Morgan Chase, Morgan Stanley ...'[16]

Other figures, whose elected task was to encourage citizens to pay taxes so that public services could thrive, included the then-serving Icelandic prime minister, Sigmundur Davíð Gunnlaugsson, who with his wife had been shown to have created a British Virgin Islands-based offshore company, Wintris Inc., in December 2007 to invest her share of the proceeds from the sale of her father's business, a Toyota importer;[17] the British prime minister, David Cameron, whose father Ian had founded an offshore fund for family money which avoided paying any tax in the UK;[18] and close associates of the Russian president, Vladimir Putin, including the concert cellist Sergei Roldugin, who owned offshore companies through which hundreds of millions of dollars were channelled to unnamed beneficiaries.[19]

Gerard Ryle, the Irish–Australian director of the ICIJ, revealed in a TED Talk something of the nature of the new leak- and Net-based investigative journalism.[20] The anonymous leaker of the Panama Papers had gone first to the left-leaning German daily *Sueddeutsche Zeitung*, who then asked for assistance from the ICIJ. To make sense of it, Ryle had to engage the collaboration of 376 journalists worldwide, beyond the ICIJ's twenty staff. The journalists worked on those papers that concerned their own nationals, and had to swear to secrecy over the months of working through the documents. A special search engine had to be created to comb through the documents for matching references, while the issues revealed in the Papers were broken down into different categories, such as sport or 'blood' diamonds, on which small specialized teams would work. Stories, said Ryle, were increasingly globalized and journalists had to drop their traditional hatred of sharing a scoop in order to collaborate on investigations which crossed national boundaries. The Net, which had destroyed newspapers, had, he said, made this kind of journalism possible. A new form of holding to account, and of discovering something of the truth of wealth and its manoeuvres, had emerged.

The Panama Papers revelations were a scoop of huge and continuing importance, playing into widespread revulsion at gross inequalities of income, made the sourer by the evidence of how much richer the rich plotted to be. They avoided the controversy of the other large leaks – the documents released by US Private Bradley Manning to WikiLeaks in 2010; and still more contested, those taken by Edward Snowden from the US National Security Agency in 2013, the controversy round the doubt that the revelations, though informing citizens of the scope and intrusiveness of the intelligence agencies, still weakened the effectiveness of services tasked with preserving the security of democracies from the attacks from authoritarian ones. The Papers, instead, attracted praise from Barack Obama, who said the Papers were 'important stuff' and took the occasion to make the social-democratic point that evasion 'means that we're not investing as much as we should in schools, in making college more affordable, in putting people back to work rebuilding our roads, our bridges, our infrastructure, creating more opportunities for our children'.[21]

The Panama Papers showed that journalism attracts and retains people who are animated by a desire to enlarge the public record to include those matters that the powerful of various sorts prefer to disguise. The passion to disclose is a precious impulse, and the journalism that employs it is only reliably possible in countries that are stably democratic and have powerful media independent enough of proprietors, state and governments, the latter of which are under pressure to act to attempt remedies, and sometimes do so.

Relatively free journalism only happens in liberal-democratic, market economies, but the workings of the corporations which produce much of the journalism in these economies are now often seen as abusing the principles of free journalism, as much as promoting them. An important instance of the former, in the 2000s, was the phone hacking practices, first uncovered by the *Guardian*, in the News Corporation's two British tabloids, the *News of the World* (a Sunday paper, now closed) and the daily paper *The Sun*. The issue was extensively examined by an inquiry headed by the judge Sir Brian Leveson, whose report recommended a state-backed regulator for newspapers, a proposal with which newspapers refused to cooperate (see Chapter Seven).

Academics, whose profession shares with the journalists' trade the search for evidence for real world events, are often horrified by journalism's practices, and – especially political scientists and sociologists – see them as inimical to democracy. The British sociologist Colin Crouch wrote that the rich people who own media companies 'do not want public opinion to focus on issues of inequality, nor do they want it to favour taxing the rich', while the increased competition in a falling newspaper and broadcasting market 'places a premium on sensationalism, distortion and using all available means (including illegal ones) to get information, whether true or false'.[22]

Paul Starr argues that 'commerce both distorts and enlarges the public sphere', while the news media became in the twentieth century 'an independent factor in politics – no less important ... than the political parties that had once held sway over them', and probably less useful to democracy.[23] The Belgian writer David Van Reybrouck believes that commercial media (newspapers, magazines, broadcasters) mounted a 'coup' over politics in the twentieth century – and in the twenty-first has increased the din of the 'cacophony' around politics, thinning it out further: 'commercial and social media also reinforce one another; continually picking up each other's news and bouncing it back, they create an atmosphere of perpetual mud-slinging'.[24]

Onora O'Neill, a Kantian scholar, gave the BBC's 2002 Reith Lectures on the subject of trust, before her retirement as head of the women-only Newnham College at Cambridge.[25] Trust in the media was her last talk (of five), with the sharp title of 'Licence to Deceive'. In it, she made a strong distinction between the freedom of speech and publication accorded to individuals and that accorded to corporations – now many leagues away from the little print shops that turned out the journals of the eighteenth and early nineteenth centuries:

> Freedom of expression is for individuals, not for institutions. We have good reasons for allowing individuals to express opinions even if they are invented, false, silly, irrelevant or plain crazy, but hardly for allowing powerful institutions to do so ... Only if we build a public culture – and especially a media culture – in which we can rely more on others not to deceive us, will we be able to judge whom and what we can reasonably trust. If we remain cavalier about press standards, a culture of suspicion will persist.

We cannot, however, rely on others not to deceive us. For apart from the mainstream news media which quite often do deceive us, we are entering – in successive waves, as the older generations, who read newspapers and watch or listen to bulletins pass out of the marketplace – a time when many websites, blogs and social media diligently undermine journalistic and expert views, and replace that part of the news media which strives for accuracy and truth, and which see their job as providing both news and opinion to a parliamentary democracy, in order to put more flesh on its promise, to be of, for and by the people. The US election of 2016 and the presidency of Donald Trump has provided a vivid example, at the highest level of exposure, of how dangerous these media can be.

FIVE

'We are in the advertising business'

As in the United States and China, the first newspaper in India was begun by a colonialist, and a disaffected one. *Hicky's Bengal Gazette* was the product, in 1780, of James Augustus Hicky, a choleric Irishman who had fetched up in Calcutta and was put in jail for debt. Released, with a store of invective, he founded the *Gazette*, much of which expressed, in overt or covert form, his dislike of the East India Company – a commercial enterprise and the effective ruler of large tracts of India before the British state took over.

His paper was a mix of whimsy, allegories, poems of his own and others' composition – one was titled: 'to a Lady who dances with her breasts uncovered, tho' they are none of the most tempting'. Eagerly read by the customers, it wasn't popular with the powers that be and would often charge Company officials with corrupt practices. The Irishman didn't like British rule, and when journalism by Indians began in the latter half of the nineteenth century, they shared that view. Their papers were modelled on Western examples and fired by indignation at the subaltern role native citizens were meant to play in the eyes and actions of colonialists. The journalism of several countries in the world, including the two largest, China and India, and the most powerful, the United States, owes a debt to the British for providing such inexhaustible fodder for searing editorials.

When the British left India in 1947, the press saw itself as cheerleader for the independence movement. It was not of one mind or voice – most clearly not between the Hindu and Muslim communities – but it was independence-minded. Radio started as a network of private stations in 1923 then was nationalized under British rule in 1930. It was taken over by the new state and, as All-India Radio, greatly extended its reach. These were midnight media, born, at the stroke of midnight, on 15 August 1947, into a newly independent state. Those existing before the British ceded the country were reborn, not just as voices for independence but also as journals of and for a new state and a new ruling class.

The journalists were deferential to Prime Minister Jawaharlal Nehru, but deference, at least among the editors and the senior journalists, was based not on trembling obedience but on shared beliefs, particularly in the claim that the state must be secular in all its official functions and manifestations. The midnight editors were not hirelings writing what the owners or the government wanted (though they gave them, by today's standards, much slack), they were men convinced of the mission to reconstruct their country as an independent state.

Born in 1930, Inder Malhotra had been the New Delhi editor of both *The Statesman* and the *Times of India*; one of the few still active journalists old enough to compare the achievements of independence with the imperial period. I met him in New Delhi in 2012, at a conference on 'Crony Journalism', where he was speaking, with some relish, about the corruption of the news media, a relish which continued in interview:

> I got a job on the United Press of India in 1949: the salaries were low, the English was Victorian but we had great pride in ourselves. There was corruption among the journalists then but it would be laughable now. I was a junior reporter; a politician offered us eight annas a line [half a rupee, or a few pence] for reporting his speech: only two people took the offer. A statement from the Baroda Bank was sent to the editor with a hundred-rupee note attached (with the implicit request that it be given prominent display): he returned it.

Malhotra said that the sentiment among most journalists of the decades after independence, encouraged by the leftist rhetoric of Nehru and others in the Congress leadership, was to look to the state rather than corporations: 'in Delhi the embrace of the state wasn't so bad but in the states they were offered houses, buildings for the editorial offices. And the effects became clear at the time of the Emergency.'

The Emergency lasted twenty-one months from 1975 to 1977, declared by Prime Minister Indira Gandhi as a response to challenges to her rule from different sections of civil society, such as trade unions and portions of the press. Electricity was shut off to all Delhi newspapers within three hours. Later, censors were posted to the main papers, and oppositionist editors arrested: 'the press was divided by the Emergency. A number of journalists passed a resolution against it at the Press Club: they were marked men. Others went to Gandhi and said – yes, this is right. They were given ... various awards.'

The Emergency ended the period when patriotism could unite the political class and much of the press. The broadcasters were under the government's control and supported the Emergency strongly: these were All-India Radio, inherited from the empire and available everywhere, and the TV service Doordarshan (the Hindi version of television: *door*/tele: far; *darshan*/vision: seeing), which had been developed under the wing of the radio service from the late 1950s. The expense of a TV set confined viewing to a minority. Later, those who had defied the apparatus of control and censorship became honoured; those who had collaborated were seen as having failed in a duty of holding the state to some sort of reckoning.

The umbilical link between state and media was broken. Liberalization of broadcasting from the early nineties made it wildly pluralistic, and saw stations competing with each other on criticism, invective and character assassination. The corporations, not the state, demanded fealty from their media holdings, and are only sometimes constrained by considerations that journalism should have priorities and values – of objectivity, investigative potential and analytical freedom. At times, they demand that the government – at federal or state levels – be excoriated. At other times, especially since the premiership of Narendra Modi, they demand positive coverage, shorn of criticism or closer investigation.

Against these pressures, a new and well-educated cadre of younger journalists now pushes for a journalism that counterpoints the sensationalism of the TV channels and the triviality of much of the press. In part, this is achieved through websites, like the lively and serious Scroll. But it is also achieved through a strong strain of criticism of journalism by journalists themselves – see Sevanti Ninan's *The Hoot* – and through the growth of new approaches to journalism, among which *Caravan* – based in New Delhi, inspired by long-form journalism in US magazines such as the *New Yorker*, *City Journal*, *Mother Jones* and *The Atlantic* – stands out. The markets for all of these are relatively small – *Caravan* sells about 40,000 copies in a country of more than a billion, but the appetite for a more informed, engaged and above all independent-minded journalism could grow as education levels rise.

Prime Minister Modi and his BJP-dominated government are committed to raising both the domestic and the international game of India, a massive undertaking which will take much journalistic unpacking to be understood. At the same time, the government's strong links to the Hindu right and the disdain the prime minister appears to have for secularism should be the subject for a fundamental debate on the nature of India. Indian journalism has the intellectual capacity, but not many of the institutions could create the conditions for such an undertaking. It should rise to these large challenges, but does so fitfully.

One of the feistiest of newspaper editors, Shekhar Gupta, then of the *Indian Express*, had in a September 2012 column in his own paper given a kind of declaration of Indian journalistic independence. Recalling that everyone in the Indian establishment knew and often listened to the long-time BBC correspondent in India, Mark Tully, and that many would not believe news of an event on Indian media until Tully of the BBC had confirmed it, Gupta noted that not one of these followers, when he asked them at a talk he was giving, could name Tully's successors as the BBC's bureau chief in India. He drew the conclusion 'as democracies grow, evolve, deepen and mature, their reliance on the international media for news about themselves declines'.[1] Indian journalism, for better or worse, is on its own.

But it is hobbled, if no longer by colonialism then by both politicians and proprietors. Prime Minister Modi, in office since May 2014, has made clear that he is available to be questioned only rarely – with few press conferences or probing interviews, and with a preference for Doordarshan and All-India Radio, where the questions can be expected to be respectful. *Quartz India* reports that

> reporters in India complained that information on the new administration was hard to come by, and that government staff had stopped responding to phone calls and text messages. Throughout Modi's term, journalists have been directed to the prime minister's speeches, press statements and Twitter feed. Ministers and bureaucrats are told to avoid the media and speak only when Modi offers an 'official line'. Some ministers are even told to refrain from speaking to journalists at all and leave it to their department's official spokesperson.[2]

This is not an authoritarian regime, more a distrustful one, with a leader with historic and present resentments against the 'Delhi press', who, like others, has discovered that social media gives him unmediated access to his people.

Poverty is the great scourge of India, deeper than in some African states. It doesn't, however, feature much in the Indian news media.

For Justice Markandey Katju, who was the chairman of India's Press Council from 2011 to 2014, this is the gravest charge that can be held against them. I talked to Katju in his official residence, one of the some thousand of large bungalows built in the 1920s within the lush, Edwin Lutyens-designed administrative zone of Delhi, and still put at the service of the senior people in the administration. Born in an upper-caste family in Lucknow and with a successful career in the law in which his family was already distinguished, Katju used his three-plus years at the Press Council to lash the press (and television, though he had no authority there) for their indifference to the want of their fellow Indians.

He is a strongly opinionated man, contemptuous of criticism. He told me, several times, that 90 per cent of Indians were 'idiots', since they voted on caste and communal lines for candidates whose fitness for office and honesty they did not examine. He believes that Pakistan is not a 'legitimate' country and has called for the reunification of Pakistan, Bangladesh and India. He also believes that gay relationships contradict women's urge to reproduce the species, blogging (after he had ceased to be Press Council chairman) the rhetorical question: 'Will a gay relationship or gay marriage serve nature's requirement of continuing the species? No.' These views give him the reputation of being an eccentric reactionary among younger cosmopolitan Indians. When I mentioned I would meet him to two Indian acquaintances, both journalists in their thirties, they said, 'But you know he's a bit mad!'

If he is mad, it's in the American-, not the British- or Indian-English use of the word. He's mad about the state of Indian journalism. He believes it's failing, more or less entirely, in reporting the true state of the majority. He told me that

> Seventy per cent of the people live on two dollars a week or less. Forty per cent of the kids are undernourished. No fewer than 250,000 farmers committed suicide in the last fifteen years: that's forty-six every day.[3] There was fashion week in Mumbai and the cotton the models were wearing

came from the farmers who are killing themselves. But 512 journalists covered this. Almost no one covers the farmers. They are an hour's flight from the editorial offices.

In India, 90 per cent of the media is entertainment. Very little attention is given to our massive unemployment; that education is in a terrible state; that there is almost no health care for the poor. Instead, they talk about film stars, sex scandals – and cricket, cricket is the opium.

Katju headed a body which, though created by statute in 1966, gave him little power. In his period, it had twenty-eight members besides him, of whom twenty were drawn from the ranks of the press. On its own estimation, it is 'one of the most important bodies that sustain democracy'. But it doesn't act like such a body. Sevanti Ninan, at *The Hoot*, told me that 'Katju shouts about ethics but he doesn't have to make his living from an audience and he doesn't have any power. There is no regulation: not of the press, not of the broadcasters.' I asked her if the newspapers themselves promulgated an ethical code and held their journalists to it. She said: 'The people with influence in newspapers are the chief financial officer and the advertising department. That's where the ethics lie.'

Katju wants to regulate, to compel the editors to raise their journalistic game, in spite of their owners.

I am not a communist: but you must have the involvement of the society in the media. The choice before the media owners and the journalists is – either pander to the people's stupidity, or try to raise the level of their understanding. I say to the journalists – *you* are doing stories with half-naked women: it's an insult to the masses! I tell the members of the Council: see what happened in Europe – with Voltaire, Rousseau, Paine; they fought for their ideas and propagated them. I tell them – I want you to be respected. Our freedom cannot go to the extent of damaging the rest of society.

Throughout his tenure, Katju pleaded publicly and futilely for wider authority, arguing that all news media should be brought under one organization – a Media Council – which would issue licences and thus be able to discipline news channels. 'The electronic media are making huge amounts of money. They are prepared to sell their mothers and their souls for a penny. But the politicians don't want to anger the TV channels.' The National News Broadcasting Council is even weaker than the Press Council: it's non-statutory, self-regulating, 'which means', Katju sniffs, 'it doesn't regulate at all'.

Dipankar Gupta, among the best known of India's sociologists, had been one of the Broadcasting Council's four 'eminent persons' on a board of twelve, on which the others were representatives of the channels. He defends it to a point: 'You will see less superstition, sex or violence on the news channels now.' But he also says:

> TV journalism isn't really professional. They don't know what to show and what not to show. We keep telling them that they should live up to the needs of democracy: we want them to check their facts. Democracy is not about gross ratings. They are constrained in what they can say, most of all by the corporations. Advertising is the great constraint.

Gupta, like Katju, sees poverty as the largest stain on India's democracy, and the largest gap in media coverage. In a book published in 2009, he argues that poverty actually rose in the decade ending in 2005, with over 50 per cent of the population 'abysmally poor by any standard'.[4] He also says that caste, the still rigid system dividing the population into hierarchical strata, often confined to particular trades, is a main cause of poverty: 'caste kills initiative because it ordains a status hierarchy based on birth'.

With Katju's and Gupta's concentration on the ignoring of poverty on the part of Indian journalism in mind, I visited the offices of Condé Nast India, a modest operation for a major publishing house in what will soon be the world's most populous country.[5] The journalists who produce its four magazines – *Vogue India, GQ India, Condé Nast Traveller* and *Architectural Digest* – tapped away at their keyboards elbow-to-elbow in cramped, workaday offices in a colonial-era building in Mumbai.

Managing director Alex Kuruvilla, fifty-two, slight, pleasant and self-deprecating, had come up with the slogan that Condé Nast – which claims 80 per cent of the luxury consumer magazines market – is 'India's most advanced publishing company'. He thought other Indian companies that started (and in some cases closed) high-end lifestyle magazines didn't properly understand the concept or how to deliver it.

Condé Nast's ambitions in India are to develop, support and flatter a cosmopolitan elite. Out of a population of 1.24 billion, Kuruvilla reckoned this elite – that is, people who make more than 100,000 dollars a year – numbers about three million, and is growing fast. He says that 300,000 of these people currently read one or more of his magazines. 'We put a lot of investment in to get it right. We might go to New York for a shoot, or fly cosmetics in from New York. Our [advertising] rate card is firm. We don't discount.'

He told me about a party he recently put on for *Vogue India*'s fifth anniversary, at the luxurious Oberoi Trident Hotel on Marine Drive – where Islamist terrorists struck in 2008, killing thirty-two people. He went on to talk about its October issue, which challenged fifty fashion houses to create differing versions of saris. 'We want to have cross-fertilization,' he said.

After seeing him, I thought he and his operation would have roused Katju to splenetic rage, and Gupta to more measured disapproval. They are at different poles of present-day India: the two older men carrying on and seeking to revitalize the socialist/paternalist traditions of the Nehruvian generations; Kuruvilla eagle-eyed for tastes of the burgeoning class, numbering the population of a small European state, who have large salaries on any measure and want to enjoy the spending (and other) power that gives.

In fact, the Indian media don't entirely ignore poverty, or its consequences. Sevanti Ninan says that 'people do write about poverty because it's all around you. But it's not a major theme.' One journalist above others has made it a major theme: Palagummi Sainath, who has written about poverty for much of his professional life, and who has been widely honoured for his work.

Sainath, from an upper-caste family in Chennai and graduate of a school reckoned to be among the five best in India, Loyola College, has rooted out the poorest in order to hear their stories, and, in doing so, has constructed, through his journalism, a journalistic history-cum-anthropology of the Indian peasant and working classes. Some of these are Adivasi – the word means original inhabitant of India; there are an estimated fifty million of these, from about 200 tribes, speaking 100 separate languages, who rely on hunting and primitive agriculture for a living. They make up a large proportion of the 'scheduled tribes' (who also include the Untouchables), and are so designated because they have special provision made for them, though that is often badly delivered.

The largest number of the lowest circles of society are the Untouchables. Government programmes have raised life chances, though they remain literally 'untouchable' by many in the higher castes, and are regarded as pariahs,[6] not least because the work they are permitted to do includes the cleaning out of the faeces in dry toilets and carrying it to large pits. On the 1991 census, some three-quarters of Indians had no toilet where they lived (64 per cent in cities); the 2011 census saw that number fall markedly – yet less than half, 47 per cent of the more than 246 million households, had a toilet, while almost half the population defecated in the open. Modi, elected prime minister in 2014, announced in his Independence Day speech that a priority of his government would be to provide toilets throughout the country – an announcement which allowed him to emphasize his own lower-caste (but not Untouchable) origins: 'I have seen poverty and the attempt to give dignity to the poor starts from there.'[7]

Sainath uncovered the way in which many of these people lived; a collection of his journalism shows its range.[8] In Nandapur, Orissa – among the poorest of states – he found a school, largely peopled with Adivasi children, in which the parents would often come to the school to take from their children most or all of the 150-rupee-a-month living allowance they got from the welfare department; they had none of their own. Another tribe could not access the benefits due to its members because at some point, a bureaucratic mistake had been made: the tribal name, Dhurua, had been wrongly rendered as Dharua – and the bureaucrat in charge refused to disburse the money.

In a rural area, he found that many of the regional health centres were not operating. In one case all the medicines and instruments had been taken by doctors who conducted private practices nearby. In Orissa and Andhra Pradesh, Sainath found labourers at brickworks 'caked in a film of brick dust', required to carry bricks in 45-kilo loads – many of them children or elderly. 'Once they have carried two tonnes of bricks, they can earn 9 rupees. Why do it? Because there is no work at all in the districts from which they come.'

Sainath's job title at *The Hindu*, Rural Affairs Editor, understated his importance in Indian journalism (he left the paper in 2014 amid internal struggles). His singularity as a chronicler of the very poor – and his eye for publicity – means he is much sought after internationally. I heard him talk at New York's Columbia University School of Journalism in September 2014; it was by some way the most charismatic of the day of talks and academic-journalistic presentations. A handsome man, then in his mid fifties, he speaks with practised passion. 'There is', he told the attendees at a conference on 'Muckraking Journalism', 'a gigantic misalliance between the Indian mass media and mass reality.' Noting that *Forbes India* had recently reported that there were 100 billionaires in India worth, cumulatively, 346 billion dollars, he said that these were the journalists' heroes, the central, pampered characters of the Indian media narrative. Citing press coverage of Modi's first hundred days, he said that 'in these hundred days, 4,600 farmers committed suicide; women are the worst sufferers: as suicides take place, they must cope with the legacy'.

The media had given up serious journalism, he argued: 'There are almost no Indian journalists who cover serious "beats", like labour, agriculture, the cities. They cover business, of course – and leisure, and fashion, and show business. And of course, sport. There is a paper in Eastern India which has a full-time golf correspondent ... The Indian media give sycophancy a bad name.' In the introduction to his collection, he wrote that the people he described were 'beyond the margin of elite vision. And beyond the margins of a press and media that fail to connect with them.'

Much of Sainath's critique seems true – certainly of news TV – though the sheer volume of channels, newspapers and magazines makes it hard to judge how much reporting of the issues he privileges goes on, especially in the minor languages. Nor is he entirely alone: one of the best known of those who write on the Adivasi issues is Dayamani Barla, herself an Adivasi from the Munda tribe of whom the majority live in the state of Jharkand in the north-east of the country.

Barla worked as a maid to pay her way through school and a journalism course. She wrote for the Hindi-language newspaper *Prabhat Khabar*, the biggest newspaper in Jharkand, which became famous nationally for uncovering a scam involving the former chief minister of Bihar, and minister of railways, Lalu Prasad – later found guilty of the large-scale embezzlement of ninety-six million rupees (1.5 million dollars) and sentenced to five years' hard labour (the sentence has not been served, and he remains head of the main party in Bihar, the Rashtriya Janata Dal; his two elder sons have high posts in the state government). Local and regional papers, in Hindi, Tamil, Urdu and others of India's many languages, can be solidly under the thumb of local politicians and business, but they can also be bold and pioneering – and are sometimes now one, now the other.

A journalist who has sought to assist the Adivasis enter into the world of news media is Shubhranshu Choudhary, who has no Adivasi background. He studied anthropology at university and moved into journalism, becoming a South East Asia producer for the BBC, a high-status, relatively highly paid post. On one assignment, he swooped in on an area of Chhattisgarh where there had been a battle between the Naxalites and the army in which seventy-six soldiers had died. Having done a series of interviews, he made it into a TV package and, after two days, returned to New Delhi. Reflecting, Choudhary had a crisis of professional conscience about 'parachute journalism', in which a tragedy is given a day of research and two minutes of TV time. He left the BBC and went back to Chhattisgarh.[9]

In a TED Talk in February 2012, Choudhary told his story through the prism of one who had, quite suddenly, seen the journalist he was, viewing the profession as 'still very aristocratic: very few decide what is news and what is not'.[10] In conversation, he likes to say that 'We are all kings in this new kingdom of democracy' – an adaptation from a poem-drama[11] by Rabindranath Tagore, the Bengali writer and scholar who remains India's most famed artist: and adapts it, to say that 'the time will come when we are all journalists, to make a better world for tomorrow'.

In 2004, Choudhary went back to the villages he had encountered as a 'vulture', and sat with the local people. He founded CGNet-Swara: CG is Central Gondwara, the name for the rural heartland of India of which Chhattisgarh is a part; and *swara* the word for voice in several languages. The system, built with the aid of William Thies, a young American computer scientist who worked at the Microsoft Research India centre in Bangalore, used the only commonly used form of technology: the mobile phone. Messages would be called in and stored in a server, before being curated by journalists in New Delhi and then put up on the website, where they could be picked up by the mainstream news media and by officials and government.

A report by Thies and two colleagues highlighted one example of success: a man named Pitbasu Bhoi had not received wages from the state for work under the National Rural Employment Guarantee Act, but needed money desperately for medical care for a sick son.[12] His story, publicized on CGNet, led to stories in the *Times of India* and *The Hindu* – and to payment of back wages within two weeks. The service is a success, if probably limited; the editor of a regional daily quoted in Thies' paper told him: 'It is my hunch that NGOs are the ones making most use of it … If you are thinking about the tribals this should benefit, then you have to remember that an individual, firstly, does not have the courage to speak out. Secondly, talking on the mobile phone to someone or something he does not know is a big thing.'

India's TV journalism is exhaustingly exciting. It has small concern with news that gives audiences rounded pictures of the state of the nation, and of the world. Instead, it focuses relentlessly on what is new, what is dramatic, what is scandalous and, at all times, what is likely to gain 'most eyeballs'.

The struggle for eyeballs, measured by ratings that are regarded as skewed and fixed by many in the industry is only in part a quest for profits.[13] Indian TV channels are about money, but not in every case about that earned by the channel itself. They are about power: the power a channel gives its owner(s) over politicians, and over other business people and corporations; the power to intimidate or flatter their way to election victories, political preferment, government contracts or advantageous mergers and acquisitions.

Thus the news channels' editors have three kinds of demands on them which editors must juggle as they believe best to conform to their owners' interests. The public service content of the news does exercise some sway; many journalists believe that journalism's duty is to report the major events in the country and abroad. But the coverage must also, in most channels, reflect the point of view and the interests of the proprietor(s) – and thus must not be critical of allies, and only hostile to enemies. Furthermore, the content must be fast, often polemical, dramatic, scandalous, deeply linked in to popular culture and to sport (above all, cricket), to attract and retain a large audience.

TV in India had been severely utilitarian in its beginnings, inspired by socialist ideas on education and community service more than by the values of entertainment. Launched, from Delhi, within the framework of All-India Radio in 1959 from a small studio and a transmitter with limited range, it had a funding of 20,000 dollars from UNESCO and used equipment donated by the US, with a brief to assist communities and to educate the population. Programmes were broadcast to some 180 television clubs within a radius of 40 kilometres from the transmitter. Programming for teachers began in 1961, news bulletins in 1965, rural programmes carrying information for farmers soon after and, at the same time, entertainment programmes. The service was extended to other large cities in the seventies; in 1976 the service separated from All-India Radio, began to air commercials and was renamed Doordarshan. In the eighties, it allowed sponsorship of programmes, acquired colour and a second channel, as well as a regional network; in the nineties, it started five satellite stations; in the first two decades of the new century, it grew to nineteen channels, ten of which were regional language channels.

The poverty of the majority of Indians meant that private ownership of a TV set was confined to the middle and upper classes – or TV was watched communally, in village halls or cafés. The first soap opera, *Hum Log* (Hindi: We People), began in 1984, and was hugely popular, set as it was in a large family, where the father is a singer turned alcoholic, the eldest son a ne'er-do-well and the younger siblings ambitious for stardom or a medical career; a social worker, a doctor and a police officer was often attached in one way or another to the main plot.

It was a defining event, and not just for Doordarshan. The show garnered fifty million viewers and its vast popularity was built round the life of a lower-middle-class family, with plots that veered between domestic comedy, social commentary and melodrama. The actors, who in some cases had not been professionals (none had any TV experience), turned into stars within weeks. Advertisers clamoured to get on; Doordarshan, after its acceptance of commercials, had become the only medium in which advertisers could address a national audience of consumers.

The plots, wrote the critic Shoma Chatterji, had as a sub-theme the aim of furthering the empowerment of women – but events were interpreted differently by the mass audience from the intellectuals who wrote and produced it:

> Bhagwanti, the mother of the family ... was a subservient, self-sacrificing, traditional Indian woman, endlessly taken advantage of and abused because she put the needs of others first. The show's producers intended that viewers would be angered by her suffering, but in fact ... 80 per cent of the women who viewed Hum Log chose Bhagwanti as a positive role model. And many men indicated they felt that India needed more women like Bhagwanti.[14]

This was the other lesson Hum Log taught. Attempts to improve people's attitudes worked, if at all, over very long periods, and characters' actions were interpreted more by the audience, in the light of their own views and experiences, than by either the actors or their writers.

Doordarshan had its origins in an era of socialism, self-reliance and import substitution: it was owned by a government that had put itself at the forefront of a call, in the 1970s and '80s, for a 'New World Information and Communication Order' in which the priorities set by the Western states and their big media corporations would no longer determine what was news. 'Fears of cultural imperialism and the domination of Western news and organizations,' writes the scholar Nikhil Sinha, 'resulted in a closed broadcasting system. Radio and television were owned and operated exclusively by the government and private broadcasting, whether domestic or foreign, was prohibited.'[15]

And then it was swept away, as the government of Narasimha Rao, inspired by its finance minister, Manmohan Singh, opened up the channels to foreign investment, increased trade, reformed capital markets and privatized large swathes of industry and services – including broadcasting. The growth of channels after 1991 was rapid. By 2015, there were around 1,250 of them, of which all in the top ten were largely entertainment channels, including Doordarshan National, its flagship channel, at number six, according to BARC ratings.

That growth was originally highly dependent on foreign channels entering the market, as the old distrust of foreign media bent, then broke. Star TV, owned by the media entrepreneur Li Ka-shing of Singapore, established five channels in India; in 1993, Star was taken over by Rupert Murdoch's News Corporation, which expanded the market to thirteen million households by 1995. News International also acquired part of the popular Hindi-language ZeeTV, and CNN created a joint venture in 2005 with the Indian company Studio 18. Much of the content was either Western – especially that aimed at the young – or highly influenced by Western styles, dress and attitudes. The political commentator Smita Gupta, then political editor of *Outlook* magazine, wrote that a new middle class was born, 'swelled post-1991 by the entry of a stream of brash, aggressive, upwardly mobile entrepreneurial types, many from the backward castes, who were increasingly acquiring money along with political power ... it also heralded a new mindset, encompassing ideas, lifestyle and moral codes'.[16]

Change was radical, and rapid. Akash Kapur confronted change in both its dynamic and destructive modes; his book *India Becoming*[17] – written after a twelve-year sojourn in the US, his mother's country – was widely lauded as a sensitive portrait of the native land he had left at the age of sixteen. He wrote that his family had wished to escape 'the economic and social torpor of India – the austerity imposed by the nation's socialist economy', yet after admiring and becoming accustomed to 'the shopping malls and shiny office complexes, with the fancy bars and the cocktails they served', he reflected that 'India would have to pay a price for its prosperity – that new money was being accompanied by new forms of inequality, that freedom and opportunities were opening the floodgates, too, to disorder and violence'. For traditionalists and for the left, as ever powerful in the cultural sphere, this was alarming and unwelcome; comments such as 'the cultural values that were championed by Mohandas Gandhi are being replaced by values produced in Hollywood' were common, and remain so.[18]

The nursery of many of the new matadors of the studio was New Delhi Television, NDTV, founded in 1988 – before privatization of the airwaves – by a married couple, Prannoy and Radhika Roy. They both came from intellectual, upper-class family milieus, with strong connections to prominent leftists. Neither Prannoy nor Radhika were revolutionaries, but they were strongly liberal; and like their TV colleagues in western Europe in the sixties and seventies, they grasped the power of television and its ability to carry narratives which, they thought, should be much more capable of asking the awkward questions Doordarshan's presenters and reporters did not ask, and should have the capacity and freedom to interpret events and political manoeuvres to a burgeoning audience.

In a lecture he gave at the Reuters Institute in November 2012, Prannoy Roy said of the first period of Indian democracy, the thirty years after 1946, that 'this was our docile phase ... when media was at its weakest and literacy lowest'.[19] From 1987 onwards, it began to change; not coincidentally, this was when the Roys, with Radhika in the lead, decided to found a small TV current affairs production company, and applied for and won a contract to do a programme for Doordarshan, on international news. Roy recalled:

We launched a weekly programme called *The World this Week*. Fortunately, in comparison with the bland news on Doordarshan ... which had virtually no visuals and was more like radio than TV ... it was not difficult to look good. We were lucky because the world [in 1988] was in turmoil ... *The World this Week* was a hit. But news on or about India was out of bounds.

The Roys were told they must submit all scripts to Doordarshan to be vetted. They agreed, but said that if anything was changed, even in a minor way, they would drop the entire story. Some stories were challenged and were dropped, but fewer, they believed, than if they had not built in the condition. The success of the programme led to a contract to broadcast coverage of some of India's many elections. In one case, an 'obnoxious but powerful' man in the prime minister's office ordered the Roys not to mention certain constituencies; they responded that they could not be censored, and would call off the programme. The official didn't budge; the sets were being dismantled; then, quite suddenly, the decision was reversed, on the orders of the then prime minister, Rajiv Gandhi, angered that the programme had been threatened.

When, at last, the Roys were allowed to do the national news, Prannoy announced on the first night: 'It's eight o'clock and the news comes to you LIVE!' At that word, another prime ministerial official took fright and demanded the right of previewing all material before it went out. The Roys again extracted a compromise: buying a computer with a large hard disk, they recorded on it the half-hour news and programmed the disk to transmit with a ten-minute delay. The show was then announced to be 'as live', satisfying the letter of the official's concern but putting a pistol to his head: accept the programme or mandate half an hour of blank screens.

They were in a tug-of-war between a corporatist bureaucracy and the market, which meant the programme was an amalgam of what was possible given the resources, what was profitable given the advertising and what kind of news would be watched, given the audience. It was the first conscious attempt to mould the 'citizen-consumer': instead of Doordarshan's obedient Indian, the Roys' ideal audience were those who needed news and analysis in order to be able to choose the politician, party and policies they preferred, often a new generation from those who had lived through Prannoy's first 'docile' thirty-year period of democracy, when media were 'weakest'. It was also a time of public reverence for independence, state building and state-controlled involvement in the political process.

NDTV prospered and broke from Doordarshan; it was hired by Star TV, then in the hands of News Corporation, to do the main nine o'clock news bulletin, and then a twenty-four-hour news channel, in both Hindi and English. Roy said that 'Rupert Murdoch financed the entire operation but had no hesitation in giving us total editorial control'. The judgement of Daya Thussu, the most prominent Western-based scholar of the Indian media, is that 'this was a convenient arrangement for both partners: NDTV could reach the homes of affluent Indians as well as the diaspora audience through the Star platform, while Star could benefit from gravitas of a serious news channel – arguably India's best television news network'.[20]

Doordarshan was forced to change. Rathikant Basu, a senior civil servant with something of a reputation for iconoclasm, was seconded from the civil service to run the broadcaster in 1993; he retained the title of Additional Secretary in the Ministry of Information and Broadcasting, to underline the continued link between state and broadcaster. Basu got investment for new programmes, charmed the press into good reviews and hired some of the bright young journalists – such as Karan Thapar, Vir Sanghvi and Raghav Bahl – to create a new service, emulating the NDTV approach. Basu succeeded so well at Doordarshan that he was hired, in 2003, by Murdoch – after one meeting in Delhi – to run Star, at a salary of 500,000 dollars, a vast uplift from his civil service pay. In the seven years he was at the channel, he greatly expanded its reach, making it a Hindi-only channel and the most popular in India.

NDTV left Star, to start two all-news channels, NDTV 24/7 in English and NDTV India in Hindi. The state's and Doordarshan's concessions to independent production in the late eighties and Murdoch's perception that the Indian market could support a twenty-four-hour all-news service were the foundations of what is now a vast panoply of voices, a semi-hysterical search for news that will entertain.

Two films, both appearing in 2010, tried to capture the nature of what was being offered to the Indian people. The tragic-comic *Peepli Live* put farmers' suicide at its centre: tragic in its demonstration of the remorseless pressures on poor peasants, while rendering it comic through the farcical hysteria that swept through newsrooms when the 'story' became the deliberate suicide of a farmer in order to secure compensation from a state programme which paid out to a suicide's family. *Rann*, starring the most durable of Indian film stars, Amitabh Bachchan, then sixty-eight, showed a TV channel owner-presenter (Bachchan) struggling to maintain ethical standards in an industry where every other news outlet is winning the race for eyeballs. The *Times of India* reviewer wrote that the film dramatized the fact that 'there is a politician-businessman-news-baron nexus at work that reduces the actual news reporter to a puppet on a chain ... and sensationalism isn't only the new buzzword in the business of news; it's fast becoming a synonym for it'.[21]

The 'politician-businessman-news-baron nexus' is rawer, more generally accepted as simply the way the game is played, than in many other democracies. Newspapers, which have grown strongly in the past three decades, are often owned or influenced by politicians, themselves linked to business groups. The evidence is that the news channel business is less for profit (many run at a loss) than for influence on government, either at state or at national levels. Prannoy Roy – the inspiration for the character Bachchan played in *Rann* – tells the story of a friend who was approached by the head of a construction company, desperate to hire him to front a news channel he intended to start – 'Money is not important! I will start it!' His friend asked him why it was so important. He answered: 'I am one of the biggest builders in this country and I put in a bid for a recent tender for a mega project in Uttar Pradesh. Everyone shortlisted was called to meet the Chief Minister. I went too, but had to wait for eight hours before he called me in ... however, anyone who had a news channel walked right in without waiting a minute!'[22]

Though NDTV, both by personal observation and by reputation, remains the satellite channel most committed to analysis and relative sobriety (if less than at its beginning), it must make money, and at first it made a lot of money. Its election coverage, which the Roys developed with the aid of the Oxford scholar and founder of the science of psephology David Butler, attracted huge audiences, with advertising rates increasing from 10,000 rupees per ten seconds to 40–50,000 rupees – and ad breaks stretching to nearly twenty minutes. The unintended consequence of coverage was – surveys showed, said Roy – that 'the TV audience at whom the advertising was targeted did not want to see farmers' suicides in rural Andhra Pradesh, pot-holed roads in Bundelkhand or parents selling children to survive in Orissa. It wished to be entertained with the razzmatazz of the election machine at work.'

Denunciations of news media are easy to find in India, and are often forcefully put; of a piece with the complaints in most democratic countries, which focus on 'dumbing down', there is a gulf between what a minority says it wishes to see and what the majority chooses to see. But the presenters who are the largest characters in the news business – the English-language presenters claim they are the most influential, since English-speaking India is nearly all of the governing, business and intellectual elite – don't buy this. They believe that they have changed and are changing Indian society for the better.

The English-language tyros are a very elitist elite, with prestigious educational backgrounds by global standards. Arnab Goswami, until 2016 the chief editor and main presenter of Times Now news channel, was the grandson of eminent lawyers and politicians, son of an army colonel who, after an education at various army schools on the bases in which his father was posted, took a Masters in Social Anthropology from St Antony's College, Oxford, then was a visiting scholar at Cambridge University. Rajdeep Sardesai, until 2014 the editor and main presenter on the CNN-IBN channel, is the son of a famous Indian test cricketer, Dilip Sardesai; he was educated at private schools and at St Xavier College in Mumbai and University College, Oxford, where he studied civil law and was a cricket blue. Karan Thapar, a presenter of several prestigious interview programmes, was the son of General Pran Nath Thapar, Chief of Staff of the Indian Army; Karan was educated at The Doon School – India's most prestigious, boys-only boarding school – Stowe public school in the UK, and at Cambridge, where he studied Economics and Political Philosophy and was president of the Union, before taking a doctorate in international relations at St Antony's, Oxford. Even the BBC, which has drawn its senior cadres disproportionately from Oxford and Cambridge, can't match that. The most prominent woman in the galaxy, NDTV's Barkha Dutt, has a slightly lower social pedigree: born in a solidly middle-class family – father an Air India executive, mother, Prabha, a pioneering newspaper reporter – she graduated from the Anglican Christian-founded St Stephen College of the University of Delhi, did a master's at the Muslim-founded Jamia Millia Islamia Mass Communication Research Centre, then took a master's degree at Columbia University's Graduate School of Journalism in New York.

Thapar, who worked at London Weekend TV's current affairs division (under the then current affairs director, John Birt, later director general of the BBC), returned to India, where he quickly became known for a forensic-aggressive style of interviewing. His style varies with the attitude of the interviewee; he did a 1999 pre-election interview on his series *Hardtalk India* with Manmohan Singh, the former finance minister, then being urged by the Congress Party to enter the Lok Sabha (Lower House) in order to be able to be appointed as prime minister, which was a dignified, restrained affair. A 2007 *Hardtalk* with Narendra Modi, then chief minister of Gujarat, in which he insistently asked Modi about the murderous riots in 2002, saw the chief minister ask for water, unclip his microphone from his shirt and say, disjointedly: 'The friendship should continue. You came here. I am happy and thankful to you. These are your ideas, you go on expressing these. I can't do this interview. Three-four questions I have already enjoyed. No more please.' He then walked out.

A more fractious interview in 2001 with Jayalalitha, three times chief minister of the state of Tamil Nadu, saw the former popular film actor become increasingly angered by Thapar's constant references to press criticism that she was 'vengeful' and 'irresponsible'. As it concluded, she snapped that she was 'Sorry I agreed to this interview'. Thapar said: 'You're a very tough woman, Chief Minister', to which she replied: 'People like you have made me so.' The politician, whose last term of office ended in September 2014, was convicted of holding assets disproportionate with her income and sentenced to four years in jail; the sentence was suspended while she was out on bail, claiming to be unwell. She was cleared by the courts in 2015, and re-elected chief minister. Her death in December 2016 was attended by scenes of mass grief.

Thapar was himself interviewed, aggressively, by the media commentator Madhu Trehan, who pressed him on his 'Pakistani sympathies', which had been alleged in press commentary about him. He responded more urbanely than Jayalalitha, but also appeared to believe that the questioning was an illegitimate line of enquiry, repeating several times that the interviewer had charged him with being a 'Pakistani spy', which she had not quite, though she did put to him that 'a politician who should know what he's talking about' had told her that Thapar had 'handlers' in Pakistan, who dictated the lines of his alleged pro-Pakistani bias.

Rajdeep Sardesai has the least aggressive (which doesn't mean soft) TV style of the leading male presenters. He spent some years on his return from the UK as a newspaper reporter – which usually dictates a more workaday deportment than TV reporting – then joined the Roys on NDTV as political editor. In a 2014 book on that year's election, Sardesai described Goswami's style as 'disturbingly chaotic and sensationalist'.[23] In an interview he did with Modi, as he toured the country to judge the depth of support for him should he decide to run for prime minister, Sardesai was told he must interview the Gujarat chief minister in a van he used for his tour. Modi sat in the passenger seat, forcing the TV journalist and his cameraman into cramped, contorted positions – 'a characteristically perverse way of reminding me of my station in life as a humble journalist interviewing a supreme leader'. He put the question on the 2002 riots and Modi 'turned away rudely from the camera', replying to a further question on whether he would move to Delhi in the future with: 'Did the people of this country assign you and the media the task of finding the next Prime Minister?'

Sardesai had, in his memoir, described Rahul Gandhi, the inheritor of the family mantle and its candidate for the premiership, as 'ensconced in a feudal political structure'. Summoned to meet him, Sardesai took a 3 a.m. plane back from Mumbai to reach Rahul's office/residence for the appointed hour of 8 a.m. in the expectation of an exclusive interview, only to find a number of fellow journalists there, jostling to get in their questions. Sardesai asked if, given that Gandhi was a family prince destined to rule, Manmohan Singh's premiership had not been merely a holding operation until Rahul took his place. Rahul flared up: 'I resent that, Mr Sardesai! The Prime Minister is doing a fine job and the question only belittles Dr Singh in a manner that I find unacceptable.' The meeting over, Sardesai, with his colleagues, was working out what to lead on, when they were told, 'Sorry, this is off the record, I don't want any controversy in the middle of an election.'

His narrative illuminates two contrasting arrogances: that of the long-ruling house of Nehru–Gandhi and that of the successful, lower-caste upstart Modi, who spent the first part of his political life in the disciplined, monkish Rashtriya Swayamsevak Sangh (RSS), the Hindu nationalist movement whose electoral expression is the Bharatiya Janata Party (BJP). His rise to the post of chief minister in Gujarat was achieved through hard work and pro-Hindu populism, with a contempt for the Delhi, Congress-dominated establishment, including the news media.

The top English-language news presenters, from Prannoy Roy on, claim fidelity to a journalism that holds power to account, the universal claim of journalism; but they meet politicians and other public figures rarely educated abroad, still unaccustomed to journalists asserting their right to question them insistently on policies and probe their past records. For Modi and Jayalalitha, insistent questioning is not a prompt – as it has for decades been for Western politicians – to find a strategy of countering the negative construction put to them by interviewers. It is simply an intolerable impudence.

Arnab Goswami, a colleague of Sardesai's on NDTV at its beginnings, goes beyond impudence to outrage. His closest parallels are figures like Rush Limbaugh, the right-wing radio host in the US, or Beppe Grillo, the blogger-cum-party leader in Italy. Like them, he places himself as a tribune of the people, a people grievously abused by the political class, who require someone with the countervailing power of the media to identify and shame the guilty or negligent people in power. Where Sardesai assumes a reportorial right, where Thapar quotes the press or some other authority's criticisms in order to confront his subjects, Goswami assumes a nation at his back and thunders: 'The Indian People want to know!'

The channel Times Now was formed around him in 2006; he was appointed the main presenter, and the chief editor. It's a subsidiary of the media company Bennett Coleman, an imperial-era company created in 1892 by Thomas Jewell Bennett and Frank Morris Coleman around several English-language newspapers whose foundations went back to the late 1830s, and which included the already prestigious *Times of India*, itself created in 1861 from an amalgamation of two Bombay (now Mumbai) business papers. It's the largest Indian corporation focused almost entirely on media of various kinds, from the *Times* to the Indian edition of *Top Gear*.

I met Goswami in Mumbai in 2012. It was, he said, a rare interview, and though he was amiability itself, he took a Rahul Gandhi view of its results, saying at the end that it was off the record. Two years later, he gave a seminar at one of his alma maters – St Antony's in Oxford – and was more forthcoming (though he forbade the organizers, Free Speech Debate, from putting a recording of it on its website): 'The journalism I do is criticized for its form but not its content. People say I shout too much: but it is transformational.'

Transformational, he claimed, because it provokes; it enforces 'punishing' levels of accountability; it breaks down the barriers of elitism; it encourages debate; makes the bureaucrats uncomfortable.

> The political bureaucratic class tries to suppress, or co-opt, the media. But [my style] has huge support. Even the kids and the women in the villages all watch me. They believe we represent a strong force of change through journalism. I'm correcting the wrongs of the last decade.
>
> The news media grew in the last quarter century – but we lost our bite, because co-opted. Between 1989 and 2010 no major case of corruption was reported. Tarun Tejpal [the former editor of *Tehelka* magazine], wanted money to start a journalists' club in Delhi, and coins were thrown at him.[24] Journalists became astonishingly wealthy; bureaucrats became wealthy. They lived in elite areas and went to each other's house to drink the finest wines.

Goswami listed a series of scams that had been revealed, many by Times Now; these included, he said, a massive scam in the allocation of 2G licences to mobile phone operators, in which the allotment of the licences was squashed. The communications minister, A. Raja, was charged with receiving a bribe worth over 400 million dollars and jailed; the former UN official Shashi Tharoor resigned from his post as Indian minister of state for external affairs in 2010 in connection with an alleged cricketing malfeasance – though no charges had been brought against him. In 2010, a scam connected with the financing of the Commonwealth Games, which saw the imprisonment of the head of the Games' organizing committee, Suresh Kalmadi, was uncovered. The most serious, a huge network of alleged corruption in the allocation, in the first place, of coal mining licences in 2007–9, had the Central Bureau of Investigation turn up evidence of so many unauthorized mines that, in 2014, the Supreme Court cancelled 214 of 218 coal blocks allocated since 1993.

A guest at Media Fest, an annual media gathering developed by the Briatoshs Trust, in March 2014, Goswami invoked his generation as 'the first post-reform generation. Corruption is a very big issue – so deep – if the media in the national capital of India is too scared to take on the powerful people then they should close down. We have the media, *we have the power* [my italics]. Why are they scared? I am not scared.' [25]

Goswami will at times take the position of one seeking the simple truth, but on one subject above all he admits a strong opinion. He is unremittingly hostile to Pakistan, and to any discussion of its claims on the disputed area of Kashmir – the northern state mostly within India but with a Muslim majority agitating for union with neighbouring Pakistan. In the Media Fest discussion, when his hostility was put to him, he replied: 'I believe we should be proud of what the army does in Kashmir. And I don't think it's fashionable to be a secessionist.' A September 2014 interview with Qamar Zeman Kaira, the spokesman for the ruling People's Party (in Islamabad), was a Goswami shouting match, with Kaira, intolerant of harsh, mocking questions, ripping off his microphone and disappearing from the screen.

Though increasingly a ranter, he still possesses a keen media intelligence and is unfazed by the grandeur of his interviewees. His 2014 pre-election interview with Rahul Gandhi became instantly famous, showing him at his best – and Gandhi at his worst. The interview makes painful watching.[26] Goswami immediately asserted his authority over the form the talk would take: 'Let's be as specific as possible on the subjects we deal with today. Do I have your agreement on that?' Gandhi, hesitant from the get-go, said, 'Yeah, we'll be specific, but, em, if I would like ... if I would like to sort of explain things in a bit ... in a broader fashion that would be okay with ... [trails off].'

As the interview unfolds, it's clear that Gandhi has decided to talk about certain issues in a certain manner, no matter what the questions from Goswami are. Pointing up the fact that Gandhi has not declared that he wishes to be prime minister, Goswami then puts to him that he 'is avoiding a direct one-to-one contest with Narendra Modi. Rahul, you must answer that now.' Gandhi: 'To understand that you must understand a little bit about what Rahul Gandhi is and what Rahul Gandhi's circumstances have been ... the real question is, what am I doing here?'

Unable to direct the interview into the channels in which he wishes it to run, Gandhi tries to turn the tables on Goswami, asking him why he decided to become a journalist: Goswami gratefully received the gift, saying that 'once I decided to become a journalist, you cannot be half a journalist ... once you've decided to get into politics and you are effectively leading your party you cannot be leading your party by half'. The question back with Gandhi, the Congress man continued the practice of referring to himself in the third person, saying that to answer the question, Goswami (and his viewers) must understand 'what ... how... Rahul Gandhi thinks'. He went back to his childhood, when he saw his father (as prime minister) 'in constant, constant combat with the system ... in India ... I saw my father die ... I saw my grandmother die.' He was asking for pity.

Goswami did not extend it. While Rahul Gandhi tried to explain what Rahul Gandhi wished to do, Goswami kept bringing him back to Modi's challenge. Goswami: 'Do you hold Modi responsible for the [2002] Gujarat riots?' Gandhi: 'That women should be empowered ... of course there is your question about the Gujarat riots and it is very important to the women in this country, giving them true power.'

The Ghandi strategy, such as it was, had reduced him to talking nonsense. The comparison with Modi – which was unavoidable – was excruciating. And Congress kept digging more deeply the hole in which it found itself. A week before the Gandhi–Goswami interview, Mani Shankar Aiyar, a former Cabinet minister, graduate of both The Doon School and Cambridge University and one notorious for his open contempt for those less elevated and educated than he, had told the annual Congress Party meeting: 'Modi will never be Prime Minister but if he wants to distribute tea here, we will find a place for him.'[27]

After the Aiyar jibe, Modi got the media to cover talks his team arranged with tea sellers on his campaign travels. He told a rally: 'See their mentality. They do not like it if a *chai wallah* [tea seller], a son of a poor mother, walks with his head held high ... The Congress has insulted the poor, mocked my origins as a tea seller.'[28] Congress, the bearer of Indian independence, the secular party promising equality for all, had revealed itself as a nest of snobs with a stumbling, self-pitying leader. Goswami's interview was a necessary revelation, in which Gandhi had been given plenty of space ... to destroy himself.

Barkha Dutt is the most prominent woman on English-language TV, constantly attended by controversy. Covering the Kargil clash between Indian and Pakistani forces in Kashmir, she reported that she had seen the severed head of a Pakistani soldier nailed to a tree – while the Indian colonel who had drawn her attention to it 'exchanged a look of shared achievement' with his men, a charge he later denied.[29]

Three years later, Dutt was in Gujarat, where Modi was first minister, covering the riots of 2002. Modi, in a TV interview, said that Dutt incited further violence by 'irresponsible' reporting, blaming her – as did others – for naming the religion of the attackers and the victims, in contravention of guidelines which prohibited such identification. Dutt, in a piece in Outlook magazine, argued: 'Gujarat was not a communal riot ... naming the community ... was the story, revealing as it did a prejudiced administrative and political system [Modi's] that was happy to just stand by and watch. Isn't it a journalist's job then to tell the story?'[30] Dutt's reporting was one large reason why the charge of Modi's involvement in the riots, in which Muslims were disproportionately the victims, was widely believed.

In 2008, Dutt was accused in the media of gross irresponsibility in her reporting of the raids, murders and hostage-taking at the Oberoi Hotel in Mumbai by Pakistani members of the terrorist group Lashkar-e-Taiba, as she gave away the fact that people were hiding in the hotel, when the army had denied it. She later said she had been told that TV reception in the hotel had been cut off.

The one scandal that appears to have hurt her is the 'Radia Tapes' controversy, in which a public relations consultant, Nira Radia – born in Kenya, educated in the UK and married to a British–Asian businessman – was taped by the Central Bureau of Investigation trying to broker deals around the sale of the 2G spectrum, deals later found to be illegal. Radia brought Dutt and the editorial adviser on the Hindustan Times, Vir Sanghvi, into the network, seeking their help in getting the main actors in the developing story to talk to each other – and by implication, assist in her effort to bring the matter to a conclusion beneficial to her clients. Transcripts of the tapes were published by a new magazine, Open, in November 2010. Dutt asked for and got a show on NDTV to help clear her name, which descended into the familiar cacophony as the five guests and Dutt all spoke at once, shedding no light on the issue.[31]

She did, however, get a small revenge on Goswami. His anger at what he saw as biased, pro-Pakistani reporting in Kashmir in July 2016 boiled over: 'Bring them to trial!' he shouted in one of his broadcasts. 'I don't care if some of these people are from the media.' The reporting, Dutt's included, had highlighted the partial or permanent blinding of young Kashmiris protesting the Indian 'occupation', against whom the police used pellet guns. Dutt claimed the privilege of the on-site reporter in contrast to Goswami, declaiming from 'the lazy comfort of a Mumbai studio table'. In a display of righteous rage to match Goswami's, Dutt concluded that 'one of the leading names of Indian media believes in censorship, wants to gag free expression, kill nuance, distort the truth and send journalists to jail'.[32]

India, more obviously than most other democracies, has a deep well of chauvinism – amounting at times to contempt for, or hatred of, women. Dutt, like most women in public life, gets screeds of such stuff. The practice of working out rape and violence fantasies on the Net isn't, of course, confined to India, but the real thing is also more common. In May 2014, the violent rape and murder in December 2012 in Delhi of a young student by a gang of men on a bus sparked large demonstrations; harsher punishments for the crime were adopted and vows made by politicians that the culture would change. A few months later, the then chief minister of Uttar Pradesh, Akhilesh Yadav, faced with questioning about another rape in his region, turned on the journalists – many of them women – and asked: 'What's it to you? You're safe.' It was a statement of deep cynicism, alarming in the top politician of India's most populous state.

Sagarika Ghose, married to Sardesai and a co-presenter on CNN-IBN, is as well connected and educated as her husband: her father was director general of Doordarshan, she won a Rhodes Scholarship in 1987, was educated at St Stephen's College in Delhi, then Magdalen College and St Antony's College, both in Oxford. No more prone to modesty than Goswami, she commented that 'Most of my critics, I have to say, are talentless elderly ladies who are probably furious that a woman who is attractive is also intelligent and also has a husband and two kids. Bit too much for them to handle, I guess.'[34] She, too, receives filthy abuse;

she, too, is seen as unpatriotic; and she, too, strives every day to remain at or near the top of the Indian news media tree, a position at once highly privileged, highly rewarded and highly contested.

In 2014, a new channel was launched: India Today TV, a product of the India Today group, which has specialized in newspapers and magazines. It challenged the noisier channels with a more analytical style. Rajdeep Sardesai and Karan Thapar were hired as the main presenters: Sardesai does the big news shows, Thapar an interview programme every weekday evening called *To the Point*, which is billed as getting under the surface of the main news 'with facts that have been ignored'. Though high pressure and insistent in their questioning, both avoid verbal scraps; in one show in January 2016, Sardesai was linked up with the Dawn network in Pakistan and an animated but relatively courteous debate on terrorism was staged, with several spokespeople from both sides taking part – a strong contrast with Goswami's mocking of his Pakistani guests. India Today won the first prize for its English-language news programmes at the 2015 Exchange4Media News Broadcasting Awards, only a year after its launch; a double night of triumph for the group, since its fifteen-year-old Hindi news channel, Aaj Tak – which takes the high ethical ground in news – also won in the Hindi section.

The kickback against confrontational news and current affairs includes the state broadcaster Doordarshan, which claims a larger audience in Hindi and English than the private channels. According to a senior executive, K. G. Suresh, 'People are now keen to watch DD News as it is against sensationalism, loud debates et al.'[35] The tabloid style, in India as elsewhere, dictates boorishness and distortion; Kunda Dixit, editor of the *Nepali Times*, harshly criticized Indian reporters who descended on Kathmandu Valley in Nepal to report the country's earthquake in the spring of 2015 (the death toll in Nepal was around 9,000; thousands more died in India): 'It was as if the reporters were selected for their archetypal crudeness and rudeness, and ability to be insensitive to survivors. Nepali villagers who had just lost relatives were treated like hard-of-hearing hillbillies who should have been thankful to be on camera.'[36]

But market news is market news. India TV, a Hindi channel founded in 2004 by Rajat Sharma and his wife Ritu Dhawan, claimed the high ground with 'responsible reporting, fresh faces, world-class technology and an international look'. But that was soon tested – to at least temporary destruction.

In July 2006, a six-year-old boy named Prince fell into a 60-foot-deep bore well in Haryana, a northern Indian state bordering on Uttar Pradesh, India TV's home state and India's most populous.[37] The day after, the channel's CEO, Chintamani Rao, arrived to learn that while India TV had broadcast a programme about a terrorist who had given the Indian police the slip, their rival channels had kept a vigil at Prince's bore hole – and everyone in the office had watched it. Rao realized the story was compelling (it also closely paralleled the plot of the 1951 Billy Wilder film *Ace in the Hole*, where a ruthless reporter lies to keep a miner trapped underground while he secures exclusive rights to the story; the miner dies): 'I said, "Shit! Guys, maybe we are missing something."' India TV dispatched its own team to cover the bore well rescue, even though Rao knew 'everybody [else] was already showing it'. But it was catch-up time, and Zee News, which had sat solidly outside the bore well from the beginning till Prince was saved on the fourth day of his accident, took 40 per cent of news viewership ratings, with India TV in single figures.

The ratings are the sun and moon in India. 'Broadcasters try to shape their programming to deliver the highest ratings; advertisers, in turn, wield considerable influence over the sorts of shows that broadcasters produce … ultimately, then, the ratings system influences the television content seen by approximately 666 million people in India's television-owning homes.'[38] Corruption is reported as pervasive, with bribery reaching down to the families that have the metering machines installed – they agree for a fee to keep their TV tuned to a given channel, while they watch their channel(s) of choice on another TV which has been donated by those paying them.

Insofar as there can be any proof of journalists' benign effect on Indian corruption, it's mixed. India is still ranked as a fairly corrupt state by Transparency International: its 2015 score, at 38 on a 1 (very clean) to 100 (very corrupt) scale, was the same as 2014, better than the two previous years by two points, and put it on a par with Brazil, Burkina Faso, Peru, Thailand, Tunisia and Zambia – all within the top half of 175 countries surveyed. However, a survey by Ernst & Young India, using responses from forty-five leaders of the media and entertainment industry, reported that 56 per cent of the respondents said that the incidence of fraud had increased over the previous two years; 83 per cent said that the central concern is the scale of the kickbacks paid for approval of rights and permissions; 70 per cent pinpointed false invoicing and over-billing by third parties; and 52 per cent believed the loss to profits to be 5–25 per cent, with 2 per cent thinking the losses were higher. Most of the companies did little to train their staff in anti-corruption practices. The Ernst & Young team concluded that their evidence 'clearly indicates that entities have been struggling with an upsurge in fraud and corruption'.[39]

The corruption cases also seem to be getting bigger. The awarding of telecom licences to companies in 2008, most of which were cancelled by the Supreme Court in 2012 – the fraud which stimulated the 'Radiagate' scandal – was estimated by the Central Bureau of Investigation to have cost the exchequer 4.6 billion dollars in lost revenue: *Time* listed it as the second most egregious scam after Watergate.[40] A cable which was part of the WikiLeaks mass leaking of US embassy cables revealed that a US diplomat had reported that an aide to the ruling Congress Party had shown 'chests of cash' aimed at bribing MPs to support a controversial agreement between India and the US which would expand the former's nuclear capacity. In March 2010, the anti-corruption head, P. J. Thomas, was forced to resign because of allegations of corruption against him, which he termed baseless. In 2010 the chief minister of Maharashtra, Ashok Chavan, was forced to resign after it became known that flats in Mumbai, destined for widows of soldiers killed in the fighting in Kashmir, had been purloined by army officers and politicians' relatives. The 2010 Commonwealth Games in Delhi, estimated to cost 270 million dollars when first proposed, ended with a bill of 4.1 billion dollars, and a report on the contracts for the Games by the state auditor alleged favouritism and corruption.

Indian governments have devolved much power to states, in some of which corruption has been the rule. Incoming chief ministers, who often feature in the scandals, have in some cases seen the post as one for self-enrichment. Transparency International's cleanest nations[41] – headed by the Scandinavians – are relatively small: the relatively large countries, if in the top ten, start around number 9 or 10, and are usually Canada or Germany.

The claim – common to journalists everywhere – that their trade 'keeps the villains honest' probably has some truth. The less corrupt countries in the world generally have the freest news media, and fear of exposure is a clear disincentive to fraud. But it's not obviously so in India. Corruption was high in India under British imperial rule to 1946, when for much of the period the press was at least partially controlled and sometimes heavily censored. After independence, it has probably got higher. A 2010 report by Global Financial Integrity revealed that the proceeds of crime and corruption more than doubled, to 462 billion dollars.[42]

Journalism was largely docile in the first three to four decades of that period; it became much more aggressive from the 1990s, and especially in the 2000s, when the scope of corruption, including in the media, broadened considerably.

Western journalism, to differing degrees of conviction, draws on a consensus that both politics and journalism should be robust, independent in judgement and fearless in revelation of what is deplorable and true. That view of the mission of politics and journalism isn't absent in India; a new and sporadically successful party, the Aam Aadmi (Common Man) party, was founded explicitly to counter corruption,[43] and most media trumpet their opposition to corruption. But its concern is shallower; and the owners/controllers of India's news media place it, in many cases, quite low in their hierarchy of concerns. All the main actors in journalism contribute to the shakiness of its base, but the crucial part is played by the owners.

In October 2012, Ken Auletta of the *New Yorker* interviewed Vineet Jain, the managing director of Bennet, Coleman & Company Limited (BCCL) – his brother Samir is the vice-chairman (their mother is chairman), but doesn't give interviews.[44] He told Auletta that the Jains have a greater interest in the money-making capacities of BCCL than in its journalism. Auletta observed that 'rather than worry about editorial independence, and the wall between the newsroom and the sales department, [the Jain brothers] propose that one secret to a thriving newspaper business lies in dismantling that wall'.

BCCL is the biggest Indian-owned media house in India; the flagship *Times of India* is the largest English-language broadsheet in the world by circulation (3.3 million daily); the company also publishes the *Economic Times*; a series of big city papers; the largest car magazine, *ZigWheels*; the largest personal finance magazine, *ET Wealth*; it has interests in film, in radio, in outdoor advertising, in TV (including Times Now, Goswami's channel), and more. Its revenues, by world media company standards, are small: between 1.5 and 2 billion dollars. But the return is very large: 25–30 per cent.

'We are not', Vineet Jain told Auletta, 'in the newspaper business, we are in the advertising business ... if ninety per cent of your revenues come from advertising, you're in the advertising business.' Further, the Jain brothers are keen that material which might promote products or personalities – such as stories on Bollywood films and stars – should be paid for. Thus stories on film releases or on film and TV stars are advertorial – so announced, but in type so small that, according to Auletta, 'a reader needs a magnifying glass to be alerted'.

The philosophy, that the newspaper is a market, not a public interest commodity, permeates the senior staff. Rahul Jansal, the executive president and 'brand chief', said that 'editors tended to be pompous fellows thundering from the pulpit, speaking in eighty-word sentences. They saw themselves as part of nation building, as part of a big dialogue. It did not connect too well with younger Indians.' As a succinct account of an age of journalism which has left the post-independence newspapers, with their Nehruvian commitment to promoting a social-democratic and secular polity in the dustbin of boring history, it's hard to beat.

The *Times* pioneered what became known as 'page-three culture', a page of (often paid for) stories on stars, shows and scandals. In 2012, *The Hindu*, based in Chennai, India's third city, attacked the *Times* in a TV and print campaign, as the older paper started a Chennai edition. The slogan common to all the ads was 'Stay ahead of The Times' – mocking the dumbing-down of the news by the *Times* with lines such as 'Because government malfunctions matter more than wardrobe malfunctions' and 'Read about political parties, not Page 3 parties'. The video commercials, each lasting a minute, showed a group of young people unable to answer a set of simple questions about Indian politics, business, sport and mythology, but reeling off the correct answers to questions about film stars. They are asked: 'Which newspaper do you read?' The answers are bleeped out, but aren't hard to decipher.[45]

English-language papers have dominated economically, and still do – but less decisively so. In her periodic review of the media business, Vanita Kohli-Khandekar notes that, till 2005, the English papers got 60 per cent of all print advertising, with Hindi and other Indian-language papers getting 40 per cent.[46] By 2013, that had been reversed. Ad rates still strongly favour the English over the other languages; space is about five times more expensive in the former. But it was, Kohli-Khandekar writes, ten to twelve times greater only seven years before. This trend is likely to last; the Hindi-only (or -largely) speaking middle class is growing strongly, and they are likely to be slower in transferring much of their reading time to online publications than the English speakers.

Though Indian journalism, in its pell-mell rush for market success, is in an ethical mess, it has many antibodies, especially among the younger journalists, who don't like what they see and read and, above all, the atmosphere in which they have to work. I came to know several who were fellows at the Reuters Institute in Oxford, all scathing about the ethics of their business. One, Anuradha Sharma, with a background in newspaper reporting, brought a particularly sharp gaze to newspaper practices and wrote of them in an essay.[47] It was unillusioned in its rehearsal of the victories which the business of journalism had scored over its practice: 'the main concern is not the fact that there has been growth in public relations and advertising, but that these are being passed off as journalism'.

Sharma gave an instance of how the journalism–corporate corruption works:

In an upmarket coffee shop in New Delhi in the autumn of 2012, two senior journalists from the Zee News TV channel were in conversation with executives of the Jindal corporation. While the journalists were fixed on the figure of Rs 100 crore [almost eleven million pounds], the company executives were insisting it was a massive amount and wondering how the figure rose from an earlier quotation of Rs 20 crore. 'If you forge a relationship with us, I'll see what best I can do,' one of the journalists promised in the end.

The meeting was part of a sting operation. Hidden cameras were filming the deal as it happened ... organized not by a news channel, as one would expect, but by the steel company to expose the 'blackmailing and extortionist tactics of Zee News'. On November 27 2012, Zee's Group Editor Sudhir Chaudhary and Business Head Samir Ahluwalia were arrested by Delhi police on charges of trying to extort a Rs 100 crore advertising deal in exchange for favourable news coverage.[48]

Some companies – such as the Tata conglomerate – are now internationally powerful, and said to be relatively clean. Others, large and small, are locked into a series of relationships and mutual dependencies with the state, which in many cases are corrupt. The FT reporter James Crabtree put it this way:

Before liberalization, corruption was a small-bore affair. But as the country opened up to globalization … a new generation of billionaire industrialists … prospered. The end result has been the creation in India of a small but powerful class of near-oligarchs … India probably now has a higher proportion of national wealth in the hands of its billionaire class than any other major emerging economy, with the exception of Russia.[49]

The figure within journalism who, on the national level, has pitted himself most powerfully against corrupt media practices is Paranjoy Guha Thakurta, a veteran of the Delhi press whose sins spur him to daily action, carried on from a spartan office in a down-at-heel mall in Delhi. Thakurta organized a 'Crony Journalism' conference in Delhi in September 2012, an event which saw an extraordinary – to me – procession of media figures, with a senior politician, one of the country's most prominent public relations chiefs and others agreeing with apparent equanimity that, in the words of R. K. Arun, the opinion-page editor of the *Economic Times*, 'Indian journalism is funded almost completely from the proceeds of corruption [and] the media cannot do anything to change this.' Rajeev Shukla, the minister of state for parliamentary affairs in the then Congress government, said that 'journalists now advise business people to get TV channels – that way you will get permission for real estate development. All levels of society are influenced by TV now: judges, politicians, business.' Dilip Cherian, head of the Good Relations PR company and one of the country's top PR advisers, said that politics is corrupt 'and as long as that prevails it influences everything else. The question is: are we as a people like this? Or are all people like this?' Pradeep Magazine, a sports writer, testified to how much coverage was determined by the finance and advertisements departments: 'the pressure to write more about sports came from the finance and ad departments. The editor's role shrank. And the media started generating business from sports journalism.'

In an investigation published in December 2009, *Outlook* magazine discovered a number of important politicians willing to admit that they paid for favourable coverage.[50] These included Haryana Chief Minister Bhupinder Singh Hooda, who said:

> when I noticed the leading paper of my state printing baseless reports on its front page day after day, I called them up and offered money to print the right picture. The paper in question apologized. They even returned the money taken from my rival to publish news items against me ... fact-finding journalism has now become a commercialized activity with the present owners having turned newspapers into a business proposition.

In 2009, Thakurta persuaded the Press Council to appoint him and a colleague, Kalimekolan Sreenivas Reddy, to a subcommittee tasked with producing a report on paid news. In their introduction to the report, Thakurta and Reddy wrote:

> In recent years, corruption in the Indian media has gone way beyond the corruption of individual journalists and specific media organizations – from 'planting' information and views in lieu of favours received in cash

or kind, to more institutionalized and organized forms of corruption wherein newspapers and television channels receive funds for publishing or broadcasting information in favour of particular individuals, corporate entities, representatives of political parties and candidates contesting elections, that is sought to be disguised as 'news'.[51]

It took Thakurta some months to force the Council to publish the report in full, though it finally did.

Much of the vibrancy of the Indian news media scene is in the quantity of publications, channels and, coming along, websites and blogs. The stories about entrepreneurs starting TV channels – usually state-wide only – to further their businesses are well attested, and these channels, which come and go, are usually run by relatively small companies. Still the fact is that TV is consolidating, and the digitization of the sector will hasten the trend; by the mid 2010s, five groups – Star, Sony, Zee, Sun and Network 18 – served 65 per cent of the audience, and Kohli-Khandekar argued in 2014 that 'the Indian TV market is set to emerge from the profit-squeezing, structural chaos that has dominated its existence so far'. Zee (Hindi), Sun (Tamil) and Network 18 (English) all have news stations, of which Network 18 was reckoned to be the most influential. In 2014, Network 18 was taken over by Mukesh Ambani's Reliance Industries (RIL), India's largest company; the takeover illuminated many of the issues at stake in the country's TV journalism.

India's richest man, Mukesh Ambani, had decreed that a stately twenty-seven-storey residence be built for him on the tony Altamount Road (officially S. K. Barodawalla Marg) in Mumbai, among the homes of Bollywood stars, wealthy countries' consulates and other rich business people. It was named, by Ambani, Antilla, after a mythical Atlantic Island to the west of Spain and Portugal, supposedly occupied by priests fleeing from the Muslim invasion in the eighth century (did Ambani's choice of a name have some religious subtext?). Looking up at the curious building, the floors overhanging each other as in a Lego construction, it seemed more an expression of power than of family refuge.

The 2014 purchase by Ambani's Reliance Industries Limited of Network 18 gave the company full control of a network in which it had invested heavily some years before, when the media group's then owner, Raghav Bahl, sought funds to tide the network over a bad patch after the 2008 downturn; Bahl then had assured everyone that Ambani had no interest in news media, that it was just an investment. But wittingly or unwittingly (opinions differ), he was wrong. Ambani did, or came to, want the network for himself. RIL, with 4G services which it was launching through its Jio Infocomm subsidiary set to roll out in 700 cities in 2015, needed 'content', and Network 18 had lots of it.

Ambani sees news 'content' in a much more utilitarian way than even the Jains of Bennett Coleman do; he sees his news media as guardians of his company's and his family's reputation. The journalism he has bought in Network 18 is 'his' journalism, not a product whose prime responsibility is to develop any sense of journalistic mission to discover the truth (though that may be a by-product); or anything other than another production centre slotted into his vast conglomerate of industries, as the floors of Antilla appear slotted one on top of the other.

Mukesh Ambani was brought into the business by his father, Dirubhai, who began in 1958, a year after his first son's birth, as a small trader in spices; until the late sixties, the family were lower middle class, living in a two-bedroom apartment. As Mukesh grew so did Reliance; sent to Stanford on a business course, the older son was brought back by Dirubhai after one year and put to work supervising the building of a yarn factory where he revealed his style – a close attention to detail.

In a *New York Times* profile in 2008, Anand Giridharadas writes that Dirubhai came from a generation which had been schooled in the ways of building capitalism in the midst of socialism – and thus, like the oligarchs of Russia, unable to assume a stable business environment, grabbed at opportunities as they presented themselves. Politicians who had administered the 'licence Raj' had their minds changed by Reliance's success: Arun Shourie, a former newspaper editor as well as a former Cabinet minister, acknowledged a year after the elder Mr Ambani's death that he had made a '180-degree turn' in his view of the company. 'They set up world-class companies and facilities in spite of those regulations,' he said in a speech in 2003. 'By exceeding the limits and restrictions, they created the case for scrapping those regulations. They made a case for reforms.'[52]

Giridharadas wrote that 'a prominent Indian editor, formerly of the *Times of India*, who requested anonymity because of concerns about upsetting Mr Ambani, says Reliance maintains good relationships with newspaper owners; editors, in turn, fear investigating it too closely. "I don't think anyone else comes close to it," the editor said of Reliance's sway.'[53] That has appeared to be the RIL attitude: a series of its interventions into the media point to a company whose boss is both touchy about any mention of his family and ambitious to take into the behemoth which is RIL a production house whose content he approves.

Though he distrusted and scorned the media, Ambani was drawn to it. When Raghav Bahl invited Ambani to invest in CNN-IBN, he put in an investment in January 2012 which totalled 400 billion rupees (640 million dollars), large enough so that, with later investments, it effectively owned Network 18, with Bahl as a minority shareholder – though it did not exercise owners' rights. In May 2014, RIL formally completed the takeover of Network 18, prompting the departure of Bahl and most of the top executives, including Sardesai. RIL thereby took control of one of the largest media organizations in India, with CNBC TV18, CNN-IBN, CNBC Awaaz; websites Moneycontrol.com and firstpost.com; print magazines *Forbes India* and *Overdrive*; the highly popular general entertainment channel Colors and Homeshop18, a television and Internet retail venture, the ETV family of some seventeen channels in various languages – among various other media and non-media businesses.

Bahl, one of the most daring of media entrepreneurs in his rapid acquisition of channels and publications, had in 2013 begun to slim down his corporation with hundreds of layoffs – and to push the channel, which had been traditionally pro-Congress and liberal, to the right, towards the resurgent BJP. The Congress government was looking increasingly weak, while Narendra Modi's challenge was looking increasingly strong, and Bahl was conscious that his majority shareholder, Ambani, had a strong interest in seeking Modi's approval. The RIL chairman has never denied lobbying fiercely for projects, and it had become probable that the next government would not be a Congress-dominated one. After the investment, which turned round the fading finances of Network 18, Bahl began meetings with his senior staff; in his meeting with the editor of Forbes, Indrajit Gupta, he asked – according to Gupta – what the editor's position would be on writing stories about RIL. Gupta said Forbes should continue to do stories as before. Bahl asked: 'Do we really need to?'[54]

Raghavan Jagannathan, appointed as chief editor of the group's magazines and websites, reportedly shouted at the journalists that they were 'doing it wrong. Forbes is about the wealthy. It's about right-wing politics. You guys are writing about development and poverty. If you guys don't get it I'm going to make sure you do.'[55] Bahl pushed Sardesai to do more, and more positive, stories about Modi, and came out openly in the Gujarat first minister's support. When the Aam Aadmi (Common Man) party briefly – from the end of December 2013 to February 2014 – ran the Delhi city government, it launched an attack on RIL on the issue of gas pricing; though RIL had not then completed the takeover of Network 18, Sardesai was pressured not to interview the leaders of the party. A report in The Mint claimed that 'They wanted a complete blackout of Kejriwal and AAP.'[56]

On the ground, however, the approach changed rapidly. Arijit Sen, the CNN-IBN reporter in the country's north-east, was told to do a package before the 2014 elections that was a 'vox pop' (interviews with people in the street) in which he was directed to ask questions about how much they wished to get rich, and what Modi's policies should be to allow them to do so. Sen resigned soon after, did a postgraduate degree in London and joined an international NGO.

When Sardesai resigned, he wrote in a goodbye note to his colleagues:

> editorial independence and integrity have been articles of faith in twenty-six years in journalism and maybe I am too old now to change! ... Putting news above noise, sense above sensation and credibility above chaos must remain a credo forever: else journalism will lose its moral compass. I hope the new management will always put journalism first and I wish them well.[57]

The most prominent critics were less inhibited. Sainath was regretful: 'Once upon a time the media took its role to question people in power very seriously. Media was the adversary. It would take on those in positions of power, whether in government or the corporate sector. Time alone will tell how that adversarial role will exist under these sort of corporate deals.'[58] Thakurta didn't think time was needed to tell: 'If India's biggest corporate conglomerate is also India's biggest media company ... It does raise concerns and questions about what happens to the voices of not just those who are contrary to RIL, but the marginalized.'[59]

Sardesai was not alone in moving on. In January 2017, Barka Dutt announced she would leave NDTV to 'explore new opportunities'. It was perhaps a wise move: the channel had been surreptitiously taken over by Reliance through large loans granted by Ambani to keep it afloat as its finances degenerated.[60] Her resignation followed a much bigger splash: two months previously, Goswami had announced his resignation from Times Now.[61] In his case, it followed an apparently well-sourced report that he had differed with managing director Vineet Jain over Pakistan – the businessman taking a markedly softer line than the presenter – as well as a demand by Goswami for 'an ownership position', deemed by the Jains as 'untenable and unjustified'. He soon announced he would start a news channel to be called 'Republic TV': rumours circulated that Rupert Murdoch might bankroll it.

Journalism always comes down to who pays the piper, and what the piper is paying for. The business people and politicians who control, in one form or another, news outlets want support for their political or commercial ambitions; the journalism is shaped to serve these ambitions. How RIL structures its 2014 acquisition of Network 18 will fundamentally influence – to use Kohli-Khandekar's phrase – the 'mood and shape of Indian news TV',[62] and thus the way in which both Indians and foreigners see the country, the way in which the people see the elite and the elite the people, and the hierarchy of priorities with which the politicians at every level have to deal.

The fears of journalists and campaigners that the corporatization of India's media could be increasingly inimical to diversity of speech and opinion, and thus to democracy itself, has passed from liberal columns and panel discussions in halls to official India. In August 2014, the Telecom Regulatory Authority of India warned in a paper that the responsibility of the news media to report accurately and truthfully 'the concern of the entire country' may be compromised by the consolidation of ownership: 'There may be thousands of newspapers and hundreds of news channels in the news media market, but if they are all "controlled" by only a handful of entities, then there is insufficient plurality of news and views presented to the people.'[63]

A report in *Caravan* magazine by Krishin Kaushik in January 2016 showed that a handful of companies and individuals – Ambani, Mahendra Nahata, an associate of Ambani's and a board member of his telecoms company, Reliance Jio; and industrialist, Abhey Oswal – have invested heavily in five leading media houses. These are NDTV, News Nation, India TV, News24 and Network 18, which include both English and Hindi language media.

In some cases, the investments have bought majority ownership; in others, large minority shareholdings. The ownership structures are complex, comprising direct loans, loans that can be converted into shares when the investor wishes and direct share ownership. The investments in NDTV, still the channel most looked to for fuller, more balanced news, is so complex that it isn't clear who controls it, but Kaushik writes, it is 'certain that these transactions have resulted in the Roys losing a significant amount of control over their company'.

Two of the ministries which could challenge the centralization of the diverse media companies – Finance and Corporate Affairs – are both headed by one of the most powerful of the BJP's figures, Arun Jaitley, who, until May 2016, had also been minister for information and broadcasting. The trend of the *Caravan* piece pointed to more controlled, government-friendly media – still diverse, but up to a lower point than before.[64]

In the mid 1970s, the British journalist Ian Jack went to write on and live in India; he came as an outsider, son of a working-class Scots family (as many such had come, in imperial times). He saw an India largely recognizable to the nineteenth-century imperial Scots:

> On a train in the seventies ... as likely as not, we would be hauled by a steam locomotive; through the dirty carriage window we would see smoke unrolling over fields that were irrigated, planted and harvested by human labour, with no other assistance outside of a camel or a bullock ... once the last urban street had been left behind, the traveller peered out into an unelectrified gloom alleviated only by oil lamps and cooking fires.[65]

The imperial sahibs, nor their erstwhile subjects, wouldn't recognize much of it now. The gloom would probably be lit by electricity – and lit, too, by a light found all over the world: the flickering white glare of television, drawing the illiterate subsistence farmer and the *Vogue*-reading urban lawyer into the narratives India now weaves for itself.

SIX

'We need a prime minister, not a Trappist monk'

The dominant figure in Italian politics, journalism and television over the two decades from 1994 to 2014 was Silvio Berlusconi, a figure for whom no biography has yet been able to do justice to the amalgam of arrogance, boldness, cynicism, determination, empathy, fantasy, grotesquerie, hope, intuition, jocularity, kindness, lying, malevolence, nobility, opacity, quixotism, romance, self-confidence, trickery, understanding, vindictiveness, wackiness, X-ratedness, youthfulness and zip that he contains. His news media were at once a protection against the many legal cases taken against him and channels of political influence on Italians; his TV channels made large amounts of money.[1]

His media were slanted, sometimes outrageously slanted, in his favour; they included the channels of the public broadcaster, Radiotelevisione Italiana (RAI), when he was prime minister, and his party and allies controlled the committee of politicians which in turn exercised most influence on RAI.

Berlusconi was that rare thing, a businessman who was successful in remaining at the top of politics; he was, however, disastrous for Italy, disguising its steady economic decline with fake forecasts of growth and entertainment. Though he did not know Donald Trump, he was a less bombastic Mediterranean version: promising to bring business expertise to the task of governing, excoriating the liberals, retaining strong links with his businesses, taking pleasure in angering allies like the Germans, making a friend of Vladimir Putin (a friendship which continued to flourish after the Italian lost power). He did not rule by Twitter, like the American, but he had much greater mainstream media power within Italy: three terrestrial channels, a newspaper, the biggest book and magazine publisher, an advertising agency, control of RAI news when prime minister. He projected a much more amiable persona than Trump, but was just as compulsively interesting to the news media, and their audiences. An Italian prime minister has nothing like the leverage on world affairs of an American president: but he established an example of one with a contempt for the established rules of politics and diplomacy.

Paul Ginsborg, a scholar of Italy, underlines the similarities between the two men:

> Once having enriched themselves to a very considerable extent, they then wanted to use that patrimony, part of that wealth, to enter politics ... [An additional motivation for both was] the need to defend themselves through changing the hands of power within democracy and making American democracy and Italian democracy autocratic.[2]

Silvio Berlusconi did not believe in objectivity any more than Donald Trump: but unlike the American, the Italian operated in a culture where most journalists didn't believe in it either. Two of the grandest figures in twentieth-century Italian newspaper journalism thought it was not relevant to the newspapers they created and edited; not just unobtainable, it was dishonest. Indro Montanelli, for decades the most distinguished journalist of the right, left *Corriere della Sera* in 1974 and founded *Il Giornale* as a liberal–conservative daily – later resigning when a new owner, Berlusconi, imposed political demands. He spent much of the rest of his life passionately opposing the new leader of the Italian political right. For him, political engagement was the core meaning of journalism. Eugenio Scalfari on the left prepared his equally audacious launch of La Repubblica in the same vein, dismissing any efforts to be fair, balanced, neutral or objective, scorning 'an illusory political neutrality' in favour of a journalism that was clearly engaged, which had 'explicitly chosen a side'.

Italian journalism in the age of Silvio Berlusconi was not his slave; on most visits to an Italian bookshop since the mid 1990s, you could find a new book on Berlusconi, usually critical, usually written by a journalist. One of the very few daily papers launched anywhere in the 2000s, Il Fatto Quotidiano (The Daily Fact), was founded to oppose him through investigation. There were many exposés, analyses, stories that showed the prime minister in an unfavourable light – as well as the thousands of pieces done by foreign media readily available, sometimes translated into Italian.

Many have been the allegations against him, on bribes paid to a variety of individuals and institutions, and on links with the Sicilian mafia; none has been finally proven in court, though many were timed out before a judgment could be made. What is clear is that he has used politics as an adjunct to business from the beginning of his rise to wealth and power. In doing so, he also spread a new kind of media experience through Italian society – which, under his tutelage, changed from being one that watched TV less than other nations into one that leads the TV viewing pack in Europe. During his period of political dominance, in and out of government, Italian society changed from one with mass popular parties to the left and right with networks of associations, clubs and institutions to one where consumption, television and individual choice was much stronger. Berlusconi was not responsible for that – the decline of parties and political engagement was a European-wide phenomenon – but he helped. And not simply helped. He made the shift from political and communal institutions to individual-family consumption into the central theme of his public pitch.

More than any other figure in Europe whose business included the production of journalism, he created a political–media world in which his interests were protected, while at the same time the TV experience was shifted decisively on to the ground of instant pleasure – in game shows, popular films, soap operas, musical spectaculars and high-impact news.

The sheer vigour of his public performance coupled with his political power, his large wealth and the media he developed meant that the period at the end of the second and the beginning of the third millennia can be called 'Berlusconi's turn'. His power period was the closest coupling between media, business and politics that the democratic world had then seen; a quite shameless display of the power of money and the seduction of television. He was the purest of market players: everything, including politics, was reduced as far as possible to an adjunct to his own business interests. Nearly a quarter of a century after Berlusconi first entered the political arena, another businessman who had used television to become famous, Donald Trump, was elected president of the USA.

The future prime minister's most important early move was to secure the close friendship of the then socialist prime minister, Bettino Craxi (1983–7), from whom he received an emergency decree legalizing his nationwide network of independent TV stations. His entrepreneurial flair worked in politics as it did in business; fearful of a legal challenge to his growing businesses, he decided in the early 1990s to enter politics and run for parliament (all deputies had immunity from prosecution), creating, from nothing, a political party based on, staffed and promoted by the executives of his advertising business, Pubblitalia. It was called Forza Italia, usually translated as 'Go, Italy!' – a phrase normally used at an international football match.

In time it did attract ordinary members, but though a formidable machine was built throughout the country, on the surface it remained a happy personality cult with little conventional party life – best expressed in the anthem, written by a member, whose chorus was: '*Presidente, siamo con te/Meno male che Silvio c'è*' – 'President, we're with you/It's a good thing there's Silvio'. The rallies, the videos, the book, largely of photographs, on Berlusconi's life which was distributed to all Italian households – emphasizing themes such as his love for his mother and how his business acumen was now applied to national problems – were crafted to make of him at once a dynamo and the man in the next apartment.

After the collapse of the Christian Democratic Party and its ally, the Socialist Party in a series of corruption scandals, Forza Italia, political infant of a business corporation, won the 1993 election and catapulted Berlusconi, as its leader, into the premiership – but only for a year, as one of his allies in the coalition he formed pulled out. It was an apprenticeship, from which he learned much, including using his media to promote his campaign, a hugely important prop for the rest of his life at the top. It lost him Montanelli: later, he would also lose the man who built his main TV channel's – Channel Five – news division, Enrico Mentana, for the same reason. These were men who could go some way with him, but who in the end believed that journalism had to preserve a measure of independent, non-proprietorial judgement, or it was a fraud.

Like the tall towers that still stand in some Italian cities, built in medieval times by warring families for their protection should the noble gang round the corner attack, so the media holdings were fortified corporations for making war, as well as for reaping political profits. Berlusconi's tower was much, much bigger than the others: 'every Italian under thirty has grown to political maturity in a country where Berlusconi and his family control half of the TV output, a quarter of the national papers, half of the news magazines and the biggest publishing house [Mondadori]'.[3] The journalist Massimo Giannini called this state of affairs 'not a dictatorship in the classic sense but ... a modern form of post-ideological dictatorship'.[4]

The most powerful carrier of journalism – in Italy as elsewhere – is television, where, until 1978, it was provided by the monopoly supplier of TV channels, RAI. It was deferential, though not entirely subordinate, to the ruling Christian Democratic Party – as much in its steady respectability, closeness to the Vatican and showcasing of high, largely Italian, culture (films, opera, concerts, plays, literary discussion) as in its broad observance of the government line in its news and current affairs output.

When the Constitutional Court ruled that this did not adequately reflect the plurality of political views in the country, RAI reorganized. It did so in a way fatal to neutrality: by giving editorial control to the main parties, who then 'owned' the channels. RAI 1, the original channel – a monopoly from 1954 when transmission began to 1963 and still the most popular – remained under the tutelage of the ruling party, the Christian Democrats. RAI 2, created in 1963, was controlled by the major coalition partner (at that time, usually the Socialists); and in 1978, when the Communists came in from the cold so far as to conclude a historic compromise with the Christian Democrats, they were gifted RAI 3.

The decision was an implicit admission that the political class did not believe in the possibility of a TV journalism that could make a convincing fist of neutrality. The assumption was that political power would always trump any such effort, and that the government should always have the last word over the broadcasts of the day. Thus the best that could be done was to give the main political tribes their protected land, reserving the largest slice of that territory for the ruling party.

As that became a settled system, the journalists and editors who produce the news became accustomed to their journalism being judged only partly on its professional quality; their careers also depended on the political line they espoused, their allegiance to parties of the left and right, and the patronage they enjoyed from leaders of these parties. The politicization of broadcasting is certainly not unknown elsewhere in Western Europe, as (in differing ways) in France, Greece, the Netherlands and Spain. In Italy, both the overt carving of the channels into spheres of influence and the manoeuvres to gain influence through placing of supportive journalists is more embedded in the daily practice of news journalism.

Italy has, in the leftist dailies Il Manifesto and l'Unita, and in the rightist dailies Il Foglio and Libero, an exceptionally lively if relatively small-circulation polemical press with national distribution, with few equivalents elsewhere. In Il Fatto Quotidiano, the stubborn investigator of Berlusconi and his circle, Marco Travaglio, founded with others a rare example of a newspaper created (in 2009) in a falling market – and succeeded for some years in gaining a circulation more than twice large enough to cover its relatively modest publishing costs.

The national papers – Corriere della Sera of Milan (founded in 1876 – closest to a paper of record); the business paper Il Sole/24 Ore (1965), also of Milan; the centre-left La Repubblica (1974) of Rome; and the liberal La Stampa of Turin (1867) – together with large regional papers, such as Rome's Il Messaggero, Florence's La Nazione and Naples' Il Mattino, are lively, competitive, with strong cultural and literary sections.

The largest inhibitors are the political and financial sensitivities of the owners. An editor of Corriere, Ferruccio de Bortoli, resigned in 2003 reportedly under pressure from the industrial interests on the board of Rizzoli, its parent company, who felt it unwise to be over-critical of Silvio Berlusconi, recently become prime minister for the first time, since they needed public financing (de Bortoli later returned to the editor's chair, from 2009 till 2015; Berlusconi was then in decline).[5]

La Stampa of Turin is owned by the Fiat Group; it cannot criticize Italy's most important company, nor damage its relations with the government of the day with over-zealous criticism. Its relations with government, hugely important for a company which produced so much for the public sector, were usually warm – including in the Fascist period, during which the firm's founder, Giovanni Agnelli, became a senator.

Il *Sole/24 Ore*, a merger between two other newspapers, is a business paper which is owned by Confindustria, the grouping of Italian industrialists and entrepreneurs; though a careful chronicler of economic, industrial, political and financial issues, it too is constrained by ownership to blandness of editorial position.

Carlo De Benedetti's Espresso Group owns *La Repubblica* on the centre-left. De Benedetti's sympathies are with the moderate left, and in financing the paper from its foundation in 1974, he assented, enthusiastically, to the long-held views of the founding editor, Eugenio Scalfari – that it would support (and to a large degree shape) a vision of the left in which 'a productive agreement between business people and workers would carry the democratic left into government, provided that this left abandon a Marxist ideology and above all, its Soviet abasements. In short, we wanted a reformist force.'[6]

La Repubblica is unique among the major papers in being co-founded by its first editor and the entrepreneur who backed him – and continued to back his successors, Ezio Mauro (from 1996) and Marco Calabresi (from 2016); with Mauro, he expressed the same agreement on the reformist socialist line as Scalfari had laid out.

The cull of papers does not pass Italy by. In the second half of the 2010s, the small-circulation papers were increasingly dependent on wealthy sponsors to keep them going. *Corriere* moved out of its imposing art nouveau headquarters in Milan's Via Solferino in 2013; *La Repubblica* and *La Stampa* merged in 2016; *Il Sole/24 Ore* made heavy losses in the same year.

Berlusconi's prime minister-aided creation of commercial national networks was as quickly successful as his later political party. RAI's monopoly had allowed the public broadcaster to be high-minded. The duopoly created was not then attended by the creation of a regulator – thus his media group Mediaset could air what it wished, proving so successful in doing so that RAI, its ratings (which were for the first time important to it) plunging, decided that the only possible strategy was to pay Berlusconi the compliment of imitation. As a result, writes Ginsborg, 'there was no public television to fly the flag of editorially independent news, civic responsibility, well-researched documentaries and quality programmes which could appeal at different times both to majorities and to special interests'.[7]

Berlusconi knew that advertising was mother's milk to television, and that in order to get it to flow generously, TV had to be friendly to the worlds which advertisers like to conjure up – happy, well-balanced, handsome people whose lives are enhanced by products (this is, of course, not confined to Italian TV). And though Berlusconi lost two out of the five elections in which he bid for power, the influence of his immensely diverting offerings have played a role both in the victories and in the narrowness of his second failure (in 2006). He brings pleasure to many millions, night after night. As Berlusconi commented soon after the launch of Mediaset: 'Basically, private TV was an act of transgression which tempted great numbers of people.'[8]

He embodied success, exuding cheerfulness, charm, a lack of inhibition in breaking the rules and courtesies of politics and diplomacy, a telegenic personality and a confident media style. Yet the direction of this energy has been to scorn, and attempt to diminish, many of the most important institutions of the Italian state and polity. The judicial system is represented as both corrupt and ideologically hostile to him – though he has managed to manipulate it so successfully that only as his power was waning was he convicted, in August 2013, of tax fraud – he served his sentence doing social work, while also being expelled from the Senate and banned from holding public office for six years.

The left – indeed, a range of opponents, including the pro-free-market *Economist* newspaper, which attacked him strongly – were, in his view, Communist. He saw parliament as a decoration, its business better handled by the party leaders deciding the central issues to avoid timewasting chit-chat. The economic reforms that he proclaimed as his vision for a more economically liberal, entrepreneurial Italy were meagre – except in those areas where the law had been changed to protect his own business interests and his immunity from prosecution. None of these targets were ill-chosen – especially the creaking and over-politicized justice system – but his attacks on them were designed to neuter what effectiveness they had, rather than improving their performance.

Politics, the endless clash of the parties, dominates Italian journalism; one of its key texts is Enzo Forcella's 1959 essay '1500 Readers',[9] a title that illuminates the care and intensity with which Italian papers cultivate and reflect politics, whose ideal readership is the 1,500 members (or so) of the political elite. Forcella wrote that, when he first aspired to be a political journalist, he had imagined he would be dealing with facts, information and news. Instead, he found that, in order to explain the world comprehensibly to his readers, he had to get below the formal events and speeches to discover what was really happening: a series of complex games, played by rules to which all except the extremes assented.

Berlusconi's journalism did break with this old order, but the new order has taken political engagement to another level: lower, rather than higher. Berlusconi regarded his media as extensions of his personal, business and political interests: his media were allowed to be relatively neutral at times, but not when his business interests were involved, or when he was under heavier than usual political or judicial attack, or in the run-up to an election. He held the popular heights – let the left and the intellectuals have their essays (a view taken also by Berlusconi's friend, President Vladimir Putin, though the latter had the advantage of working within an authoritarian state and was much more thorough in his suppression of independent media).

Hyper-militancy does assist sales and ratings. Alessio Vinci, the TV presenter who took over the *Matrix* current affairs discussion show – after Mentana left Berlusconi's employment, unable to agree that the current affairs and news should be instrumentalized in the service of the owner's political aims – said that if he put on a 'responsible' programme about health care, which should concern almost everyone, the programme's ratings fell far below those he could expect for one in which opposing sides shouted at each other across a studio floor. Commenting on the superheated polemics of the 2000s, the British-Italian writer Tim Parks quoted the nineteenth-century writer Giacomo Leopardi, who said that Italians 'do nothing but torment and deride each other', adding that 'Leopardi would only be confirmed in his opinion if he were alive today. Radio and TV debates invariably degenerate into shouting matches. Opponents are presented not so much as wrong but as losers, or better, sexually inadequate ... a political loser and a sexual loser are the same thing.'[10]

In a hyper-politicized environment, where the media are the tools of powerful and wealthy individuals and where the dominant media are very largely controlled by a wealthy individual who is also prime minister – and who recognizes few of the walls which have traditionally separated the estates of democracies – everything is designated as a matter of opinion. Journalists are, willy-nilly, corralled into the confines of one side or the other. Vinci, the *Matrix* presenter, formerly a reporter for the US news channel CNN, said this was a matter of deep regret for him. He envied his predecessor, Enrico Mentana, who had, he said, been given, for some years, a relatively free rein to build up a news division whose output could not be written off as propaganda, but whose defining and most obvious feature, after decades of the stiff RAI way with the news, was its 'looser, less formal' approach. Vinci told me:

> You couldn't do it like that today; what matters is the frame within which the programmes are set, and the country was not divided then [in the nineties] as it is now. I'm seen as on the right simply because I work for Mediaset. We invited Ezio Mauro [the editor of *La Repubblica*] to the programme – he wouldn't come, saying, 'I'm a journalist: you are something else.'

That, it seemed from his demeanour, had hurt.

—

The 'Italian exception' is not, on the face of it, so exceptional; everyone in the news business around the world is frenziedly trying to attract audiences from the pool of people willing to ingest news. The commercial success of right-wing Fox News and left-wing MSNBC in the US, of Al Jazeera in the Middle East and of the strongly polemical channels in India and elsewhere points towards opinionated news and current affairs as a viable business model. This is, after all, the way news was usually, in the past, communicated – through polemic, debate and argument. In this, Italy was ahead of the game.

Berlusconi's channel did not transmit simple propaganda; although the channel Rete Quattro, its news under the direction (till 2012) of Emilio Fede, the most conspicuously and unashamedly loyal of the prime minister's media associates, did approach, if not North Korean, then Venezuelan levels of admiration for the Leader. But Canale 5 was relatively balanced, at least outside of electoral campaigns, which was a conscious political act on the part of its owner, who wished to have it, and programmes like *Matrix*, act as ambassadors to the section of Italy that were not part of his project, including his opponents on the left and his sometimes doubtful allies on the right.

Once political interest, coupled with commercial success, becomes dominant, everything else – even an attempt at balance – must be made subordinate. This subordination was, as a number of former directors of RAI news and current affairs have testified, greater than that experienced under the Christian Democrats. Though the director of the news and current affairs division would generally be expected to lean towards the country's main party and its coalition allies, he would also be expected to report relatively fairly.

However, when Berlusconi was prime minister, this was not the case. It was especially not the case when the prime minister was fighting for his political life, as he was when RAI's news division was under the directorship (2009–11) of Augusto Minzolini, one of the most talented and opportunistic of Italy's journalists, with strong views on politics which aligned him ideologically, and quite openly, with the prime minister. Minzolini's RAI 1 news was increasingly partisan. This was underscored both by Minzolini's own editorials and by those of Giuliano Ferrara, the ex-Berlusconi minister and editor of the rightist Il Foglio, who took prime broadcast time after the main RAI 1 news programme, TG1, every weekday evening to give his own, usually original and witty, take on current events.

Less obviously, RAI downplayed or did not carry some stories which may have reflected badly on the prime minister. In July 2003, Berlusconi had an altercation with a German MEP, Martin Schulz, the leader of the Social Democrats' representation in the Brussels parliament (later president of the parliament). The German had criticized the Italian premier for his conflict of interest. The prime minister responded: 'I know there is a man producing a film on the Nazi concentration camps. I shall put you forward for the role of Kapo [a guard chosen from among the prisoners]; you'd be perfect.'[11] It was a revealing moment – Berlusconi's frame of reference is naturally that of popular culture – but also an embarrassing one, since he had just likened a German Social Democrat to a Nazi guard-slave who ushered the condemned into gas chambers (the Social Democrats of the thirties were among the first to be herded into concentration camps). He refused to apologize. RAI 1's main news showed Berlusconi in the parliament but did not play any of his retort, commenting merely that he was replying to a deputy who 'attacked him'. The silences were not confined to issues which directly affected Berlusconi business or personal interests: in 2009, when the Italian state airline Alitalia, in deep financial trouble, underwent a prolonged and largely unsuccessful rescue operation, TG1 did no in-depth story or analysis of one of the most important issues in Italy's economic life. Though a probling analysis would have been uncomfortable for the then government, its lack was not only due to an implicit or explicit bar on producing such a programme. Analytical broadcast journalism – a difficult and usually unpopular medium – is underdeveloped in Italian broadcasting.

The prime minister himself used TV as an extension of government in a way no other European or North American leader has – until Donald Trump, who used not TV but Twitter as a governing tool. In most democratic societies, the heads of government and of the state are interviewed by senior journalists, and are expected to deal with difficult questions on the style and substance of their government. In some cultures – as in the French – the tone has been respectful (less so under Nicolas Sarkozy and François Hollande than under Jacques Chirac and his predecessors). When Prime Minister Tony Blair took the UK to war against the tyranny of Saddam Hussein in Iraq, he faced questioning that could approach overt criticism on the part of the interviewer; he was also put before panels of citizens who were against the war, and who were not shy about giving him a hard time.

Silvio Berlusconi rarely had to face sharp interrogation; he prefers as his interlocutor the agreeable host of the long-running late-night talk show on RAI 1, Bruno Vespa. Vespa, who in 1996 created and for many years presented the show, *Porta a Porta* (Door to Door), does not ingratiate in the Fede manner, but he can usually be relied on not to press on sore points. It was on that show that Berlusconi made his contract with the Italians to give them good, clean, low-tax government, signing it with a flourish before the admiring gaze of Vespa. Almost none of his promises, including those made in this televised 'contract', were kept, but he had, till his fortunes turned decisively down in mid 2011, assumed that TV viewers have short memories. Berlusconi's close associate and former head of Pubblitalia, Marcello Dell'Utri, was quoted as saying that 'the medium of TV was profoundly congenial to Berlusconi's character. It inspired him because of the speed with which he could put into practice the ideas which went through his head. I'd go further: TV *is* Berlusconi.'[12]

This is very far from Fascism. Mussolini, after all, sought to discipline Italians (whom he privately saw as hopeless), while Berlusconi wished to make them happy. It was a kind of moderate Bonapartism of the screen.

More, it was a Bonapartism of entertainment: where the French emperor helped to spread the ideas of the French Enlightenment, in particular those of Voltaire, Berlusconi gave practical content to the best-known phrase of the Canadian scholar Marshall McLuhan, 'the medium is the message', which he defined as how 'the personal and social consequences of any medium – that is, of any extension of ourselves – result from the new scale that is introduced into our affairs by each extension of ourselves, or by any new technology'. In this context, Berlusconi saw that its most important characteristic is that it addresses individuals and families – until the second decade of the 2000s, usually in their homes.[13] On that, he could build a national movement. After observing a Rome in the grip of World Cup fever in the summer of 1994, in which Italy lost on penalties to Brazil in the final, played in the US, the Italian–American writer Alexander Stille wrote an analysis of Berlusconi and his political weight during his first premiership, using a line from W. B. Yeats:

> one senses that a terrible new power – mixing television, sports, entertainment and politics – had been born [moving from] the print-based culture of the 19th and 20th centuries, in which politics was about clashing ideologies, into a world where personality, celebrity, money and media control are the driving forces … Berlusconi is a man of a different age, of the age of TV and mass media, in which image and perception are all that really matter … 'Don't you understand,' he told one of his closest advisers, 'that if something is not on TV is doesn't exist? Not a product, a politician nor an ideal!'[14]

Until Matteo Renzi, then the mayor of Florence, erupted into the leadership of the centre-left Partito Democratico in 2013 before gaining the premiership (from which he resigned after losing a referendum in 2016), the left had not been able to match Berlusconi's firepower on television. They did not have a figure who could break with the past of the left, as

Berlusconi did with the past of the right. Both Christian Democrats and Communists were uncomfortable on television – or, better, television was uncomfortable with them. They were used to giving their views at some length and the interviewers rarely pressed them to be briefer, or to stick to the point of the question. The style which Mentana created for Berlusconi's current affairs was sharper, less deferential and lighter.

Berlusconi had made the centre of politics his own – everything referred to him – and as long as he could give a convincing impression of strength and as long as Italy's economy could be represented as being in good shape, he would usually win. Enrico Mentana told me that 'With the disappearance of the left, it means that journalists have picked up the baton and play the real role of the opposition.' The 'real role of the opposition' was played out, not just in the committed papers of the left, with La Repubblica in the lead, but more potently in the current affairs-cum-talk shows on RAI, which often took a radically different line from the news. Berlusconi and his allies, who complained bitterly about the bias in these shows, were largely right. These have long been, and remain, largely critical – and not just on the dedicated leftist channel, RAI 3.

Leading the regular programmes was AnnoZero, a show that was calculated to enrage government supporters. For many years it was presented with ferocious polemical vigour on RAI 2 by Michele Santoro, who had as his regular guest Marco Travaglio, the co-founder of Il Fatto Quotidiano (Santoro shifted, after several rows, to a new vehicle, Servizio Pubblico, broadcast by La Sette). He caused particular offence when, in September 2009, he interviewed an escort named Patrizia d'Addario, who had taken part in parties organized for Berlusconi at one or other of his residences, and claimed – unlike others, who produced accounts of a wholly platonic relationship – that she had spent the night with him; she later came out with a book, Gradisca, Presidente (Enjoy Yourself, Prime Minister). AnnoZero was seen by the Berlusconi camp as so outrageous that Il Giornale, the family paper of the prime minister of Italy, called on its readers not to pay the *canone*, or licence fee, to RAI in protest.

In March 2006, Lucia Annunziata, a prominent journalist of the left, had been able to pose a rare series of sharp questions to Berlusconi, provoking him to walk out from her show; she later said that he had handed her a list of questions she was supposed to ask. In September 2011, the presenter of another programme, *Ballaro* (I'll Stir Things Up), Giovanni Floris, also a committed man of the left, attempted to phone up the prime minister while on air, and appeared to get through, but no voice came from the other end. Floris provided a teasing commentary throughout.

None of these programmes and hosts had the slightest doubt that their job was to oppose Berlusconi, to return fire with fire. They had much to aim at, and they knew their man, since some had worked for him, or at his appointment; Annunziata had been president of RAI for a little over a year, resigning in May 2004 (the tradition has been that the president, a largely powerless figure, is drawn from the political current of the opposition). Mentana was not of that group; he went to La Sette, in 2010, with the explicit aim of presenting the news objectively. He said that 'the problem is not that there is no anti-Berlusconi opinion. There is, plenty of it. The problem is with the facts: and making sure these are put to the audience.'

Mentana believes that journalism and journalists were wholly unprepared for the Berlusconi effect; not so much because of the power of his media, but, he told me, because of the power of his audience:

Ninety per cent of Italian journalists are moderates, or of the left. They saw the audience through their own political lenses. They did not see that politics had changed. There had not really been a right in Italy – because of Fascism, people shrank from it. The Christian Democrats were of the centre: often, through Catholic social teaching, of the moderate left. Berlusconi's genius was to create an area of the right.

This is a democracy, with a civil society: people make choices, and many made the choice for Berlusconi, freely. And so of course they should be represented in the media. *Giornale* and *Libero* don't attack Berlusconi, because their readers don't want them to. And I must say: foreign correspondents based in Italy often see Berlusconi through the eyes of the left, because that's what they read. You will not understand Italian journalism if you think that the left is the norm and the right an exception.

In part, the target which Berlusconi presented was that which commercial TV everywhere has usually presented – that is, it does relatively little in the public interest, but much to interest the public. Edward Murrow, the US radio and television reporter and presenter who became famous for his wartime radio broadcasts from London, had warned that

if … this instrument is good for nothing but to entertain, amuse and insulate, then the tube is flickering now and we will soon see that the whole struggle is lost. This instrument can teach, it can illuminate; yes, and it can even inspire. But it can do so only to the extent that humans are determined to use it to those ends.[15]

Berlusconi's TV was, above all else, an instrument to 'entertain, amuse and insulate'. Many of the programmes on his channels were of the *Big Brother* or *Island of the Famous* kind, or were quiz shows in which men and women from all walks of life pitted their wits against sets of questions for large prizes; with these, he was giving a number of new openings for people who lived materially much better lives than their grandparents, but were subject to the condition of mass urban society: anonymity. Through Berlusconi's shows, they could be, if briefly, someone – or at least they could watch people like them becoming someone, and sometimes someone with a large cash windfall. These shows, in a country where the great mobilizing ideologies of political Christianity and Communism were much weakened, had real political and social, as well as media, meaning.

Both the pro- and anti-Berlusconi sides could find some justification for their views of how the state broadcaster should comport itself in RAI's statement of ethical values: 'the principle of pluralism ... constitutes the fundamental value of RAI'. That pluralism, rather than neutrality or objectivity, should be so is not surprising, in a state that had a few turbulent decades of democratic rule after unification, then over twenty years of totalitarian rule, culminating in a disastrous war for which the country's military was ill-prepared. Pluralism, the existence and clashing of differing parties, explains much about the media as well as the politics of the country: the politicization of RAI, the attachment of journalists to a specific political interest, the state funding of newspapers of differing political views.

This explicit politicization also means that there are myriad informal links between politicians and RAI journalists. Members of parliament, especially those with some seniority, see interventions in the output of the public broadcaster as natural, while RAI journalists often have, indeed often need, political patrons and defenders. The importance of this means that political positioning is at least as important to RAI journalists as is the public service element of their journalism. Incorporating and responding to the official and unofficial pressures from the political class in a manner which privileges the government in news shows is the corporation's version of serving the public interest. But understanding of the main issues of public life suffers.

Berlusconi's television and press output, during his time in office and in opposition, were directed to see it as their public duty to take up arms to protect his interests, in every sphere of life – and to confound his enemies, from whichever part of the political spectrum they came. Because his actions and motivations were often questionable, the opposition media were bound to be dragged into the fight; the posture of Olympian detachment, sorting right from wrong, was simply unavailable. In a lecture in Oxford in 2007, the Florentine academic and former senator (of the left) Stefano Passigli summed it up:

> Everything fits in nicely: power over the media makes it possible to win political power, and political power makes it possible to change the criminal law in order to thwart the efforts of the judiciary, while power over the media guarantees that public opinion does not see this operation to be in violation of the fundamental principles of morality ... the situation has produced a particular situation which is almost like the tyranny of the majority – a majority based on the overweening media power exercised by Berlusconi.[16]

While that road was followed, the public interest was not just damaged: it had been made, to a significant extent, impossible to serve.

Although it has long been imagined by northern Europeans as a place of sexual licence, Italy's national newspaper and TV journalism excluded most sex scandals and celebrity eruptions from its pages and bulletins – at least in news and current affairs. Gossip and film magazines were of course a different matter, but also occupied a quite different sphere, if one within which Berlusconi acquired some political power. The British press is much more promiscuous than the Italian press (or the French, or the American) has been; celebrity, sex and politics rub against each other in the same paper, sometimes on the same page, most sensationally in the same story. Italians, including Italian journalists, when asked about this discrepancy, often respond that sexual affairs on the part of politicians, or other (usually) men of power, are simply not interesting because there would be no surprise, and thus no story, in their revelation. In any case, when politics was a duopoly between the Christian Democrats and the Communists, the leaders of both led outwardly (and perhaps inwardly) lives of apparent respectability – and where they did not, their transgressions were known, but not chronicled.

This was changing by the eighties. The Socialists – whose leader, Bettino Craxi, was prime minister of a Socialist–Christian Democrat coalition from 1983 to 1987 – often lived the high life; Gianni De Michelis, the long-haired foreign minister, was famed for ordering his ministry's diplomats to find the most exclusive discotheques for evening diversions in foreign capitals. But these habits were at best a minor media theme, until Silvio Berlusconi.

Berlusconi's goatishness has been well attested – in stories and gossip, in wiretaps that inevitably found their way into the press, in the many books and, slyly, in his own jocular admissions. The most famed and most effective was, in July 2009, that 'there are tons of good-looking girls out there. I am not a saint, but you all know that' – adding – 'I hope those at *La Repubblica* also understand it.' This was effective because, like many other sayings, jokes, apparent slips of the tongue and boasts, it was so close to the way in which many people lived their lives.

The *Corriere* commentator Angelo Panebianco said that these few words ('I am not a saint') 'burst the moralism of the PD [Partito Democratico, the main centre-left party]'.[17] One of his most waspish editors, Vittorio Feltri, underpinned the hardly necessary admission by saying, 'We need a Prime Minister, not a Trappist monk.'[18] The prime minister ensured that a few beautiful women, some with careers as models and starlets (*veline*), join his party, become MPs at a regional and national level, and in one case, that of Mara Carfagna, a former model, become a minister – of equal opportunities.

Twice married, Berlusconi had left his first wife, Carla Dall'Oglio, for the beautiful actress Veronica Lario. He had two children with his first wife and three more with Lario. Though he has, based on her many accounts, been a largely absent father, his children have stayed (or become) close and loyal; Marina and Pier Silvio are senior executives in Mediaset, and have publicly defended him.

In 2009, the 'Noemi' affair was made public; this was a relationship the prime minister had developed with Noemi Letizia, an attractive girl of seventeen, who was the daughter of a modest family in Naples. Lario, who blew the rumours into the public arena with a letter to La Repubblica, in which she said she could no longer tolerate living with one who consorted with minors, later sued for divorce. In 2010, another story surfaced of an alleged liaison with Ruby Rubacuori (or Ruby Heartstealer), a Moroccan girl whose real name is Karima el Mahroug, whom Berlusconi insisted be released from detention in a police station, later protesting that he thought she was the niece of the then Egyptian president, Hosni Mubarak. In both cases, the stories gave details of parties attended by many girls and young women in Berlusconi's residence, at which an unexplained 'bunga bunga' erotic game was played. Accounts varied from these being wildly orgiastic to cheery affairs, in which the prime minister played the role of an indulgent wealthy uncle, distributing gifts of value and attentive to the aim of giving his guests a pleasant evening.

There was much here, especially in Berlusconi's inconsistent and often improbable accounts of the relationships, with which an investigative journalism could and should have done – and with which La Repubblica did have a great deal to do, concocting ten questions, angled at the more improbable parts of the story, to which, it claimed, it was in the public interest to have on-the-record answers. The paper kept up the campaign for months, printing and reprinting the questions to keep them in the public mind, eliciting international support for its initiative – though its aim, to force a resignation, did not succeed, and news of the affairs faded. Berlusconi's ratings did not seem to suffer: he would argue that they got better.

Italian journalism was developing an interest in the private life – albeit of one who had so mixed and stirred the ingredients of his personal, commercial and political lives that the one could scarcely be adequately described without the other. Like French President Nicolas Sarkozy, with whom the Italian prime minister is sometimes compared, he wanted to show the audience/electorate what a virile and attractive man he was, but was quite willing to call foul when the coverage became damaging. This was a position in which British and more recently American politicians had often found themselves, though the occasions in which they were caught transgressing were accompanied by embarrassment and humble apologies, not the 'So what?' defiance of Berlusconi. One of his jokes, in which he may have been casting some irony on his own habit of producing statistics on everything, was that a poll showed 'sixty-five per cent of women said they wanted sex with Berlusconi, the rest already had'. In worse taste, he commented, after some instances of violent rape, that the state would need as many carabinieri to stop them as there are beautiful women in Italy.[19]

A tabloid approach began to develop within the carapace of formerly serious political newspapers. When Dino Boffo, the editor of the daily *Avvenire*, the organ of the Italian Catholic hierarchy, launched an attack on the prime minister because of the Noemi affair, there came a response from the Berlusconi family paper *Giornale* in the form of a scathing article on Boffo by its editor, Vittorio Feltri – and a news story which accused Boffo both of harassing a married woman and of being homosexual. Berlusconi dissociated himself from it, saying that 'the principle of private life is sacred'. The story was later found to be largely false.[20]

Giuliano Ferrara, who takes an indulgent view of this, says:

> There isn't much of a journalism of the right in Italy: for example, when Mentana did the news at Canale 5, it was really left-wing news within the channel of a right-wing owner. What there is, is the journalism of *Giornale* and *Libero* [a daily founded in 2009 by Feltri, and edited by him until he moved back to *Giornale*]: and it's not really pro-free market and liberal, it's tabloid journalism, for the first time. Feltri is perfectly willing to fight scandal with scandal. So, if Berlusconi is accused of making love to starlets, Feltri will accuse Boffo of being a homosexual. And then the left complains!

The only man who bested Berlusconi in the media was one who moved to a medium Berlusconi could not control: the Net. Beppe Grillo, for decades one of the most popular comedians in Italy, has succeeded in an outstanding example of technological–cultural–political entrepreneurship. He reached a new, generally young audience, by developing a line of political indignation against the political class as a whole and gathering huge crowds in many piazzas up and down Italy for his *Vafanculo* (roughly, Fuck Off) days, where he always addressed the crowd at length. The political movement he founded, Movimento Cinque Stelle, grew in strength until, in the 2013 elections, it secured 25 per cent of the vote – the largest for any single party (though the coalition of the left received nearly 30 per cent).

The Movimento depends heavily on Grillo's egocentric and energetic personality, but it is also shrewd in tapping into not just anti-Berlusconi sentiment, but more broadly the disgust with politicians who have given themselves higher salaries and more privileges than their equivalents in most other countries, and to the corruption and supine quality of the public administration. Grillo did what a web-based show can do best: use the freedom of the medium to channel many different flows of information, to which it can link for purposes of either support or mockery. It is journalism with a campaign, or a campaign with journalism, with a show to attract the crowds.

The Movimento's career in mainstream national politics, which it is programmed to despise and wishes to abolish in favour of a web-based referendum politics, has been at best mixed. Grillo proved himself an authoritarian leader, expelling deputies who transgressed against the party line which he laid down; by the end of 2014 and into 2015, the party was polling in the lower teens. But it did not disappear and, by 2016, it was back up in the high 20s, a little behind the government. In the mayoral elections of that year, it won in Turin and in Rome – in both cases the candidates were young women – and it began to be seen, for all its inexperience, as able to form a government. *The Economist* wrote: 'For as long as Italy's economy continues to flounder and its mainstream parties lurch from one corruption scandal to another, [Grillo's] appeal can be expected to endure.'[21] When, in late 2016, Matteo Renzi resigned from the premiership after failing to persuade Italians to approve, in a referendum, a constitutional change to reduce the powers of the Senate, Grillo ramped up his rhetoric and his claim to political leadership in the country. Among his proposals, early in 2017, was the creation of 'people's juries' to judge the veracity of the news on television and in print. Grillo said that the news media were 'the main creators of fake news'[22] – a line he had consistently taken since presenting himself as a political force from the mid 2000s, and which put him in perfect synchronization with the newly elected US president.

In a memoir published in 2011, the journalist Giampaolo Pansa, who in a long career had served on *La Stampa*, *Corriere della Sera*, *La Repubblica* and *Libero*, recounted the story of how Berlusconi had one night called in to a show on La Sette called *L'Infedele*, presented by the experienced talk show host Gad Lerner – another of the many shows which put the prime minister in their sights time after time.[23] The show concentrated on Berlusconi and had as panellists three women strongly opposed to him, one who supported him and a man who was said to be neutral. They saw, first, a montage taken from Pier Paolo Pasolini's *Salò, or the 120 Days of Sodom*, and Liliana Cavani's *Night Porter*; the first showed the last days of Mussolini's shrunken republic at the end of the war, ending in a round of desperate sensuality, the second told the story of a deportee who became the sex slave of a Nazi officer.

The point being made was that Berlusconi, then facing charges of having consorted with a minor – in this case Ruby Heartstealer – lived in an environment similar to the debauched end of the Fascist republic. When Berlusconi was put through to the studio, he was nearly inarticulate with rage, spraying words like 'disgusting', 'repugnant', 'cowardly' (he was right: it *was* an absurd parallel). He demanded that his one supporter, the singer Iva Zanicchi, make her protest by leaving the studio (she didn't).

His voice hoarse with anger, he accused Lerner of having insulted Nicole Minetti, who, it turned out, was a woman who worked for him, including, reportedly, as the organizer of his 'bunga bunga' parties with girls at his villa at Arcore.

Pansa saw in this a terrible mistake: an admission, not of guilt, but worse – of impotent rage. He saw a man reaching the end of his tether, with skin like wax, his belly grown fat and slack, still tricked out in platform shoes to gain height. Pansa had thought that his villa had been a 'political sanctuary, set aside for select meetings, hosting formidable thinkers of the centre right ... come to work out strategies for the government'. Instead, it had been revealed as 'a private brothel, a court of miracles stuffed with little girls, ready to satisfy the wishes of a man in his seventies, still able to have sex with the energy of a twenty-year-old'.

All around him were women who spoke of the parties – some (like Ruby) insisting that they had not slept with Berlusconi, others, like the escort Nadia Macri, claiming in the course of a long interview on Sky on 28 November 2010 that she had gone to bed with Berlusconi at least three times, at Arcore and again at his villa in Sardinia. Nadia had either a good memory or a vivid imagination: in Pansa's account of her interview, she described a prime minister 'with his belly and everything else on show, emerging from a warm swimming pool to where five or six girls waited for him, including Nadia. And after a bath he received one after the other in an adjoining room. Here, with the cry – "Next!" he took them all with the rapacity of a stallion in heat. Was it true? Or false? For sure, it was ridiculous.'

Thus, wrote Pansa, was the reign of the 'Sultan' (as the social scientist Giovanni Sartori had called him) ending: in ridicule and the loss, finally, of respect.

That the leader of a major European state should pass into his political endgame in such a way is indeed extraordinary; and as extraordinary as the radical breaking of every rule of assumed propriety was the fact that he should feel he could ride the storm. Alexander Stille's charge, that Berlusconi 'would not have lasted a year with an aggressive and capable press',[24] is exaggerated but still demands an answer. Were the Italian news media – confronted with one whose actions were often deeply questionable where they were not illegal, shaped for his own convenience where they were not damaging to the country he governs, surrounded with mystification and ambiguity where they were not downright lies – simply not up to the job?

Part of the charge must stick. The refusal of either right or left to reform RAI because it would mean the loss of the capacity to suborn it to their political programme when in power; the attachment of many of both the broadcasters and the most prominent newspapers to a reporting style that contented itself with quoting each side and leaving an issue largely unexamined; a journalism which explicitly or implicitly negated the primacy of the fact; and finally, the tolerance of too many journalists – well paid and secure, though that was changing – with the state of affairs; all of these must be weighed in the answer to the charge.

Berlusconi was terrible for the politics of Italy, bad for the economy which he did too little to reform and disastrous for journalism in his period in power. But Italy is a free country, with institutions and movements which both uphold the workings of a democratic state and express, often with mass appeal and to mass response, opposition and views contrary to the majority which elected and re-elected the parties that supported the premiership of Silvio Berlusconi. Enrico Mentana, concluding our talk, said harshly: 'If you think freedom is precious you must win it: many journalists don't try.'

SEVEN

'Some of the stories ... were more or less true'

British popular papers – the tabloids – are terrible newspapers, if judged as media attempting to describe, in some detail, significant events, trends and the actions of the powerful. They had been edited to do some of that in the first part of the twentieth century, and continued to do so into the sixties; the news was phrased more simply and dramatically, the editorial stance was more polemical, and there was greater use of design, humour and personality than in the upmarket papers. But a citizen reading the *Daily Mirror* or *Daily Express* or *Daily Mail* could expect, if s/he read dutifully, to know in outline much of what upmarket paper readers might know in greater detail.

From the seventies on, that bit by bit ceased to be the case, especially in the 'red tops' – *The Sun*, *Daily Mirror* and *Daily Star*. The popular papers declined in readership – in part disguised by the rapid success of *The Sun*, and the turnaround in the fortunes of the *Daily Mail*, both positioning themselves strongly on the right, where the *Mail* had always been and where *The Sun*, which had been on the left, rapidly settled itself after being bought by Rupert Murdoch in 1969. The two papers had, at their height, a joint circulation of between six and seven million, dominating a market in which both the *Express* and the *Mirror*, and their Sunday editions, were steadily declining.

Daniel Boorstin writes, in *The Image*, that for journalists from the sixties on, 'The question, "Is it real?", [became] less important than, "Is it newsworthy?"'[1] A tabloid editor increasingly had to choose the latter of Boorstin's choice, and usually did. No law says that a tabloid, or any other, newspaper must be true, or even attempt to be. But its status as a commercial enterprise inclines its owner to expect that it makes a profit, even if that owner also wishes it to increase or express political power. So it must attract, and that has increasingly meant entertain much more than to inform.

'Tabloid' derives from the name given to the first medicines marketed in 1880 by Burroughs Wellcome, which compressed powder into handier and more portable pills. The word then became synonymous with compression; other uses of it have been lost, and it has come to apply only to popular newspapers. From the 1960s onwards, the word came to mean a journalistic style, rather than the shape of the paper. That, when handled by the new masters of the style, no longer fought against the limited space, but used it to give the stories and features punch, the power of the short sharp shock.

In the US, British-style tabloids do exist in New York (often edited by British journalists) – the *New York Post*, owned by News Corporation from 1976 to 1988, and again since 1993, and the *New York Daily News*, owned by the real estate investment tycoon Mortimer Zuckerman – but US tabloids beyond the *News* and the *Post* in New York are generally recognized as taking upon themselves the job of telling tall stories, urban, rural and galactic myths, inhabiting a world of aliens, fantastically gruesome sexuality and such headlines as 'SKYDIVER DEVOURED BY STARVING BIRDS' or 'ARMLESS VETERAN BEATEN FOR NOT SALUTING FLAG'.

Because US tabloids are less overtly anchored in real-world events than the British, they can be more lurid. The American novelist Robert Stone worked as a young man for several tabloids in New York in the sixties – from one of which, the *National Mirror*, the headlines above are drawn. It was modelled on the leader of the tabloid pack, the *National Enquirer*, 'though it lacked the delicacy and the taste of the original'. Stone wrote, in a short memoir, that after the first shock at the nature of the paper – the lurid stories had no truthful basis whatsoever – the new hires who stayed, as he did, 'eventually lost all sense of decent restraint'.[2]

In one incident, a story he had written on a murdered female vampire was to be illustrated by the head shot of a woman with fangs – which it was then decided to ink out, in order to have the story rather than the picture reveal the fact of vampirism. As the ink was applied, it spilled, covering the lower half of the face; the page had to be at the printer's in half an hour, the vampire story was lost and a new one had to be created: 'In black and white the ink looked for all the world like blood. I started playing with grotesque headlines, sizing them into the space allowed. Suddenly ... I had it: "MAD DENTIST REMOVES GIRL'S TONGUE".'

Stone batted out a story, which had the mad dentist's assistant walking in after the amputation: 'I could see the stump of the tongue with its jagged edge and strands of blood vessels hanging loose ... as I looked round in the direction of Dr Ingermill [the mad dentist] I saw the most disgusting thing possible to imagine.' The point was the gory readability, the invitation to discover what was the most disgusting thing possible – and that it was nonsense. Stone moved to another tabloid, Inside News, and was distressed to discover 'that some of the stories behind the headlines were more or less true ... the notion that what we were publishing reflected human behaviour was disturbing'.

But this disturbing business of reflecting actual human behaviour was what their British colleagues were doing every day, if with less editorial freedom; however lurid the stories, there usually was some truth. Kelvin MacKenzie, editor of The Sun (1981–94), pushed the truth/fiction confusion as far as he could, directing his staff to get the most dramatic stories possible, while keeping them out of the courts. He did not always succeed, as when the singer Elton John was accused, in a January 1987 front page, of having had sex with under-age rent boys. A later story alleged that he had had the vocal chords of his guard dogs removed so that they would not disturb his sleep. Both were judged false, and the singer was awarded the highest damages of the time, one million pounds. MacKenzie later commented, 'I think The Sun should have its million quid back. It hasn't damaged him at all, has it? Libel can only have a value if there has been some kind of damage, right? Where is the damage? Where? There's nothing wrong with him. So no, I don't feel bad about him, not at all.'[3]

He would occasionally appear penitent – as when he admitted that he made 'a serious mistake' when The Sun wrongly blamed drunken Liverpool fans for a crush at the Hillsborough Stadium in Sheffield, where their team was playing a Football Association Cup semi-final, and which resulted in ninety-six deaths and nearly 800 injuries. But he was generally aggressive in his defence of his actions. Confronted with stories that were untrue, he answered: 'When I published those stories, they were not lies. They were great stories that later turned out to be untrue – and that is different. What am I supposed to feel ashamed about?' The authors of Stick It Up Your Punter! (one of the two authors, Peter Chippendale, was a Guardian journalist) recounted MacKenzie shouting at a reporter whom he deemed over-liberal:

You just don't understand the readers, do you, eh? He's the bloke you see in the pub, a right old fascist wants to send the wogs back, buy his poxy council house, he's afraid of the unions, afraid of the Russians, hates the queers and the weirdos and drug dealers. He doesn't want to hear about that stuff [straight news].[4]

One of the most revealing books about British tabloids, The Insider, was written by one of MacKenzie's disciples, Piers Morgan, who had worked on The Sun's show business column, 'Bizarre'.[5] In 1994, Morgan had been elevated at age twenty-eight to be editor of the News of the World, then was stolen from the News International stable – in which the News of the World was the most profitable runner – and made editor of the Daily Mirror. He was fired from the *Mirror* by Sly Bailey, the head of the Trinity Mirror Group, in 2004, because he had published photographs of 'torture' meted out by British soldiers to Iraqi captives, which turned out to have been faked.

By his mid to late thirties, Morgan had been at or near the top of the main tabloids in the country. Based on his diaries, *The Insider* is valuable because it is the account of an intelligent and ruthless man – like MacKenzie, he was privately educated but did not go to university – who has much of the brass neck of his mentor, diluted only occasionally with reflections such as 'what a vile business politics is, almost as vile as journalism', which were not meant, probably, to be taken seriously. Unlike MacKenzie, he made forays into positions that were seen as leftist, including opposition to the Iraq War, and when at CNN as main interviewer, he initiated a campaign against gun ownership. The *New York Times'* leading media reporter, the late David Carr, commented:

> There have been times when the CNN host Piers Morgan didn't seem to like America very much ... Mr Morgan's approach to gun regulation was more akin to King George III, peering down his nose at the unruly colonies and wondering how to bring the savages to heel. He might have wanted to recall that part of the reason the right to bear arms is codified in the Constitution is that Britain was trying to disarm the citizenry at the time.[6]

Yet the sheer bloodiness of a gun culture – as in a Charleston, South Carolina, church in June 2015, when nine black worshippers were killed by a young white supremacist in a state which had made the purchase of guns about as easy as buying a chocolate bar – gave retrospective justification, if one was needed, to Morgan's stubborn campaign and rendered Carr's judgement tawdry, as if it were illegitimate for a British presenter on CNN to campaign against gun ownership because his country had been the colonial power more than two and a half centuries before. Yet Morgan's previous existence as a gossip king haunted him: in a more detailed critique, Laura Bennett admitted his persistence, but wrote:

> Pumped full of a sense of his own mission, he is a caricature of what gun owners imagine their antagonists to be: smug, patronizing urbanites. So he often ends up playing into the anxieties of right-wing extremists rather than puncturing them ... he has reduced one of the most sensitive, knotty issues in US politics into a mere soapbox for the Piers Morgan brand.[7]

In *The Insider*, Morgan wrote of a lunch with Diana, Princess of Wales (also attended, at her home, by her eldest son, William, then thirteen), as if it were an entrée into a holy place, where a goddess, speaking – it seemed – quite naturally gave him 'three fantastic scoops in thirty seconds'. He was editor in the heyday of the Diana craze, when she was tabloid and magazine-cover gold worldwide, and understood clearly her value to his trade.

In his second book, *Don't You Know Who I Am?*, he disdains politicians as 'dull, slippery', for avoiding talking about policy and ideology, while he is reduced to 'prising some gaffe out of them'. When offered the job of editor of a paper that the then Harrods owner Mohamed Al Fayed was considering starting, he quotes the Egyptian billionaire as saying, 'Between us we'll get rid of these Labour bastards who are ruining the country.' Morgan replies: 'But then we'd just get the Tory bastards back again' – to which Al Fayed replies, 'You're right they're all bastards, aren't they?'[8] It was a piece of banal bile that prompted Morgan to muse: 'All papers should be owned by megalomaniac billionaires with axes to grind: they'd be so much more entertaining, not to mention fearless.' As if courage could be displayed, in twenty-first-century Britain, by calling politicians 'bastards'.

Morgan tried to maintain something of an ironic distance from the journalism he wrote and edited; his attacks on US gun culture was one of several forays into the terrain of serious comment. But those who carry out contemporary tabloid news successfully must be single-minded in obtaining it, and must see it as at least as important as serious news.

By the 2010s, the US site TMZ had become the most successful tabloid site in the world; its creator and boss, Harvey Levin, believes that the stories the site breaks are of real importance, but are tailored to make an impact among ordinary people, not just the readers of books and upmarket papers.[9] In February 2009, TMZ ran a story that a private US bank, Northern Trust, which had received 1.6 billion dollars from the government in bailout assistance, hosted a party in Los Angeles at which star acts – Chicago and Sheryl Crow – performed and Tiffany bags were distributed.[10] The piece attracted much condemnation of Northern Trust, including from John Kerry, then a senator. Levin later said that it was the most important thing TMZ had done, telling the *Los Angeles Times*, 'It's hard for people to wrap their heads around $800 billion in bailout money [Levin is referring to total bank bailouts, not Northern Trust]. It's much easier to understand paying for a Sheryl Crow concert.' In a 2013 radio interview, Levin said that the approach TMZ reporters took to their work was on the same level of care and accuracy as straight reporting: 'You could take me, put me in Afghanistan, and I'll use the same principles I'd use with Britney Spears.'[11]

Tabloid journalists need a few facts, but above all they need to stimulate or imitate emotion, an approach now leeched into straight news. In the years in which he had made celebrities the centre of his journalistic life, Morgan had established himself as a celebrity. After leaving the *Mirror*, he presented a number of TV interviews, one of which, with the then UK prime minister, Gordon Brown, in February 2010, had Brown (his wife, Sarah, was in the audience) with his eyes full of tears as he recounted the death of their first child soon after her birth in 2002.[12] Though the interview went on for nearly an hour, Morgan barely touched on the issues that he had earlier said were essential to be illuminated, such as policies and ideology. The object of the interview with Brown was to lead him into raw emotion; a lead which Brown seemed willing to follow, to the point where he was accused of orchestrating the encounter in order to make him a more sympathetic and thus more popular figure, thereby improving his low approval ratings.

TV presenters must be, or become, at least somewhat narcissistic; it's a professional necessity if they wish to stay at the top. Morgan was never in the celebrity premier league, but he was in the one below, and while that level allows time off for bad behaviour without paparazzi necessarily present, it also imposes the discipline of being, in his case, the perennial controversialist, the – as he described himself – big mouth. It means treating others at the same level as competitors, with whom a public spat might be good for the publicity. Morgan had such a spat when he was a rising power in 1996 at the *News of the World*, with Ian Hislop, the editor of *Private Eye*. The latter had bested him in a trade of insults on the BBC comedy panel show *Have I Got News for You* in 1996; Morgan responded, some time later, by putting the reporter Graham Brough on a mission to dig up all and any dirt on Hislop to assuage his anger – only to find none, reportedly to Morgan's irritation.[13]

As that shows, tabloids must be cruel. By the seventies, there had become no other way to do a popular tabloid, since delight in others' humiliation, even the cultivation of hatred, are such widely held emotions that any inhibition in indulging them on the part of the editors or owners fell away. In his history of the tabloids, Matthew Engel writes that 'writing for a mass audience is not an intrinsically debased form of literature ... but it has become debased. Over a hundred years much of British journalism turned into an institutionalized force for distortion and half truth.'[14]

As that happened, the tabloids became shriller, more militant in defence of the supposed attitudes of their readers and more proactive in shaping these attitudes. The most popular of these came to be owned by politically engaged figures of the right – in the UK, *The Sun* and the *News of the World* were owned by Rupert Murdoch's News Corporation; in Germany, *Bild* was owned by the Axel Springer group, founded by the journalist of that name. For their part, the Greek newspapers, and not just the tabloids, were more vicious: the right-wing paper *Democracy* pictured Chancellor Angela Merkel in a Nazi uniform on their front page in April 2012.[15] In February 2015, the left-wing paper *Avgi* (The Dawn), close to the ruling Syriza party, easily topped that by depicting the German finance minister, Wolfgang Schäuble, as demanding to 'make soap from your fat' and saying 'we are discussing fertilizer from your ashes'[16] – two uses to which the SS in the concentration camps put the corpses of the slaughtered.

Bild provoked one of the most literary denunciations of tabloids after it demonized the author Heinrich Böll, a supporter of the mainstream centre-left Social Democratic Party, when he objected publicly to the treatment of the small terrorist group RAF by the German state.[17] In a piece written for *Der Spiegel* magazine, Böll strongly criticized the tabloid's lack of concern for accuracy and its habit of assigning guilt without proof; he was himself subjected to a tabloid attack (as well as reasoned criticism from the right, and from the centre left).

His novel, *The Lost Honour of Katharina Blum*,[18] features a naive young woman, the eponymous heroine, whose love for a radically minded criminal, whom she helps to escape from the police (she was ignorant of his crimes), results in her life being ruined by *The News* – a tabloid paper like *Bild* – which twists her words and those of her friend and her mother, who was interviewed on her hospital deathbed by a reporter who had tricked their way into her room. In the end, Katharina, driven to desperation by *The News*, takes her own life.

Annalena McAfee's novel *The Spoiler*[19] captures the resentment, a necessary companion of the production of *schadenfreude*, in which the British tabloids specialize. A muddled, semi-educated young woman, fearful of losing her tabloid commissions, is sent to interview an eighty-year-old woman who was a much-lauded photographer and friend of the famous. The latter, affronted by the reporter's ignorance and personal line of questioning, turns her out. The reporter then resorts to spying on her, and discovers she has a regular caller who is a handsome youngish man: tabloid gold struck. Set in the mid nineties, the novel is inhabited by cynical reporters and editors, living on faked expense accounts, in return for degraded prose and casual brutality of its subjects, while the whole industry teeters on the brink of technological obsolescence.

As a counterpoint to these literary demolition jobs was *The Diaries of a Fleet Street Fox*,[20] a jaunty celebration of British tabloid practices and mores by one who affected anonymity but was easily outed as Susie Boniface, who worked mainly for the *Mirror*. In the MacKenzie tradition, she revealed that 'Trespass, theft, speeding offences, impersonating people I shouldn't – I have done and will do any and all of these things and a few more if the story justifies it. I'd hack a phone, too, if I thought it was the only way to prove a truth that needed to be known.' The stories that need to be known are largely sex scandals. Reviewing the book, Annalena McAfee remarked that it might have some value as it gave 'a tangential insight into the boorish, bullying tabloid mentality'.[21]

Tabloids must be resentful, and must use people in the public eye, in the upper political and social classes, as objects of resentment. It has long been a feature of the popular papers in Britain; however, in the early half of the twentieth century they were constrained by deference and fear. After the Second World War, deference lost its grip and there was a backlash against the ruling classes. Under the editorial directorship of Harry Guy Bartholomew, before and after the war, the *Mirror* journalists were encouraged to take a strong anti-establishment tone, and to aim the paper – formerly a staid middle-class journal – at the working class, and at servicemen and -women. It had a circulation of around 1.5 million before the war, which rose to 4.5 million by the late forties, and then – under the editorship of Hugh Cudlipp – topped 5 million through the fifties and early sixties. This period in the *Mirror*'s history was viewed in the 2000s with much nostalgia by elderly leftists; it was sharp and radical and unswervingly for Labour and social-democratic policies, but Bartholomew had modelled it on the earlier New York tabloids, and knew well the value of gossip, scandal and covering the rich and famous.

In the eighties and early nineties, the frame within which the upper classes were defined changed: they came to be portrayed less often as the wealthy and titled, more often as leftists who were out of touch with the desires of ordinary people and opposed to the free-market reforms of Margaret Thatcher. The former Labour Party leader Ed Miliband (2010–15), son of a Marxist politics professor, Ralph Miliband, was a natural target, one made more attractive by his robust condemnation of the tabloids during the phone hacking revelations. Little was more welcome to the right-wing tabloids in the run-up to the British general election of May 2015 than the story that Miliband had two kitchens in a north London house said to be worth two million pounds.

Trade unions, which had been largely venerated by the pre- and post-war Mirror, came to be represented as barriers to progress, the preserve of ideologically driven and self-serving leaderships. Even the Mirror's adherence to Labour, though it remained, was severely diluted. Under Piers Morgan, it dived as gleefully into the scandal and sex celebrity pool as The Sun and the News of the World. The more serious and politically committed (to the right) Daily Mail, which partook of both tabloid and upmarket elements, was ferocious in its naming of the 'guilty men and women', largely of the left, who were holding back the country.

The focus of tabloids shifted to the lives and scandals of celebrities, who have the advantage of being well known because of appearing often on television, or in films, or in sports, especially football, and thus needing no introduction. They employ PR aides who are skilled at entering into negotiations with the various media on which parts of a celebrity's private life should be the content of a story, and smooth journalists' paths into stories which are lightly scandalous or sensational. The prize for the tabloids, and for the celebrity sites – such as TMZ, Yeeeah, PopSugar,

Celebitchy, Dlisted, Popbitch, Egotastic, Hollywood Tuna, PerezHilton and others – is a celebrity embarrassed, whether because of an exposed nipple or a row with a lover or assistant or photographed drunk or on the way down from whatever celebrity height achieved. The head of social activation at Horizon Media, Keith O'Brien, says that 'these sites are visited by all types of people so it's possible to reach a wide audience, even if some are just coming for the *schadenfreude* and may not return until the next scandal. Everyone loves a celebrity's fall from grace.'[22]

Princess Diana, divorced wife of the British Crown Prince Charles and the greatest celebrity of her age, fell not from grace but from life – in a fatal accident, as the car in which she was being driven, trying to outrun a posse of paparazzi on motorbikes, hit a pillar in a tunnel running alongside the Seine in Paris in August 1997. It was an end which focused blame on those who pursued her, as they had done since she was engaged to Charles, at the age of nineteen, when they caught her in a diaphanous skirt against the sun, thus showing the shape of her legs.

Hilary Mantel, at the height of the fame she enjoyed from the reception of her novels *Wolf Hall* and *Bring up the Bodies*, wrote a piece said to be controversial because it described Kate Middleton, Duchess of Cambridge and wife of Charles' elder son William, as 'precision made, machine-made, so different from Diana whose human awkwardness and emotional incontinence showed through in every gesture'. Diana, by contrast, 'was more royal than the family she joined ... something in her personality, her receptivity, her passivity, fitted her to be the carrier of myth'.[23]

Mantel's piece misses the proactivity of Diana in conducting her own public relations, and her colossally inflated self-image as a divinity, able – as she said in her last interview with the Paris daily *Le Monde* – to take on the characteristics of a goddess, in being able to instantly come to the side of anyone who expressed a need for her, a quotation which is carved on her tomb in the park of her family's mansion of Althorp. But Mantel is right that the impression of passivity and receptivity, which Marilyn

Monroe also had naturally, drew millions to Diana, each feeling that she held something special for them.

Proactive passivity can be a successful posture. The footballer David Beckham gained from it, appearing to be the man of infinite amiability, on whom anyone can write what they wish, in the spaces between his tattoos. Beckham, like Diana, made vulnerability his trademark, developing and displaying a feminine side and a readiness to admit emotional pain – as when he told his former teammate at Manchester United, Gary Neville, in an interview: 'Over the years people have looked at things that have gone on in my career and sometimes that's overshadowed what I've done on the pitch. As much as I say that doesn't hurt me, of course it does.'[24] None of this saved him from a grilling over alleged affairs with a personal assistant, a Manchester United fan and the singer Catherine Jenkins, both of which were denied, yet though they were well covered by the tabloids, they were careful not to leave him with a permanent 'love rat' tag. Diana was the People's Princess; Beckham was the People's David.

The highly competitive field in which the British tabloids operate – there are five daily and six Sunday tabloids – drives them deeper and deeper down into the mines of private life.

When, in the 1990s, reporters discovered that they could, with the help of private detectives, hack into mobile phones and retrieve voice messages, they opened up the richest seam of potential scandal – ironically, allowing them to be more accurate than they had ever been before. The phone hacks, which had ballooned to include thousands of phone conversations and messages, were first revealed by the *Guardian* investigative reporter Nick Davies, whose researches, largely into the practices at the *News of the World* (though the practice was later found to be widespread among the red-top papers), were confirmed by a team for the *New York Times*.

When public outrage was aroused by a (partly mistaken) report on the hacking of the phone of the thirteen-year-old murder victim Milly Dowler from Walton-on-Thames, near London, the Conservative-led coalition government felt impelled to appoint an inquiry on the practices of the press, presided over by the appeal court judge Sir Brian Leveson. After a year of hearings, Sir Brian published his report on the issue in November 2012.[25] It is a lengthy and hugely informative report: the judge sees a sweep of history, in which the press gradually won the independence and power it needed to become a medium for holding power accountable – down to the late twentieth/twenty-first century, when press power could threaten democratic practice at least as much as bolstering it.

On a practical level, he found that although the Press Complaints Commission, which was set up in 1990, did some useful work, it really offered no proper protection against press intrusion. He noted, too, that the argument made by both John Milton in the 'Areopagitica' and John Stuart Mill in On Liberty – that in the collision between truth and error, truth will win – is, when applied to the press, wholly uncertain. He quoted one of the academic witnesses, Dr Neil Manson, a senior lecturer in philosophy at the University of Lancaster, as saying that 'there is nothing to stop a free press ... from freely deciding to support corruption or to be involved in it. We cannot assume that a free press, or specific agents within a free press, will be motivated to provide the kind of content that is, in fact, in the public interest.'

Leveson himself was dismissive of the view – strongly put by most of the journalists appearing, especially those from the tabloids – that the government, or the state, were actual or potential suppressors of their freedom. To the contrary, he found that 'in recent years there are, I think, examples only of Parliamentary law-making in respect of the press which is clearly focused on strengthening rather than restricting the freedoms of the press'.

And what had the tabloids done with this freedom? Leveson rehearsed some of the good that the newspapers did, such as the Daily Mail's campaign for justice for the family of the murdered teenager Stephen Lawrence, together with other campaigns for justice that were vigorously pursued and were often, like that of the Lawrence campaign, successful; *The Sun's* investigative work on various individuals' plans to commit crimes – one of which uncovered a plot by a jailed doctor to kill his former lover and baby because they had helped convict him – possibly saved lives; the *Daily Star's* revelations of the violent culture in the English Defence League; and the *Daily Mail's* raising of sixteen million pounds for the victims of the 2004 South Asian tsunami, a record for any British newspaper.

Tabloids do many pieces of this kind; and their suspicion of establishments, while selective, often includes the unmasking of abuses of power. But in his enquiries into the practices of the red-top tabloids and the *News of the World* in particular, Leveson met the 'What? Me worry?' insouciance about veracity not only from Kelvin MacKenzie of *The Sun*, but also from Paul McMullan, former deputy features editor of the *News of the World*, who said he believed completely and proudly in the public service role played by his paper, and in his diligent servicing of one of the mass needs of the British people. Leveson drew attention to 'one of the most provocative statements made to the Inquiry', that of McMullan saying of a story he wrote on paedophiles which prompted a mob, searching for paedophiles in their neighbourhood, to beat up a man who had a sign on his door advertising the fact that he was a paediatrician – 'in a bizarre way, I felt slightly proud that I'd written something that created a riot and got a paediatrician beaten up, or whatever was the case'.

Leveson viewed the *News of the World* man with barely disguised, fascinated horror; he quoted him again as being 'at the extreme end of the lack of respect for privacy' when McMullan said that

the only people I think need privacy are people who are doing bad things. Privacy is the space people need to do bad things in. Privacy is particularly good for paedophiles, and if you keep that in mind, privacy is for paedos, fundamentally no one else needs it, privacy is evil. It brings out the worst qualities in people. It brings out hypocrisy. It allows them to do bad things.

On a further comment by McMullan, Leveson commented that 'it is perhaps a true measure and reflection on the man' that he asserted that 'phone hacking is a perfectly acceptable tool, given the sacrifices that we make, if all we are trying to do is to get to the truth'.

This is not confined to tabloids. The *Guardian*, which for many months played a solitary role in pursuing the hacking story, was, with the *New York Times* and the German weekly news magazine *Der Spiegel*, proud to have published many stories based on WikiLeaks' documents, and more momentously some of the estimated 1.7 million National Security Agency files stolen by Edward Snowden, when he was a contractor in one of its centres. These were state property and they were put in the public domain through theft; in both cases, especially the latter, there was and remains a real risk that an informant who had passed information to the US or UK security services could be identified and killed; and a probability, which for the security services was a proclaimed certainty, that terrorists would change their behaviour once learning what the US's National Security Agency and Britain's Government Communications HQ were likely to know about their modus operandi. For the papers that published the selection of files, the issue which trumped all others was that they revealed a huge breach of privacy, of which the citizens of the UK and the US were for the most part unaware, and about which they should have been informed: the public interest in that revelation was uncontroversial, assented to, usually privately, by many senior intelligence officers. Their publication drove huge traffic to their websites, which they – along with most other newspapers – hoped would be their financial salvation as the sales of physical copies relentlessly declined.

Leveson could not be aware, or if aware could not feel sympathy for, the fact that those immersed in celebrity journalism – like McMullan, and Mazher Mahmood, the *News of the World's* investigative reporter often trading under the nom de plume 'the Fake Sheikh' – saw this as an area where privacy had not just been given up, but traded for money, fame and, above all, attention. The celebrities who appeared in tabloid papers were devotees of the Wilde doctrine: that to be talked about could be purgatory, but not to be talked about was hell. Many of the stories were deals, calculated indiscretions or staged confrontations. Where the Leveson view saw victims of gross intrusion and distortion, the journalists saw a field of battle, where sometimes you won a round against a coverage-hungry celebrity or a cheating spouse or a shifty politician or a trade union leader 'guzzling' in a Michelin-starred restaurant – and sometimes you lost.

In an essay on 'Privacy, Secrecy and Human Bonds', the British sociologist Zygmunt Bauman quotes the French sociologist Alain Ehrenberg as dating the 'birth of the late modern cultural revolution' from when, in the 1980s (no more precise date is given), an 'ordinary French woman' said on a TV chat show that because her husband suffered from premature ejaculation, she had never experienced an orgasm in all of her married life.[26]

It became clear, wrote Bauman, that 'the true significance of the event was an effacing of the once sacrosanct division between the "private" and the "public" spheres of human bodily and spiritual life'. This happened in France, a society where privacy had long been ferociously guarded, especially by an elite who had the means to have it policed. French political life had to wait for the presidency of Nicolas Sarkozy (2007–12) for one who deliberately displayed elements of his private life to bolster his public image – a lowering of the walls of discretion on the part of the news media which had been maintained round the presidential palace, and which his successor, François Hollande, was unable to rebuild, to his cost.

It had happened much earlier in Anglo-Saxon societies, and the *News of the World* had long been in the vanguard of lowering what walls there were. Its reporters were connoisseurs of the trade between private and public, the price and conditions attached to the transitions between the two – and were necessarily skilled at organizing these transitions, usually in emotionally taxing circumstances. They came to disbelieve – at least this was their public attitude – in the protestations of hurt and violation. Leveson had a vivid example of this, from one of the central figures in the phone hacking scandal, Rebekah Brooks, former editor of both the *News of the World* and *The Sun*, and then promoted to be chief executive of News International.

Once again, it dealt with the emotions of the Gordon Brown family, which was curious, since Brown was the most rational and intellectual of front-line politicians, yet seemed doomed to have his private life trawled through time and again. In 2006, when Brooks was *The Sun*'s editor, she had obtained a story that Fraser, the four-month-old son of Gordon and Sarah Brown (he was then Chancellor of the Exchequer) had cystic fibrosis. It was a story which the health board in Brown's home county, Fife, believed to have been sold to *The Sun* by a board employee, but which Brooks insisted had come through someone whose own son had the condition. Brooks phoned Sarah Brown to say *The Sun* would run the story.

Brown told the Inquiry that there was 'no question of explicit permission' to publish the story. Brooks, by contrast, said the Browns 'were absolutely committed to make it public', a statement which Leveson commented, 'defies belief'. Brooks said, several times, that she and Sarah were friends, even 'good friends', and that she felt sympathetic to their plight – 'I was very sad for them.' But her friendship and sympathy had no bearing at all on her determination to publish. Brooks also said that after the story appeared, the good friendship appeared to remain intact; the Browns came to Brooks' fortieth birthday party and to her wedding. When asked why, Brown said that his wife 'is one of the most forgiving people I know'; of his own actions in continuing to see Brooks socially, he said, 'we had to get on with the job of doing what other people expect a politician to do, run a government' – leaving Leveson to comment that 'the imperative of continuing to get on with News International was abiding'.

Leveson heard much more. He heard that the *News of the World* obtained a diary kept by Dr Kate McCann, whose daughter disappeared during a family holiday in Portugal and has never been found, and ran excerpts without securing permission. He heard that several tabloids, including *The Sun* and the *Daily Mirror* (which went furthest in imputing guilt), blackened the name of a retired teacher, Chris Jefferies, strongly implying he was the murderer of Joanna Yeates, a tenant of his, in December 2010. He heard and read of the obeisance which successive government ministers, and prime ministers, paid to the tabloid editors and proprietors – vividly displayed in Gordon Brown's relationship with News International through the figure of Rebekah Brooks, the same commanding figure whom Tony Blair wooed and to whom David Cameron sent email messages ending 'LOL' in the mistaken impression it was the acronym for 'lots of love' (it's 'laugh out loud').

All this led Leveson to comment that, 'taken as a whole, the evidence clearly demonstrates that, over the last thirty to thirty-five years and probably much longer, the political parties of UK national government and of UK Official Opposition have had or developed too close a relationship with the press, in a way which has not been in the public interest'. But the tabloids went after these stories because they knew that they interested the public – the public being masters of the tabloids, for whom journalists blackmailed, spied, lied and traduced.

One major press figure – the largest, for many – was Paul Dacre, who has edited the *Daily Mail* since 1992 and was appointed editor-in-chief of all the *Mail* titles (*Mail on Sunday*, *Scottish Daily Mail* and *Irish Daily Mail*) in 1998. Dacre – though he was modest in his evidence to Leveson, crediting his 'brilliant' reporters, editors and columnists rather than himself – was among the last of the dominant Fleet Street editors, whose vision infuses the paper. For him popular journalism and the emphasis on sex scandals is not a matter of mere titillation in pursuit of circulation.

Pressed on his view in his time before the Inquiry, Dacre quoted the professor of journalism at the University of Kent, Tim Luckhurst (an uncommon sign of approval of a media academic by a popular newspaper editor, though Luckhurst had been editor of the *Scotsman*, and was a rare voice of the right in media studies), who wrote: 'the notion that moral failures such as adultery are entirely private and do not matter to the wider world is an affront to the very idea of community'.[27] Though he did not say so explicitly, Dacre was taking a quite different direction from that of most of his tabloid fellows. He was locating revelatory journalism not only as 'a bloody good story' but as a moral pointer. The paper can be vicious and underhand in its stripping of public figures, but there's little doubt that a moral force – often a ferocious one – is strongly claimed to be behind it.

Dacre sees the 'liberalocracy which runs Britain' as his main target, and thinks that 'no day is too busy nor too short not to find time to tweak [their] noses'.[28] In a sustained attack on a judge, David Eady, who handled many libel cases and who had strong views on the need for privacy, Dacre accused him of making 'no moral distinction ... between marriage and those who would destroy it, victim or victimizer, between right and wrong'. Eady's decision that the then head of Formula One, Max Mosley, revealed in 2008 by the *News of the World* as having had a masochistic orgy with several women, should receive 60,000 pounds damages from the paper, was, according to Dacre, an example of Eady's 'ruling out any such thing as public standards of morality and decency'.

This approach is a major factor in making the *Mail* 'the most powerful newspaper in Great Britain', as a profile[29] of April 2012 put it, though, the profile also said, the Mail Online is the most popular newspaper website in the world, which is famous for a long trail of PR-provided pictures and stories about celebrities, most often lightly dressed, beautiful women, catnip for male and female readers. Dacre does not, he says, approve of the way in which sex scandals are handled in the 'red top' tabloids, and has said he 'would not have it [the *News of the World*] in the house' (when it existed);[30] but he is adamant that scandal must be provided, otherwise popular newspapers will fail – which would be bad for the freedom of the press.

No one who has read Leveson's long report could fail to conclude that, with all allowance for the good reporting, public interest investigations and charitable projects, the tabloids, when out hunting for victims to smear and debase, were mud machines. And thus Leveson saw every possible good reason to argue for a regulatory framework, backed by the state, to restrain the wolfish instincts which had been revealed to his Inquiry, and to protect future would-be victims.

The government, having so roundly condemned phone hacking and having put so many ashes on their heads for genuflecting to the newspaper proprietors and above all to Rupert Murdoch, accepted the report and set up a body – a Recognition Panel – under the aegis of a Royal Charter (a medieval mechanism also employed for the BBC), which would confer recognition on any regulator that conformed to the criteria set out by Leveson. In fact, Leveson had suggested that the communications regulator Ofcom do the job, but the various parties thought this too draconian, and settled on the Royal Charter as a way of giving the state some purchase over the behaviour of the press.

The newspaper industry, deciding that a period of contrition was over, ignored it. By 2016, nearly all newspapers and magazines had joined the Independent Press Standards Organisation, a body conceived by Guy Black, executive director of the Telegraph Group, and not recognized by the Recognition Panel; or, like the *Guardian* and the *Financial Times*, had preferred to join no regulator, arguing that it was the editor's job to set and keep standards. The government seemed content to let the matter be; by 2017, with a vote to leave the EU dictating a radical reorientation of Britain's foreign and trade policy and with an opposition Labour Party locked in a savage internal war, any plan to attempt to corral newspapers into an organization that would secure recognition was so far down any agenda as to be invisible.

Leveson was wrong to propose a state mechanism to act as a backstop to newspaper regulation. British journalism requires a cleansing by its journalists – rather than being niggled at round the edges by a semi-statutory instrument of medieval provenance, which was the lowest common denominator the political parties could agree on.

The men and women who aspire to be journalists could make a break with those of preceding generations who either – because 'it's a job' or because they enjoy it – produced the tabloid press of the past few decades, and refashion popular journalism into something worthy of their readers' time. And not just tabloid journalism; the practices and carelessness of the upmarket press, where mistakes, slurs and fabricated stories are dismissed with indifference or even admiration, can also be large. The development of a culture of real independence, depending as it must on real responsibility, is no quick fix. But a state-approved regulator is no fix at all.[31]

EIGHT

In the market, but free?

Dr Neil Manson, the British philosophy scholar whose evidence to the Leveson Inquiry was quoted in the preceding chapter, has done some practical thinking on the nature of a free press. In a memorandum submitted to the Inquiry, he wrote:

> when we consider the public interest in a free press we need to consider closely the nature of the press in question. That is, we should not ask whether a free press ... is in the public interest, but we should focus, rather, on the various ways in which a free press may, or may not, be in the public interest, depending upon what that free press is both able and disposed to do.[1]

'Able and disposed' summarizes well the constraints either imposed on or self-administered to the news media: frequently, both are in play. The examples here are of journalism practised without much or any state interference – but highly constrained by other forces.

i 'The most important story ... is the one that cannot be covered'

The failure of the Mexican state, its corruption, and that of its police and armed forces, keep the most vital part of Mexican journalism – that which should expose the non-state tyrannies of the country – in a state of fear, punctuated by acts of great, and often fatal, courage in pursuit of the truth.

On 18 September 2010, the daily *El Diario* in the Mexican border town of Ciudad Juarez ran an editorial headlined '*Qué quieren de nosotros?*' – 'What do you want from us?', which ranks among the most poignant pieces of journalism published. It addressed the 'Gentlemen of the different organizations that are fighting for Ciudad Juarez plaza', noted that two reporters had been killed (without attributing agency for the murders), and continued:

> As information workers, we ask that you explain what it is that you want from us, what you intend for us to publish or not to publish, so that we know what is expected of us. You are at this time the de facto authorities in this city because the legal authorities have not been able to stop our colleagues from falling [dying], despite the fact that we've repeatedly demanded it of them.

Control by crime often works in concert with parts of the state. This control can be found in different places – in Russia, for example, especially in the 2000s – but it is most visible, and most bloody, in Latin America, and most of all in Mexico. Control here means that a significant part of the news media cannot safely report the details of organized crime; at times not even the most neutral facts of their murders. Those reporters bold enough to face down those threats often pay for it with their lives.

Mexico is a market economy, with mostly private media; indeed, Carlos Slim, the man who has been the world's richest (he sank to only fifth richest in 2015, with a fifty-five-billion-dollar fortune, as the peso depreciated against the dollar and his telecom company America Movil suffered from tougher antitrust laws), owns large shares in media businesses – including a 17 per cent stake in the *New York Times*. But the inhibition on journalism in Mexico is not the strength, but the weakness of the state. It cannot protect the country's journalists from the drug gangs, and sometimes, through the medium of the police, it preys upon, and murders, them itself.

Ciudad Juarez, in Chihuahua province, has been called 'the most dangerous city in the world'; the feuds between rival narcotics gangs have killed thousands in the city. The journalist Anabel Hernández wrote that '1,500 people [were] executed in 2008, 2,660 in 2009 and by 2010 the figure was 3,116, or about eight murders a day'.[2]

In November 2008, the *El Diario* crime reporter Armando Rodriguez was shot in his car; he was with his eight-year-old daughter, whom he apparently shielded with his body. She survived the attack, but Rodriguez died at the scene. He had received death threats, but kept on working; in the weeks before his murder, he was working on uncovering links between the Chihuahua state attorney general, Patricia Gonzalez Rodriguez, and the drug cartels. The story appeared on 13 November: later that day, he was killed. The case became a high-profile one; the president, Felipe Calderón, who had declared 'war' on the drug mafias, became personally involved and later told a delegation from the Committee to Protect Journalists (CPJ) that the murderer had been found. He was Juan Soto Arias, recently imprisoned for another murder and serving a 240-year sentence.

The Mexican-born journalist Alma Guillermoprieto, one of the most prominent chroniclers of Latin America since the 1970s, was told that Soto Arias's confession had been obtained by means of torture by the military, and that he was not guilty. In any case, the investigation was dropped. The news editor at El Diario, Rocio Gallegos, told her that the paper had given up on much of its reporting: '[There were places] where you simply couldn't send a reporter out alone ... it would be three in the morning and I'd find myself comforting a reporter who was weeping because she'd just received a death threat on her cell phone.'[3]

In 2010 – a high watermark for cartel power and state and journalistic submission – the dominant gang, the Zetas, felt secure enough to develop and enforce a public relations strategy. In Ciudad Victoria, the capital of Tamaulipas state, an editor on one of the local newspapers (unnamed), Martha Lopez, told the CPJ representative Mike O'Connor that the Zetas gave press releases to a local crime reporter – whom they paid – who then passed them on to the city's news media.[4]

At first they received three or four a month, then the frequency grew to two or three a week. They were mainly designed to highlight the real or alleged brutality of the police and military, but differed when they dealt with the local police, assumed to be in the pay of, and complicit with, the Zetas.

O'Connor comments: 'In Tamaulipas ... cartels have penetrated the police and city governments to the point that the cartels almost have free reign, according to reporters in the state's five largest cities. But ... the most important story – that the citizens have lost control of their cities to criminals – is the one that cannot be covered.'

The tempo of killing appears to have moderated since 2010, though not the intimidation. More journalists have been attacked in Mexico City than before; the Article 19 free speech NGO recorded 222 attacks on journalists in 2013 – the majority, extraordinarily, perpetrated by public officials, who all went unpunished.[5] Anabel Hernández writes:

> The drug traffickers impose their own law. The businessmen who launder their money are their partners, while local and federal officials are viewed as employees to be paid off in advance, for example by financing their

political campaigns. The culture of terror encouraged by the federal government itself, as well as by criminal gangs through their grotesque violence, produces a paralyzing fear at all levels of society.[6]

I spoke to Hernández when she was on a trip to the UK, promoting her book *Narcoland*. Though one who faces death threats to herself and her family, she seems cheerful and is wholly determined to use her experience, contacts and intelligence to continue reporting. She stressed that the main point, and impact, of the book was that she was able to pin down a specific and high-level example of corruption: that of Genaro García Luna, who rose to the pinnacle of law enforcement under Presidents Calderón and Fox, creating in the latter's presidency the Federal Investigation Agency.

García Luna, she revealed, climbed to the top of the tree with many public protestations – aimed at the US as much as to a domestic audience – of commitment to enforcing the law and justice, while he was in fact collaborating with the cartels at the highest levels, and surrounding himself with, and protecting, senior officers who were accused of corruption, theft and rape.

On another issue Hernández was also insistent: 'I was and am in more danger from the police than from the gangsters. Everyone knows about the gangs, but to denounce policemen or a police chief is something different' – since they, as state officials, had the protection of the government.

President Calderón ended his presidency in 2012 after two years of unprecedentedly high killing rates. He and his officials saw this as a sign that the strategy of taking war to the gangs was working: they were, said Calderón, fighting among themselves, as well as with the police and military.

Yet it was clear that the culture of the police, in particular, was slow to change. In September 2014, a group of some 100 students, who had travelled to Iguala to protest against what they saw as funding which favoured city colleges over their own rural college, were confronted by police who later claimed the students had hijacked buses and drove off in them. In fact, they had been taken out of the city by the police. Several students were killed and the remainder were rounded up by the police and handed over to a local gang named the Guerreros Unidos (United Warriors) who – the evidence suggests – murdered them. Discounting those students who died before being handed over, and others who managed to escape, forty-three were unaccounted for. However, remains found at the site to which they were taken showed that they had been executed there. Extensive protests followed for months, and the case remains among the most terrible of recent years, and the most destructive to claims that underlying problems were being tackled.

Mexico's neighbour to the north has long given encouraging encomiums to successive presidential initiatives. A better guide to US administration views came when a cable from the US embassy in Mexico City, part of the diplomatic cable trove leaked to WikiLeaks and published by the *Guardian*,[7] showed that US officials believed that President Calderón's push could not match up to the sophistication, firepower and intimidation of the gangs. The cables also showed panic on the part of Mexican high officials: Geronimo Gutierrez Fernandez, the undersecretary for governance, told US diplomats that 'pervasive, debilitating fear' had infected even relatively safe parts of the country. The cable's author comments that 'he expressed a real concern with "losing" certain regions'.

The cable continues:

Mexican security institutions are often locked in a zero-sum competition in which one agency's success is viewed as another's failure, information is closely guarded, and joint operations are all but unheard of. Official corruption is widespread, leading to a compartmentalized siege

mentality among 'clean' law enforcement leaders and their lieutenants ...
[The gangs] are sophisticated players: they can wait out a military deploy-
ment; they have an almost unlimited human resource pool to draw from
in the marginalized neighbourhoods; and they can fan complaints about
human rights violations to undermine any progress the military might
make with hearts and minds.

—

Brazil, the largest Latin American state, is less noted for the control the
crime mafias exercise over the news media and the police: but that control
appears to be growing, the more so as the government weakened in the mid
2010s. This is in part due to corruption scandals, which in many citizens'
eyes (and the law's) puts it on a level with criminals.

In 1985, the country emerged from a dictatorship when the military
government, having lost the support of the elite, held elections and lost
again. Though economic reforms were started under Fernando Collor de
Mello, the first elected president after the end of the military dictatorship,
the country had a weak, corrupt government for nearly a decade. Only
in the mid nineties, when Fernando Cardoso, first as finance minister
then as president, launched his 'Royal Plan', did the economy stabilize.
Cardoso was blamed, however, for growing inequality; he ceded power
in 1992 to a Workers' Party administration headed by Lula da Silva,
who as president radically modified his previous attachment to statist
socialism, stuck to the main lines of an IMF-approved programme and
used economic growth in Brazil to initiate broadly successful social
programmes for the poor.

He picked as his successor Dilma Rousseff, who, as in Lula's time,
faced large corruption scandals in her Cabinet but lacked her predecessor's
popularity in dealing with them; she only just survived a second presidential
election in 2014, beating the Social Democrat Aecio Neves with 51 per cent
of the votes, and was forced into resignation in 2016.

The economy continued to decline: the fiscal deficit rose to 10 per cent in 2015, and 1.5 million workers lost their jobs. The murder rate rose, sharply in the north-east of the country; the grip of the mafias grew, with the two largest domestic criminal gangs, the First Capital Command and Red Command, expanding their interests in drug supply in one of the biggest cocaine markets in the world. The gangs are also active in extortion and kidnapping; a business in which militia groups, made up of police and others, are involved.[8]

Thus, for similar reasons to Mexico, Brazilian journalism is a relatively dangerous trade. 'Brazil is a large, dynamic country where wealth is often expanding faster than the rule of law. That can make things dangerous for journalists and civil society activists who challenge powerful and wealthy interests.'[9] These interests have become savvy in the ways of using privacy legislation to stop the news media covering allegations of corruption or criminality on the part of the powerful.

The reporter John Otis has described how the *Diario de Pernambuco* (which claims to be Latin America's oldest paper), ran a story about allegations of influence peddling by Guilherme Uchoa, the president of the legislature in the state of Pernambuco, which was picked up by the other state media. Then, quite suddenly, the paper went silent, as a judge decreed that any news medium which ran the allegations would be fined 21,500 dollars a day (on appeal, the injunction was lifted).[10]

More lethal action is disturbingly common. The state reporter Keating cites the case of Valerio Luiz de Oliveira, who presented a sports programme in Goiania, who was assassinated outside his studio. De Oliveira had been strongly critical of the management of the city's football team, Atlético Goianiense, and the team's vice president was charged, together with others, for being an accessory to the murder. In May 2015, the body of Evany José Metzker was found in a ditch outside the town of Padre Paraiso in the state of Minas Gerais: his head had been severed from his body. The sixty-seven-year old wrote a blog, Coruja do Vale, which concentrated on corruption in the impoverished north of the state; his wife, Hilma Silva Borges, said that 'given the barbarity of the murder, it was because he hit on something. He investigated mayors, politicians, cargo robberies, prostitution.'[11]

In the same month, the radio journalist Djalma Santos de Conceição was found murdered, with signs of torture on his body, near the small city of Conceição da Feira in the state of Bahia. An unnamed police officer was quoted by the Committee to Protect Journalists as saying that the journalist 'pulled few punches when reporting about and demanding action on local crime and corruption'.[12]

Some journalists charge the police with threats or worse: Enderson Araújo, a blogger and founder of the Midia Periferica, a blog which reports on poor communities not covered by the mainstream press, says he was threatened by a policeman after he had written critically of young men killed in a shootout with police in the city of Salvador. The officer told him to 'stop moving your fingers and criticizing those that really provide security otherwise you might not get any yourself'. Araújo left town. Anna Freitas, who blogs about sexism, was subjected to streams of abuse, with faeces, maggots and sex toys posted to her. The CPJ comments that this kind of abuse, levelled disproportionately at women, 'is increasingly seen as a problem that limits freedom of expression for journalists, bloggers and even commentators'.[13]

Violence against Brazilian journalists has been increasing, and most murders are unsolved. The example of Mexico is a malign warning; after a certain point has been passed, the gangs need to murder less, since they have enforced a rule of terror which almost no one dares break. This inhibition on journalism is largest in the areas that need it most, and blogging, less obviously visible and audible than the press or broadcasting, is no protection. It can be done much more cheaply, can make a rapid effect and can feed and feed from social media: but it means, as Freitas found, that you become an object of concentrated, venomous messages.

'Bello', *The Economist*'s column on Latin America, opined that 'many of the region's democracies are riddled with corruption and conflicts of interest. If democracy itself is to survive and prosper, such abuses by the powerful must be exposed so that they can be punished.'[14] These are the right civic sentiments, but the region's boldest journalists have found that exposing abuses by the powerful has resulted in *them* being punished, often by death.

ii 'We did not grasp what was happening'

In the Communist states, press policy derived from the view that, as Lenin put it in *What is to be Done?*, 'the press should be not only a collective propagandist and a collective agitator, but also a collective organizer of the masses'.[15] This was written in opposition and exile, but the basic purpose of the press remained the same when Communists became the state power.

They put propaganda and exhortation first, and did not adhere to the view that there was an objective truth in events to which journalism should strive. Instead, there was a Communist version of the truth, which was that capitalist and imperialist oppression must be fought, and socialist organization enjoined and encouraged. The newspapers were under party rule.

Vladimír Hudec, Dean of the Faculty of Journalism of Charles University, Prague, in the 1970s and '80s, wrote that 'all journalism – central as well as local – is ... subordinated to the party leadership, it is responsible for its activities to the respective bodies of the Party or the National Front and the socialist state ...'[16] The name of the main Czech newspaper of Communist times made that clear, as the Soviet Union's *Pravda* before it had: *Rudé Právo* (Red Truth). The truth was red: there were no alternatives.

The Czech Republic is the result of a 'velvet divorce' in January 1993, when the new administrations in the Czech and Slovak parts of the country agreed to peacefully separate into two sovereign states. The Czechs had long been considered the most hard-working people of Communist Central Europe – a popular saying was that 'the Czechs can make even Communism work', a feat which gave it the highest GDP per person in the Communist bloc. Its capital, Prague, was among the most beautiful and best preserved in Europe, with some of the loveliest baroque and art nouveau buildings in Europe: even some of the Communist-era housing was distinguished.[17]

Yet it also had Václav Havel, the playwright and dissident who emerged in the revolt against the Soviet Union in 1968, and then again in the 1970s and '80s, as the most stubborn enemy of Communism and the most consistent upholder of liberal values in the region. He was the leader of the 'velvet revolution' in 1988–9, addressing vast rallies and giving voice, it seemed, to a national disgust at a particularly reactionary Communist Party and the then-weakening grasp of the USSR.

Elected president in 1989 by the national assembly – first of Czechoslovakia and then, from 1993, of the Czech Republic – he remained president till 2003, dying at the age of seventy-five in 2011. In an obituary, the writer and scholar Timothy Garton Ash wrote of him that he 'was the epitome of a dissident because he persisted in this struggle, patiently, non-violently, with dignity and wit, not knowing when or even if the outward victory would come'.[18]

In an essay written in 1990, at the height of his world fame, Havel wrote of his country:

Thanks to [the Communist] regime ... the stifling pall of hollow words that have smothered us for so long has cultivated in us such a deep mistrust of the world of deceptive words that we are now better equipped than ever before to see the human world as it really is.[19]

Havel was wrong about his fellow Czechs. During his own two terms as president, the Czech Republic did not produce a governing class worthy of its president's ideals, nor were the people free, in the main, from the blandishments – from the new political classes, often not to Havel's liking – of 'generalizations, ideological platitudes, clichés, slogans, intellectual stereotypes, and insidious appeals'. He himself soon lost some of the aura of the nation's moral guide (it was never assented to by everyone); he was assailed by 'the other Václav', Václav Klaus, finance minister then prime minister of the Czech Republic, who once told me that he regarded intellectuals as nuisances spouting about unrealizable utopianism. (Havel was the European model of an engaged public intellectual, though one who had had to suffer imprisonment for long stretches for his fidelity to his ideas.) In an interview when he was finance minister of Czechoslovakia in the early 1990s, Klaus answered my question about the corruption that was then said to be surrounding his privatization process by snapping: 'There is no sense in dividing dirty money and clean money'; Havel, on the other hand, deplored it – but was powerless to stop it.

Corruption, especially the collusion between the new politicians and the new class of business people who bought up the privatized enterprises at bargain prices, remained a feature of the Czech political economy. In a 2010 cable from her embassy in Prague (leaked by WikiLeaks), the US chargé d'affaires, Mary Thompson-Jones, wrote:

Corruption is a serious problem here, inhibiting business, including US business, and poisoning domestic politics ... ultimately the solution to the corruption problem will require electing a strong, committed leader who has a like-minded Cabinet. Unfortunately, no such political leader has yet emerged. Until one does, the Czech public will remain rightly skeptical of its leaders, equating politics with 'corruptionism'.[20]

Scepticism about leaders has seemed to be the right posture. After a first brief premiership of the Communist-turned-dissident Petr Pithart, Klaus was prime minister from July 1992 to January 1998 – stepping down when a scandal linked to privatizations enveloped his Civic Democratic Party (ODS). Josef Tošovský ran a caretaker government from January to July 1998, during which he was accused of having collaborated with the STB Communist-era secret police. The social Democrat Miloš Zeman was prime minister for the next four years (President from 2013); he was much criticized for public behaviour while apparently drunk, and his strongly pro-Russian views and agreement with Klaus on the environment alienated many, left and right. Vladimir Špidla's two-year term till June 2004 was free from scandal. Stanislav Gross's nine-month premiership ended with a series of allegations of corruption and nepotism. Jiří Paroubek (to September 2006) was accused by a police chief of contacts with criminals and covering up a murder; Mirek Topolánek (to May 2009) resigned after questioning the moral character of gays and Jews; earlier, he had been photographed naked, sexually aroused, at a pool in Silvio Berlusconi's Sardinian villa, with several topless women close by. Jan Fischer's year-long government was relatively scandal-free. The three-year term of Petr Nečas (to June 2013) ended as his chief of staff Jana Nagyová was investigated for involvement in organized crime (she was released, and they later married). Jiří Rusnok's government lasted only six months, to January 2014. Bohuslav Sobotka, leader of the Czech Social Democratic Party, remained premier through 2017.

For journalists, some of whom see themselves as charged with the responsibility of uncovering scandal, the common view that the republic's polity and business culture are deeply compromised is at once a challenge and a reproach. The transition from a widely disliked regime (though not by all: the Czech Communist Party retained a large membership and a bedrock vote after the Communist government's collapse) had been seen by many Czech journalists as a relatively simple process of substituting truth for lies, freedom to inquire against prohibition on inquiry, openness to the world as against a confinement to the Communist bloc. They stepped confidently into a new era – and found themselves unarmed.

Shallowness of understanding is journalism's greatest bane. Journalists in authoritarian societies do not need to understand too much: it is enough that they obey. But for those journalists who work in news media which exist in relative freedom, scepticism must be their default position, but it is one requiring a working knowledge of the subject(s) covered, or it becomes mere cynicism. The journalists who emerged from communist societies had a further problem: they had to grapple with economies whose very hard-wiring was foreign to that in which they had been brought up.

István Léko is the editor of *Lidové Noviny* (People's News); founded in 1893 in Brno, it moved to Prague and became well known for the high literary quality of its writing. The paper was suppressed by the German authorities during the Second World War, briefly revived after it, then closed by the Communist regime in 1952. It began again in the late 1980s in samizdat form and was restored legally in 1989. Léko, who has been on the paper from the nineties, believes that the first years of 'liberated' journalism were a failure. He told me that

> We did not grasp what was happening. We saw ourselves as on the same side as the new politicians and as Havel; and we wrote about the Communists, and the STB, and the past. We were too soft. Everyone who was doing something for the country was 'good'. Meanwhile the relationships between the politicians and the new business people were being quickly formed and the new time of corruption was beginning.

Léko was an economics correspondent, and though he knew something of the capitalist system, it was largely new to him – and even more to his colleagues. Much that was happening was simply not understood; the new journalists were young – typically in their twenties and early thirties – and usually had limited economic knowledge or experience. Léko's colleague, the paper's managing editor Veselin Vačkov, says that 'there were no business journalists here. Everyone was overjoyed that the Communists had gone, but the Czech journalist community was just not prepared for the new era.'

Quite soon, the attention of journalists – always easily seduced by the obvious drama of high-level hatred – was distracted by the increasingly overt sourness of the relationship between the two Václavs, Havel the president and Klaus the prime minister. Journalists formed camps round each man, even within the same newspaper, with each side using the two leaders' arguments as a basis for power. These opposing forces carried on even after Havel's death in December 2011, in different forms, when Klaus, who had succeeded him as president in 2003, was still in office.

One of the consequences of Klaus's economic liberalism was openness to foreign investment, and the entry of German publishing companies into Czech journalism; a takeover so complete that, by the mid 2000s, nearly 90 per cent of Czech journalism was produced by companies with their headquarters in Germany. The two 'upmarket' dailies, *Mladá Fronta Dnes* and *Lidové Noviny*, were owned by the German concern Rheinisch-Bergische Verlagsanstalt; the business daily, *Hospodářske Noviny*, and several magazines, by the German business daily *Handelsblatt*; the tabloid *Blesk*, the *Daily Sport* and the magazine *Reflex* by Ringier; and *Deník*, which changes its editions to serve the various regions, by Passauer Neue Presse.

In a strongly critical essay, Jan Jirák and Barbara Köpplová of Prague's Charles University write that the new publishers

> found the Czech market interesting, also because it was not impeded by
> the existence of traditional titles – and therefore offered good conditions
> for a full and unrestrained development of business strategies leading to

minimization of costs and maximization of profit ... despite declarations
to the contrary, the essence of the transformation was not democratization
of society but creation of a prospering and effectively functioning media
sector.[21]

Many journalists don't think so. Petr Dudek, head of current affairs at
Czech public radio, says that German ownership sharpened reportorial
skills and introduced a more ethical atmosphere into what had been a
fairly anarchic and at times self-enriching practice. Alexandr Mitrofanov,
the chief commentator on the upmarket daily *Právo*, says that the Germans
wanted profit, which, after making considerable investments, they got –
and were not interested in Czech politics; the editorial choices made by the
Czech editors were largely endorsed.

Právo bucked the trend. Its US correspondent, Zdenek Borybny,
returned to Prague, persuaded the still-existent (and still quite popular)
Communist Party to release its paper, took off the *Rudé* (Red) from its
title and refashioned it into a centre-leftish paper, which over the years
has passed into the centre. Mitrofanov, its hyperactive columnist (two
columns a day, with tweets, blogs and radio appearances thrown in),
joined in the nineties as a political reporter and had never been a member
of the party. He says others, who, like President Zeman and President
Klaus before him, are strongly pro-Russian and anti-EU, balance his own
views – strongly pro-Western liberal. The idea is to give a range of views,
and to report straight. Borybny and his paper represented that strand
of Czech Communism which had – like the late Soviet, Gorbachev circle of
aides and supporters – become essentially social-democratic, and which
resisted the plunge into market fundamentalism.

But the Germans retreated in the mid to late nineties, then more rapidly
as the 2008 crisis hit and the profitability of their Czech holdings declined.
The vacuum they left was filled by Czechs, who quickly became a larger
civic problem than the Germans. The new owners were soon known as

the oligarchs, following the example of the Russians who became rapid billionaires in the mid 1990s. Several of them, too, had benefited hugely from privatization, and were surrounded by allegations – usually not conclusively proven – of criminality and corruption; they, too, bought into the news media in part for power, in part for protection, in part from patriotism.

Of these, the best known is Andrej Babiš, who, in the mid 2010s, was deputy prime minister and finance minister and then the most popular politician in the country. He was founder and head of the ANO party (Akce Nespokojených Obĉanů, or Action of the Dissatisfied Citizens – the acronym, ANO, means 'yes' in Czech), owner of the chemicals company Agrofert; his Mafra media group owns the upmarket dailies *Mladá Fronta Dnes* and *Lidové Noviny*; and Rádio Impuls, the most popular commercial radio. Next to him is Zdeněk Bakala, the US-educated banker who built up the coal and coke company New World Resources into one of the biggest in the world; through his Economia group, he has the business daily *Hospodářské Noviny*, the weekly current affairs magazine *Respekt*, as well as the news website Aktuálně. Daniel Křetínský, a lawyer and main shareholder in the EP energy group, owns *Blesk*, the most popular paper in the country.

These purchases meant the exit of several leading journalists, objecting to the 'oligarchization' of the Czech media; one of these, the former head of the Mafra group's internet activities, Dalibor Balšínek, founded a new group, Echo24, saying at a seminar on the media, early in 2015: 'We did not want to work for an owner who has a political party and is one of the biggest employers in the country. We simply could not imagine that we could work for someone like that.'[22] The Echo24 website covers many issues, but tends to return often to stories and commentary which shows Andrej Babiš in a bad light.

The use of the news media for protection is well attested in the Czech Republic. Marek Dospiva, a founder of and partner in Penta, remarked that the best reason for buying media was that they acted as a deterrent against those 'who would irrationally attack us';[23] while Babiš has said that once he became a media owner, journalists started treating him with greater respect.

Babiš is at the centre of attention in political and journalistic Prague, because more than any other figure since the Velvet Revolution, he most resembles a Russian oligarch to the east[24] and Silvio Berlusconi to the south (he is sometimes known as Babisconi). Like the Russian oligarchs Boris Berezovsky and Vladimir Gusinsky, he benefited greatly from privatization and the liberalization of the economy; like Berlusconi, he became very rich through skilful and successful management of entrepreneurial projects, founded a party, ANO, from nothing, became an influential figure in politics, has said that the country should be run like a business and that he is too rich to be corrupt.[25]

Babiš's popularity was rarely less than easily ahead of all rivals. He has expressed, often, his disdain for parliamentary debate and procedure, and for his fellow politicians. All the non-Babiš-employed journalists to whom I spoke said that Babiš interfered in the editorial line of *Mladá Fronta Dnes* and *Lidové Noviny*. Erik Best, an American who has lived in Prague since 1991 and puts out a lively publication called the *Fleet Sheet*, which chronicles the worlds of Czech politics, business and media with a sharply sceptical eye, told me that he believes a handful of oligarchs now largely control Czech society. He also believes that these worlds are mired in corruption – instancing Prime Minister Topolánek's remark during his premiership (2006–9) that it would be good if the rake-off paid to middlemen in business deals involving the government was reduced from an average of 25 per cent to 7 per cent. Best thinks this corruption, and the growing media power of very rich people, is the true story in the country, one which journalism ignores. This is in part because it isn't understood, in part because the 'rule of the oligarchs' is too complete and stifling.

In one well-documented case, the TV channel Prima, whose major shareholder is Ivan Zach, a friend of President Miloš Zeman, whipped up strong opposition to asylum seekers, tens of thousands of whom were, in the autumn of 2015, stranded in Central Europe.[26] President Zeman had expressed strong hostility to immigrants and seemingly in response Zach ordered his station to drop all pretence at objectivity and campaign against entry for any of the refugees. In an audio recording of an editorial meeting where this order was transmitted to the staff, Jitka Obzinová, the editor-in-chief, ordered the journalists to push the new line, saying that 'the custom here is that the broadcast management is God, and one just doesn't talk back to God.' In this case, God took the shape of Luboš Jetmar, the vice president of the parent company, who told the meeting that the crisis was potentially 'the beginning of the end', that 'there are now a few hundred thousand [migrants] here [in Europe], maybe a million, I don't know ... but, as of the moment there are lots of them here, they really won't respect our rules'. If they were allowed in, he said, they would begin to 'really, really push their truth, their way of seeing the world, their religion, and their rules'.[27]

The public broadcaster, Czech TV and Radio, should be, and to a degree is, an antidote. The services, re-established as public rather than party/state broadcasters after the Velvet Revolution, provide by most consent a reasonable service – with better news coverage than any other broadcaster, including analysis and even some investigation in their current affairs output, which reaches a much larger audience than the newspapers. Petr Dudek says that the ethical level of reporting at the service is now high and bribery is rare, but the politicians continually attempt to influence the broadcaster, and complain that it pays too little attention to politics, or to their party, or to their policies.

When you ask about the broadcaster, most people refer to a story which features President Zeman, going to Czech TV at night, after it became clear he had won the January 2013 presidential election. The cameras were following him as he had to be helped from his car, walked shakily into the building, nearly fell over as he missed a step then flopped down, took out a cigarette and asked the director general, who was attending him, for an ashtray. The ashtray was produced, though the building was strictly non-smoking. The story is told in part to highlight the president's frequent appearances when seeming to be drunk, and also to show how servile the station is to the political power.

All the states in Central Europe have struggled with corrupt government–business deals, usually arising from the breakneck privatizations, which the reformers, Western politicians and experts saw as necessary in order to deprive the former *nomenklatura* of economic and media platforms on which they could regroup and attempt a comeback.

In Poland, the most economically successful of the post-Communist states, a scandal in 2002 enveloped the most famed post-Communist paper, *Gazeta Wyborcza*, founded by the Solidarity-aligned journalist and former dissident Adam Michnik. A film producer, Lew Rywin, apparently a government intermediary, asked Michnik for 17.5 million dollars in return for Rywin ensuring a change in the law that would allow the company publishing the *Gazeta* to obtain a TV channel. Michnik did not publish anything on the offer for six months, saying he wanted to protect Poland's negotiation on accession to the European Union; he then published transcripts of the meeting with Rywin in *Gazeta*.[28]

In Hungary, the authoritarian Fidesz government of Victor Orbán introduced in 2011 a regulatory system with sweeping powers to suspend or cancel licences, examine the content of publications and broadcasters, levy fines and limit appeals against the regulator's judgements. The government is also starving the struggling left-wing media by severely limiting government advertising in them. In Romania, the public broadcaster is on a tiny budget and has a very small audience, while business interests dominate the press and private broadcasters, which ensure that they stick closely to the party or the business lines.

In all of these states independent-minded journalists continue to protect space for enquiring journalism in the available media and/or take to the Net to provide parallel journalism which may suffer from few resources but is relatively independent. They work in a society that has become more comprehensible, but which falls far short of the soaring ambitions Václav Havel had for it, and in which he and other journalists of his and the next generation believed the media would play a role, as guardian of the state's ethical probity. In none of them has the stifling control of the monopoly party been reasserted, but the experience of pluralism and the market has been disappointing, or worse, corrupting.

iii 'The intellectual tradition in East Asia ... is that the intelligentsia, including journalists, are part of the power structure'

Japan is a wealthy, pacifist-inclined parliamentary democracy with a purely symbolic, though widely revered, emperor and an increasingly lively civil society. In spite of its eastern position, it is an honorary member of the democratic 'West'. However, the country saw its place in the press freedom ranking compiled by Reporters Without Borders decline sharply in the early years of the 2010s.[29] The Paris-based institute, which orders states on a 'top to bottom of the class' scale, marked it down from a position in the 20s among some 180 states to, in 2016, 72. What had Japan done?

In 2013, the government of Shinzō Abe, who was prime minister from 2012, passed a Law on Specially Designated Secrets, which lists penalties including stiff jail terms for divulging classified information in the categories of defence, diplomacy, counter-terrorism and counter-espionage. The move was welcomed by the US, which had long deplored the relative laxity of Japan's security provisions.[30] The law annoyed journalists, and Lucy Birmingham, president of the Foreign Correspondents' Club of Japan (2013–15), wrote that the bill 'suggests that freedom of the press is no longer a constitutional right' and that it poses a 'threat to both journalism and the democratic future of the Japanese nation'.[31]

Abe's period in government has been proactive in threatening broadcasters and newspapers with retaliation, either through regulation or through denial of access. But there appears to be little solidarity among journalists in opposing the harsher climate, and some evidence points to the government's ability to cow the press and broadcasters. And while the government's legislation may 'chill' some investigation, many of the inhibitions from which the Japanese news media suffer stems from the still dominant culture within Japanese journalism.

In August 2014, an investigation by the *Asahi Shimbun* into the details of the Fukushima power plant's meltdown and release of radioactivity in March 2011 was based on a leaked testimony from the plant's manager, Masao Yoshida, but was sensationalized in some respects. This prompted a scathing response from the authorities, but also from other journalists and the conservative papers, especially the powerful *Yomiuri Shimbun*.

However, the testimony, which had not been made public, did show that the official version of a manager standing by his controls aided by dauntless workers was itself greatly exaggerated – a fact not featured by other news organizations, who preferred to bash the *Asahi*. Martin Fackler, the *New York Times* bureau chief, said in an interview that instead of following up on the details of the transcript to hold the power company, Tepco, to account, the critics 'had instead focused their ire exclusively on Japan's leading left-wing newspaper and antagonist of the Prime Minister'.[32]

Three TV presenters with liberal views – Ichiro Furutachi of Asahi TV, Shigetada Kishii of TBS and Hiroko Kuniya of the dominant public service broadcaster NHK – were all let go, for reasons connected with their coverage of the Fukushima incident.[33] In the last case, Kuniya had presented the station's main investigative programme for twenty years and the reason for her departure, according to colleagues, was her probing interview of the government's chief cabinet secretary and close Abe aide, Yoshihide Suga, on whether or not new legislation on security could lead to involvement in conflicts abroad. Kuniya's approach was reportedly relatively polite if insistent, but it was held to have flouted the unspoken rules for questioning a high-state functionary.

Suga operated as Abe's enforcer in the media. In March 2015, at a press conference, he objected to comments made by a former fellow bureaucrat, Shigeaki Koga, who had set himself up as a critical commentator on TV Asahi, and who had resigned on TV after lashing out at Abe's pressure on the news media. Suga warned that 'we will be closely watching how the channel handles the issue in line with the Broadcast Law'. The following month, TV Asahi executives, with their NHK counterparts, were called in to meet a panel selected by the ruling Liberal Democratic Party, and told they were out of line; the executives returned to the studios and reprimanded the producers of Koga's show.

Koga, who has broken ranks with the bureaucratic class and gone over to those whom that class would regard as the enemy – the liberal media – says 'the Japanese system is structurally biased in favour of the government, since the Ministry of Internal Affairs and Communications grants – and refuses – TV station licences, without an independent intermediary, thus TV stations are under constant supervision and fear losing their right to operate if they challenge the government'. Further, the stations' senior management often cut out editors, and set about 'micromanaging' journalists and coverage, while 'many journalists, recognizing that their bosses are obedient to the government and themselves eager to protect their own careers, hesitate to be critical of the government'.[34]

The 2011 underwater earthquake, the huge and deadly tsunami it caused and the Fukushima power plant meltdown have been at the centre of polemics about press negligence, or inertia, in digging for the details and for criticizing both the power company Tepco and the government. An indictment on the tofugu.com website claimed that the members of

Tepco's 'kisha club' – Japan's unique system of groups of journalists given privileged access to government and corporate leaderships, so long as outsiders to the sanctioned group are kept out of the loop – 'never quite got round to asking the questions the Japanese public most wanted and needed to know ... those independent journalists who did make it into these press conferences were often shouted down by kisha club members if they dared to ask any off-script questions'.[35]

The tsunami-prompted disaster was a terrible one: some 16,000 people were killed, more than 6,000 injured. Explosions and meltdowns were triggered in three of the plant's units; there were no radiation-connected fatalities, and long-term cancer rates were thought to increase only marginally.[36] Still, there were an estimated 160 deaths in the vicinity of the plant over succeeding years that were traceable to the radiation leaks, while there was widespread panic throughout the country over contaminated food and water.

The stakes were high, and there was a focus on the way in which events were reported which hadn't been so strong before. At the centre of this was the kisha club.

Kisha clubs owe their origin to a struggle for freedom to report the Imperial Diet, or parliament, which on its inception in 1890 excluded reporters. The battle to convey to the public what their legislators – for whom few could vote – were saying, was first fought in Britain, from the seventeenth century onwards, until the de facto lifting of reporting restrictions in the early nineteenth century. Britain still has the parliamentary lobby of accredited political correspondents, who are briefed twice a day in a private meeting by the prime minister's media aide who is not named; the US presidency has the White House press corps which is televised and, in the Trump presidency, famed for the aggressive relationship between the press secretary, Sean Spicer, and the White House Correspondents. The same is true in some form in most democracies.

These lobbies are official, in the sense that both sides recognize certain rules – the main ones being that only members of the lobbies will be briefed, and that when briefings are off the record, that is respected. When I covered labour issues for the *Financial Times* in the 1980s, I joined the Labour and Industrial Correspondents' group, organized by the reporters themselves but quickly recognized by companies, unions and government. Membership was obligatory, if one wanted to be briefed. The group was, unusually for such bodies, riven by left–right arguments, and its attempts at excluding non-members broke down as organized labour itself weakened, and the numbers in the group declined.

Kisha clubs spread from the parliament to the ministries, to local government, to the Tokyo Stock Exchange, to corporations. In many of these, there is a room or rooms set aside for journalists, where they can both work and receive briefings and press statements. They also visit the homes of the boss or a senior official of the institution they are covering, usually late at night when he – invariably he – gets home. They are invited in and given views and gossip into the small hours; none of it for publication, but to give officially slanted background, and to cement the bonds between institution and press.

The guidelines provided for the clubs by the Japan Newspaper Publishers and Editors Association emphasize their voluntary nature,[37] and their determination to serve the public's right to know: 'the kisha club is an institution and system fostered by Japan's media industry for over a century in pursuit of freedom of speech and freedom of the press'. Four of its five principles are balancing couplets: 'Freedom and Responsibility', 'Accuracy and Fairness', 'Independence and Tolerance', 'Decency and Moderation' and 'Respect for Human Rights'.

Foreigners who know Japan and speak its language are generally critical. The clubs, taken together with Prime Minister Abe's pressure on the news media, are in considerable part responsible for Japan's low rating in the Reporters Without Borders scale (though in my view, too low). The writer Ian Buruma, who has studied and written widely on Japan, told me:

> the intellectual tradition in East Asia generally is that the intelligentsia, including journalists, are part of the power structure. You dissent from that at your peril. The dissenters from this within journalism are very often those who have been correspondents in the West, especially the US. The magazines take up some of the slack which the papers leave; they get real scoops together with scandals and sex, but they aren't part of the club system.

The dissenters are becoming more numerous, it seems – and better organized. Yu Terasawa, a doughty freelancer, with many investigative scoops to his credit, especially from reporting on the police and crime, founded with others the Free Press Association of Japan. It had its first meeting two months after the Fukushima meltdown, and explicitly linked the perceived need to that. The press conferences are open to all: the first was with the former leader of the opposition Democratic Party, Ichirō Ozawa, who told an interviewer that the mainstream media 'only use the negative parts of his remarks'.[38]

The clubs are less exclusive now because of reforms made by the previous Democratic Party administration in 2009. Foreign correspondents and even freelancers can in theory attend press conferences, though in some cases, if clubs organize these, they keep them out – or forbid them to ask questions, which in any case must be given in advance. Kimiko Kuga, who worked as a freelancer then joined a doctoral programme at Oxford University, interviewed several senior club members for an article she wrote, and found the system working as well as ever. One economics reporter, in the club at the Finance Ministry, told her he visited a senior ministry official at home almost every night. Another, in the Tokyo metropolitan police club, leaked a video of a murder suspect – and was suspended by his fellow members for a month. She wrote that 'all of my interviewees admitted that it was difficult for them to criticize their sources and mostly they tried to find something congenial to say based on the information with which they were provided'.[39]

Hiroyuki Abe (no relation to the prime minister) was a journalistic high-flier in a secure, high-paying job: in his forties, he was the New York bureau chief for Fuji TV, one of the main private networks. Back in Japan, having been exposed to the much more aggressive culture of US journalism, he became frustrated by the passivity of his colleagues, especially in the coverage of the Fukushima meltdown. He told me: 'I was pushing the idea that people should have been evacuated more quickly – why not? But nobody else was running this line. It is obvious that the old [non-Net] media don't think they have the duty to propose, or to criticize.'

In 2013, he resigned, and now runs a more or less one-man website which does what he says the mainstream doesn't – proposes different ways of tackling problems, and criticizes. He says: 'The most serious thing is that the TV companies are so easily intimidated. The clubs are so much part of the system, so tied in to the power structure. You need to break that up, and I think the Net will do it, though it will take time.'

iv 'I think that when journalists come to Israel they leave behind their professional tools'

In the 2010s, politics in Israel shifted to the right. In an article in *Foreign Affairs* magazine in June 2016, the editor of the liberal daily *Haaretz*, Aluf Benn, wrote:

> Israel – at least the largely secular and progressive version of Israel that once captured the world's imagination – is over ... Israel's current leaders

– headed by Prime Minister Benjamin Netanyahu, who metamorphosed after the election from a risk-averse conservative into a right-wing radical – see democracy as synonymous with unchecked majority rule and have no patience for restraints such as judicial review or the protection of minorities. In their view, Israel is a Jewish state and a democratic state – in that order ... Extreme as it sounds, this belief is now widely held: a Pew public opinion survey published in March found that 79 per cent of Jewish Israelis supported 'preferential treatment' for Jews – a thinly veiled euphemism for discrimination against non-Jews.[40]

For all that the right is in the ascendant, two-state liberals are a large group, though are probably more influential in the media, certainly in academia, than with most of their fellow citizens. Polls show a majority of Israelis favour a two-state solution, though the scepticism about its reality is common. Israel's government is also officially attached to the position, though with several ministers signalling dissent. It seems clear that the two-state route is increasingly a formal commitment, no longer one actively pursued, and though they genuinely believe it must be pursued, the liberals accept there can't be a sudden devolution of real power to a Palestinian government and the pullout of the IDF and all settlements.

In a talk in his Tel Aviv University office, the political scientist Asher Susser told me that Israel should make 'unconditional withdrawals' from the West Bank, pulling back the growing number of settlements on West Bank hilltops, while keeping the main settlement blocs, and an IDF presence in the region. He recognized that this would neither solve the issue nor necessarily lessen Palestinian hostility, especially among hardliners like Hamas, but it might start a ball rolling.

He believes that

as the Palestinians proceed to build the institutions of their state, we should withdraw from considerable territories in the West Bank, gradually

– withdraw settlements, particularly – leave the military in many places where we still need them. Thereby we will create the possibility of what I call a 'two-state dynamic' – instead of what we are presently creating ourselves, which is a one-state dynamic, working against our own long-term interests.[41]

For liberal Israelis, who wish for movement now towards a two-state solution, political life exists between two hard facts, which must live in tension. Firstly, that the fight to secure the state in the 1940s, fuelled most of all by a desire for a defensible space after the experience of the Holocaust, was achieved with many Arab deaths and the exile of some 700,000 Palestinians, and that this has left the Palestinians with a burning grievance. Secondly, they cleave to the belief that were they not to have a large, well-equipped and well-trained military ready to strike back at those, such as Hamas in Gaza, intent on destroying Israel then they would be wiped out. Moshe Dayan, when Army Chief of Staff in 1956 (later foreign minister and defence minister), described the dilemma thus: 'We are a generation of settlement and without the steel helmet and the gun's muzzle we will not be able to plant a tree and build a house. Let us not fear to look squarely at the hatred that consumes and fills the lives of hundreds of Arabs who live around us. Let us not drop our gaze, lest our arms weaken.'[42]

The Israeli journalist who has re-presented this dilemma most vividly (and who quoted Dayan's speech) is a *Haaretz* columnist and editorial board member, Ari Shavit, who in his best-selling book, *My Promised Land*, wrote:

Although I oppose occupation I am responsible for occupation. I cannot deny the fact or escape the fact that my nation has become an occupying nation ... on the one hand Israel is the only nation in the West that is occupying another people. On the other hand Israel is the only nation in the West that is existentially threatened.[43]

It's often quoted (the book was very successful), and though honest, it risks posing Shavit, and all Israelis of liberal views, as one who will live with the occupation but, unlike the right, be guilty about it. For a liberal who remains and cannot change government policy, there's probably no way out of that.

The news media had long been largely tied to one version of secular liberalism, and retained, till the shift in public sentiment which Benn describes, many of the anti-right reflexes which had been the dominant media mindset. But in this period, they have themselves reflected the shift to the right – if not enough for the prime minister, nor, perhaps, for many Israelis. Amit Segal, the political correspondent of Israel's most popular TV network, Channel 10, says that

> the media is 'very Tel Aviv' – liberal. My father's generation didn't go into the media; they left it to the left. But then there was a commentator called Uri Orbach. He wrote in *Yedioth Ahronoth* [which had been, till recently, the most popular paper] a column saying that 'good people should go the media'. He meant that people on the right should go into the media – and it is happening. They went into IDF Radio – I do a show there now. And you see a change beginning. Now with social networks, where you are hearing the voices of people, they have to change. There's a strong sentiment against the [liberal] media.

The image of Israel is a central issue of government policy, of which the Israeli media themselves are an important part. So central is it that Prime Minister Netanyahu commands the Communications Ministry portfolio himself, and takes an active part in it – one reason for a downgrade from 'free' to 'partly free' by Reporters Without Borders. Another was that the daily tabloid *Israel Hayom* (Israel Today) was founded and is paid for by the US billionaire Sheldon Adelson, with an investment totalling, in 2016, fifty million dollars, and is a very strong supporter, not so much of the right, as of

Netanyahu personally. Keren Tenenboim-Weinblatt, an expert on media at Jerusalem's Hebrew University, told me that 'it isn't there to make money. It has a political agenda – it is there to support Netanyahu. The first pages are all him – thereafter there's more diversity. It is polemical, but also a tabloid, lots of entertainment, celebrity. The level isn't very high, but it's not low.'

The paper is very aggressively marketed: distributors offer it in restaurants, place copies on café tables and push them through bus and taxi windows. It has displaced *Yedioth Ahronoth* (Latest News) from its once-unchallenged position as Israel's most popular paper – and, in the opinion of many, made that centrist, mainstream paper much more anti-Netanyahu, though not more hostile to government policies, than it was previously. The free newspaper is widely believed to have given Netanyahu an immense boost, at least as much as *The Sun* gave to UK Prime Minister Margaret Thatcher in the 1970s and '80s.

Adelson's tabloid is not the prime minister's only supporter. More judicious bolstering of his government's record, and an argument against those who claim it is veering off into authoritarian territory, comes from Haviv Rettig Gur, the senior analyst at the *Times of Israel*. In a lengthy piece in April 2016 – 'The End of Israeli Democracy?'[44] – Gur mocks what he sees as the overheated charges of the left (and, later, the right) that Netanyahu is pursuing an increasingly authoritarian course. He argues that bills seeking to curb liberal NGOs receiving foreign funding and to introduce the death penalty for terrorists were defeated not by the weakened left but by the right. The death penalty motion was beaten by ninety-four votes to six, though foreign-funded NGOs became subject to a law requiring them to divulge foreign funding if it made up more than half their income. This move was seen by many NGOs as discriminating against leftist and liberally oriented organizations, since they depend most on foreign funding.

Gur sees the battle between the hard tribunes of the right and the civil rights defenders of the left as a kind of self-interested game; he told me that this debate about Israel's democracy, both at home and among those overseas who take their cues from Israel's domestic politics, is mostly driven by the faux stridency of powerless demagogues – by rightists who propose unpassable bills in undisguised bids to become the left's latest bogeymen, and by leftists whose hand-wringing ensures them both their foreign patrons and their mobilizing ethos of victimhood.

Those on the left of Israeli politics see Netanyahu's influence over the period since his re-election as one in which the Israeli media are under threat. Noa Landau, the news editor of *Haaretz*, told me: 'He's in control, in one way or another, of most of it.' He appears to have exercised some of that control over Channel 10, Israel's second most popular terrestrial channel, which had been running on a temporary broadcasting licence. It had been near bankruptcy, but a successful strategy of rebalancing the output towards more news and current affairs by the CEO, Yossi Varshavsky, saved it. It was taken over in May 2015 by a consortium headed by the RGE media group, owned by the London-based Russian-American billionaire Len Blavatnik, and then granted a fifteen-year broadcasting licence.

Channel 10 is generally thought to be somewhat to the left of the more popular/populist Channel 2. In its darkest days in 2014, before Varshavsky's recovery plan had succeeded in stabilizing the channel, it ran a picture of the prime minister with the caption – 'In three days, Channel 10 will close. The Prime Minister, Benjamin Netanyahu, who serves as the communications minister, refuses to find a solution.' (Varshavsky later criticized the decision to run the picture and caption.) The channel features Israel's best-known investigative reporter, Raviv Drucker, who, in a series of reports beginning in 2011, alleged that, when foreign minister, Netanyahu, with his wife, Sara, and in some cases their children, had enjoyed free foreign travel paid for by various foreign institutions. The charges ballooned over the years and in a report in December 2015 by the

State Comptroller, Joseph Shapira, it was claimed that some of the prime minister's trips were paid for by foreign institutions, were not cleared by the Knesset and may have been double-billed.[45] Netanyahu has also been plagued with allegations of receiving illegal funding for his campaigns from Arnaud Mimran, a French businessman on trial in France, in mid 2016, for large-scale fraud; at the same time, the Attorney General, Avichai Mendelblit, was reported as having opened another inquiry, undertaken by an anti-corruption unit, into unspecified allegations involving the prime minister that are said to be 'more serious' than the Bibitours or the Mimran allegations.

I talked to Drucker in the Channel 10 offices; he had just broadcast a programme – *Jerusalem: Divided City* – which, to Varshavsky's delight, had received a high rating for a current affairs programme, and which, Drucker said, 'showed how the city was not undivided as they [the government] say – but as it is. The places outside of the fence – a no man's land – it's a refugee camp for 100,000 people. It is part of Jerusalem, but conditions are very bad.'

In early June 2016, the shareholders appointed a new chairman, Rami Sadan, a public relations executive and lobbyist, reportedly close to the Netanyahu family, who soon caused a row by proclaiming that the channel should broadcast more programmes for those of low intelligence, and for the orthodox believers – even though the main orthodox party, Shas, was, he said, led by 'that thief Aryeh Deri. But we, as the elite, have to broaden the channel's circles.'[46]

As a means of issuing an order to change the editorial direction of the station, it was – assuming reports to be true (Sadan denied them) – maladroit. Both Varshavsky and the head of the channel's news division, Golan Yochpaz, separately confirmed the statement. Deri, at the Interior Ministry, appeared to believe them, issuing a veiled threat that if the prime minister did not force Sadan's resignation, Shas would not remain loyal to the coalition, but would 'vote as it sees fit'.

Channel 10 is clearly an irritant for Netanyahu, and may yet be brought to heel, with or without Sadan at the head of its board. Yet Channel 2 has also been to the fore in reporting criticisms of the prime minister. In May 2016, it aired a series of interviews with the recently retired head of the domestic intelligence agency, Mossad, Meir Dagan, who, when commenting on the most important security threat to Israel in the medium-term future – the possibility of a nuclear-armed Iran – said of Netanyahu, 'I did not trust him. I still don't. I see his conduct. Instead of fighting Iran, he's fighting the US. Instead of Israel working with its closest ally, he's turned them into an enemy. Does that seem logical to you?'[47]

The prime minister's struggle with the news media is aided by the prevailing views of Israelis – who support many of the positions taken by him, even if they dislike the man himself. During the Gaza invasion, Walla, the prominent news website, started a campaign called 'Israel First', aimed at having journalists recognize that they were first of all Israelis, and then journalists. Drucker, the Channel 10 investigative journalist, told me that he prompted it; on a panel discussion during the Gaza War, he began to say he was 'fed up' with complaints about the coverage of the war – only to be cut off by a senior Walla editor, who said, 'You must remember you are first of all Israeli!' Drucker said, 'People applauded this, which made him happy so they started a campaign, Israel First, to get attention.'

I asked Benn, in his office next to the *Haaretz* newsroom, about the campaign (Haaretz Group owns part of Walla). He said, 'The campaign didn't go very far. The fact is, nobody here supported Hamas during the war.' Yet while none supported Hamas, *Haaretz*'s most controversial columnist, Gideon Levy, wrote a column during the Gaza War – 'Lowest deeds from loftiest heights' – which very harshly criticized the Israeli Air Force pilots' part in the Gaza battleground, as in this excerpt: 'It's a war game. They determine life and death, from their lofty place in the sky they see only black dots running around in panic, fleeing for their lives, but also some who wave their hands in terrible fear from the roofs.'[48]

The column sparked anger from many *Haaretz* readers – a greatly expanded group, since the paper is now available via Facebook, so that Israelis who might rarely or never read it can now access it easily. One of the most compelling responses, printed the day following the column's publication, came from a former pilot, Nehemia Dagan, whose son is also a pilot: Dagan invoked the holocaust as a comparison to Israeli military action – a frequent trope. He wrote: 'Levy's implied comparison to the Nazis' blind obedience is infuriating; if only the inhabitants of the Warsaw Ghetto had the options the Gazans do. We're fighting against people who are trying to kill us and, at the same time, without any hesitation, are killing their own people. The elderly, women and children – a helpless population.'[49]

Israeli news media are like the media in every developed state: much more populist than in the past, much less dependent on the opinions and agendas of the political elite. In his book *Telepopulism*, Professor Yoram Peri, former head of the Chaim Herzog Institute for the Media, writes that the first prime ministers, from Ben Gurion to Begin, 'regarded dealing with the media as secondary to the real work of government ... "speak to them less, and the less the better" said Golda Meir to her bureau chief, Simcha Dinitz.' By contrast, 'Netanyahu's daily question was: "What shall we sell to the media today?" The basic conception behind this question was that statesmanship – namely, steering the affairs of state – means foremost setting the public agenda, and this is done through the media.'[50]

One of the most successful shows on Israel's Channel 2 is *Eretz Nehederet* (A Wonderful Country). Among the programme's most popular items is a satire of a BBC news item, featuring a reporter wearing a blazer and a cravat, speaking English in an exaggeratedly drawling voice, whose interviews with West Bank Palestinians (speaking Arabic) are represented as bewailing ruthless and savage Israeli attacks, while an interview with a Jewish Israeli policeman (speaking Hebrew) is translated as the overweight official talking about eating Palestinian children. The BBC, more than other foreign news media that are not obviously hostile, is widely thought to be biased against Israel – though many of those thinking so are unlikely to have seen much of the coverage.

Amit Segal of Channel 2 emphasized that the show was created by leftists and yet they still saw the BBC's coverage as skewed. He had studied for a master's degree at University College London in 2009–10, and says that

> I think that when journalists come to Israel they leave behind their professional tools. I didn't see a single story in the UK that wasn't biased. It's a structural bias. The preconception is that the settlers are to be blamed for the problems of the Middle East. See what Obama said in his Cairo speech: Israel is a colonialist creation and superpower. Anything that the journalists find won't change this perception.

When I asked Benn at *Haaretz* what he thought of the foreign coverage of his country, he replied that 'the reporters who come here don't really report Israel. They are here to report war and peace. That's what this country means to the foreign news media. You can plot it on the hits of our website. The peaks of the traffic are during a war, the troughs are peace. The reporting follows the view of the Western elites: that is, that Israel must give up the West Bank.'

Elhanan Miller, a former reporter on Arab Affairs for the *Times of Israel* and now a writer for the online features site *The Tablet*, spent six weeks on a placement with *The Times* of London in early 2016; he says that his impression was not of pro or anti views, but of indifference: 'They've had enough of us. There's conflict fatigue.' Miller said that when he was in London, the Israeli embassy hosted two IDF officers, both of whom were Israeli Palestinians. He thought this was newsworthy, running against the conventional view that Israeli Palestinians play no part in their country's army; he suggested it to *The Times'* news desk, but no story was commissioned.

> I don't think there is hostility on the part of UK and other foreign journalists to Israel; they try to be fair. In some situations, as in Gaza, where the conditions are difficult and they are completely dependent on translators and fixers, then the coverage can get skewed. There was no direct Israeli coverage because Israeli journalists were not allowed in by the army. Except in one instance where they were taken in to view the tunnels.

At the *Times of Israel* in Jerusalem, Haviv Rettig Gur told me that he sees a foreign press blinded by its own lack of ability to seriously analyse Israel's present conjuncture:

> The 2000 intifada convinced the left that there should be no further movement in that direction. The Jews are not the French in Algeria who came back to France. This means we will never give away the West Bank. There is nowhere else to go. So there is nothing that [John] Kerry [US Secretary of State] can do. And so most of the foreign coverage is prejudiced. It's not, most of the time, anti-Jewish – it's just ignorant. It assumes that we are negotiable. They don't report that the political conditions make it impossible to negotiate.

At the Hebrew University, Tenenboim-Weinblatt says that part of the media narrative is that 'the world is against us. This came out at a meeting journalists had with a Knesset committee. People do follow this narrative, that the country is being picked on. People say – "they look at us only and not the other countries which are worse. They don't understand how we live here."'

Many on the left, especially the veteran Peace Now activists, see critical foreign coverage as wholly justified. I spoke to the lawyer Tzali Reshef in the offices of his law firm, Reshef and Shiff, in a Jerusalem business park. He was a co-founder of Peace Now, one of several former serving soldiers who had come to believe that Israel's position was unjust and repressive. He said:

> I'm not trying to eliminate the threat and say it doesn't exist. But I'm saying that the current position is totally unacceptable to me. I can agree with the world's disapproval. I think this will become worse and worse. The number of Muslims in Europe is growing and growing and this will have an effect unless we change our attitude to the Muslim world. We use the Palestinians for hard labour and to work in restaurants. We sell them our second-rate products.

Reshef believes that boycotts and sanctions are 'ineffective', but says that 'you do need pressure'.

One of the strongest critics of foreign reporting is Matti Friedman, a Jewish Canadian, who was a reporter and editor in the Associated Press bureau in Jerusalem between 2006 and 2011. In an essay in *The Atlantic*, Friedman argued that the Western press has become

> less an observer of this conflict than an actor in it, a role with consequences for the millions of people trying to comprehend current events, including policy makers who depend on journalistic accounts to understand a region where they consistently seek, and fail, to productively intervene ... the cumulative effect has been to create a grossly oversimplified story – a kind of modern morality play in which the Jews of Israel are displayed more than any other people on earth as examples of moral failure. This is a thought pattern with deep roots in Western civilization.[51]

He criticizes the use of liberal NGOs as the main sources of information for journalists:

This alliance consists of activists and international staffers from the UN and the NGOs; the Western diplomatic corps, particularly in East Jerusalem; and foreign reporters ... confusion over the role of the press explains one of the strangest aspects of coverage here – namely, that while international organizations are among the most powerful actors in the Israel story, they are almost never reported on ... Journalists cross from places like the BBC to organizations like Oxfam and back. The current spokesman at the UN agency for Palestinian refugees in Gaza, for example, is a former BBC man.

He sharply criticized his own organization, Associated Press (AP), for its neglect of facts that did not fit the 'Palestinian victim' narrative:

The AP staff in Gaza City would witness a rocket launch right beside their office, endangering reporters and other civilians nearby – and the AP wouldn't report it, not even in AP articles about Israeli claims that Hamas was launching rockets from residential areas. [This happened.] Hamas fighters would burst into the AP's Gaza bureau and threaten the staff – and the AP wouldn't report it. [This also happened.]

AP refuted Friedman's charges, and Steve Gutkin, the AP bureau chief while Friedman was there, wrote at length defending his own and other colleagues' coverage, arguing that Friedman's examples were either false or reflected a legitimate difference of opinion of what constituted a worthwhile story.[52]

Such is the concern about Israel's image that it's given rise to a particular concentration on a certain kind of public diplomacy, named 'hasbara' (explaining). It is designed to meet what a report from the Reut Institute called:

a global campaign of delegitimization [of Israel] ... the work of a worldwide network of private individuals and organizations ... many of [the participants] are European and North American left-wing activists.

> The Western left has changed its approach to Israel and now sees it as
> an occupation state ... if in the 1960s Israel was seen as a model for an
> egalitarian, socialist society, today it epitomizes Western evil.[53]

The government has funded social media activists to counter anti-Israel material and encourages citizens to pass on egregious examples of anti-Israeli propaganda, as well as articles and posts praising its democratic institutions and polity. It arouses some scepticism on the left: it's called 'washing' the country's image (calling attention to Israel's tolerant attitude to gays, and to Lesbian, Gay, Bisexual and Transsexual marches and demonstrations, which is known as 'pink washing'). Landau at *Haaretz* told me that 'Promoting liberal policies doesn't cover up the illiberality of the state, or the effects of the occupation. People see them rightly as different things. The first doesn't excuse the second.'

The illiberality of the state was foreshadowed early in 2017, when opinion and trustworthy reporting, to which Israelis were strongly attached, were being bartered away for political gain – with, if the stories were right, the participation of both the political and the journalistic bosses. One of several charges against the prime minister was that he had secretly met Arnon Mozes, owner of *Yedioth Ahronoth*, to 'offer financial and business advantages to Mozes in exchange for positive coverage of the Netanyahus'. It was reportedly discussed that *Israel Hayom* would be wholly or partly shut down – restoring dominance in the newspaper market to *Yedioth Ahronoth*.[54]

In Israel, both the domestic and the foreign media set a context within which the country is viewed. As Benn says, reporting on Israel is reporting on war, not peace, and peace is increasingly seen as being ruled out by the Netanyahu administration, both by internal critics and by a growing constituency abroad, including in the diaspora. Journalism is always important in determining how a country is viewed. In Israel, it approaches the existential.

NINE

'There is no model for newspapers'

'At the nation's founding ... Americans were concerned with building not just a continental nation but a republican one ... [Their activity] reflected the powerful confluence of democracy and capitalism in eroding certain forms of restricted communication.'[1] The sociologist Paul Starr thus sums up the early American interleaving of commercial and political interest as a freedom of the market, and of thought.

The medium used to spread the effect of the free press was a state enterprise, the Post Office, which sent newspapers through the mail for free. (Public expenditure doesn't get enough credit in the US: the inventiveness of the Pentagon's research arm, DARPA, brought forth the Internet.) The Europeans levied taxes on periodicals, to keep them out of the hands of the potentially revolutionary classes, prone to be enthused by the American and the French revolutions.

The journalism of the United States is the most influential in the world. It is mainly in English, now the world's lingua franca; the big media corporations are still disproportionately American, able to project their journalism most forcefully and, till the 2000s, fund it most generously. American companies, such as Apple, Facebook, Google, Microsoft, Twitter, YouTube and others are now the world leaders in presenting and redefining news, entertainment and communication. American popular culture, in which journalism is increasingly embedded, is hugely attractive beyond the US.

The concern, sharpened by the strong critique of the news media from the right during the US presidential election campaign of 2016, with 'post truth' journalism, is paradoxical, since US journalism has, more than any other national form of journalism, insisted on the facts, and on their revelation; its steady conviction has been, and in most of the mainstream news media remains, that at least a sketch of the truth is available, that journalism's task is to discover it; and that in doing so, it is performing a public good. It has been its appeal to journalists around the world. None of these attributes are unique to the US, but they have been pursued most energetically and exported with an almost missionary zeal.

As the newspaper – the main institution of journalism for the past three centuries – attempts to prolong its life on the Net, it is from the US that models for funding the continued production of journalism which informs and investigates is likely to come. That is because journalism in the US is closer to the centre of public concern than in other societies and there are more centres for its study and development; because the social and legal climate is more supportive of experimentation; and because of the large and rich communications companies which have grown through fashioning the Net into a variety of user-friendly mechanisms. And there was, in the Trump presidential campaign and in his presidency itself, an unexpected gift: the anti-journalism president was very good for journalism. The BBC's Amol Rajan reported that the *New York Times*, CNN and the *Guardian* – all committed opponents of Trump – were experiencing boosts to subscriptions and traffic, as people were avid for news about the new president.[2] In the report, the CEO of the *New York Times*, Mark Thompson, commented that the president's actions and words 'are causing hundreds of thousands of Americans who've never paid for news before to pay for it for the first time ... it's not a political point, it's purely a commercial point: the Trump era seems to be a very good era for quality journalism'.

Journalism is nothing if not a practical trade: 'from early in its history, American culture was oriented more to facts than to theory, more to practicality than to literary refinement'.[3] US journalism drew on a nineteenth- and twentieth-century American tradition of pragmatism evolved by several US thinkers, such as John Dewey (1859–1952), who had a greater influence on journalism than most philosophers because he cared and wrote so much about it, arguing fiercely about its role with Walter Lippmann (1889–1974), the most influential journalist/intellectual of the time.

The scholar–journalist Louis Menand writes that 'Dewey thought ... an idea has no greater metaphysical stature than, say, a fork ... "it is an instrument or organ of successful action" [Dewey's italics].'[4] The pragmatists spoke to 'a generation of academics, journalists, jurists and policy makers eager to find scientific solutions to social problems'. The years in which the group spoke most clearly to the rising generation of influential people were those in which optimism about the power, reach and moral strength of the United States were at a new height, and when journalism could see itself as more than an appendage to political parties; even – to a degree – independent of their employers. Contemporary US journalism's formative years were in these decades, when the foundations of its investigative and analytical mission were being laid, proving robust till today.

A reporter is set to discover a series of facts which can be verified, and which can be made into a narrative form. Stories, often centred on one or a few individuals, really *are* stories, narratives, the most attractive way of understanding facts and events. For the popular city press, this style was shaped to describe the notable events, scandals, celebrities and movements of the urban sprawls. The fact-based narratives provided a basis for grasping the main elements of public life. Journalism had to be written in a way that drew from the techniques of fiction (and sometimes *was* and *is* fiction), but its main democratic purpose, much trumpeted, was as a teacher of civic enlightenment.

That purpose was, and still is, its Sunday best. In the hands of proprietors such as Gordon Bennett, Joseph Pulitzer and William Randolph Hearst, the 'yellow' press of the late nineteenth and early twentieth centuries hadn't many ethical issues to deal with, since it didn't have many ethics. Yet for contemporary journalists, the view that they are engaged in thousands of acts of public enlightenment every day is particularly attractive; it is in that belief that they can insist on a privileged space in which to investigate, to expose, to comment and to insult while being strongly protected from state or judicial censorship, a situation which the judiciary has taken increasing care to guard. 'The [US] press is more free of government restrictions than in any other nation on earth,' writes Columbia Journalism School's Michael Schudson.[5]

The Progressive Era at the turn of the nineteenth/twentieth centuries nursed investigative and campaigning journalism into existence; as journalists broke their links with political parties, of which many had been more or less agents; and as politics and elections became at once less corrupt and more professionalized. Journalists came to own the First Amendment ('Congress shall make no law ... abridging the freedom of speech, or of the press') and see it as a bulwark, against the state first of all, but also as a means of underpinning their status as men and women of consequence with a publicly important mission to accomplish daily.

The amendment has become more powerful, interpreted more fundamentally, in the twentieth and twenty-first centuries than in the eighteenth and nineteenth.[6] In 1971, the Supreme Court upheld decisions of the lower courts not to permit President Nixon to stop the *New York Times* from publishing the Pentagon Papers – leaked to the *Times* by Daniel Ellsberg. In a powerful opinion, much quoted since, the liberal Justice Hugo Black wrote that 'in the First Amendment the Founding Fathers gave the free press the protection it must have to fulfil its essential role in our democracy. The press was to serve the governed, not the governors.' [7]

Journalism's mission, in its most militant defenders' eyes, brooks no dilution – even by patriotism, in a country renowned for its displays of patriotism. In the autumn of 1987, an episode of a PBS series named *Under Orders, Under Fire* had two prominent news show presenters, Peter Jennings of NBC's *World News Tonight* and Mike Wallace of CBS's *60 Minutes*, being questioned by a Harvard professor on an ethical dilemma.[8] A hypothetical situation was outlined, in which the US had sent advisers to 'South Kosan' to assist the military in their fight against 'North Kosan'. The TV reporters, Jennings and Wallace, had got themselves embedded with a crew in North Kosan – and the platoon they were filming had prepared an ambush for a group of South Kosanese and American soldiers. Would they try to warn their allies and fellow Americans? Or would they film? Jennings said he would try to give a warning. Wallace, who affirmed that he would stay quiet and film, turned on Jennings to say he was 'astonished, really ... I'm a little bit at a loss to understand why, because you're an American, you would not have covered that story.' Jennings folded, saying he should have remembered that it was his duty, as a journalist, to remain neutral: 'I chickened out.'

The senior military men on the show greatly deplored the stance of the journalists, and expressed their disgust. Marine Colonel George Connell said that were the journalists later to be hit by stray gunfire, his men would be sent to bring them back, 'and that's what makes me so contemptuous of them. Marines will die going to get ... a couple of journalists.' James Fallows, who related the episode as part of an essay on why the news media were unpopular, commented that 'In other important occupations people sometimes face the need to do the horrible ... when Mike Wallace said he would do something horrible, he barely bothered to give a rationale.'[9]

In 1942, with America at war against the Axis powers, Henry Luce, creator of Time Inc., asked Robert Hutchins, chancellor of the University of Chicago, to set up and chair a committee to determine the present state and future prospects of the freedom of the press. The committee, mainly composed of academics with no journalist on it (though many were interviewed), published its report, 'A Free and Responsible Press', in 1947.[10] It was a call to moral leadership; a high-water mark of American mainstream journalism. It called on the news media – mainly, in the forties, the press – to supply what the public in a democracy needed: it is a daunting list:

> First, a truthful, comprehensive and intelligent account of the day's events in a context which gives them meaning; second, a forum for the exchange of comment and criticism; third, a means of projecting the opinions and attitudes of the groups in society to one another; fourth, a method of presenting and clarifying the goals and values of society; and fifth, a way of reaching every member of the society by the currents of information, thought and feeling which the press supplies.

Hutchins thought this could be done, taking the news media as a whole: but was critical of the way it presently was being done. Important matters, such as the march of new technology, the transformations of labour, the growth of leisure time and ways of enjoying it, education, a growth of liberal attitudes – all these were at best dealt with briefly, 'crowded out by stories of night-club murders, race riots, strike violence and quarrels among public officials'.

The US media didn't live up to the demands of the august committee, but it probably did more than other journalistic cultures. Newspapers, highly profitable, widely read, provided hundreds of reporters to cover the federal government, with thousands more in the states' senates and congresses, courts, police precincts and city halls. Its main TV news channels were embedded in wealthy media corporations, lavishly subsidized by entertainment. If, as Clay Shirky wrote, Wal-Mart paid for the newspapers' Baghdad Bureaus, then popular programmes, such as

What's my Line?, allowed the CBS bosses to make their chief newscaster, Walter Cronkite, and his successor, Dan Rather, into multi-millionaires.

In the high period of US news media – from the fifties through the nineties – money was so plentiful it wasn't discussed (at least by journalists), merely spent. Maureen Dowd, the *New York Times* columnist who worked at *Time* magazine in 1981, recalled in a column that

> on Friday nights, when the magazine was going to bed, there were sumptuous platters of roast beef rolled in, and bars in editors' offices ... It was a plummy time when a top editor could arrive in Paris and think nothing of sending a staffer from Paris to London to fetch a necktie he had left in his hotel room, or of sending a minion flying off to fetch a box of his favourite cigars.[11]

That world has largely gone; much of the commentary on US journalism over the past decade has been on how great it was.

The Net, satellite and cable ripped the cladding off the privileged systems of the mainstream news media, leaving them shivering in cold blasts of public indifference or migrating to more diverting spectacles. The certainty of decline grew in the first decade of the 2000s, though it was the previous decade in which the forces of globalization, bounding free after the collapse of Soviet Communism and the switch to Party-controlled capitalism by the Chinese Communist leadership, were first felt keenly. In its Newspaper Outlook for 2005, the US-based International Newspaper Marketing Association wrote that 'industries which once marketed themselves based on unique value suddenly found themselves competing on price, cutting costs and consolidating ownership ... newspapers are caught up in the same effect'.[12]

Ken Doctor, who feels the pulse of 'newsonomics' for the Nieman Lab, tracking the fortunes of the mainstream and emerging news media, wrote in early 2015 that 'The industry hasn't overall seen revenue growth at all (much less with inflation taken into account) since 2007.'[13] In January 2016, Doctor wrote that 'nothing can stop the decline of newspapers' and linked to a site which showed many of the great newspapers of the nation losing readers at a rate of well over 100 every day.[14]

Mary Meeker, of the Silicon Valley-based venture capital firm Kleiner Perkins Caufield & Byers (KPCB), who posted her annual assessment of trends in the media markets through the early 2010s, turned the knife by comparing ad spend with time spend, i.e. the amount of time and attention people gave to print compared to other media.[15] In 2013, that was down to 5 per cent – advertising was 'overvaluing' print by nearly 400 per cent: that is, assuming a value to advertisers of audience attention to their advertisements of, say, 100 dollars, they were actually paying 400 dollars. Clay Shirky wrote that 'many of their [newspapers'] most passionate defenders are unable, even now, to plan for a world in which the industry they knew is visibly going away ... there is no model for newspapers, to replace the one the Internet just broke'.[16]

One of these passionate defenders was John S. Carroll, who had been one of the most prominent newspaper editors in the land, his career climaxing at the *Los Angeles Times*, which – with large injections of cash by Otis Chandler, a member of the family that owned the paper – had grown its newsroom to rank itself with the east coast *New York Times* and *Washington Post*.

In 2000, the Tribune Company, a corporation based on the *Chicago Tribune*, bought the *LA Times*, and as sales and advertising turned down, the company demanded cuts. Carroll came to the paper in 2000; in his five years as editor, the paper won thirteen Pulitzer prizes. He hired Dean Baquet, later editor of the *New York Times*, and Michael Kinsley, former editor (at twenty-eight) of the *New Republic* and founding editor of *Slate*. These were the achievements from whose lustre an editor, before the 2000s, could have basked. Instead, the paper's new owners, who saw advertising and circulation falling, asked Carroll to make cuts in 2003, then more, and more, leading him to resign in 2005. A year later, he gave a speech to the American Society of Newspaper Editors. It was a eulogy for a noble profession overtaken by hucksters, and a warning to a great nation, undefended by its news media, prey to every kind of unexamined political chicanery and unchallenged demagogue:

> If, at some point in America's newspaper-free future, the police decide that the guilt or innocence of murder suspects can be determined perfectly well by beating them until somebody confesses, who will sound the alarm, as the *Philadelphia Inquirer* did in 1977? Or, if some future president secretly decides to nullify the law and spy on American citizens without warrants, who – if the *New York Times* falls by the way-side – will sound the warning? Our corporate superiors are sometimes genuinely perplexed to find people in their midst who do not feel beholden, first and foremost, to the shareholder. What makes these people tick? they wonder. The job of any employee, as they see it, is to produce a good financial result, not to indulge in some dreamy form of do-gooding at company expense ... even outside the corporation we have lost stature. We might see ourselves as public servants, but does the public see us that way?[17]

Carroll's speech was a patrician journalist's revenge on the money-grubbers who had made his editorial chair untenable. 'Serving the reader' was a public good; 'serving the shareholder', though the basis of US capitalism and a fiduciary duty on company leaders, was ultimately selfish, even shady.

He contemptuously dismissed bloggers as being merely parasites. The speech ignored other centres of account-holding: the government and its institutions, the Congress and Senate both at the federal and state levels; the huge range of NGOs of every kind; the courts and the law enforcement agencies. Carroll fell into the journalists' trap of regarding all of these – with the partial exception of NGOs, many of which have made an implicit compact of mutual support with the media – as only requiring, not exercising, account-holding. Yet government, the legislatures, the courts and of course NGOs exist, in part, to hold powers other than themselves to account: it was, after all, a government which agreed the US Constitution, and wrote in the First Amendment, and a supreme court which delivered the judgment that has been its shield ever since. Modern democratic society is a web of institutions which both wield and question power.

Five years after he wrote about how US newspapers were created, Paul Starr had come to the conclusion that they were being destroyed, and their public role had to be found elsewhere. In a 2009 essay, he wrote:

> If we take seriously the notion of newspapers as a fourth estate or a fourth branch of government, the end of the age of newspapers implies a change in our political system itself ... if we are to avoid a new era of corruption, we are going to have to summon that power in other ways. Our new technologies do not retire our old responsibilities.[18]

These voices – many others were heard in the same vein – spoke the truth as they saw it. The more aggressive Netizens, however, saw them as Jeremiahs protecting dead tree production, like a Home Guard with ancient rifles. As the latter recited the defeats of once-proud newspapers reduced to wisps of their former selves or to the indignity of Net-only existence, the new guard pointed to news organizations new and old configuring their services for iPad and iPhone consumers, leaving the old guard nodding over the *New York Times* in an East Village café.

The energy still being pumped into the news media in America is the largest hope journalism has that it will find a way of paying for itself when newspapers are killed by the Net, television news and current affairs are cut and trivialized and TV channels themselves abandoned for YouTube and social media. How US journalists and would-be journalists refashion the trade for the Net, and how far they acquire audiences for holding-to-account journalism, is central to its continued, popular existence.

In America, that which is new, welcome or not, arrives more quickly than elsewhere. The fundamental challenges of the Net came in the early 2000s, as it became the main carrier of journalism. There's some dispute about how complete its domination will be: some believe there will be a more than vestigial survival, especially of the global brands, as The Economist, the Financial Times, the International New York Times and the Wall Street Journal.

Lionel Barber, the editor of the Financial Times since 2005, believes that financial papers will survive by making money from digital circulation, where they can charge premium prices, and possibly as newspapers. He told me:

> Why will we survive? Because of accuracy, which we put a lot of time in to ensure. The information is reliable. And If you pay a lot more for the paper, you don't lose: you make money by reading it. General news is a commodity now: so general newspapers find and will find it much harder.
>
> When I came as editor in 2005, we decided to go digital, aggressively. We raised prices. We wanted to get off the newsstands and become a subscription business. And it worked. We had much going for us. We could deploy expert people to cover the central institutions of the world economy, as the central banks. We have world-class commentators.
>
> And going for us also – the English language. And you have to say that the financial crash [in 2008] was a fantastic opportunity for us, in terms of making it understood.

A little before we talked, in March 2016, Nikkei Inc., the owner of the Japanese business newspaper of the same name, bought, for 844 million pounds, the Financial Times from Pearson, its owner since 1957. The Nikkei sells nearly three million copies daily, but has only 400,000 digital subscribers; the FT's paper circulation was by the mid 2010s under 200,000, but its digital subscribers were rising above 600,000. (I was a reporter for the FT for many years and remain, at the time of writing, a contributing editor.)

Barber may be right or wrong. Certainly, in the mid 2010s, the success of the FT is in marked contrast to the financial struggles of other UK papers, including the *Guardian*, which had a series of important scoops in the 2010s that made its name known globally. But it's quite conceivable that a new website, or a series of websites, could, if well financed (possibly by Bloomberg or Springer, the latter of which competed with Nikkei Inc. for the FT), carve deeply into the areas the FT has made its own and fight it on to the canvas. No niche is also a fortress.

No one knows what will happen next; in any case, the challenges remain the same, whether digital sweeps the board or is merely dominant. In the report of the committee that bears his name, Robert Hutchins listed five 'ideal demands' of journalism: to provide a factual, truthful and context-rich account of events every day; to offer space for the widest spectrum of comment; to be fair in the presentation of the actions and beliefs of groups or individuals; to fully and fairly describe the motives and activities of government; and to grant as full access as possible to current information. Journalism ceases to have a purpose if these are not at least attempted.

The unbundling of newspapers and to a lesser degree broadcast news separates out the elements which made up the packaged product, and subjects them to market tests from which they have been shielded. For those who feel deprived of the close attention newspapers gave to federal and state politics, a very wide range of sites have been developed that specialize in politics, spawning sites still more specialized and niche.

Nate Silver, a talented pollster, developed a blog named FiveThirtyEight which he deployed to great effect in predicting the results of state-wide and presidential elections in 2008 and 2010. Hired by the *New York Times* in 2010, he stayed till 2013, attracting the attention of a significant part of the readership who relished his hard-fact-based journalism, retaining a high degree of accuracy in his predictions. He was less popular with his *Times* colleagues than with the public, and while the then editor, Jill Abramson, tried to keep him, the CEO, Mark Thompson, was reportedly cool on whether he stayed or went.[19] In March 2014, Silver took a generous offer from the sports channel ESPN to host his site, which, with a staff expanded from two to twenty, also worked on predicting economic issues and science as well as sports, especially baseball scores.

In a manifesto, Silver said he launched FiveThirtyEight because he believed that 'there is both a need for more data journalism and an opportunity to build a business out of it ... the news media, as much as it's been maligned, still plays a central role in disseminating knowledge'.[20] Interviewed as he was setting up his new site by *New York* magazine, he was brutal about his competitors, saying that many of the most distinguished journalists wrote 'bullshit', and went on:

> the op-ed columnists at the *New York Times*, *Washington Post*, and *Wall Street Journal* ... don't permit a lot of complexity in their thinking. They pull threads together from very weak evidence and draw grand conclusions based on them. They're ironically very predictable from week to week. If you know the subject that Thomas Friedman or whatever is writing about, you don't have to read the column. You can kind of auto-script it, basically.[21]

Here was a proud defiance of one of the rules of the more cautious journalist – don't give your future critics, in a tank full of piranhas, reasons for ripping your flesh by proactively tearing into them. Leon Wieseltier, for many years the literary editor of the *New Republic*, took direct issue with Nate Silver, writing that 'the intellectual predispositions that Silver ridicules ... are "nothing more than beliefs". What is so sinister about beliefs? ... Without beliefs we are nothing but data, himself included, and we deserve to be considered not only from the standpoint of our manipulability.'[22]

Paul Krugman, a Nobel Prize winner and, with Martin Wolf of the FT, one of the two most famed economic journalists in the world, came back hard. He thought that the data-laden pieces lacked context, and levelled other such charges, before concluding that 'so far [FiveThirtyEight] looks like something between a disappointment and a disaster'.[23] Silver said this showed that Krugman, 'with his pundit hat on, had made no attempt to be fair'; Krugman, perhaps thinking that Silver had seen nothing yet, responded that FiveThirtyEight was 'sloppy and casual opining with a bit of data used, as the old saying goes, the way a drunkard uses a lamppost – for support, not illumination'. This slugging wasn't elevating, but it was spirited.

Ezra Klein (born 1984; Silver was born in 1978) had blogged intelligently since his late teens, was an associate editor of the *American Prospect* in his early twenties and lifted the drifting circulation (or slowed the drift) of the *Post* in his mid to late twenties with a blog which apparently fed a general desire for more explanation. Vox Media, itself a new series of sites on various subjects, hired him to refashion his blog in early 2014. In his manifesto, Klein told the slow learners: 'New information is not always – and perhaps not even usually – the most important information for understanding a topic ... [Now, however], there's space to tell people both what happened today and what happened that led to today.'[24]

Klein thinks journalists should get to understand things well enough to explain them to audiences who don't, or only partially do, and thought that the conventional route into journalism was no longer of use. He commended a critique of journalism schools by Michael Lewis (of *The Big Short* fame) in a 1993 *New Republic* piece, in which Lewis argued:

> Those who run, and attend, schools of journalism simply cannot – or don't want to – believe that journalism is as simple as it is. The textbooks,

the jargon, the spell checkers – the entire pretentious science of writing journalism only distract from the journalist's task: to observe, to question, to read and to write about subjects other than journalism. They have less to do with writing journalism than avoiding having to write journalism at all.[25]

Better, thought Klein, to do the maths, and understand process; after all, 'pretty much everyone in journalism can write'.

Journalism schools everywhere in Western societies do face an existential question: why pay money for a course when you can't get a paying job in a market which the Net is shrinking? The financial journalist Felix Salmon, who credited himself with intelligence, good (liberal arts) education and high literacy and numeracy, believes that while these attributes had served him well in journalism twenty years ago, they were of little use now:

Labour has almost no leverage over capital any more, which helps explain the rash ... of start-ups: they're nearly all based on the idea that there is a bottomless pool out there of people with smartphones willing to do just about anything (drive a car, go shopping, do laundry, clean an apartment) for fifteen dollars an hour. If a company loses one of those workers, it's no big deal, it just replaces that person with someone else who's just as good and just as cheap. Now just apply that model to journalists.[26]

The aristocrats of the old media continue, as long as they can, to look through their lorgnettes with scorn at the new media. Chris Matthews of MSNBC, when asked to comment on a Vox post on the US response to ISIS, responded with contempt for what he sees as a lower order of journalism than the polemical broadcasting he practises: 'Why would I respond to something like that? ... Let me deal with the grown-ups – let me deal with the political people and not get involved in the blogs and the websites, okay?'[27] Matthews' response was a more than usually overt expression of disdain, which showed a surprising underestimation in a senior media figure of the serious attention the 'political people' and the 'grown-ups' were showing in sites like Klein's.

Yet the largest and most damaging criticism came from Klein himself. In an essay published in April 2014, he highlighted the work of the Yale law scholar Dan Kahan, who, with others, had done some research into why objective, scientifically verified evidence didn't resolve political and other disputes – and concluded that the combatants didn't want enlightenment which might contradict their position – they wanted to win: 'To spend much time with Kahan's research,' he wrote, 'is to stare into a kind of intellectual abyss ... Kahan's research tells us we can't trust our own reason. How do we reason our way out of that?'[28]

Klein tried – and could only come up with the 'hope' that faulty evidence would be found out (as on climate change) because of the damage policies based on it would do and thus face a reckoning at the polls. It's admirably honest, the kind of self-reflection which Net journalism, with its more freewheeling, open style, encourages.

The media commentator Jack Shafer wrote of an interview Klein and his colleague Matthew Yglesias had in February 2015 with Obama that

> they're less interested in interviewing Obama than they are in *explaining* his policies [Shafer's shocked italics: a journalist *explaining* a politician, when his obvious job is to *trash* him]. Again and again, they serve him softball – no, make that Nerf ball – questions and then insert infographics and footnotes that help advance White House positions ... I've seen subtler Scientology recruitment films.[29]

For Shafer, Klein committed the largest sin in the current political journalism book: he wasn't aggressive – even though, as Shafer also wrote, aggression and attempts at trick questions don't get anywhere with practised interviewees.

In fact, Klein got a real insight into how Obama sees the media – and how he is determined to work round them. The president said that

> my advice to a future president is increasingly try to bypass the traditional venues that create divisions and try to find new venues within this new media that are quirkier, less predictable. You know, yesterday I did three interviews with YouTube stars that generally don't spend a lot of time talking about politics ... when you talk to them very specifically about college costs or about health care or about any of the other things that touch on their individual lives, it turns out that you can probably build a pretty good consensus.

His successor as president did go round the traditional venues, but also charged into them, seeing them as enemies.

New projects, scrambling to fill the hole that the collapse of newspapers is leaving, seek to defy the pessimism of those, like John Carroll and Paul Starr, who see in that collapse a tragedy for democracy. The Texas Tribune, an all-digital not-for-profit news site, supported by donations, is using its growing reputation to host conferences and other events to increase its income. The Global Post, also founded in 2009 with 8.5 million dollars in private funding, specializes in news from abroad – 'an American voice in foreign news'. It is a for-profit organization (though it may not yet make a profit), which has built a revenue stream from syndication agreements with broadcast channels. CALmatters, launched in the summer of 2015, is dedicated to covering Californian politics. It was founded by a former public relations executive named Simone Coxe who noted the cull of reporters from Sacramento, the site of California's government and legislature, and, tired of people complaining about bad government, determined to explain the issues more clearly and more fully.

CALmatters' funding illuminates the nature of many of the new journalist ventures. It's a non-profit (ventures like this might be better called yes-loss), but its location in California and its public mission to enlighten appealed to the large community of new-tech-rich in Silicon Valley, many of whom have contributed. They include John Doerr and his wife Anne; Doerr is a venture capitalist in Menlo Park in the Valley, with a net worth of 4.1 billion dollars (*Forbes*, 2015) – he is ranked the 135th richest man in the world; Mick Hellman, founder and managing director of HMI Capital, a San Francisco private equity firm; Craig McCaw and his wife Susan – he is a cell phone entrepreneur, she is a former ambassador to Austria; and Tom Sudberry, founder and chairman of Sudberry Properties. The list also includes the former National Security Council director, then Secretary of State (in the George W. Bush administrations) Condoleezza Rice, and the former Secretary of State (in the Reagan administration) George Shultz. Its list of supporters suggests that a money-losing venture can survive with the support of rich sponsors; how stable that will be is a large question.

Many of these start-ups are formed for strongly liberal reasons, based on the view that journalism which enlightens also develops better citizenship. The Global Post, which has struggled for much of its life, merged with, or was taken over by, Public Radio International in 2016; the merged entity pledged to use in-depth reporting to 'create a more informed, connected and empathetic world'. PRI/Global Post has a large newsroom and many correspondents, but most of the news start-ups have staffs of around ten (the Texas Tribune is a giant, with fifty staff). Many have less than ten and they often work furiously hard, even – most of all – when they're famous. The former *New Republic* editor Andrew Sullivan, who blogged to a large fan base since the mid 2000s, has written enthusiastically of the experience: 'for all the intense gloom surrounding the newspaper and magazine business, this is actually a golden era for journalism. The blogosphere ... has exposed a hunger and need for traditional writing that, in the age of television's dominance, had seemed on the wane. Words, of all sorts, have never seemed so now.'[30]

Yet Sullivan gave up in 2015. The Dish, the website he created in 2013, had relied on financial support from its readers, and though Sullivan's fame and fine writing secured him an initial splurge, it thinned out. Furthermore, he was exhausted: 'After years and years of intense, always-on-deadline work – not just editorially, but also these past two years in running a small business. We're a very tight ship as we are, with a drained crew. The seas ahead would be extremely rough, and the danger of sinking without a captain quite high.'[31]

From the mid 2000s on, a series of sites were launched, some of which grew into new kinds of hybrid news, social and entertainment platforms. Vice, which has its beginning as a jobs site in Montreal in 1994, grew in twenty years into a multi-media organization which first hosted entertainment then branched into news. Some of its success relies on a disdain for the canons of journalism. One of the founders of Vice, Shane Smith, did an interview with David Carr of the *New York Times*, describing the Vice style of journalism in ways that would have shocked the Hutchins Committee. On a reporting trip he had made to Liberia, he said, 'I don't know Liberia, I don't know what's going on, I don't pretend to, I'm not there to solve the problems of the world, I didn't get flown in on a special ... thing, I'm just a regular guy, but I've been to some places and I thought, this is fucking insane.'[32] The interview then cuts to a clip of a young Liberian man who says: 'Before a battle we kill an innocent child and we drink his blood.' Then cuts back to Smith, who says, 'Cannibalism, that's fucking insane ... and the *New York Times* is meanwhile writing about ... surfing ... and I'm saying, you know what, I'm not going to talk about surfing, I'm going to talk about cannibalism because that fucks me up.'

Carr, sharply, tells him that 'before you ever went there' *New York Times* reporters had written at length about the genocides in Liberia, 'and just because you put on a fucking pith helmet and went there doesn't give you the right to insult our coverage'. Smith, unabashed, continues, 'I'm just talking about what I saw there.'

In an interview with CBS's *This Morning* in March 2014, Smith said there was 'a changing of the guard' in journalism, in which Vice was a leader: that style was, in part, 'where we press the button [on the camera] and let the story tell itself'. He said that Vice had defied the conventional wisdom, which held that viewers, especially youth, wanted short and trivial news: Vice did long-form documentaries and serious subjects. 'Young people are angry,' he said, 'they're affected more than anyone else by unemployment … What we've seen so far [in protests] is going to be a picnic.'[33]

Smith – whose net worth from his share in a company worth 2.5 billion dollars in 2014 was estimated by *Forbes*[34] at 400 million dollars; he was reported to have spent 300,000 dollars on dinner for thirty people in Las Vegas in February 2015[35] – is some measure away from the young people with whose anger he sympathizes. But he has done well from their viewing habits.

In the mid 2000s, Vice still trailed BuzzFeed in audience – less than thirty-three million unique US views in mid 2015 as against BuzzFeed's seventy-four million, though this excludes its exposure on TV through HBO, YouTube and videos.[36] It is held in high regard by the market for its strong connection with the millennial generation. It targets its demographic cannily, doing some pieces which normally elude the mainstream media, such as having the film-maker Medyan Dairieh embed with ISIS in the summer of 2014, a bold and risky venture that yielded some fine insights, including a catechism given to an eight-year-old boy by his father, both recently arrived from Belgium, on why the *kuffar* (apostates) must be killed.[37] At the same time, Dairieh included no condemnation, implicit or explicit, of ISIS: in a note on his filming, he expressed his gratitude to his hosts for conducting him back to non-ISIS territory safely. Andrew March in *The Atlantic* questioned whether or not it could, under current US legislation, be considered a crime.[38] It contrasts with the comments made after the embed by the seventy-four-year-old German journalist Jürgen Todenhöfer, in 2014, who said that the group was both more dangerous and more brutal than it had been represented.[39]

In 2015, Smith did two interviews – one with Justin Trudeau, leader of the Canadian Liberals before the Federal election,[40] which the Liberals won, and another with US President Barack Obama.[41] In both, Smith privileged issues like the environment and the legalization of marijuana – both men were convinced of the need to do more to preserve the earth's ecology; Trudeau was for marijuana legalization, Obama against. In both, too, Smith adopted the position not of a mainstream interviewer with a stock of difficult questions, addressing the assumed weak point of the interviewee's position, but rather that of a sympathetic interlocutor. He grunted sympathetically through both, or said 'sure, sure' approvingly. With some of the questions, especially on the environment, he took the attitude of a fellow activist, encouraging his interviewee's commitment to change.

The Vice style, in both its interviews and its many documentaries, is largely to eschew a point of view and to employ a manner of questioning that is almost the opposite of the insistent, aggressive approach of many mainstream reporters, who wish to be seen as taking no nonsense or evasions from politicians.

BuzzFeed, founded in 2006 by Jonah Peretti, had begun life as a laboratory for creating viral content. Peretti had been inspired when, while teaching computer science in New Orleans, an exchange with Nike over his request to print 'Sweatshop' on a pair of the brand's shoes went viral after he forwarded the emails to ten friends.[42] So widespread was the response – Nike had been embroiled in accusations of using sweatshop labour – that Peretti was invited on the *Today* show to debate, with a Nike executive, labour practices in the Far East. Peretti, from his stumbling upon the phenomenon of memes with his Nike exchange, has built a new Net empire on it.

A meme, the word invented by the biologist Richard Dawkins, is an idea or story that spreads rapidly. Peretti saw, more clearly than other entrepreneurs working in the new media, its huge possibilities for making money. A profile of Peretti and of BuzzFeed commented that 'beneath BuzzFeed's cheery gloss lies a data-driven apparatus designed to figure out what makes you click. Peretti is aware that if he really has divined that secret ... he will have developed an asset of immense value.'[43] Thus readers of the BuzzFeed material set the hierarchy of news value, usually through Facebook preferences, while the wall between editorial and advertising is lowered to the point where one can step lightly over it.

In November 2014, BuzzFeed's editor-in-chief, Ben Smith, announced that his site had signed a deal with Facebook to gain access to the latter's research into the feelings, thoughts and dreams of their users. Writing on his website, Smith enthused: 'This data will be drawn from a Facebook project working in the tricky field of "sentiment analysis", the attempt to analyse people's feelings based on what they write.'[44]

BuzzFeed and Facebook are both working to re-engineer the media into a new relationship with politics and the state. They want to explore and affect the sentiments, thoughts and private preferences of citizens in a more powerful and direct way than the mainstream media have been able to do. Because sites like BuzzFeed and Facebook have made it their business to collect and analyse the individual natures of their users, they are set to take the stage as the major media determiners of electoral success or failure. In his website post, Smith wrote:

At some point in the next two years, the pollsters and ad makers who steer American presidential campaigns will ... eventually, realize that the viral, mass conversation about politics on Facebook and other platforms has finally emerged as a third force in the core business of politics, mass persuasion. Facebook is on the cusp – and I suspect 2016 will be the year this becomes clear – *of replacing television advertising as the place where American elections are fought and won* [my italics].

Though both Smith at Vice and Peretti at BuzzFeed are enthusiastic boosters of their millennial-friendly offerings, they face continuing hostility from the mainstream media, which see both their journalism and their business models as a lowering of standards – firstly, by being reluctant or unable to challenge power, and secondly, by structuring their sites to attract as much advertising as possible, wooed in by an environment which doesn't much distinguish between editorial and ad copy. Jeff Zucker, the CNN president, said: 'I don't think Vice and BuzzFeed are legitimate news organizations. They are ... native advertising shops. We crush both of them. They are not even in our same class.'[45]

Vice, at least, has also been getting a bad name among its contributors. A critical piece in the *Columbia Journalism Review* claimed: 'journalists who have worked for Vice tell CJR that the company published their work without paying them for it, promised them assignments which were later rescinded, and asked reporters for their help with documentaries that covered issues they had written about without any plans to pay them for their work.'[46]

The exploitation is alleged to be universal: two experienced French journalists were phoned continually by a Vice producer to give leads and advice on the Paris Muslim community after the 2015 attack on *Charlie Hebdo* – but all requests for payment were ignored or set aside with promises to come back later. A Moroccan reporter, Aida Alami, who received the same treatment, retaliated by sending out, to a list of freelancers held by the *Review*, a '"Warning for freelancers re: Vice". Within minutes, my inbox was flooded with emails from other journalists who had suffered similar misfortunes with Vice. Most of the stories were worse than my own.'[47]

Political communication is changing because political journalism is changing; its citadels of excellence are now trembling, collapsing, even disappearing. One of the privileged sites from which to survey what's happening is *Politico*, the Washington-based website that aspires to be the closest watcher and holder to account of the most powerful complex of governing institutions in the world.

John Harris, one of its two founders, came into journalism in 1985. His was a blessed entry: days after graduation, he was accepted as an intern in the *Washington Post*, and twenty years later, became the paper's national politics editor, top of the political journalism heap in the US.

Yet within a few years, he was planning an exit, and with Jim VandeHei, the *Post*'s White House correspondent, he left the paper and founded – across the river, in an office tucked behind a TV station's studios – *Politico*, with the explicit mission to cover US politics more closely, even more intimately, than a newspaper could or did (VandeHei left *Politico* in 2016). Speaking in a small office overlooking the newsroom, he said:

> For some years after that I thought, everyone thought, that what was on the front page of the *New York Times* or the *Post* was by definition important. By virtue of their sources, ability to promote, the writers.
>
> Then there was a kind of – holy shit! What is this about, this new world? – moment. We thought – we don't want to be at the old party any more, we want to be at a new party. Our strategy back seven years ago was to create a niche – that the future is more robust with a niche model than a general one. I grew up in the old world, I liked the fact that I worked for a paper that did cover the world. But the old world is now deconstructed – and it's deconstructed along specialities. *Politico*'s is not going to work unless we cover politics better than the *Washington Post*.

Harris thinks that he and his colleague got out just in time, because there is a new vision of journalism – call it the auteur school – in which the business shifts from being organized by institutions to being organized around individual journalists with discrete followings. That's a new notion, this solipsistic brandedness [of journalists like Nate Silver and Ezra Klein]. The old organizational notion in journalism was exactly the opposite. There were never enough readers interested in one subject or one writer so you created a package of many subjects and writers, sharing the attention and the rewards. This was an older method of traffic aggregation. Everybody benefited from the combined heft and influence.

I wouldn't want a whole lot of twenty-two-year-olds trying to be Ezra Klein, that would be a pain in the ass – but I do think it's true that people should early in their careers acquire expertise. For my generation the recipe for success was: be able to cover any type or style of story. The key now is for people to identify themselves round a niche specialism: as – I cover economic policy-making better than anyone else. I'm an expert on energy – so if the *New York Times* is looking for an energy reporter they will be looking for me ... You work your way up the ladder that way – the damn ladder isn't there anyway. So make yourself the indispensable franchise.

Politico quickly became significant. Its staff grew to some 300, with (according to the analytics firm ComScore) seven to eight million unique visitors and fifty million page views in an average month, and users each spending an average of thirteen minutes on the website. In mid 2015, it founded a bureau in Brussels, believing the European Union was being covered badly. The belief that covering it better would gain a substantial audience was a risky one, but by the end of 2015 it seemed to be paying off: Harris announced a large expansion in staff and coverage, saying in a memo that 'every critical indicator – audience engagement and growth, advertising revenue, Pro subscription revenue – is ahead of the forecasts in our original business plan'.[48]

Politico is high-minded – in the sense that it believes many people want to know and should know a lot about politics, which isn't just about how awful politics and politicians are. The writer on media Michael Wolff wrote that 'much of the country may still find politics to be an execrable and mind-numbing proposition, but *Politico* has built a far-flung network of actual and armchair political professionals who find it not just exhilarating but habit-forming. They're on the edge of their seats.'[49]

It has – so far – done what Harris describes should be the route for the aspiring young journalist. It has an audience wide enough to support a large staff (by news start-ups standards); and it has emerged as a site for people who do not just tolerate, but eagerly devour, a long piece about politics. Indeed, it has expanded its ambitions since its beginnings, founding a magazine in 2013 in which pieces can run to over 7,000 words.

The assumption that Net readers would not tolerate lengthy articles has yet to be proved. Jill Abramson, a year after being ejected from the editor's seat at the *New York Times*, teamed up with Steve Brill to develop a long-form journalism site which would publish one long word piece each month, with a generous fee of 100,000 dollars. Mooted in 2014, it was 'on hold' two years later.[50] But when Belt Publishing began a magazine for journalism about the Rust Belt in the autumn of 2014 – a risky proposition, one would think – it was, in mid 2016, still going strong, featuring a long and intriguing piece by Oliver Lee Bateman on the white racists of Pittsburgh.[51] JSTOR, the academic digitalized documents site, started a JSTOR Daily – 'Where news meets its scholarly match' – which mixes readable academic papers with specially commissioned analyses.[52] The move to length isn't confined to print: the LA Times teamed up with Direct TV to broadcast a series of documentaries – challenging Vice and BuzzFeed's experiments in documentaries and fiction films. These and others are known as 'explainers' sites': they assume a large audience which wants to know, and will take time to learn about, complex or quirky or public interest subjects.

Bill Keller, the former executive editor of the *New York Times* (2003–11), carried the paper through (but not out of) the rough waters of circulation drop, and large expansion of the digital offering. Soon after leaving, he announced he would set up and edit a news website called the Marshall Project, which launched late in 2014.

Keller isn't optimistic about mainstream news organizations surviving; he thinks his old paper will, he thinks National Public Radio will – because it's non-commercial, and its supporters and sponsors will keep it going. Beyond that, it's going to be a landscape of specialists, who will make up, in diverse and discrete ways, for the ever-greater failings of the mainstream media. The Marshall Project is named for Thurgood Marshall, the reforming justice of the Supreme Court (1967–91), who was the first black lawyer to reach the summit of the legal profession. It springs from Keller's belief that the justice system in the US is badly broken, and that informative, analytical and investigative journalism can make something of a difference. It's a gamble on the existence of two appetites: one, for a constant running commentary on a specialized area; the other, a willingness of readers to absorb complexity.

Speaking to me early (for journalism) one morning in still empty offices, he explained the rationale behind his venture:

> Taken as a whole, coverage of the criminal justice system has been a casualty of the economic trauma of our business. It's complicated, time-consuming investigative or quasi-investigative work; it's just something that most of these organizations don't feel they can afford any longer. As a result, I think that state legislatures have become more corrupt, more ineffectual. So justice isn't the only area, but it's certainly one area which needs attention.
>
> We needed more digging, but also more explaining. It's issues of law enforcement, prosecutorial conduct, sentencing, the conditions in our prisons and the population in our prisons, alternatives to prisons, parole,

probation – and then acutely dramatic subsets like executions – these are really complex subjects. Easy to cover in a tabloidy and sensational way, which tends to be the mantra of the local TV – if it bleeds it leads.

And the criminal justice system disproportionately targets the poor, the blacks and the Hispanics. Sixty per cent of the people in prison are black or Hispanic. And there's a little voice in the back of publishers' heads which says – this is not our demographic. Advertisers are not clamouring to reach out to the impoverished areas of America. And maybe our readers aren't dying to read about these areas. Yet traditionally there has been a sense of responsibility, which means that these areas should be covered.

Keller, feeling a little incongruous in a small-staff start-up, believes in the restorative power of journalism, the ethic which has sustained the trade in the US for a century. American journalism, which like journalism everywhere can be awful, retains its optimism for the future, and retains, too, the ambition to be an example for the rest of the world.

TEN

'We've got the ability to go directly ... to the people'

In the authoritarian world, as the originally hopeful third millennium unrolled a little further, the limited spaces given to independently undertaken and forcefully pursued journalism were, as I've written above, quite sharply reduced. In countries with both formal democratic institutions and active, deeply rooted civil societies, journalism underwent a quite different shift. Accustomed to dominating the 'national conversations', it became increasingly subaltern – first to public relations, including that branch of PR which is political communication, and then to social media, which benefits both the voiceless and the powerful, and which has encouraged, along with pleasurable conversation, the appearance and rise of fake news.

People are stimulated much more by emotion than by facts, even if the latter are necessary for everyday life. Journalism has long known this, and there has been for centuries a split between journalism that informs and journalism, generally more popular, that stimulates the emotions. Both partake of elements of the other and there is no firm border. In the twenty-first century, social media, through which a steeply rising percentage of citizens now receive their news, eroded the market models of newspapers and, to a lesser degree, broadcast news and current affairs, a shift which introduced an even more promiscuous mixing of fact and fantasy than had always been present in journalism.

In *The Political Brain*, psychology professor Drew Westen writes that 'a dispassionate mind that makes decisions by weighing the evidence and reasoning to the most valid conclusions ... bears no relation to how the brain actually works'.[1] Westen meant the book to prompt US Democrats to wake up to that central statement since their perverse belief in rationality had tended to lose them elections. The Democratic Party did go on to lose the 2016 presidential election: its candidate was a super-rational, even hyper-rational, policy intellectual, Hillary Clinton, whose long immersion in practical politics, both domestic and foreign, coupled with an incisive intellect and capacious memory, had made her one of the most formidable politicians in the US, if apparently not sympathetic enough in her self-presentation to attract sufficient support. Her failure brought to the White House a man, Donald Trump, demonstrably ignorant of most of the policy areas which she commanded, and who appeared to show little desire to address the large gaps in his understanding of the polity of the country he was aspiring to lead.

That such a person should come to power at the expense of such another, and that Trump larded his speeches and statements and interviews with so many untruths, focused attention on the nature of truth in active politics. This was more the case since the candidate excoriated the news media as 'dishonest', 'liars' and 'scum', picking out for particular obloquy those news media – such as CNN, NBC, the *New York Times*, the *Washington Post* and others – that most pride themselves on their devotion to accuracy.

As he approached the beginning of his presidency on 20 January 2017, Trump continued to revile the news media, at one point (in a press conference a little over a week before his inauguration) shouting down the CNN political reporter Jim Acosta, forbidding him to put a question,[2] because, Trump claimed, the cable channel had been one of the first to report on unverified allegations of his indulging in sex with prostitutes in a visit to Russia years before, and fears on the part of the US intelligence services that he could be blackmailed, as president, by the Russian authorities. Trump labelled the report 'fake news'.

He had also understood that journalism, which has never been so available, so varied and so accessible to comments, corrections and arguments from its audience, also suffers from the closures and cuts to one of its main institutions: the newspaper. (Even so, newspapers accounted for most of the reporters in the US as Trump came to power.) Putting out a quality newspaper with wide coverage and high standards of fact-checking and reliability is becoming increasingly hard – as advertising rapidly deserts paper for the Net, usually Google and Facebook. All newspapers struggled to adapt to the digital age; some with present success, others with continued heavy losses.

Broadcast and cable news fared well in 2015–16 – in large part due to the popularity of their coverage of Trump's campaign. Leslie Moonves, CEO of CBS, said in spring 2016 that Trump's campaign 'may not be good for America, but it's damn good for CBS'. But mainstream media are regarded with suspicion by a large majority of Americans: a Gallup poll in September 2016 showed that those with a large or fair amount of trust in news media 'to report the news fully, accurately and fairly' dropped to 32 per cent (14 per cent among Republicans), a new low.

Many historians believe that fundamental shifts in communication are significant causes of shifts in political organization. The Harvard historian of America Jill Lepore argued that the US two-party system 'is a creation of the press', and that further changes to that system were shaped, for example, by mass literacy and newspaper reading, and then by broadcasting, before going on to write about the increasingly dominant twenty-first-century method of communicating and receiving information:

> The Internet, like all new communications technologies, has contributed to a period of political disequilibrium, one in which, as always, party followers have been revolting against party leaders ... It is unlikely but

not impossible that the accelerating and atomizing forces of this latest communications revolution will bring about the end of the party system and the beginning of a new and wobblier political institution ... at some point, does each of us become a party of one?[3]

The party system looks shaky, but it doesn't seem to be ending yet; indeed, far from new technology leading to parties of one, it is giving individuals the means to dominate their parties. Trump's posture is of a piece with those of other populist leaders, such as Beppe Grillo, leader of Italy's Movimento Cinque Stelle (Five Star Movement). At the end of 2016, when the Movement was the country's most popular party, he called for citizen juries to judge journalists' accuracy, echoing Trump's view that they were the main source of 'fake news'.

For all who take the populist route in politics, news media that attempt a coherent, fact-based narrative of current events are a natural enemy. The Net, with its promiscuous mixture of fact, conjecture, partisan spin and fake news, deliberately constructed to gain attention and income, is a much more attractive medium within which to work. Thus Grillo has risen to challenge more conventional Italian parties through his blog, and Trump appears to command the US political scene through Twitter.

Kellyanne Conway, a seasoned political aide and pollster, who was Trump's campaign manager for part of his campaign, often had to put a thick gloss on the candidate's statements and on the trend in the polls, which mostly pointed to a Clinton win. One of the most creative of these, however, came some weeks after he had trounced the polls and won the presidency, when she was invited to respond to an attack on Trump by the actor Meryl Streep, speaking at the Golden Globes ceremony in January 2017. Expressing her revulsion at Trump's apparent mimicking,[4] during a speech in November 2015, of the jerky movements of the *New York Times* reporter Serge Kovaleski, who suffers from a congenital condition, arthrogryposis, that limits the movements of his joints, Streep had said: 'This instinct to humiliate, when it's modeled by someone in the public platform, by someone powerful, it filters down into everybody's life ... disrespect invites disrespect, violence incites violence. And when the powerful use their position to bully others we all lose.'[5]

Conway appeared on CNN's *New Day* programme the day after Streep's speech. The anchor, Chris Cuomo, said that Trump's explanation – that he was merely mimicking a reporter 'grovelling' while denying a story he had written for the *Washington Post* about Muslims rejoicing over the collapse of the Twin Towers in September 2001 – could not be believed because his imitation was 'a gesture that is so keenly tuned to what Serge's vulnerability is'. Conway replied: 'You're saying you don't believe him. You're saying he's a liar and you shouldn't ... *Why is everything taken at face value? ... You always want to go by what's come out of his mouth rather than look at what's in his heart* [my italics].'[6]

It was among the most remarkable pieces of spin produced about Trump – perhaps about any public figure. Conway was giving a piece of advice to journalists which was, in current journalistic practice, impossible to follow: in the case of a president, or a president-elect, words coming out of his mouth or on documents approved by him are by far the largest source for reportage and understanding. And how can a reporter report on what is in a public figure's heart?

Yet Conway voiced something that was a proxy for the truth. Taking Trump's words at face value – getting the quote right, explaining its significance, quoting it in context, going by what comes out of his mouth as if it were a statement of fact or a settled view – was no longer the correct approach. Trump's radicalism lay very substantially in the constant evanescence of what came out of his mouth. It may be something which he would disavow the next day, or the next month or year – or it may not (his heart remains another matter). Why take it at face value?

All politicians in a democratic polity must appeal to the public for support on the basis of pledges of future action and policies. It is the logic of the ballot. Such pledges are most often sincere, at least insofar as the politician pledging wishes to deliver them, though the difficulties of sticking to a pledge are generally less stressed, if mentioned at all. They are not designed to be evanescent, disappearing as soon as they have done the trick of attracting support, but are contingent on favourable circumstance. Even before his presidency began, Trump moderated, backtracked on or contradicted some pledges – such as barring all Muslims from entering the US, immediately deporting eleven million Mexicans, having guns in classrooms and criminalizing abortions. It was thus hard to determine how far he would attempt to convert pledges, or random ideas, into law. Reporters could not go by what's come out of his mouth.

Two dogs in a room. One, sitting on a chair before a computer screen, turns to the other, sitting on the floor, and says blithely: 'On the Internet, nobody knows you're a dog.' It was reckoned to be the most-reproduced cartoon the *New Yorker* had ever published; its creator was Peter Steiner, a regular cartoonist for the magazine, who came up with it in 1993, when Net use was still, for most, in its infancy. He said he had no particular expertise, or even great interest, in the Net, and that it was not the result of a contemplation of its nature: 'There wasn't any profound tapping into the zeitgeist. I guess, though, when you tap into the zeitgeist you don't necessarily know you're doing it.'[7]

The Net's zeitgeist has become clearer in the decades since the dog cartoon, and the central importance of the anonymity it confers on users – the cartoon's insight – has only become greater. No one need reveal anything which is factually correct (though they may, in their construction of an ideal self, reveal truths: as Kellyanne Conway would say, what's in their heart); in the virtual world, virtual identities thrive. At the same time, the rapid growth of social media allows powerful and popular individuals to construct huge networks of followers who are addressed – as it were – 'directly', and can be themselves addressed 'directly'.

'Directly' is between quote marks because it's likely that powerful individuals don't spend much time communicating with their followers. Mark Zuckerberg, the co-creator and CEO of Facebook, posts often on the medium he invented, and these are typically shared some 200,000 times. He posts pictures of his family, his dog, his meetings with the Pope and President Xi Jinping; however, Bloomberg's Sarah Frier reported that they are not his own work: 'Typically, a handful of Facebook employees manage communications just for him, helping write his posts and speeches, while an additional dozen or so delete harassing comments and spam on his page, say two people familiar with the matter. Facebook also has professional photographers snap Zuckerberg, say, taking a run in Beijing or reading to his daughter.'[8] Does that make the posts 'fake news'?

The posts, such as those mixing in domestic pictures of the Zuckerberg family with those of a Facebook project to create an intelligent home device-cum-servant, for example, conflate the image created for Zuckerberg – a regular guy, open, accessible and genuine – with his company: 'Within Facebook, it's an article of faith that Zuckerberg's image is pretty much synonymous with the company's, employees say. If people think Zuckerberg is innovative and charming, so is Facebook.'

Celebrity tweeting/posting is a relationship, which can have a large meaning for the followers of the powerful individual. It may be antagonistic and hateful, but more often, from followers, it is admiring, even adoring. Both Grillo and Trump have succeeded in building communities of millions of followers – since they are seen as representing people frustrated by mainstream politics and media, burdened with a feeling of powerlessness and neglect, avid for change in the circumstances of their lives, willing to accept as a leader one who promises to tackle the source of their desperation by promising security in the face of terrorist threats, protection from immigrants and job-destroying products and above all respect, and understanding of their frustrations.

The paradox of the virtual world is that it is at once non-corporeal, divorced necessarily from the solid human being, a world of trillions of digits whizzing about, all labelled as to destination – and yet capable of rousing the most torrid emotional effects, of moving multitudes. Emotion here is nearly all: the adored one receives the love and trust of millions, and in turn strokes their resentments and hatreds into more active life, forming them into a community of injured souls, their patience too long tried, their passivity too confidently assumed.

And their opinions firmly held. One of the amusements which the liberal media had in 2016 – when the general assumption of the media and political worlds was that Trump would, in the end, flame out and Clinton win – was to interview Trump supporters and reveal the ridiculousness of their views. *The Daily Show*, long presented by Jon Stewart and since September 2015 fronted by the South African-born comedian Trevor Noah, did a number of them. One outing, featuring Jordan Klepper, a reporter for the show, saw him go to Trump rallies and interview participants, leading them to speculate on Hillary's health, among other subjects.[9] She has AIDS, said one man, contracted from her husband who had been 'messing around with Magic Johnson', the former baseball star who had contracted HIV from, he said, multiple (hetero)sexual partners and who then became a leading activist in combatting the disease. Asked about Obama, then still president, one woman said, 'Obama is a Muslim, he's a terrorist, no one will ever tell me different.' Asked how she knew, she replied, 'Do I have proof? No. Do I have articles? No. My mind is made up.' A man said Obama was a Muslim because he wore jewellery in a Muslim fashion, such as not wearing his wedding ring during certain months. The man who believed Hillary Clinton had AIDS also wondered why Obama had absented himself from the Oval Office during 9/11 (that is, more than seven years before he became president).

Though it was unpleasant to see a clever, slim, youngish man pull apart, for laughs and on camera, mostly older men and women of apparently

337

modest means, many of whom were overweight and lacked reasoning ability on this issue (Look! Aren't they *stupid*?), it was depressingly clear that the interviewees, who may have been selected for their naivety, depended little or not at all on fact. Like the woman who admitted, with a laugh, to having no proof for a conviction as momentous as that her president was a violent jihadist, they started and ended with belief, or a grudge, or prejudice. They came to the rally to have the baselessness of their views flattered and expanded.

The exposing of ignorance via street interviews isn't confined to the left. Mark Dice, a writer and broadcaster of the right, who has published a number of books on secret societies which control the world,[10] regularly conducts interviews which reveal huge ignorance. In June 2016, he did a number of brief interviews with mainly young people on a beach in San Diego, California[11] – a regular outing for him, this being the sixth time he had asked, 'Why do we [Americans] celebrate the Fourth of July?' Most confessed total ignorance: one man said 'independence', but did not know from what or whom (on 4 July 1776, the representatives of the thirteen British colonies in America signed a Declaration of Independence from the UK). In other interviews, interviewees struggled to name even one Founding Father of the US, with two naming Abraham Lincoln, who was president nearly a century after the Declaration (1861–5).

'Fake news' has long been more popular than well-attested, carefully checked and strongly sourced 'real news'. Much of the material that filled the news sheets circulating from the early seventeenth century in Europe was based on rumour, or was paid-for copy to boost or destroy a reputation, or was simply made up. Only in the nineteenth century, with some newspapers – *The Times* of London playing the most prominent part – did accuracy become a major criterion. Even so, the cynical judgement of Jasper Milvain, the literary journalist who succeeds in the journalistic rat races described in George Gissing's *New Grub Street* (1891), emphasizes that the tyranny of demand, not the ethics of supply, governed the trade for most: 'Literature nowadays is a trade ... your successful man of letters is your skillful tradesman. He thinks first and foremost of the markets; when one kind of goods begins to go off slackly, he is ready with something new and appetizing.'

Much of the 'news' published in authoritarian states is false, or grossly distorted; in the tabloid culture, accuracy is sacrificed to impact. Yet 'fake news' suddenly became a large issue in the US election year of 2016. This was a result of the growth of ultra-polemical politics and above all the anonymity, ease of publishing and ineradicable confusion between the true and the false permitted by the profusion of the Net. The Net provided the conditions for both the creation and the projection of journalistic-like stories into wide circulation, which had been created entirely for the market. Demand trumped truth.

The liberally inclined news media, which had elevated fact, checkability, sourcing and neutrality as the laws by which journalists lived (or should live), were challenged by a wave of narratives taking their inspiration from the lies and exaggerations of Donald Trump – their rapid growth prompted by the heat of the fascination he held for audiences right and left. Brian Stelter, the CNN media reporter, says: 'There are more news outlets [on the right] designed to feed fake news than on the left, and it's true that there has been more appetite for it on the right – but now [after Trump's election] there's a growing appetite on the left for anti-Trump BS.'

In December 2016, a *New York Times* article by Sabrina Tavernise investigated the spread and appeal of fake news. She interviewed Larry Laughlin, a retired businessman who had built up his own small metal-finishing plant, who told of his admiration for Mark Dice, especially his sarcastic interviews and his witty, rapid-fire commentary. (One such example: on his own YouTube channel in January 2017, Dice mocked CNN's Stelter for having drawn critical attention to Fox News having an 'all-white-male line-up' of presenters and pundits in prime time after the defection of the high-profile Megyn Kelly to NBC – commenting that he was surprised that Stelter had objected, asking, while making a limp-wrist gesture, what he had against 'all-male line-ups', suggesting Stelter was gay.)[12]

Laughlin – from a broken home with an alcoholic father – described his preference for journalism of the right, framing it in emotional terms.[13] Recalling a liberal friend of his son's saying to him, 'You have a nice house and got it made because you are a white guy,' he said, 'My struggles in life are just dismissed ... there are all of these preconceived notions that I'm a racist, idiot, a bigot, and oh, uneducated.' Speaking about the mainstream media, he stated, 'It's like an inside joke for people on the left, and we are the butt of the joke. At some point, we stopped listening.' Following the election of Trump as president, Laughlin looks for the most 'intense' content on the Net celebrating the victory and mocking liberals – 'this is like sweet release'.

He does, however, draw the line at news he can identify as fake, and said he was embarrassed by an incident in December 2016 in which a man from North Carolina, enraged by a fake story about a sex abuse ring run by Hillary Clinton from a back room in a Washington DC pizzeria named Comet Ping Pong, went to the restaurant with an assault rifle and other weapons, fired some shots, injuring no one, and was quickly arrested. Laughlin said that the incident 'adds to the stereotype that we're all nutters'.

But it isn't a case of being 'nutters'. It's a case of preferring to consume news that gives satisfaction above information, conforms to a certain view of the world and gives 'sweet release' like a drug, or sex. Laughlin, like many on the right, rejects what he identifies as fake news because it would be a false friend, lacking the stamp of reality and at least some fact; he does not wish to live in falsity, but in grounded triumphs – such as Trump's win. He seeks intensity; and the hyper-partisanship of US politics, attaining a new height in the Trump campaign – which reached into areas of fantasy and narcissism never before deployed in modern presidential races – encouraged the search and enjoyment of strong pleasures, both true and false in origin.

CNN's Brian Stelter, speaking at a seminar in London in January 2017, divided fake news into three main streams: first, 'the basic, made-up story, the purest form of fake news, been around for ever'. Then the hybrid: some truth, but partly or mainly fake – 'more sophisticated and dangerous'. Finally, the hyper-partisan stories which, like the hybrids, have an element or base of truth, but then take off into an area which speaks to preconceptions and prejudices of an individual or a group, and deepens them. Hillary Clinton's health is a good example: the reality seems to be that she takes some medication to prevent blood clotting, other medication to treat hyperthyroidism, which means that the thyroid gland is less active than normal, and thus extra hormones need to be taken. She has in the recent past suffered concussion, a broken elbow and had an operation to prevent a blood clot on the brain. In September 2016, she was forced to leave a commemoration ceremony and staggered as she reached her car, supported by bodyguards. It was later announced that she had a bout of pneumonia.

Thus stories about her health have some foundation. Though her personal doctor, Lisa Bardack, said in a statement in mid 2015 that 'she is in excellent condition and fit to serve as President of the Unites States',[14] the fact that the public record shows some non-threatening illnesses provides a sufficient base for every kind of speculation – as the *Daily Show* reporter Klepper discovered. Those who opposed her – hated her, many said – wanted to believe her seriously sick or dying.

If emotion powers the consumers of fake, or hybrid, or hyper-partisan news, money is the main attraction for the producers. In 2016, what might be termed JAM, the Journalism of Absolute Mendacity, was boiled up in former Soviet Georgia, in former Yugoslavian Macedonia and in the US itself. In every case, when JAM journalists were interviewed, they attested to being uninterested in politics – at times personally opposed to Donald Trump – but dedicated to cranking out material boosting his chances of success, usually by spreading powerful lies about Clinton.

Cameron Harris, from Annapolis, Maryland, a recent graduate from Davidson College in North Carolina, had debts to pay off, and heard Trump – apparently preparing fans in early autumn for later defeat – tell an audience in Columbus, Ohio, that 'the election is going to be rigged'.[15] He had an idea: to provide proof for Trump's vague claim.

He was already in the fake news business, having put out stories such as 'Hillary Clinton Blames Racism for Cincinnati Gorilla's Death', but the ballot rigging story, inspired by Trump's accusation that votes would be tampered with, and headlined 'BREAKING: "Tens of thousands" of fraudulent Clinton votes found in Ohio warehouse', was his best effort, attracting thousands of hits and making its creator some 5,000 dollars within a few days through the micropayments he earned from advertisements Google had put on his site. To give his stories greater moral weight, Harris had bought, for five dollars, an expired domain, 'Christian Times.com', which became the publisher of his pieces.

The story was accompanied by a picture – taken from a British newspaper, the *Birmingham Mail* – which showed a worker standing behind a stack of ballot boxes, helpfully labelled 'Ballot Boxes'. These boxes, the story explained, held the fake voting papers organized by Clinton's campaign. A worker, Randall Prince, was invented and, in order to explain his late discovery of the boxes, was quoted as saying, 'No one really goes into this building.' The story went out on 30 September, to be shared by six million people. Asked about his success, Harris said: 'At first it kind of shocked me – the response I was getting. How easily people would believe it. It was almost like a sociological experiment.' Though he appeared 'thoughtful' when asked if he felt guilty at having made a sizeable sum from stories that were pure lies – 22,000 dollars during the campaign, for an estimated twenty hours' work, with many written after the ballot rigging story, though none as profitable – he took refuge in protestations that 'hardly anything a campaign or a candidate says is completely true'.

The US presidential campaign was fake news's finest hour, but it didn't initiate the form. An early success was the National Report, first registered as a site in February 2013. Though it – sporadically and not prominently, it seems – warned readers that it was satirical, the main stories were presented as real, and some were treated as such, getting limited traction on Fox News, and the tech site Boing Boing. In an interview with Caitlin Dewey of the *Washington Post*,[16] its lead writer, Paul Horner – who specialized in taking on the virtual identity of the popular British graffiti artist Banksy – made clear he treated his work, which brought him well into six figures annually, as a joke, part of which was for his own enjoyment, when more mainstream sites ran the stories as true.

The story that Fox ran – only once, Horner said, before 'they learned to use Google during the commercials, or something' – was headlined 'Obama uses own money to open Muslim museum amid government shutdown'; the only accurate part was that the piece went out during a shutdown of federal offices. Insisting that his stories 'always had a point', usually to reveal the hypocrisy of his subjects or that of the gullible, he did a story about marrying his dog, which a Los Angeles chat show asked him to talk about on television – 'it was just to make fun of the fact that super anti-gay people are like – what's next? A toaster?'

Fox is inclined to put more stress on stories that lean to the right, just as its rival MSNBC has a bias to the left, but it also wishes to be seen as a serious news channel, an ambition probably strengthened after the resignation of its creator and CEO, Roger Ailes, in 2015, after charges of sexual harassment. Three days before Trump's inauguration, the presenter Tucker Carlson, succeeding Megyn Kelly, had torn into a man named 'Dom Tullipso', who had presented himself as the leader of a many-hundreds-strong group which were paid to protest at Trump rallies – by then a familiar trope on the right. Switching between aggression and mirth, Carlson and Tullipso sparred, with the latter, somewhat ineptly, continuing to speak to the fantasy that he was the organizer of an army of protestors who – on the pay scales that he had claimed were then current – cost nearly sixty million dollars a year to run, but ended by thanking Fox for fact-checking, and debunking him.[17]

Horner left the National Report in 2014 – since January 2017, it's no longer available – but he couldn't give up so profitable and amusing a pastime. Speaking again to the *Washington Post*'s Caitlin Dewey in November 2016, soon after Trump's victory, he boasted – satirically or not – 'I think Donald Trump is in the White House because of me.'[18] He had posted stories about protestors paid to appear at Trump rallies by pro-Clinton organizers, which had quickly gone viral and were quoted widely. Horner continues to see the activity as a joke – but one which, since Trump (whom he 'hates') took the prize, he now feels bad about:

His followers don't fact-check anything – they'll post everything, believe anything. His campaign manager posted my story about a protester getting paid $3,500 as fact. Like, I made that up. I posted a fake ad on Craigslist. Just 'cause his supporters were under the belief that people were getting paid to protest at their rallies, and that's just insane. I've gone to Trump protests – trust me, no one needs to get paid to protest Trump. I just wanted to make fun of that insane belief, but it took off. They actually believed it … that's how this always works: someone posts something I write, then they find out it's false, then they look like idiots. But Trump supporters – they just keep running with it! They never fact-check anything! Now he's in the White House. Looking back, instead of hurting the campaign, I think I helped it. And that feels [bad].

Horner is in the US to see, and regret, first hand, the results of his fakery. Many of the most active are not: fake news about the US election was outsourced. In the Macedonian town of Veles, reporters from BuzzFeed – which was early to take up the fake news story – found a group of young men who had discovered that they could earn good money from making up news for sites with names like WorldPoliticus.com, TrumpVision365.com, USConservativeToday.com, DonaldTrumpNews.co and USADailyPolitics.com: 'Teens and young men who run these sites told BuzzFeed News that they learned the best way to generate traffic is to get their politics stories to spread on Facebook – and the best way to generate shares on Facebook is to publish sensationalist and often false content that caters to Trump supporters.'[19]

None of those interviewed – most insisted on anonymity – said they supported Trump: they looked upon him and his supporters as a profit centre and, interviewed shortly before the election on 8 November 2016, they hoped for his victory, since a Clinton win, according to a sixteen-year-old, 'means that there will be no more politics worth covering'.

The Macedonian youngsters, clearly intelligent but inexperienced in US politics, often plundered straight or satirical US websites for ideas and bases for their stories. The same technique was used by fakers in Tbilisi, the capital of Georgia: twenty-two-year-old Beqa Latsabidze told *New York Times* reporters that he took a story from a site in Vancouver, Canada – the *Burrard Street Journal* – which claimed that Obama would move to Canada if Trump won.[20] The *Journal* was a clearly marked satirical site, but Latsabidze, who does true and hybrid stories as well as wholly fake pieces, touted the story as true – as he did with a successful story which claimed that Mexico would close its border if Trump won. He explained: 'My audience likes Trump. I don't want to write bad things about Trump.' Like Horner, he professes amused contempt at the gullibility of his readers: 'I don't call it fake news, I call it satire. Nobody really believes that Mexico is going to close its border. This is crazy'; and like Horner, and others, he is not a right-wing partisan. Though many of his stories have an anti-Muslim slant, he says, 'I am not against Muslims. I just saw there was interest. They are in the news. For me this is all about income, nothing more.'

President Obama left office believing that fake news, and the context within which it succeeded, is a danger to the world. A short while after Trump won, Obama told David Remnick that the new media ecosystem

> means everything is true and nothing is true ... An explanation of climate change from a Nobel Prize-winning physicist looks exactly the same on your Facebook page as the denial of climate change by somebody on the Koch brothers' payroll. And the capacity to disseminate misinformation, wild conspiracy theories, to paint the opposition in wildly negative light without any rebuttal – that has accelerated in ways that much more sharply polarize the electorate and make it very difficult to have a common conversation.[21]

Up to the nineties, he said, 'there was a baseline of facts that we could work off of. And now we just don't have that.'

Fake news spread mainly through Google, Twitter and Facebook, and increased their income. They have protested that they are not publishing, but technology, companies: a claim Patrick Walker, head of Facebook partnerships in Europe, the Middle East and Africa, still leaned on at the London seminar on fake news[22] – 'the Facebook news feed is only ten years old. We don't do news ourselves, we work with partners.' But he and other Facebook, Google and Twitter executives became conscious, by late 2016, that they were expected to take some action against it, and claimed they had begun to do so. Walker added to his denial that Facebook 'does news' the assurance that 'we signal things which are unconfirmed or untrue. We work with fact-checkers in the US and internationally.'

The culture, the pressure to make money, however, weighs against a deep change. One former Facebook worker told the *Financial Times* that 'the way the company is run may have exacerbated the distribution of fake news. Its engineers focus on improving engagement – clicks, likes, comments, shares – as the primary measures of success of any new feature. New projects are typically released after six-month "sprints", during which pressure to increase those metrics is intense.' Another former manager added: 'engagement is a dangerous drug. Nobody is incentivized to think critically about unintended, often long-term consequence.'[23]

Two important media figures, Sir Martin Sorrell of WPP, the world's biggest global advertising and PR corporation, and Robert Thomson, chief executive of News Corporation, both dismissed any claim made that the communication companies were not also publishers. 'Of course they are publishers,' said Thomson, 'and being a publisher comes with the responsibility to protect and project the provenance of news. The great papers have grappled with that sacred burden over decades and centuries, and you can't absolve yourself from that burden or the costs of compliance by saying, "We are a technology company."'

In November 2016, three days after the US election, Mark Zuckerberg dismissed the criticism that Facebook carried stories which had a malign effect, telling a conference in California that 'the idea that fake news on Facebook, of which there is a very small amount of the content, influences the election is a pretty crazy idea'. A little over a week later, he had changed his mind and his tune, saying he took seriously the job of weeding out falsehoods, and stressing that there was 'more to be done'.[24]

The communications corporations, now dwarfing other media companies in revenue and increasingly in audience, may adopt some of the ideas being pressed upon them – such as developing algorithms that will flag up doubts about a site or a story, or the appointment of a (human) public editor based on the model of some newspapers. But their default position is a quasi-absolutist attachment to complete freedom of publication, not making a distinction between free opinion, fake and accurate news – distinctions in which the leaders of the companies did not seem much interested.

Fake news was not Donald Trump's invention, but it thrived mightily under his wandering star and he gratefully used it to label stories he disliked. It was not confined to the right, but the demand for fantasy and 'intensity' in stories, especially those on Hillary Clinton's health, competence and truthfulness that could be to her detriment, was greater on the right, among supporters of Donald Trump – who, even before he began his official campaign, had a habit of insouciantly tossing out gobbets of news that were obviously, or likely to turn out to be, false. These stories included giving credence to the 'death panels' which the Affordable Care Act (Obamacare) prescribed to determine if elderly patients would be deprived of care and left to die; his years-long insistence that Obama's birth certificate was a fraud and that the former president was born outside of the US, thus disqualifying him from the presidency; and the revelation of a secret deal Obama had made, before his re-election in 2012, with the Saudis to flood the oil market so that the price remained low, thus helping him win.[25]

During the campaign he alleged that the father of Ted Cruz, the junior senator from Texas and his closest rival in the primaries, had associated with Lee Harvey Oswald before Oswald killed President John F. Kennedy in 1964, and that a protestor who had attempted to mount the stage at a rally in March 2016 was a member of the Islamic State. After an election in which Clinton won the popular vote by over 2.8 million but lost the crucial electoral college vote by a wide margin,[26] Trump claimed that he won the popular vote 'if you deduct the millions of people who voted illegally'.

That one should become president with such an evidently slight regard for fact was a blow to democratic practice in the United States – and, because of its power and influence, the rest of the world. It reduces the US to the level of those authoritarian states which habitually use lies to bolster the power of the leader or the party – especially Russia and President Vladimir Putin, to whom Trump seemed anxious to be friendly.

Zuckerberg, however, may have been at least partly right in his earlier dismissal of the importance of fake news in the presidential election. The economists Matthew Gentzkow of Stanford University and Hunt Allcott of New York University published a paper soon after Trump's inauguration, arguing that the effect of fake news had been significantly overestimated, and that most people continued to get their news and attitudes from TV, while often not remembering what they had read or heard about on social media.[27] They concluded: 'Our data suggest that social media were not the most important source of election news, and even the most widely circulated fake news stories were seen by only a small fraction of Americans. For fake news to have changed the outcome of the election ... [it would need to have] a persuasion rate equivalent to seeing thirty-six television campaign ads.'

Yet TV and other news media routinely used social media, especially Trump's tweets, as their content, endowing them with great importance and bringing them into the TV-watching screens of the nation. Trump, in his rise to power and in his Twitter messages, strove throughout his campaign to prove that the mainstream ('lamestream') media were liars. Near the end of his campaign, he turned on the security services, because they produced reports which pointed to Russian hackers having hacked into the database of the Democratic National Committee, probably on the orders of Putin, and publicizing the emails through the good offices of WikiLeaks: he also blamed the services for leaking a dossier containing serious allegations about his activities in Moscow. The dossier – research, by a former MI6 agent, Christopher Steele, commissioned by anti-Trump members of the Republican Party, then by Democrats[28] – reported that Trump had, on a visit to Russia, engaged the services of prostitutes to urinate on the bed in the room in the Ritz Carlton Hotel which Trump had hired, which was bugged and where President and Michelle Obama had slept during a Moscow visit, thus laying him open to blackmail. It also detailed a series of links between high Russian officials and former members of Trump's campaign team; and alleged that Trump, in seeking business opportunities in Moscow, had paid several bribes. None of the allegations have been independently verified.[29]

The US news media have, more than other journalistic cultures, insisted (though now with increasing exceptions) on their commitment to neutrality and a discipline of checking: in this lies their claim to be trusted. Part of their commitment to neutrality was to report, fully, on statements via the social media from the man about to be president – and because they were often so novel and incendiary, they received top billing. For journalists who care about the craft, seeking and publishing as much of the truth as they can discover remains the reason for their power and privileges, and for trust to be placed in them. The intelligence services, which provide a synopsis of highly classified material to the Oval Office every day before 8 a.m. in the form of the President's Daily Brief, would find their work rendered meaningless if the administration, led by the president, dismissed it as either intrinsically flawed because of past error or politically partial (during his campaign, the president declared he had no need of such a briefing).[30]

President Trump came to office after a campaign to destroy trust in two of the institutions most requiring it as the basis of their existence. In doing so, he has both implicitly and explicitly demanded that trust be placed only, or at least mainly, in him. He is where the truth begins, and ends. He can be in direct communion with his people: media, get lost.

In the US, public relations began to take an organized form in the late nineteenth century, and, for much of its history, its largest task has been to attract the attention of the news media. Like journalists, the PR people had to be adroit at sensing and using the currents of the times; they acted, and act still, as a conduit between public movements and tastes, journalism and the corporations and institutions which hired them.

In 1928, one of the trade's founders, Edward Bernays, won a contract from the American Tobacco Company, which wanted to access the large, and largely new, market of women smokers. Bernays consulted Abraham Brill, a psychoanalyst, who advised him that feminist-inclined women used cigarette smoking as a testimony to their determination to attain equality with men. Bernays translated that movement into a 'Torches of Freedom' march, where women, demonstratively smoking cigarettes, joined the Easter Day Parade in New York in 1929.[31] The influence of Sigmund Freud, then still in Vienna, hung over the event; Brill was Freud's original translator into English and claimed to be the first to introduce his theories and methods in the US; Bernays was Freud's nephew.

The stunt was catnip to reporters and photographers, and illustrates the dilemma – not acutely felt by all journalists – that has plagued journalism. PR exploits, if well done and with some social or economic content and with strong visuals, are attractive to audiences; reporters and editors know quite well the commercial imperative behind them – but rush to cover the event, in part because the PR executive has done much of the work of attracting eyeballs for them.

A successful stunt costs more these days than paying some young women to smoke while strolling; the inflation in what constitutes an event worth covering has been large. In 2012, the Halo 4 video game, published by Microsoft Studios for the Xbox 360 console, was launched. The game is, like its Halo 1, 2 and 3 predecessors, built round an interstellar war between humanity and a theocratic alliance of aliens led by warrior priests named the Prophets; less socially important than turning thousands of women on to tobacco, but still demanding a debut consonant with its virtual momentousness. For it, the organizers of the event took over large parts of the tiny Principality of Liechtenstein, 25 kilometres long and bordered by Austria and Switzerland, with a population of 37,000. The organizers used a landmark, the thirteenth-century Balzers Castle, as a 'futuristic military fortification' and staged mock battles across part of the principality's territory. The day-long event was directed by the Hollywood director David Fincher (The Girl with the Dragon Tattoo, The Social Network); eighty journalists were invited, CNN covered it and it generated a huge response on social media.[32]

The coverage by mainstream media was welcome, but secondary; the blogs, tweets and Facebook posts, in their millions, were the true prize since they went more directly to the target audience. Most of the web-based journalists present at the event were part of the large gaming community, writing from the inside – able to judge the effectiveness of the game but sure to be overawed by the spectacle. The game grossed 220 million dollars on its launch day, 300 million dollars in the first week on sale.

Getting round the mainstream media, rather than getting in them, increasingly became the mantra. Weber Shandwick, a US company with a strong presence in Europe, won the PR Week Global Agency of the Year award in 2015, largely based on its ability to break through 'traditional service lines to integrate the social, digital, content, publishing, advertising, PR and public affairs services that drive business results' for its clients. This unconventional approach 'produced unconventional results'. Its European head, Colin Byrne, says that 'the idea is that companies won't have to rely on journalists to get their message out. Companies can become, more and more, general interest channels, it's usually a matter of finding out what people are interested in.'[33]

In March 2013, Byrne and his colleagues had announced a new content marketing unit called Mediaco, which the company's global head of digital, Chris Perry, says brings together 'newer sexier native advertising, to the social side of things'.[34] Perry says clients now want to create a 'compelling content model', and to distribute the content as widely as possible. On its website, a video insistently displays the message: 'Every company is a media company', and shows how advanced Weber Shandwick is in writing and designing content for each of its clients, so that their story may be dramatized and brought to life, to pass – as a PepsiCo manager said – from passive websites to 'active story telling'. Journalists, one Mediaco worker says, had been good at telling stories: his work was to apply these techniques to companies. In the spring of 2016, Weber Shandwick announced it had formed an 'Innovation Council' in response to 'accelerating change' in media, tasked to advise companies on how to better create narratives for their brands.[35]

Parallel with the media-tization of corporations, and the increasingly subaltern position assigned to the mainstream media, runs a greatly increased confidence in the importance of PR – which is no longer limited to conventional PR, but has shaded into counselling on social and political issues, internal relations within the company and shaping the messages which companies put out on their websites, Facebook pages, blogs and Twitter feeds. The bosses of the big companies are not just rich, but are large global players. They run very big businesses, now often conglomerates uniting advertising with PR and consultancy firms; they include Maurice Levy, since 2013 joint CEO of Publicis; John Wren, head of Omnicom (these two failed to merge in early 2014); Richard Edelman, whose company is the largest PR business still privately held; and Sir Martin Sorrell, head of the WPP media group – the world's largest advertising and PR group – one of the few very high-paid corporate leaders who publicly justifies his vast pay packet.[36]

These are men whose wisdom on how the world of business, or even the world, is going is expounded in arenas like the Davos World Economic Forum, in lectures and in opinion pieces in the prestigious press. Public relations people now take on large, strategic tasks, which reach deeper than before into political and social issues, and often define them. One CEO of a large London agency whom Laura Toogood and I interviewed for research done for the Reuters Institute – who asked for anonymity – instanced work for a famed, multinational engineering company, for which the agency had long done largely financial PR:

> Suddenly the company is interested in a much broader range of issues, they've decided they want to have a debate round the role of value added

in manufacturing in the UK economy, the need to rebalance away from an over-reliance on financial services – so suddenly you're making an essentially political case to a political audience. You're, yes, mindful of media reaction – but you've also got politicians, the labour movement, NGOs – suddenly you're part of a debate about what the British economy is going to do. It's a much broader job, broader constituencies.

At London's Portland PR, CEO Tim Allan, a former press adviser to Prime Minister Tony Blair, says that one large client – whom he would not name – had retained the firm to advise on a relaunch after the new CEO decided that the company had become 'toxic' to the public – 'Now that's really interesting, high-grade work, complex and absorbing. You need really good people for that: we now employ people with first-class degrees from Oxbridge.'

The British–Dutch Unilever's CEO since 2009, Paul Polman, has, with other CEOs, taken part in a series of 'Conversations with global leaders', organized by McKinsey, the consulting company. A significant part of the conversation – an interview with Adam Bird, a McKinsey director – allowed Polman to boost his company through linking the reduced spending power millions of people were experiencing with products designed with tighter budgets in mind, such as ready meals – a Unilever product – to eat at home rather than eating out. Brands, though, are no longer just brands, they are social artefacts, and must be put into the swirling circles of the Net and social media to compete, in narrative power, with the messages from journalism: 'this requires a brand manager that is in tune with society; that is agile, very close to new technologies; frankly, increasingly more global, and doing that with a broader perspective than just selling the brand from the brand benefits ... lots of the social missions of the brand coming in are different stakeholders. So, it is becoming a job that is a little bit broader and more of global scope.'

Unilever has products which can help the world, Polman believes. Asked by Bird what concrete steps he is taking, he seized on the ice-cream division, which Unilever had had to restructure after its purchase:

Ben & Jerry's is a good example of that – a key fighter against climate change and nuclear weapons ... the consumers' trust in business is, unfortunately, lower than we would like it to be. And the standards that the consumer sets – the expectations, her own proactiveness and influencing with her purchase decisions and her own beliefs, are only going to increase ... so companies with a strong social mission will be companies that are more successful long term.[37]

The successful twenty-first-century public relations companies are now moving into the space which a defensive mainstream journalistic culture is reluctantly vacating. They do so with a certain *schadenfreude* demonstrated by its practitioners, the older among them having been the butt of scorn by journalists for years. In doing so, they see themselves not merely as much greater beneficiaries of the Net's takeover of the media, but as more ethical – because social media now makes everything, including the PR corporations themselves, more transparent, more easily called out. Paul Holmes, who publishes the annual Holmes Report on the state of the PR industry, commended in his 2016 Trend Report both the Republican presidential candidate Donald Trump and the Democrat Bernie Sanders for their 'authenticity', and says 'that's a quality people believe is lacking in mainstream politicians and mainstream corporations'.[38] He quotes, in similarly militant vein, Rod Cartwright, director of the global corporate and public affairs practice Ketchum, as saying that the PR business 'is about brands and corporations realizing the scale of the opportunity – and arguably a responsibility – of being brave, taking a stand, having a voice on social issues, leading much-needed conversations or helping right wrongs'. Exactly what a crusading editor would have said, and some still do say.

—

Political communication or consultancy had as its aim, in its beginnings and early years, the imprinting of an image or images of the candidate as a politician of integrity and energy – and the opponent as one not to be trusted, even to be despised. Aides of aspiring or settled political figures had long used that dichotomy; when the trade became professionalized, it naturally defaulted to the same approach. Among the first – perhaps *the* first – political communication firms, Campaigns, Inc. was founded in California by two former newspaper people, Clem Whitaker and Leone Baxter. Hired by the Republicans, horrified by the prospect of the socialist writer Upton Sinclair winning the gubernatorial election in 1934, they put into operation a strategy for beating Sinclair that would seem to justify his name for them: 'the Lie Factory'.[39]

They ran an ad in the *Los Angeles Times* headlined 'Sinclair on marriage', with the line underneath: 'The sanctity of marriage ... I have had such a belief ... I have it no longer'. But it was not Sinclair's belief about marriage; after divorcing his first wife on the grounds of her adultery, he married his second wife and remained married to her for nearly fifty years, until her death a little before his own. The quotation was from one of his novels, *Love's Pilgrimage* (1911). As Baxter said later, when it didn't matter, 'Sure, these quotations were irrelevant. But we had one objective: to keep him from becoming governor.'

The couple were writing a template for a new trade. Their practice included injunctions like 'woo voters', 'make it personal', 'attack the opposition' (if there isn't one, invent one and attack it), 'claim to be the Voice of the People', 'see subtlety as your enemy', 'simplify simplify simplify', 'never shy away from controversy', 'win the controversy' and 'put on a show!'

These injunctions passed into the common sense of the profession and some emulated the brutality and mendacity of the Campaigns, Inc.

approach, with great success. The most celebrated, feted and loathed was Lee Atwater, Republican political communicator of the 1970s and '80s, crafter of the successful presidential campaign of George Bush the elder in 1988. In his critical biography of Atwater, *Bad Boy*, John Brady argues that from his tactics 'was born a new breed of hired gun, consultants who brought a specialized knowledge of today's enormous communications network and sensitivity to the perversities of human nature. They ran polls, conducted focus groups and created a candidate's image, they manipulated the press and invented news ...'[40]

Atwater's tactics are not copied everywhere, and there are some more constraints on those who wish to emulate him. But his negative campaigning and his spreading of damaging rumours remain a stock-in-trade of many. Bush's son, George W. Bush, benefited when a group supporting him, the Swift Boat Veterans, heavily backed financially by wealthy Texas Republicans, published allegations that his Democratic opponent in the 2004 presidential election, John Kerry, had lied about his record as an officer in Vietnam – allegations that were shown to be untrue even before the vote, but were judged to have damaged Kerry.

Consultants face different kinds of media, which now tend to be more politically committed, especially in the US – where TV channels, such as Fox and MSNBC, together with the (most successful on the right) radio talk shows, give a more raucously polemic tone. The legions of bloggers, Facebook messengers and tweeters, some in the news media but millions more not, are increasingly in command; though television remains the dominant medium for news and political coverage, it more and more uses social media as content.

At the same time, the decline of the political reporting fire power of the still potent legacy press can bother the political consultants who remember another time. Kevin Madden was communications director for Mitt Romney when the former Massachusetts governor and CEO of Bain Capital ran as the Republican candidate for the presidency: I talked to him in his office in Washington. For Madden, inexperience is more trouble than it's worth

> The papers have pulled back their reach. You can see it at the level of people who cover campaigns now – as that in 2012. They didn't have any of the institutional knowledge you need when you're covering states' races – and because of the speed with which these things are done, you need endurance, so they go for young people. And given the way it's changed, a lot of good smart journalists don't see it as the best place to be to cover the race, they realize that there is this dumbing down, a Twitterization of the news, that they want no part of – it's not what they find interesting, it's not what they think will inform the wider electorate.

In that, they were wrong: Twitter emerged, in 2016, as a – sometimes *the* – major medium for informing millions, and supplying large amounts of content to the mainstreamers.

Mike McCurry, Bill Clinton's press spokesman in the White House, now a consultant, told me that 'When I get on my hobby horse I say that the new trends have dumbed down political discourse because they have made everything sharper – angrier, more designed to elicit an emotional response.' Joe Klein, one of the most prominent political writers of the past thirty years, rides his hobby horse harder: his *Politics Lost* is a mourning for a political coverage now gone, replaced by a politics become bland and protected in every phrase, by consultants – while broadcasting is captured by partisan shouting matches and stunts.[41] His listing of the reasons why, as he put it in a *Los Angeles Times* column,[42] 'the inanity and ugliness of post-modern public life has caused many Americans to lose the habit of citizenship' include the encouragement by Richard Nixon of a new breed of political consultant, who helped him win the 1968 presidential election – among which number was a young Roger Ailes, the creator of Fox News, whom Nixon made his executive producer for television. Ailes said after the election that 'this is it. This is how they'll be elected for evermore; the next guys up will have to be performers.'[43]

The pushing of senior politicians into the entertainment zone would seem to bear Ailes out. The most intellectually fastidious of presidents, Barack Obama was put up for chat and comedy shows, with some signs of enjoyment. In March 2014 he traded mock insults with the actor Zach Galifianakis on his spoof interview show, *Between Two Ferns*.[44] Commenting on the show, the president's chief communications strategist said that 'we have to find ways to break through. This is essentially an extension of the code we have been trying to crack for seven years now.'[45] Mike McCurry, quoted in the same article, was more hesitant, saying that 'we have to worry about the dignity of the presidency, there's a limit about how much you can do' – adding, however, that 'the shifts in the popular culture and the way people are entertained and get information almost mandate new strategies'.

The new strategy which arose in 2016 was not the expected one: it came at the insistence of both the losing Democratic contender for the presidential nomination Bernie Sanders and the successful Republican contender Donald Trump, who wanted to campaign on being their own man. They had some PR help: Sanders had old friends and colleagues at the head of his campaign, led by Jeff Weaver, his chief of staff, who first worked for the Vermont senator in 1986, when he was but twenty. The more professional campaigner was Tad Devine, who worked for Al Gore, Michael Dukakis and John Kerry and was 'as cosseted in the Beltway power establishment as a consultant comes'. Devine was a founding member of the consultants Devine Mulvey Longabaugh, and was estimated to have been paid at least ten million dollars for his work with Sanders.[46]

Trump had, among others, Hope Hicks, now White House Director of Strategic Communications, formerly of Hiltzik Strategies, whose father had run Ogilvy PR in the Americas.[47] Kellyanne Conway traded her campaign manager post for one of consultant in the Trump White House and continued to appear on TV shows. The Trump campaign chairman, Stephen Bannon of Breitbart News, who loves to hate liberals and who is, in turn, accused by liberals of racism and misogyny,[48] did not appear or speak for Trump before the campaign though after the victory in November 2016, in an interview with the *Hollywood Reporter*, he said that 'we're going to build an entirely new political movement' and could rule 'for fifty years'.[49] He was later named as 'chief strategist' in the White House.

In his campaign, Trump emphasized themes which professional advisers saw as toxic; that they proved to be popular is forcing the PR trade to revise their prompt books – and show that communication techniques have not rendered all policymaking and government activism wholly dependent on them, as the critique often assumes. Trump did attempt to fix certain images, especially of his opponent, e.g. 'Lying Hillary'. But much of his rhetoric was of the moment, which would transform shortly after: accusations that the intelligence service had acted as if they were working in Nazi Germany simply dissolved when, in a speech after his inauguration to CIA officers, he said 'he loved' the Agency.[50] The discipline which consultants and campaign managers like to impose on candidates – 'stay on message' – was replaced with off-the-cuff statements and rambling talks, pledges sworn and dropped, accusations made with no factual base. It was addressed, it seemed, not to audiences who would punish inconsistency or lying, but to those who would reward the invoking of a mood music with words that had meaning only as attractive chords, not as statements of present fact or future commitments.

The enhanced status of PR and the denigration of the mainstream media by one become, by most measures, the most powerful political leader in the world are quite separate events, united in one important sense. Both reflect the increased power given to already powerful players in business, politics and celebrity occupations by the Net, gained at the expense of the mainstream press. The Net does allow individuals to become their own publishers, and a few individuals with no previous public visibility have become famous, usually briefly, while new organizations which meet or create a public mood or need can have a longer and successful life on the Net. But the Net, and social media, work within the bounds of a given social structure – and within that structure, powerful people with large resources use it to avoid the established media and appeal directly to an audience.

For many mainstream politicians, the Net isn't a means for 'deconstructing the state', but for deconstructing the press. It isn't confined to the American right: Jeremy Corbyn, elected in 2015 as a far-left leader of the British Labour Party, criticized the British news media both for intruding into his family's privacy and for coverage heavily biased against him – a bias partly deriving from the right-wing positions adopted by most UK newspapers, more substantially by a growing belief among his colleagues in Parliament and his leftish sympathizers in the media that he was incapable of presenting a coherent enough narrative to the electorate. He also sees the mainstream media's days as numbered and 'prefers to wield his influence on social media or through grassroots campaigning. Here, Corbyn feels he can talk directly to the electorate and reach out to the disenfranchised away from the filter of journalists.'[51] But it's fair to say the view is stronger among politicians of the US right, since they have a larger, mainly Net-based infrastructure of right-supporting media with a wide reach. Ted Cruz, one of the leading contenders for the presidential nomination in the Republican primaries, told Fox News in February 2016 that there was no point in 'whining' about anti-conservative media bias, instead they could 'do what Reagan did, go over the head of the media ... we don't live any more in a world of three networks that have a stranglehold on information. We have got the Drudge Report. We have got talk radio. We have got the social media. *We've got the ability to go directly around, and go directly to the people* [my italics].'[52]

In transferring their efforts to reach out to the Net and social media, politicians usually charge the mainstream media with lying, gross inaccuracy, arrogance and ignorance, to all of which these media could, on any given day, plead guilty. Trump has the highest profile in making such claims; the public relations and political communications worlds do it more *sotto voce*, often off the record, since they need the mainstream media still, even in its retreat. Yet the grounded belief of journalism – that it seeks a truthful narrative – has remained an ideal, an aspiration, more precious and more sought after by some than others, often eluding even the eager seekers. But journalism remains to make a credible claim for its essential presence in the construction and maintenance of a democratic state with a powerful civil society – of which the news media are part.

Insofar as the shift of power is also a war on observable, provable, checkable facts, it is not only an attack on pre-Net journalism, but also on one of the necessary elements for a democratic polity: the primacy of the fact.

PART III

FREEDOM

INTRODUCTION

'Journalism's first obligation is to the truth'

The constraints on journalism in authoritarian states spring from a fundamentally different view of its utility: for authoritarian leaders, it is useful in informing the citizens, but only with facts deemed appropriate that they should know. The larger duty is to follow the lines the leadership has laid down, and rally the media audiences to the support of the regime. In democratic societies, the position taken by governments is that independent journalism is an indispensable element in civil society – however much they may at times seek to diminish its effect (rightly or wrongly) and however gritted their teeth must be when invoking its democratic necessity. In democratic societies, individuals and corporations command most of the news media, imposing a restraint on governments, but also on journalists, who seek to overcome, or at least widen the boundaries of the restraint. Freedom, or greater freedom, of journalism resides in these efforts – some of which can be enfolded into democratic practice, some of which fail.

One way of looking at journalistic freedom is to define it as the partner of responsibility. The more journalism is responsible to its core mission, the freer it will be. The core mission is that set out as the first of the ten principles which Bill Kovach and Tom Rosenstiel propose in their *Elements of Journalism*[1] – 'Journalism's first obligation is to the truth'. The truth sets journalism free, or free-est, the argument goes, because whatever constraints are placed upon journalists, their belief in Kovach and Rosentiel's first commandment most securely expresses their autonomous and socially necessary existence.

The first two examples here – public service broadcasting and investig-ative reporting – work under that belief. The second two – a radical approach to reporting, privileging the unmediated voices of working people, and a journalism of revelation through leaking of confidential information based on the view that the state works against the interests of the citizenry – reject that belief.

ELEVEN

Roads to freedom

i 'Your work has always been essential'

Investigative journalism is that part of the trade that follows lines of enquiry down numerous tracks, many of which are invisible at the outset. Enquiries are often pursued, as James Ettema and Theodore Glasser note approvingly in their *Custodians of Conscience*, to right wrongs and assert a moral framework. In liberal democratic societies, the results of investigative journalism are often contested, denied and can prompt legal action, but the right of journalists to pursue is not fundamentally contested; the liberal democratic states are usually less fragile than the autocracies.[1]

More than any other forms of the journalists' craft, investigative journalism depends on unwritten agreements among the government, the state, the judiciary, the police, the secret services and companies. These agreements flow from an understanding, which has become more complete in the past half century, that journalism has – and should retain and develop – the ability to lay open what has been hidden and what is important. The details are fought over: the practice must be supported.

Investigative journalists are thus ideally more free than others, because they are directed, or direct themselves, to find the truth, or the best version they can of that elusive commodity. It operates more routinely in the borderlands of acceptability, both to the state and to the public.

A scandal, in free societies, need not be based on an illegality. It is what the news organization wishes to designate as a scandal. In popular journalism, much of the energy behind investigations is to unmask sexual affairs, usually adulterous. Adultery is not illegal in most states – but its discovery among the celebrated and the powerful is based on the still-prevalent view that, in spite of it being common, it is morally wrong. More to the point, experienced journalists know their audiences will enjoy the embarrassment and pain of those caught in the glare of the revelation. To simplify: the upmarket media tend to investigate in the public interest, the tabloids in what the public is interested in. It's a simplification, because both do both.

The expenses claimed by British MPs revealed in 2009 by the *Daily Telegraph* with information taken from a stolen computer disk purchased by the newspaper were mostly not illegal and were, set against government expenditure, trivial. But they offended against a general opinion that Members of Parliament should be scrupulous about the use of public money. The torture of the MPs was prolonged for weeks as the paper published daily revelations to raise circulation and deepen agony, the whole lying between *schadenfreude* and public interest.

As this chapter was written, a scandal broke in the *Sunday Mirror*, one of the UK's tabloids. It concerned Keith Vaz, a long-serving Labour Member of Parliament, who was chairman of the House of Commons Home Affairs Select Committee – a powerful body whose remit covers crime, policing, immigration, prisons and drugs. The *Mirror* story revealed that Vaz had engaged the services of two male prostitutes, and asked them to bring banned drugs with them to a session in his flat. The issue was dismissed as a private affair by the Labour Party leader, Jeremy Corbyn, but both Conservative and Labour members of the committee made it clear they could no longer support him. Their argument was that one whose remit included drugs and Home Office policy on prostitution could not be seen as neutral: an argument made by the newspaper when charged with intrusion into private life. After some days' delay, Vaz resigned. The story was unusually clear in its mixture of private sexual activity and public responsibility.

An example of a more 'pure' public interest investigation was carried out in the late 1980s, initially by Reuters then more fully in *The Hindu*, a daily in the southern India city of Chennai (previously Madras) into the securing of a contract for howitzers for the Indian army by the Swedish arms company Bofors. It was a probe, the first of such a size in India, into large-scale bribery. The company paid ten million dollars in kickbacks to politicians, senior officers and officials, and its discovery contributed to the defeat of the party then in power, Congress, though it did not result in convictions of the guilty. This stimulated a tradition of investigative reporting in India, especially in the magazine *Tehelka*, founded in 2004, and in Sweden, where the Centre for Investigative Journalism owes its inspiration to the Bofors scandal.

As it has grown stronger over the last few decades, investigative journalism has been given more and more official – government and judicial – support, and is being held up as a necessary civic endeavour. Networks of investigation centres, based in and outside of news organizations, increasingly conduct joint work and provide models. In 2012, for example, an investigations unit in Japan's *Asahi Shimbun* daily, vulnerable to closure, was revived and expanded after a visit by executives from the paper to the *New York Times* and the New York-based ProPublica centre.

The independent centres presently flourish. ProPublica is a prolific producer of long pieces of illuminating journalism, and has covered subjects as diverse as a series on the continuing US racial divide, the role of the tyre company Firestone in the conflict in Liberia and the failure of robust regulation of Wall Street. Correctiv in Germany did a forensic piece of reporting on the downing of the Malaysian airliner over Eastern Ukraine in 2014; and Baltica in Latvia revealed the large exodus of wealthy Russians to the Baltic states as it endeavoured to 'find out who is running away from Putin's Russia'. The International Consortium of Investigative Journalists has had the greatest recent coup, working through millions of documents leaked from Mossack Fonseca, the world's fourth largest offshore law firm, which led to the publication of the Panama Papers – reams of embarrassing, and in some cases potentially criminal, revelations about tax evasion.

It's a commonplace among journalists that all journalism is, or should be, investigative, or it's just a press release, but that isn't the case. It's true that any meaningful definition of the investigative genre has to make a distinction between a story which chronicles an event – such as an aeroplane crash – and one which, as the Correctiv project attempted through multiple interviews, discovery of documents and access of expert opinion, attempts to get the likely truth behind the cause of the crash. But the first type of story is not the outcome of a press release: if well done, it's an effort to put known facts of a significant event into the public sphere as soon as possible – inevitably, at first, relying partly and at times heavily on official sources and explanations. That sort of information is hard to suppress, even in a highly controlled state like China, where the 2011 Wenzhou train crash could not be buried, both literally or figuratively. That incident showed, as had the earlier massive Sichuan earthquake in 2008, that straight reporting can be at least potentially subversive to authoritarian governments. Where such reporting is commonplace and largely unimpeded, readers and viewers tend to take it for granted: yet it is the first draft of a process which – if the incident is major, such as an earthquake or a large-scale train crash – will include expert reports and judicial inquiry.

Democratic governments just have to take the fallout from investigative reporting (if it's accurate: there's no point in not objecting to an inaccurate piece); and mostly, they now do. Of the major states, French leaders have done most to protect themselves against investigation, though even that citadel is crumbling. When President François Hollande was revealed, in

2014, to be having an affair with the actress Julie Gayet while his partner, the journalist Valerie Trierweiler, was the official first lady, the president took no action against the revelations, saying it would not be proper for one who has legal immunity, as a president does, to take another party to court. Gayet, however, did initiate a suit against *Closer*, the magazine which had published the original photograph of Hollande riding to a tryst at her flat on a scooter and which took pictures of her in her car, which is considered a 'private place' under French law. Photographs taken of her entering the building which Hollande also subsequently entered were not a subject of the suit, since the street is regarded as a public place. In March 2014, she won 15,000 euros in damages and *Closer* was ordered to publicize the judgment on its front page.[2]

President Obama, much criticized by investigative journalists for attempting to stop leaks by ensuring officials who leaked were tried, made a speech in March 2016, in memory of the former *New York Times* national political reporter Robin Toner, which combined implicit criticism of Donald Trump – then storming ahead in the Republican primaries – and an explicit endorsement of investigative and well-informed reporting. In one passage in the speech, which went far in praising serious reporters, he outlined the necessity of an investigative free press to a functioning democracy:

Whether it was exposing the horrors of lynching, to busting the oil trusts, to uncovering Watergate, your work has always been essential … too often, there is enormous pressure on journalists to fill the void and feed the beast with instant commentary and Twitter rumours, and celebrity gossip, and softer stories.

And then we fail to understand our world or understand one another as well as we should. That has consequences for our lives and for the life of our country.[3]

ii 'The BBC has ... a liberal bias'

The implicit assumption in the US is that the market media can be trusted more than those funded by the state, because the former are numerous, naturally competitive and, in extremis, less punitive: that is, the journalists cannot normally be fined or jailed by private corporations, though they can be fired. The state, for Americans of the right, and for some on the left, is an object of suspicion, with no business in many areas of public life – such as the regulation of journalism. In Europe, by contrast, a prevailing view has been that the state is more capable of looking after the public interest than private enterprise, and has the right and duty to tell broadcasters that they must cover certain areas – such as news, current affairs or arts coverage – in return for their licences to broadcast.

This belief combines, often implicitly, different strands of argument. One is state paternalism: broadcasting is too powerful to be left entirely to non-state actors. Another is a concept of public service, which is based on an assumption, and often on experience, that private media corporations choose not to provide what's judged to be full, unbiased, balanced coverage of issues that may be of public concern and interest, and are disinclined to spend large sums on expensive analysis and investigations. Thus the state must repair the market failure by its own provision.

Public service broadcasters argue that only a public/state broadcaster can bind the nation together, emphasizing national values, showcasing the central national events, covering debates in Parliament and elsewhere, and invoking, at critical times, the national spirit. The BBC is sometimes promoted as the Church of England on the air: an institution, long since reconciled to losing its monopoly, which provides an overarching ethos for the nation, within which other providers – of faith and of journalism – can find their place.

Above all others, the clinching argument is that the state can be neutral and that the public broadcaster, financed from taxes or by public subscriptions through the state, is the best way to allow its journalism to get closest to the truth. For the BBC, the truth is possible to achieve, and helps to set citizens free. In eschewing any right to have a voice of its own, it underscores the primary task of being a resource, both proactive and passive, for engaged citizenship.

In 2015 David Elstein, who had headed several independent TV companies, held a satellite-enabled TV exchange with Norman Fowler, a former Conservative Cabinet minister, on the BBC, during which Fowler pitied Elstein for being in New York, with such paucity of viewing. Afterwards, Elstein wrote that he 'found the usual fifty channels in my hotel room that evening, including subscription channel Showtime offering *Masters of Sex*, followed by *Ray Donovan*, followed by *The Affair*: three dramas better than anything offered by all UK channels combined in the previous twelve months'.[4]

Anecdote is endlessly flexible: yet as this was written, the part-state-backed Channel 4 had recently put out a gripping German espionage series called *Deutschland 83* and broadcast another, intriguing French media and politics series called *Spin*, while the BBC had just aired a luscious version of *War and Peace*, capitalizing on its long-won ability to do period dramas very well, before moving on to an expensively shot and gripping adaptation of John le Carré's *The Night Manager*.

The BBC regards itself as the best public service broadcaster in the world, and it is probably right to do so. Central to such broadcasters – who typically cover the range of programming, through sport, comedy, drama, game shows, soap operas, history, schools programmes and music – is their news and current affairs divisions, their journalists, and the freedom and confidence with which they can tell the audience that *this, or that, happened.* The BBC has sufficient resources to be among the first and the fullest in reporting significant events; it can also claim to be among the select few of public broadcasters which have a large degree of independence from the government of the day. The economic commentator Martin Wolf wrote that 'the BBC is a public institution but not the government's lackey. That is what made it trusted in the UK and around the world. The BBC is not the elite's property. It belongs to the people because the people pay for it directly.'[5]

Funding for the BBC from all sources approached four billion pounds in 2010–11, but is estimated to fall to near three billion in 2020–21. The Conservative-dominated coalition government elected in May 2010, and the Conservative government elected in 2015, pressed heavily on the BBC, and it now has to bear the cost of the BBC World Service (previously borne by the Foreign Office) and that of providing free licences to the over-seventy-fives – already a large part of its audience and forecast to grow. That would cost the Corporation an estimated 725 million pounds a year, which is another large bite out of its revenue, so large that in January 2016, the BBC asked those over-seventy-fives who could afford it to continue paying the annual licence fee voluntarily.

Criticism flows from two main sources. Firstly, broadcasters funded by advertising and/or subscription argue that the size and power of the BBC so dominates the marketplace that competition, especially in radio (where the BBC has some 85 per cent of the market), is heavily skewed to favour the public broadcaster. Secondly, a particular trope of the political right is a complaint that the Corporation does not uphold political neutrality and observe political balance.

The shift from broadcasting to the Net blunts the force of the first of these complaints, and throws the charge back at the complainers. US sites such as BuzzFeed, Vice and Huffington Post have all grown strongly in the UK market; that British-developed Net-based journalism should not have produced a major news medium isn't the fault of the BBC, and may speak more to the continued dominance, in opinion as well as news, of a still potent and highly polemical press.

The second charge has more force. In a remarkable session of self-criticism put on by the BBC in October 2006, mainly an internal affair, one of its most prominent current affairs presenters, Andrew Marr, argued that 'the BBC is not impartial or neutral. It's a publicly funded, urban organization with an abnormally large number of young people, ethnic minorities and gay people. It has a liberal bias, not so much a party-political bias. It is better expressed as a cultural liberal bias.'[6]

At the same gathering, the then US editor, Justin Webb, said that he had complained of anti-US bias on the part of the BBC (this was during the George W. Bush presidency), giving the actions of the administration 'no moral weight' – and revealed he had asked the deputy director general, Mark Byford, to correct this. The business editor, Jeff Randall, said he had complained to a 'very senior news executive', about the way in which multiculturalism was promoted within the BBC and was told: 'The BBC is not neutral in multiculturalism: it believes in it and it promotes it.' When Randall said he would wear Union Jack cufflinks, he said, he was told (by whom he didn't say), 'You can't do that, that's like the National Front!' (He did wear them, on air.) The head of news, Helen Boaden, said a Radio 4 programme revealing that black youths were bullying whites at a young offenders' institutions had been produced, but scrapped – until she stepped in and ordered its broadcast.

It was a cathartic moment for the speakers, both liberal (such as Marr) and conservative (such as Randall), to be able to express what they believed the BBC's default position was, and it had, it seemed, some effect. The 'cultural', urban bias which Marr described continues, all but inevitably, yet Webb was brought back from the US to be a presenter on the BBC's most influential current affairs show, Radio 4's *Today* – with, as a co-presenter, Nick Robinson, who had been active in the Conservative Party as a student (but whose neutrality has never been seriously questioned, except by the Scottish National Party). Its bias against the large constituency of politicians and others who favoured exit from the European Union, which had been marked, disappeared; coverage of the EU membership campaign in the spring of 2016 was carefully calibrated – to the point where disappointed 'Remainers' complained that its even-handedness gave equal weight to important pro-Remain economists and obscure pro-Brexit ideologues.

It remains, however, a complaint among many in the Jewish diaspora, and in Israel, that the BBC is biased against Israel and supportive of the Palestinian case, an issue pressed most passionately by the columnist Melanie Phillips.[7]

Public broadcasters everywhere are now losing out to private corporations in the competition for popular programming. The *Financial Times's* Henry Mance reported in August 2015, 'In the US PBS lost the best rights to *Sesame Street* after forty-five years because it could only cover about one tenth of the show's cost. Weeks earlier, Europe's public broadcasters were outbid for the rights to air the Olympics by Discovery Communications, owners of Eurosport.'[8] A public broadcaster now treads a ground dotted with deep pits: falling in one and failing to get out quickly can be fatal.

That seems to have happened to the Canadian Broadcasting Corporation (CBC), which has an audience share of only around 5 per cent, and which must compete with commercial Canadian stations, with Net-carried programming and with the hundreds of channels pouring across the border from the US. In the mid 2010s, it was dealt, or dealt itself, a series of blows that started when its most popular show, *Hockey Night in Canada*, was snatched from it by Rogers Communication, owner of a commercial network, which paid 5.2 billion dollars for the right to broadcast the games, and gain the lucrative advertising, over the next twelve years.[9]

Then, late in 2014, one of CBC's biggest talents, Jian Ghomeshi – a lively and popular chat-show host – was arraigned on charges of sexual assault on several women in the early 2000s, while another CBC host eviscerated a Corporation executive who claimed, it seemed falsely, that he had closely investigated Ghomeshi. *Maclean's*, Canada's news magazine, commented that the network had 'a labyrinthine bureaucracy that seemed to permit all manner of wrongdoing; a destabilized workforce shaken by some $230 million in funding cuts over the past three years that made it vulnerable to the demands of a coddled star [Ghomeshi]; a management that seems determined to stand by its faulty decisions – if it says anything at all'.[10]

Ghomeshi was cleared of most charges in March 2016, and a final charge dropped when he signed a 'peace bond' guaranteeing good behaviour.

The affair bore a close resemblance to the BBC's woes and obfuscations, as more and more evidence emerged in 2012 of the sexual predations of the one-time star presenter and disc jockey Jimmy Savile (who died in 2011). It was revealed that a programme prepared on the disgraced star by the BBC had been suppressed, while the rival ITV came out with its own investigation. The issue forced the new director general, George Entwistle, into retirement after fifty-four days in office – the immediate cause being a stumbling interview on BBC Radio 4's *Today* programme. Leaked details of a posthumous report into Savile's behaviour by Dame Janet Smith, a former High Court judge, pointed to a culture that rendered stars 'untouchable', and towards whom managers, who held themselves to be 'above the law', were 'deferential'.[11]

Before Savile, the most high-profile event, both in content and in effect, for which the BBC had been pilloried was a prank, in which comedian Russell Brand and presenter Jonathan Ross phoned the actor Andrew Sachs on a radio show they were co-hosting in October 2008. When there was no answer, they left a message on his answerphone, in which Brand recalled that both he and Sachs had appeared on the police TV series *The Bill*. At that point Ross called out, 'He [Brand] fucked your granddaughter!', referring to Georgina Baillie, a musician then performing with a group named Satanic Sluts.

The BBC received a handful of complaints; however, when the *Daily Mail* wrote an outraged feature about the show, the complaints to the BBC and to the communications regulator Ofcom ran into the tens of thousands. Both Brand and the controller of Radio 2, Lesley Douglas, resigned from the BBC, while Ross was suspended from his weekly TV show for twelve weeks without pay.

In March 2015, the *Top Gear* presenter Jeremy Clarkson, returning late to his hotel from a day's filming, demanded a steak; on being told that the kitchen staff were no longer available, he punched a producer, Oisin Tymon, and called him a 'lazy Irish cunt'. Clarkson's contract was not renewed; his strongly anti-politically correct, on occasion right-wing, views had long put him at odds with the politically correct, liberal culture of the BBC, but he was wildly popular and *Top Gear* was a top earner. His replacement, the disc jockey Chris Evans saw the programme's ratings crash, and he resigned, in favour of the former *Friends* actor Matt LeBlanc. Clarkson and his fellow *Top Gear* presenters were hired by Amazon, then building up its TV network, where he is reportedly paid ten million pounds a year, making him the highest-paid presenter on British TV.[12]

CBC attracts the same charges from the Canadian right for its leftist and 'preachy' tone. Philip Cross, an economist, wrote in the *Financial Post* that the network employs 'a chorus of CBC reporters and producers affirming their assumed superiority by churning out a constant stream of intellectual bigotry that alienates its listeners. The latter are migrating in droves to the proliferation of media available on the Internet.'[13]

CBC's terrible ratings are a kind of memento mori for public broadcasters and show what happens when they lose their grip on the loyalty of a sufficiently large slice of the nation they claim to both serve and represent. Yet though both the BBC and CBC have at times been charged with being under their respective governments' thumb, they can't plausibly be described as servilely doing the administration's bidding, nor do they construct the news so that the nation's political leaders always appear in a positive light. During both the Conservative Margaret Thatcher premierships in the UK (1979–90) and the Conservative Stephen Harper premierships in Canada (2006–15), the

BBC and the CBC were criticized for being leftist oppositions to the government, while the BBC's presenters treated the Labour ministers during Tony Blair's three terms in office (1997–2008) at least as harshly as they had their predecessors.

That degree of independence and *lèse-majesté* isn't the case elsewhere in Europe. In April 2015, the state broadcaster Radio y Televisión Española (RTVE) stood accused of blatant favouritism to the ruling Partido Popular (PP). A *Financial Times* report claimed that 'the channel's own journalists have grown so concerned about political interference that they sent a delegation to Brussels this month to make a formal complaint to the European parliament. In a seven-page document, they describe RTVE as "a propaganda instrument in the service of the government" – and chronicle a series of alleged journalistic lapses and manipulations.'[14]

Among other stories, the channel is accused of playing down corruption within the ruling party, as well as the rise of the Catalan independence movement and of the anti-establishment Podemos movement.

A group from the International Press Institute led by the former BBC executive Stephen Whittle visited Spain and produced a worrying report. Among other criticisms, it said that

recently, the newly appointed chairman of RTVE has boasted of his political affiliation to the PP and overseen a process of putting known government supporters into the newsroom and in key reporting posts. His own appointment was made thanks to an executive order that changed the law to allow a simple parliamentary majority rather than a qualified one when appointing the membership of RTVE's board. This is a dangerous precedent. Decrees which override existing laws should only be used for emergencies – not to upset a fundamental principle of good governance in relation to the public broadcaster.[15]

Spain continues to operate a 'spoils' system, in which the victorious party seeks to ensure that the institutions that it can control have leaders and key staff who are reliable supporters of the government; and that, when needed – such as at an election – they will demonstrate their loyalty with overt or (in the case of the broadcaster) semi-overt support. However, the most vivid case, and one most damaging to the reputation of public broadcasting, is the example of Radiotelevisione Italiana (RAI) (see Chapter Six).

Germany's public service broadcasters, ARD (founded in 1950) and ZDF (1961), have higher incomes than any other public service networks, and a share of viewing higher by 5–10 per cent than that of the BBC. Their output of news, current affairs and talk shows on political and social issues far outweigh that of other public service providers, though they aren't yet major players on the world TV drama scene, where US, UK and recently Scandinavian and French productions are in command.

ARD was given a remit by the post-war occupying powers to do 'serious, independent and objective reporting'.[16] The then senior US administration official Edmund Schaechter said that 'it is our deep conviction that radio stations should no longer be a mouth-piece of the respective government ... stations should represent every level of society and give all political groups and parties the opportunity to voice their opinion.' The fact that German broadcasting was so comprehensively re-founded after the end of the war and the Nazi period – along with the size of the public spending on the channels – has left the country with a practice and an ethic which emphasizes explanation and analysis, often at lengths which are seen as excessive by less devoted public service organizations.

The governing broadcasting councils in every state are required to represent all major parties and leading social actors. The parties are the most active participants, seeing rightly that the way in which television represents and characterizes them impacts directly on their electoral performance. It can be fractious, and doesn't escape a weaker form of the Italian trap: in 2009, Roland Koch, the Conservative leader of the state of Hesse and a board member of ZDF, forced a vote against the renewal of the contract of ZDF's editor-in-chief, Nikolaus Brender, on political grounds.

Public, or state-backed, TV channels remain quite popular in Europe. In the mid 2010s, the BBC channels took about 30 per cent of viewership, almost double that of the two main commercial networks, ITV and Channel 4; the German public broadcasters ARD and ZDF both top the most popular commercial channel, RTL; RAI usually has a few percentage points over Mediaset, with near 35 per cent of viewership; France Télévisions' three main channels – France 2, France 3 and France 5 – have a share of around 27 per cent, significantly below the three most popular commercial channels, TF1, M6 and D8, which have around 35 per cent, while the most popular commercial channel, TF1, is at over 21 per cent, 7 points ahead of the first state channel, France 2. This is a long way down from the state-protected dominance of television broadcasting in its first decades, but some way, too, from CBC-style collapse.

State-backed intervention in the market in order to produce and protect analysis and investigation is only good in practice where the public broadcaster can count on the fullest independence from the state, while not arrogating to itself any kind of political posture. And it's only possible where the funding for the news and current affairs divisions is enough to ensure their effectiveness, their reach and their grasp. In the 2000s and 2010s, they are under increasing pressure both from commercial media and their newspapers, who criticize them for 'distorting the market', and from the perverse effect of their own attempts to observe ethical standards – resulting in more scandals.

Most are seeing their income cut by governments. The service they provide, which has been a considerable addition to public understanding and to debate, may now be duplicated and effectively substituted by the vast choice offered by the Net, and the licence fee must – as critics like

Elstein argue – be replaced by subscription. They have posed as the main, even the only, 'destination' for viewers interested in news, current affairs and serious discussion: though many, usually older, viewers and listeners still cherish the publicly funded channels with which they were brought up when young, that position is likely to weaken further.

The claim that public service broadcasters can most convincingly represent the true facts of any case is, however, not a redundant one. The 'BBC approach' to neutral, balanced and truthful reporting, as it has developed over the decades since the founding of the BBC as a public corporation in 1926, remains an aspiration that acts as a spur to all public service networks and to those who would hold them to that standard. It has been adopted by many privately owned broadcasters for their news divisions, though it's likely that the numbers of more politically committed news channels will increase.

iii 'Nous sommes un journal'

In February 2014, the 190 journalists on the Paris daily *Libération* went on strike over a management plan developed by its then editor, Nicolas Demorand, to stop printing the rapidly declining newspaper and build up its website, create a social network and a big café/debating space in the Marais district of Paris. The majority backed printers' ink, and had a front-page banner headline printed that read: 'NOUS SOMMES UN JOURNAL: *pas un restaurant, pas un réseau social, pas un espace culturel, pas un plateau télé, pas un bar, pas un incubateur de start-up*' (We are a newspaper: not a restaurant, not a social network, not a cultural space, not a television studio set, not a bar, not a start-ups incubator). Demorand resigned. The paper, as of 2017, continues to print, at a large loss. Its paper sales sink continually, but it was still, in the mid 2010s, *un journal*, a *newspaper.*

It's no longer, though, a newspaper that defies the market. Its attempt to do so was perhaps the most audacious among daily newspapers in the twentieth century: its early success came at a time when the far left had a strong influence and considerable buying power, which permitted the paper to run through its early years without paying advertisements. Like the more famous *Le Monde*, *Libération* has had to embrace wealthy sponsors to keep publishing; in doing so, it retained much of value – but lost its revolutionary *raison d'être*.

It sought freedom (ironically under the influence of the then most despotic state in the world, China) by breaking the chains of bourgeois journalism, supplied by careerist writers. It existed to give freedom to the people to speak for themselves. In exercising that freedom, its founders believed, journalism could get closer to the truth of the human condition.

The philosopher Jean-Paul Sartre was a co-founder of the paper in 1973, and its editorial director in its first years. Like others in the paper's founding group, he was attracted to Maoism: it was popular on the French left of the 1970s, and had other adherents, such as the Communist philosopher Louis Althusser, Michel Foucault, and the writer Simone de Beauvoir, Sartre's partner. Neither Sartre nor de Beauvoir joined a Maoist group, but they did sell a Maoist newspaper, *La Cause du Peuple*, after it was banned; Sartre was the nominal editor of that, too. Both saw the Maoists as preferable to the French Communist Party, whose compromise with the state after the events of 1968 they abhorred. Neither denounced, nor even admitted, the murderous tyranny which China became under Mao, and saw demands from fellow intellectuals that they do so as evidence of reactionary views, even of CIA membership.

Sartre took a close interest in the newspaper, but he was already ailing when the paper was founded – he was nearly blind – and died in 1980. Along with Serge July, who became the editor, the central figure in its founding was Jean-Claude Vernier, who in his twenties had created a Maoist press agency in 1970, called the Agence de Presse Libération; its principle was to put journalism at the service, not of the market, but of the masses.

In an interview he gave at his retirement, he said that, when he joined the Maoist group (and wrote for *La Cause du Peuple*), he went, as had many of his comrades, to work in a factory: 'I didn't go to the factory to get to know the workers, because my grandparents were metal workers, but to listen to the masses, like a good Maoist ... for me, a journalist is first of all someone who inquires, then transmits what he has seen. It's being a spokesman [porte-parole], it's the words of others which are important.'[17]

The political philosopher Géraldine Muhlmann sees in the early years of *Libération* a sustained attempt to overcome the false objectivity of the mainstream journalist's 'gaze'. Its initial manifesto, published in 1972, committed the paper to 'attack secrecy, help the people speak ... by relying on the direct expression of the people ... everything that is discussed at work and in the community will be at the heart of the newspaper'. Sartre, she writes, came to see the paper 'as a means of unification of the people'[18] and he stated that 'the essence of our thinking ... will permit the unified people to demand from the State and the administration control of everything that goes on in these organizations. The government must no longer have any secrets. We must demand this.' Here, Sartre anticipated the demands of Julian Assange by four decades.

Soon after the paper began regular publication, a strike broke out at the Lip watch factory at Besançon – a plant founded by Emmanuel Lippman as a clockwork workshop in the 1860s, and as a watch-making plant in 1893. The paper sent several journalists to Lip, where they wrote reports which emphasized that they were transmitting the views of the workers, and celebrated the amity which grew up between the workers and the journalists. Muhlmann quotes a journalist writing of 'an unskilled worker using the familiar "tu" to the tie-wearing correspondent of *Le Monde* ... one of the women who works there says to us, "we would never have believed that a bronzed lady journalist from *Paris Match* could live with us for several days".' The aim and the result were, as Muhlman observes, 'to keep to this wholly insider viewpoint'. The view of the management was that given to the journalists by the workers, as were the 'contradictions' among these views; observations of contradictions in the workers' views by the *Libération* journalists were not countenanced. The desire to be pure conduits of the words and views of those whom they wished to represent – the search for a non-stylistic style and non-authorial authorship – caused many ructions, which culminated in Serge July's resignation and the paper ceasing publication in 1981.

He returned, however, and publication was resumed – though July had, increasingly firmly from the late seventies onwards, opposed a journalism which treated its subjects as the voice and themselves as the megaphone. *Libération* had to accept that it was a newspaper, with journalists – and they had agency, not merely passivity. It was a repudiation of the Maoist approach: the *I* – the fallible reporter – even if a very limited witness, was nevertheless telling a story, not merely taking dictation. *Libération* remained idiosyncratic, still on the left (but a social democratic, not revolutionary, left), and found the 2000s increasingly hard going. In July 2005, desperate for extra capital, it was proposed that the banker Édouard de Rothschild take a stake in the paper; after some argument it was agreed. There followed a year of disruption and the layoff of more than fifty staff provoked a strike. July asked for more investment and was refused – and resigned, this time permanently. One of the co-founders, and the managing director of the paper, Bernard Lallement, commented in an interview that Rothschild had introduced 'an economic and capitalist logic ... *Libération* always hated money. Throughout its history it always had fortunate people who supported its destiny, who brought in funds, I the first among them, without expecting any particular profit ... but *Libération* couldn't escape economic reality ... *Libération* is becoming a newspaper like any other.'[19]

Not quite. Journalism always attracts self-publicists, who may or may not be talented: *Libération* has several who are both. The paper's long-time correspondent on the European Union, Jean Quatremer, is one such: his reporting was hard and detailed enough to help end the Santer-led Commission in 1999 due to an expenses scandal. He has pronounced dislikes: of José Manuel Barroso, the former president of the Commission; and of Jean-Claude Juncker, who succeeded him. In his blog Coulisses de Bruxelles (Brussels Offstage) he writes with a mix of venom and detailed knowledge – such as this waspish piece on Juncker:

> No one has forgotten that he coveted that job in 2009, when he was never a candidate for the presidency of the Commission. Nicolas Sarkozy, then French President, blocked his progress then, because he believed this bon vivant (too many cigarettes, too much booze) had allied himself a little too much with German thinking, and didn't show himself active enough at the beginning of the crisis in 2007–8. At that time, Merkel supported the French President.[20]

This is the opposite of *Libération*'s founding aspiration; Quatremer is, within his field, the celebrity journalist par excellence, the man all must read because *he* is writing, and not transmitting the views of others. Sonia Delesalle-Stolper, a correspondent for some years in London, told me that *Libération* has become a place for individuals, not transmitters: 'I worked for Agence France-Presse, where you can't have your own style; and for *Figaro*, where you really can't either. But in *Libération*, you can, and it will not be changed.' *Libération* had become, not a peoples', but a journalists' paper.

The paper, she says, is still bold – not just in its opinions, but in its actions. The day after the murders at *Charlie Hebdo* in January 2015, it published the offending cartoons on the front page – then hosted the *Charlie* staff in its office, a stylish if slightly grubby reconstruction of a parking garage, with the corkscrew of ramps still intact. From 2015, the dominant shareholder has been the French–Israeli entrepreneur Patrick

Drahi – the richest man in Israel, third richest in France – who built up a sizeable communications and media group, which includes, beside *Libération*, the magazines *L'Express* and *L'Expansion*, as well as the Israeli TV channel i24News.[21] He moved the paper out of its central Paris offices to a standard office block further out; and is pushing it towards Net-only publication.

The successive rescues of the paper took it further and further away from its founding ideals. Yet these ideals leaned heavily on an ideology – Maoism – that was hopelessly compromised by the massacres committed in its name, and its suppression of liberty of every kind. Its founding contradiction was that it sought freedom from bourgeois morality – liberation – by adopting the ideology and the practices of one of the most repressive and murderous movements of the twentieth century.

iv 'The Internet is a threat to human civilization'

Leaking is as old as journalism: it is the dissemination of any information which has not been authorized to be released. In the 2010s, however, the new era of leaking became identified with the downloading and publishing of huge quantities of confidential files. The first such load were those held by the US State Department, leaked by Private Bradley Manning and published by Julian Assange's organization, WikiLeaks, in 2010. A larger haul, both in quantity and in impact, were those taken by Edward Snowden from the US's National Security Agency, and later published widely, in 2013. In 2016, the Panama Papers, 11.5 million files taken from a Panamanian tax haven law firm, Mossack Fonseca, giving details of the determination of the rich and powerful to keep their earnings out of the maw of the state, were published worldwide. These leaks are seen by those who obtain and those who publish them as a more militant journalism, free from the entanglements and compromises of the mainstream.

—

Journalism keeps a kind of public record. 'Papers of record', which are now on the decline almost everywhere, detailed the main events, institutions and deliberative councils of the town, or the region, or the nation. No newspaper now would print long accounts or verbatim renderings of council or parliamentary debates. Nor need they, since they're usually available on the Net, or in the case of national parliaments, televised by the public broadcaster.

But constant availability isn't the whole point. When set in the pages of a newspaper, accounts or speeches took their place with other significant events, and often had pride of place; they were there to inform, but their presence also expressed an assumed bond, created by the journalists, between the reading citizens and the elites of various sorts, including the elites in the root sense of the word – the elected.

Parliamentarians joke sourly that the best way to keep a secret is to make a speech about it in a legislature, or in a committee open to press and public. That's not true, of course, but it has a kind of half-life truth. Much of what is churned out on the record by legislatures and by administrations everywhere is unseen by the news media, and some of it, when sifted, can be as important, even as dramatic, as the secrets that have to be dug for, or which are leaked. The US journalist Izzy Stone put out *I. F. Stone's Weekly*, a Washington insider's newspaper revealing much that insiders didn't know, fifty-five years before the founding of its nearest successor, *Politico*. He told me a few years before his death in 1989 that he drew most of his content – which was often revelatory – from committee hearings and official publications ignored by his more febrile colleagues: 'A lot of the news that we should know and isn't in the papers is lying there, published, at the taxpayers' expense.' Stone was using material openly available: 'the whistleblower' was the public record of one or other section of the political establishment. The leaking culture of the 2000s isn't like that.

Leaking has gradations, and they include – probably most commonly – authorized leaking, where an institution agrees that one of its members or employees tells one or more journalists something which it has not made, and perhaps will never make, explicitly public. It's the 'between you and me ...', the 'don't quote me but ...' sort of leak, which has a particular objective in mind and is nearly always to benefit the institution, or part of the institution (since many such leaks are the product of internal battles), or the individual, from which the leak comes. Journalists tend to be scornful of the authorized leaker, even as they use the leaks that are given. Diligent journalists aren't controlled by their sources; if the authorized piece fits – and if, as far as can be ascertained, it's true – then it adds to the many parts that go into making a good story.

There's a lot of leaking that floats in a grey zone, which has aspects of confidences, aspects of calculation, or aspects of intimacy. To have a confidential source who leaks on a regular basis can be an intimate relationship, with over- or undertones of domination and acceptance. In the first series of the US political drama *House of Cards* (2013), which is both acute and melodramatic about the relationship between politics and journalism, a novice who is being secretly fed stories by a senior politician is asked abruptly by a jealous older woman colleague: 'Who are you screwing?' The older journalist adds that she could not get such quality material without offering sex, and that she had made such bargains herself.

Personal intimacy in journalism, whether sex-based or not, excites overt disapproval among the guardians of journalistic ethics; but some degree of it can't be avoided, because of the emotional nature of the transaction. It's more overt, or maybe less hypocritical, in some journalistic cultures, such as in Europe. In an interview for a book I wrote in 2004, the then political correspondent of the French business paper *Les Echos*, Françoise Fressoz (she later moved to *Le Monde*) told me that: 'the curse of French political journalism is the connivance between the political class and political correspondents; they live, work eat and sometimes sleep together ...

you go to a press conference and you get a lot of official stuff which means little. You meet a politician for lunch and at the end of it, when he's relaxed, he'll tell you a whole lot of stuff which you can't attribute – and which may or may not be true.'[22]

Leaking has – had – certain protocols. Alex Jones, who wrote about the media for the *New York Times* and then became director of the Shorenstein Center on Media, Politics and Public Policy at Harvard, argues that 'many of the most critically important pieces of watchdog journalism depend on … anonymous sources' – and that it is a matter both of honour and of common sense to tightly guard the identity of the leaker/source. Failure to do so, Jones believes, is a 'betrayal'.[23] Heroes are those journalists who elect to go to jail rather than divulge the source to law enforcement agencies pursuing the leaker; that is, they are imprisoned for breaking the law. More to the point, he states that 'widespread breach of these promises would be crippling journalistically, as sources would no longer trust reporters'.

Jones, as one of journalism's thought leaders, assumes that mainstream journalism works – when working at its best in exposing abuses and lies – in opposition to established authorities, including the state, and that those who pass information on to journalists must be protected by a code of silence which, in practice, could mean defying the law. And sometimes it does. In 2005, the *New York Times* writer Judith Miller went to jail for eighty-five days rather than reveal her source of information on a CIA agent, Valerie Plame; she provided partial information, and was released. And in June 2014, the *New York Times* investigative reporter James Risen refused to testify on his sources for a revelation he made, in the paper and in a book, on the CIA's efforts to disrupt Iran's nuclear programme. A district judge had ruled that Risen did not have to testify, but the state won its case on appeal when, on a 2:1 vote, the appellate judges determined that the First Amendment did not protect reporters from the authorities' demand that they reveal a leaker. The Supreme Court rejected his appeal, but Risen reiterated his refusal to give information: there's a stalemate at the time of writing.

However, the possibility that journalists will betray them is no longer a source's main issue; it's more the ease with which they can now be identified via smartphone data and other surveillance.

The best of deals for the journalist is that offered by a whistleblower, who is often ethically affronted by the institution for which s/he works. Because it's done for moral reasons, the deal has the satisfaction of the moral imperative and the journalist is thus the handmaiden to the purest form of journalism, with no quid pro quo for the story except its publication.

The best-known heroes of post Second World War whistleblowing in the mainstream are Daniel Ellsberg, who leaked the Pentagon Papers – a history of the Vietnam War, which revealed that the political leadership had for some time believed the war was being won by the Viet Cong, while they publicly insisted it was being won by South Vietnamese and US forces – to Neil Sheehan of the *New York Times* in 1971; and the Watergate informants for Bob Woodward and Carl Bernstein of the *Washington Post* in 1972 – all Americans. There was much whistleblowing, less globally celebrated, elsewhere, such as the French agents who leaked to *Le Monde* details of the sinking of the Greenpeace ship *Rainbow Warrior*, blown up by French foreign intelligence because it was sailing to disrupt atomic bomb tests, in 1985 – it prompted the resignation of the head of the agency. Germany's weekly *Der Spiegel* magazine specializes in reports based on leaks – it's one of the major publishers of both WikiLeaks and Snowden's revelations. But it also regularly reveals less explosive but still confidential information. A report in the magazine in September 2010 was based on a leaked document from the Bundeswehr's [German armed forces] Future Analysis department, and spoke to concern of future conflict in the world because of shortages of oil.

The people who organized the mass leaks of US diplomatic cables, and of the NSA files, are often compared to the central characters of past disclosures. But the differences are important – more important, especially, for an understanding of the contemporary news media in much of the democratic world. Both Woodward and Bernstein, separately, criticized aspects of the leaking of the NSA files by Edward Snowden – Woodward more dismissively, telling Larry King that Snowden 'clearly broke the law ... I certainly wouldn't call him a hero.'[24] Bernstein called Snowden's travels to Hong Kong and then to Russia 'operatic', adding that the former NSA contractor should have stayed in the US to face the consequences of his act. He also said that 'most of the [NSA's surveillance] programs that Snowden revealed were already known to the public' and that 'as far as we know, the program has not been abused and safeguards are in place domestically'.[25]

Woodward and Bernstein were reporters who pulled on a thread, tentatively at first, which turned into a rope thick enough to hang a president. They worked within – though they enlarged – already established protocols for reporting in depth. Daniel Ellsberg was more radical; he wrote in the *Washington Post*, soon after the first stories based on the stolen NSA files appeared, that 'for the whole two years I was under indictment, I was free to speak to the media and at rallies and public lectures ... I couldn't have done that abroad, and leaving the country never entered my mind. There is no chance that experience could be reproduced today.'[26] But Ellsberg worked within the system, albeit in opposition to the administration's policy: he was given (covert) assistance by a fellow researcher at Rand, Anthony Russo, and by members of the staff of the Democratic senator Edward Kennedy. He believed in the ability of the political system to digest the findings of the study and to use them to inform debate about the nature of the Vietnam War. He wanted to rally support against a war which he believed to be failing – as it was. He thought that opposition within the political system could help stop the war – as it did. Though he has expressed solidarity with Snowden, he is a very different political phenomenon.

—

Today's leakers are people of the Net and the screen – men and women for whom the vast space of information flows, and the technology which give access to it, is their natural domain. In Julian Assange's book *Cypherpunks*, one of his co-authors, the German hacker Andy Müller-Maguhn, says in a concluding symposium that 'we don't understand ourselves as living in Germany, we understand ourselves as living on the Internet'.[27]

Julian Assange was also a man of the Net, one who, in a sometimes-chaotic childhood and adolescence, found solace, order and control online. He also found targets for his anger over the belief that the Net was being used as a tool for a deepening and all-enveloping worldwide repression.

The first few pages of *Cypherpunks* ('Not a manifesto: there is not time for that') sees the world 'galloping into a new transnational dystopia ... the Internet is a threat to human civilization ... left to its own trajectory, within a few years global civilization will be a postmodern surveillance dystopia from which escape for all but the most skilled individuals will be impossible. In fact we may already be there.'

There is, however, a way out: 'Our one hope against total domination' is that it is 'easier to encrypt information than to decrypt it'. The cypherpunks, endowed with the secrets of encryption, are superheroes, saviours of the universe. They can 'abstract away our new platonic realm from its base underpinnings of satellites, undersea cables and their controllers ... to create new lands barred to those who control physical reality. And in this manner to declare independence.'

That Assange sees himself as an extraordinary man with a mission to save the world was given strong underpinning by Andrew O'Hagan, the British novelist whom Assange had agreed should assist him in writing a book about his life to date (Assange was then around forty).[28] Much of what Assange told O'Hagan fitted *Cypherpunks*' apocalyptic view of the world's future and the role that they must play in order to avert it: 'there is a new vanguard of experts, criminalized as we are, who have fastened onto the cancer of modern power, and seen how it spreads in ways that are still hidden from ordinary human experience'.

O'Hagan, though patient, came to see him as a mixture of a fantasist and a narcissist: 'Assange referred a number of times to the fact that people were in love with him, but I couldn't see the coolness, the charisma he took for granted. He spoke at length about his "enemies", mainly the *Guardian* and the *New York Times* ... He hardly mentioned the right-wing press that called him a criminal and a traitor.'

The novelist did manage to complete a book – *Julian Assange: The Unauthorized Autobiography*; though the 'autobiography' was written by O'Hagan, Assange refused to recognize it and railed against the publisher Canongate for, in his view, breaking the terms of the contract. Still, O'Hagan, with whom he remained on reasonable terms, managed to get down some (probable) facts, which sketched in a remarkable nomadic life. After escaping with his mother from a vengeful partner, he turned, soon, to the cybersphere and in the book's most lyrical passages, he describes how, in his mid-teens, 'it was the computer I spoke with ... where selfhood dissolves into history ... I was giving myself to my computer ... new life was burning within me ...'

To that new life was added, in his twenties, a view of government as a conspiracy, which it became his duty to destroy, not by conventionally violent revolution, but by breaking into the secret banks of data and networks of power. He became a pioneer in this new form of crime and warfare, which has since become much more common, and threatening. He was an experienced and bold hacker, who had the technical means and, by the mid 1990s, the mission – which became WikiLeaks. But the fame and importance of WikiLeaks depends very largely on the decision of a young, often depressed and lonely US Army private in a base in Iraq, whose raw and sensitive nature was shocked by the material he was handling and who decided to become a whistleblower, so that the world would know what was going on below the conventional press radar.

It's quite hard to see Bradley – now, after a decision to come out as a trans woman, Chelsea – Manning as anything other than a butterfly broken on a wheel. His (using the masculine form for the time before Manning came out as a trans woman) parents were divorced; his mother, who was Welsh, was a heavy drinker and attempted suicide. Aged thirteen, he moved with her from the small town of Crescent, Oklahoma, to the larger town of Haverfordwest on the English–Welsh border; then, at seventeen, he returned to the US to live with his father and stepmother, but left once more after arguments and – following a couple of years of low-paid jobs and temporary stays – he joined the US Army, aged twenty. He was gay and had come out in his teens, but quietly, fearing bullying. And although he was intelligent, he had little further formal education after school.

He was a computer whizz and had, like Assange, retreated into the Net as a child. When examined by the army, he was found to have high enough IQ and the skills to be assigned to duty as an intelligence analyst.

Deployed to a base near Baghdad in 2009, Manning was given access to a huge mass of classified material. Reading the war logs and other material, he became disillusioned and cynical about the US presence in Iraq and Afghanistan. He had a brief affair with a musician named Tyler Watkins, who was in a circle of 'hacktivists' round the Massachusetts Institute of Technology in Boston – but who, during a leave, turned away from him.

He had become aware of WikiLeaks before being sent to Iraq; in a statement he made at his trial in January 2013, he noted that – contrary to the critical and hostile tone of an army counter-intelligence report he had read – WikiLeaks 'seemed dedicated to exposing illegal activities and corruption'.[29] Manning, by temperament and experience accustomed to being outside of whatever form conventional society took, was caught between two sharply differing worlds: that of the military, fighting an unpopular and failing war, and that of WikiLeaks and its supporters, for whom the US Army was at least a virtual enemy. The knowledge he was imbibing through his work, he said in his trial statement, 'burdens me emotionally'. Leaking to WikiLeaks was to unburden himself.

By the time of his mid-tour leave in January 2010, he had stored a great deal of secret information on his laptop (initially to insure against computer crashes) and had come to believe 'that if ... the American public had access to the information ... [it] might cause society to re-evaluate the need or even the desire to engage in counter-terrorism and counter-insurgency operations that ignored the complex dynamics of the people living in the affected environment each day'.

On leave, he tried to contact the *Washington Post* and the *New York Times*, only the first of which showed any interest, but did not follow it up. He considered *Politico*, but didn't pursue it. That left, in his mind, WikiLeaks, and thus began the uploading, and later publication on the WikiLeaks site, of material which included a 2007 incident in which a US helicopter gunship, patrolling above the streets of Baghdad, shot up a group of men on the ground who were engaged in innocent activities (they included two Reuters employees, who were killed); Afghan and Iraq War logs; and later, 250,000 diplomatic cables.

In May, he contacted Adrian Lamo, a former hacker and occasional journalist, and, encouraged by a promise from Lamo that he would not betray him, he spoke about what he had done. Lamo reported Manning to US Army counter-intelligence – he was arrested at the end of May and later sentenced to thirty-five years. In custody, he came out as a trans woman, naming herself Chelsea Manning, and in 2014 requested hormone therapy.

She could not know how the material would be used, and thus if unredacted would endanger her army comrades, or others in different branches of US state service, such as diplomats and their sources – a fact she does not seem to have considered. That last insouciance on her part explains the harshly exemplary sentence, which clearly warned others who might be thinking of emulation. The 'butterfly on the wheel' impression remains, because more than any other of the participants in the mass leaks, she was the least prepared for what was about to descend on her.

Edward Snowden, by contrast, came from a military family: his maternal grandfather was a rear admiral in the US Coastguard, then an FBI official, and his father was also a senior coastguard officer. Glandular fever meant he was off school for months and at around the same time – in his late teens – his parents divorced. He moved with his mother to Ellicott City, outside Baltimore, within a few miles of his later employer, the NSA. Shy and introverted but described as pleasant, he, too, was a creature of the screen, taking computer courses, though he never finished high school.

As an adolescent, he had inherited his father's patriotism, joining the army to serve in Iraq 'to help free people from oppression'. Invalided out of Special Forces training because he broke his legs, he found a job as an information technology specialist with the CIA, thereafter rising quickly because of 'exceptional' IT skills. He was a libertarian of the right, dismissive of social problems like unemployment, strongly patriotic and hostile to newspaper revelations – such as, in 2009, the *New York Times* disclosures of a secret Israeli plan to attack Iran to neutralize its nuclear weapon capacity. But acquaintance with CIA techniques meant that he came to realize 'that I was part of something that was doing far more harm than good'.

Transferring from the CIA to two different civilian contractors working for the NSA – the computer company Dell, then the consultants Booz Allen Hamilton – Snowden found himself, in 2013, first in Japan then in Honolulu, where his advanced computer skills netted him a large salary and access to a vast trove of top-secret information, which he downloaded on to thumb drives and smuggled out of the underground facility where he was based. In May 2013, he told Booz Allen he needed time off because of epilepsy difficulties: in fact, he was beginning a new life. He flew to Hong Kong, checked into a hotel, and began to contact those he wished to help him unload his trove.

He had completed one kind of transition – from a patriot who thought that whistleblowers 'should be shot in the balls', as he put it in his guise as trueHOOHA on the Ars Technica site, to one who saw his trade as having grossly surpassed its proper limits: 'what I witnessed, over the course of my career, was the construction of a system that violated the rights not just of Americans but of people around the world – and not just constitutional rights, but human rights'.

Snowden, in both his private and his professional life, was as much a creature of the Net as Manning and Assange. The *Guardian* writer Luke Harding quotes his colleague, Ewen MacAskill – appointed by the *Guardian* to contact Snowden in Hong Kong – as saying after a few meetings with Snowden that 'he's comfortable with computers. That's his world.'[30] From his late teens, when he signed on to Ars Technica, Snowden was, writes Harding, 'passionately attached' to the Internet.

Passionate – even moderate – attachment to the Net is prompted by the freedom it offers. The social scientist Sherry Turkle writes that, on the Net, 'we are encouraged to think of ourselves as fluid, emergent, decentralized, multiplicitous, flexible, and ever in process'.[31] For the Net-adept, as Manning, Assange and Snowden became from an early age, any barriers to the freedom to search or to read or watch run against the grain of the Net life, where they believe everything should flow freely.

Snowden chose three journalists to whom to leak his material – Barton Gellman of the *Washington Post*, who had covered the uses and failures of intelligence before and during the Iraq War; Glenn Greenwald, a lawyer who blogged for Salon and wrote columns for the *Guardian*, his writing also concentrating on methods of surveillance, especially by the NSA; and Laura Poitras, an award-winning documentary-maker who had made two films on different theatres of the war on terror. Snowden chose them because of their choices of subject; significantly, only one was from the mainstream press.

Greenwald later said that Snowden did not contact the *New York Times* because it didn't publish an investigation by its reporter James Risen that the NSA was eavesdropping on US citizens without warrants for fifteen months – and only did so in 2005 because Risen was about to publish a book which told the story, thereby scooping his own paper. The story anticipated by some years many of the most important details which Snowden's files revealed.

Snowden's contacts with the initially uninterested and distrustful Greenwald and Poitras bore fruit when Greenwald, having been instructed in encryption techniques by Snowden, received from him a handful of files formerly in the sole possession of 'one of the world's most secretive agencies in the world's most powerful government'. One of these files was a description of a programme under which some of the most highly valued corporations in the world – Google, Microsoft, Apple, YouTube and others – allowed NSA collection of billions of messages from their servers. Then and later, Greenwald was too elated to keep reading without breaks of delirious joy. After panhandling for little traces of gold for years, he had been gifted a fabulous, world-changing mother lode. He and Poitras, having enlisted the backing of the *Guardian*, set off for Hong Kong, their delighted celebrations over the files they were reading on a sleepless flight waking other passengers.

In a memoir-cum-polemic, Greenwald summarizes what he glimpsed in these first minutes of delirium – a joy prompted by the realization that the issues he had blogged about for years now had a material base, and that his suspicions about the 'security state' had been confirmed. The 'mountain' of documents 'indisputably laid bare a complex web of surveillance aimed at Americans [who are explicitly beyond the NSA's mission] and non-Americans alike. Crucial, overarching documents at the front of the archive ... disclosed the agency's extraordinary reach, as well as its deceit and even its criminality.'[32]

Poitras worked on films of the events surrounding the leaks, and she, with Greenwald and a clutch of others, mainly investigative reporters, later joined the staff of The Intercept, a website which concentrates on revelations and investigations, and is funded by Pierre Omidyar, the billionaire creator and owner of eBay. Gellman continued to produce a series of original stories for the Post drawn from the Snowden files, but, unlike the other principals in the Snowden affair, remained bound by the protocols of US reporting.

In a story written on 5 July 2014 with Julie Tate and Ashkan Soltani, Gellman used some of Snowden's purloined documents to show that 'ordinary Internet users, American and non-American alike, far out-number legally targeted foreigners in the communications intercepted by the National Security Agency from US digital networks'.[33] The story contained the statement that 'The Post will not describe in detail, to avoid interfering with ongoing operations', the contents of the Snowden-provided files. It also says that 'At one level, the NSA shows scrupulous care in protecting the privacy of US nationals and, by policy, those of its four closest intelligence allies – Britain, Australia, Canada and New Zealand'; it then qualifies this with a paragraph which points out that some individuals are not so protected. It is evidence of a journalistic style which wishes to avoid the charge of marshalling facts in a purely polemical fashion.

Glenn Greenwald, who has mixed polemic with reportage since begin-ning his journalistic career, is by some way the most prominent of the Snowden group, in part because of that much less constrained position – and because he takes an aggressive stance to all critics, most of all to those within the journalistic community who have been critical of the Snowden leaks and of the newspapers, especially the Guardian. Greenwald and Assange, much more than the low-key Snowden, are the harbingers of a new form of journalism which they believe is growing and will ultimately escape from the womb of the old.

Greenwald and Chris Blackhurst, then editor-in-chief of the *Independent* titles in the UK, had an exchange on the issue in October 2013, which illuminates Greenwald's approach to journalism. Blackhurst, while making many genuflections to the importance of whistleblowers, wrote that he would not publish any Snowden revelations because he could 'not get wound up' about the fact 'that the security services monitor emails and phone calls, and use Internet searches to track down terrorists and would-be terrorists ... what [is it], exactly, that the NSA and GCHQ are doing that is so profoundly terrible?'[34] He added that he did not publish the material the paper did get from the Snowden files because the government had asked him not to, on grounds of national security.

Greenwald replied in white-hot rage. Blackhurst, 'a career journalist', had, in obeying the state's request not to publish, 'perfectly encapsulate[d] the death spiral of large journalistic outlets'.[35] Blackhurst was 'subservient, obsequious'; he was 'a good journalistic servant [of the UK state] ... it does not surprise me that authoritarian factions, including (especially) establishment journalists, prefer that none of this reporting and debate happened and that we all instead remained blissfully ignorant about it ... when they do so, they do us a service, as it lays so vividly bare just how wide the gap is between the claimed function of establishment journalists and the actual role they fulfill'.

Of all of those who have spearheaded the mass leaking movement, Greenwald has been the most explicit in his contempt for both US and UK media – and the most explicit in believing what all in the leaking movement, in one form or another, take as gospel: that the US, with its subaltern state the UK, has lost any legitimacy because it has enthusiastically embraced surveillance technology, which is used to oppress both their citizens and foreigners. This lies at the core of their claim that journalism must elevate itself to a new stage, one in which the state is an object of a priori suspicion.

In his memoir of his large part in the publication of the Snowden files, *No Place to Hide*, Greenwald contrasts the 'iconic reporter of the past [as] the definitive outsider' on low wages, when 'a career in journalism virtually ensured outsider status', with the present corporate creature, 'peddl[ing] media products to the public on behalf of that corporation ... those who thrive within the structure of large corporations tend to be adept at pleasing rather than subverting institutional power'.[36] (In fact, the 'iconic reporter of the past' tended to be more under the thumb of powerful editors, politicians and owners than their professional descendants, since they were more dependent on these figures for retaining their jobs and had little independent status.)

A straight-'A' high-school student, Greenwald attended the private George Washington University in Washington DC, an institution constantly credited with being among the 'most politically active' colleges in the country, with a high proportion of its graduates entering politics. He took a degree in philosophy, then a further degree in law at a second prestigious and private institution, New York University. He received fifteen offers from the foremost law firms in the land, choosing the most 'prestigious and selective among them', Wachtell, Lipton. He interned at the firm while completing his degree, and worked there for over a year after graduation, receiving 'uniformly and enthusiastically positive' performance reviews. He then set up his own, successful practice, which over a decade grew to a firm employing six lawyers with a US-wide practice specializing in constitutional issues. He published three books – *How Would a Patriot Act?*, *A Tragic Legacy* and *Great American Hypocrites*, all vigorous, and quite popular, attacks on Republican politics in general and the Bush presidency in particular.

Greenwald has been explicit in seeing journalism as in permanent opposition to political and, to a much lesser extent, corporate power, and that it should eschew any pretence at objectivity. In a dialogue with Bill Keller, then executive editor of the *New York Times*, in October 2013,

Greenwald dismissed 'this suffocating constraint on how reporters are permitted to express themselves, [which] produces a self-neutering form of journalism that becomes as ineffectual as it is boring ... [it] rests on a false conceit ... We all intrinsically perceive and process the world through subjective prisms.'[37]

Keller replied:

I believe that impartiality is a worthwhile aspiration in journalism, even if it is not perfectly achieved. I believe that in most cases it gets you closer to the truth, because it imposes a discipline of testing all assumptions, very much including your own ... A reader doesn't have to go back very far in the archives – including the archives of this paper – to find the kind of openly opinionated journalism you endorse. It has the 'soul' you crave. But to a modern ear it often feels preachy, and suspect.

Most radically, Greenwald believes – a belief which puts him close to Assange, though Assange remains the more rhetorically extreme – that journalism should be an act of aggression against the government. The 'check' which the notion of a Fourth Estate is supposed to provide to government 'is only effective if journalists act adversarially to those who wield political power'; the largest sin is to be 'subservient to the government's interests, even amplifying rather than scrutinizing its messages and carrying out its dirty work'. This is vague (what is government's 'dirty work'?) but it seems to mean that *any* government policy should not be approved or supported.

Keller, and journalists in his mould – liberal, professionally sceptical, practitioners and/or editors of investigative reporting – are at least as much suspect in Greenwald's eyes as journalists and commentators of the right. The characteristic O'Hagan had seen in Assange – 'he expended all his ire on the journalists who had tried to work with him and who had basic sympathy for his political position'[38] – is not wholly true of Greenwald, who expends a lot of ire on the right, but he does see liberal journalists, like Blackhurst of the *Independent* – a paper which, before, during and after his editorship, had not shown notable 'subservience' to the government of the day, and employed strongly radical reporters, such as Patrick Cockburn – as traitors to a cause which, as he defines it, should mandate root and branch opposition to government.

Keller believes in revelation, but when *New York Times* editor he held back stories and cut details in others because of government requests. In July 2006, in a joint declaration with Dean Baquet, then editor of the *Los Angeles Times* (and since May 2014 editor of the *New York Times*), Keller said journalists and other citizens had a common interest in defeating terrorism; and attested to occasions when after discussions with administration officials, they had held or cut articles. They affirmed the basic credo – that freedom brings responsibility, 'a corollary to the great gift of our independence' – and also affirmed that 'the virulent hatred espoused by terrorists … is also aimed at our values, at our freedoms and at our faith in the self-government of an informed electorate. If the freedom of the press makes some Americans uneasy, it is anathema to the ideologists of terror.'[39]

Early in 2014, Greenwald – having broken off his ties with the *Guardian*, for which he had written regularly – joined the First Look Media company, founded by Pierre Omidyar, already owner of a website, the Honolulu Civil Beat, which covers civic affairs in Hawaii. Omidyar, learning that Greenwald, Poitras and Jeremy Scahill of *The Nation* had decided to create their own website, persuaded them to join forces with him, and The Intercept – the name came later – was born.

Omidyar, child of Iranian parents, born in Paris and living in the US since his childhood, sees investigative reporting as needing to push beyond the implicit limits in which it had worked before, as in the Watergate tradition. Jay Rosen, a New York University academic who blogs illuminating essays on PressThink, wrote: 'Omidyar believes that if independent, ferocious, investigative journalism isn't brought to the attention of general audiences it can never have the effect that actually creates a check on power.'[40] With Greenwald at its centre, Omidyar pledged 250 million dollars to build up The Intercept as an online investigative news site, specializing in security and privacy issues; other well-known names were hired, including, as editor-in-chief, John Cook, who had run the Gawker site. It had a slow start, but by 2015, material of weight, beyond the Snowden leaks, appeared on it. In May 2015, a lengthy, poignant piece by Peter Maas described in great detail the case of Stephen Kim, a Korean–American State Department official jailed for leaking classified information about North Korea – evidence of the tough approach the White House was taking on officials passing classified information to journalists.[41]

Omidyar, who had been approached about buying the *Washington Post* (which Jeff Bezos of Amazon did buy), said that he was concerned by the growing pressures on journalism round the world and wanted to support 'independent journalists with expertise, a voice and followers', so that they could come together to do their journalism in concert. He believes it important to have a well-funded organization, with a strong legal team behind them, because (again according to Rosen) 'the kind of journalism [The Intercept] intends to practise is the kind that is capable of challenging some of the most powerful people'.

The journalism of leaks and the attitude of resolute enmity to authority, which, in the view of Greenwald, must accompany it, foreshadow a new stage in the trade. It is one that encourages the theft and publication of confidential information which bears on the strategic choices and hidden disasters of states and corporations, secret services and armies. Yet for its impact, much depends on the state of mind of the citizens who are the object of its publication.

Though the Snowden leaks bore mainly on the US and the UK, protests in both were significant but not extensive. Germany produced the largest reaction, in part because the chancellor's phone was revealed as bugged, which upset her and she called for an apology. But there, too, the protests subsided quite quickly; the fear of terrorism, as incidents multiplied in Europe in 2015 and 2016, encouraged a huddling round the secret services and the other security services, who were seen as protectors rather than oppressors.

The aftermath of the big leaks, especially that from the NSA, was on one side good news for administrations and the security services, as the public, everywhere, continued to look to them to protect them, and soon seemed to forget the breach of civil liberties which the publishers of the leaked documents insisted had been made. But the reality of the situation in which the agencies find themselves is worsening: Thomas Rid, professor in security studies at King's College London, told me that 'there are ways of protecting information. Which means that to do bulk collection on the part of the intel agencies is now much more difficult. It used to be that there was, as it were, a broad pipe of information that was relatively easily accessed. Now there are many very narrow pipes, which are encrypted and difficult to see. There is much more encryption at every level. Google has changed itself and put more encryption on.'

The greater encryption is itself a consequence of the Snowden leaks. The big communication companies, deeply embarrassed by the fact of their cooperation with the agencies in allowing monitoring of their traffic, have become hyper-protective of their clients' information, while users have become more security conscious. These companies still profess an anti-state ideology at times, says Rid, 'but that no longer matters much in the Valley. They're not extremist or anarchist. It's all about money and competition. Their cry to government is – "Leave us alone!"'

One leak was more marked than others in its effect. The theft, by one still unknown at the time of writing, from the Panamanian offshore law firm Mossack Fonseca and the publication of some of the 11.5-million-plus files taken showed how the super-rich of the world, and the politically powerful – from the Kremlin through Downing Street and Reykjavik's prime ministerial office to the presidential palace in Buenos Aires – benefited, directly or indirectly, from astute 'tax planning' in offshore havens. The content of the files met a spreading discontent at the seemingly unstoppable widening of the gap between the extremely wealthy and the getting-by – while the very poor, in most states, remained very poor. The leaker went first to the left-of-centre German daily *Suddeutsche Zeitung*, which then called in the International Consortium of Investigative Journalists to unpack the impact of the files from country to country.

The mainstream media were still capable of 'challenging some of the most powerful people' of the world, but now in concert with those prepared to steal large quantities of information from state or private institutions. The claim that these raids on banks of files and the subsequent publication are closer to the truth than other journalistic attempts has real force; this is the raw material, the goods, millions of documents any one of which, in the recent past, might have provided a front-page or top-of-the-bulletin story. They were obtained and published with an explicit and militantly moral purpose: so that the people should know the truth about what was being done in their name with their tax money, or what the rich were doing to avoid shelling out tax money.

They also bring journalism closer to asking fundamental questions about its purpose and its limits. When, in their joint statement, Baquet and Keller argue that freedom brings responsibility, a corollary to the independence of the US itself, they accept what they should do with material which has been leaked to them: check it out with the government and/or the security agencies. If the decision is made to publish material which authorities have argued is sensitive, even dangerous, then the editors put themselves in the position of one determining, possibly, the safety of their city or country. They would be publishing the truth, but the truth, as well as setting free, imposes constraints.

Increasingly, as it became clearer that Russia was prepared to hack western agencies and institutions and use the revealed material, with well-targeted propaganda, to damage democratic and civil processes, the question of how far purloined material, when published, could aid anti-democratic forces became more urgent.

CONCLUSION

This happened

Journalism is about what happens in the world. How events are shaped and presented to the public depends on the space that the largest powers in the world – the state and private capital – accord to the sometimes servile, sometimes semi-autonomous, but always weaker, power of the craft itself. Journalism is always dependent and can only lessen its dependence, and develop a consistent concern to get at as much of the truth as possible, in democratic states with strong civil societies.

The ways in which journalism can be packaged and presented is changing greatly in the early decades of the third millennium. The Net gradually colonized and began to destroy the older media; and the burgeoning possibilities of social media opened a new chamber, in which connections could be made, information passed, mobilization furthered – and, as President Trump demonstrates, a country governed.

The delivery mechanisms of all kinds of messages, including journalism, were represented by Marshall McLuhan as being largely deterministic: 'The medium is the message'[1] was his capsule of this insight. Journalism in the twenty-first century is now being delivered in radically different and continually changing ways, yet the content remains the most important, conveying real facts, fake facts and views as it always has. However, the huge difference digital media have brought, allowing consumers the opportunity to be creators, is having a profound effect on what that content is and how it is perceived and acted upon.

The best analysis of the technologies and effects of the new journalism is in the report 'Post Industrial Journalism'[2] by Emily Bell, head of the Tow Center for Digital Journalism at the University of Columbia's Journalism School, with Chris Anderson, assistant professor at the City University of New York, and Clay Shirky, the scholar and writer on new media issues. Journalism, they insist, is in the midst of a great disruption, and will stay there. Much of what is said and written about the trade is a lament, often by older journalists, some of whom have lost jobs they have done for decades. Others find it hard to be at ease with the constantly developing technology which journalism demands, and are terrified by the prospect that much routine journalism can be better done by computers, believing, perhaps self-defensively, that these shifts dilute the real point of their craft, which is finding, and digging for, stories. Bell, who had been head of digital content at the *Guardian*, is respectful to these concerns, and accepts that

> journalists can be much more efficient than machines at obtaining and disseminating certain types of information. Access and 'exclusivity' or 'ownership' of a story is created through interviewing people. Making phone calls to the White House or the school board, showing up at meetings and being receptive to feedback, sharing views and expressing doubt all make news more of the 'drama' ... central to the concept of a newspaper. These very personal and human activities mark journalism as a form of information performance rather than simply a dissemination of facts.

But having patted the old boys and girls on the head, she goes on to say: 'the most exciting and transformative aspect of the current news environment is taking advantage of new forms of collaboration, new analytic tools and sources of data, and new ways of communicating what matters to the public.'

Bell and her colleagues note that one of the best things that is happening to journalism, most rapidly in the US, is the creation of a myriad of special-interest sites. One, which Bell likes to highlight when she gives talks on the report, is 'Scotus' – not the fourteenth-century, Scots-born theologian Duns Scotus, but a site which uses as its title the acronym of the Supreme Court of the United States. SCOTUSBlog was started by two lawyers, the married couple Tom Goldstein and Amy Howe, joined by the former reporter on the court (for over half a century) Lyle Denniston. The purpose was to chronicle and analyse the cases in front of the court in some detail, but in plain English, so that the often technical arguments are accessible. It makes no charge, presenting itself as a public service. Thus the public mission of journalism is, in sites like SCOTUS, not just preserved but deepened – a perspective often lost in the flood of criticism of the Net, and its predisposition to promote 'fake news'.

She is certain that the struggles of newspapers to keep as much as possible of the old way of doing journalism while cutting back to minimize inevitable losses is doomed:

> Even publishers willing to bet their businesses on this kind of salvation should consider alternative plans for continuing to produce good journalism should the advertising subsidy continue to decline ... The past three years of decline have taken place during a period of economic growth; in addition to the cumulative effects of revenue loss, the inability to raise revenue even in a growing economy suggests that legacy media firms will suffer disproportionately when the next recession begins, as it doubtless will within a few years.

At the core of the disruption is a new actor: the consumers, the audience, or – in Jay Rosen's phrase – The People Formerly Known as the Audience.[3] They – in various forms, individually and en masse, scattered or together in one group or institution – must be both addressed and co-opted into the act of journalism, which many (sometimes without knowing it) already commit: 'Each of the acts that make up journalism might best be done inside or outside the newsroom, by professionals or amateurs or partners or specialists. It all depends upon the economics of the ecosystem and, ultimately, the needs of the users.'

Journalists themselves (as in many other trades and professions) can no longer assume a 'corporate ladder' kind of career, from intern to international correspondent, with a fine pension at the end of it. The new digital journalism can and should produce institutions – Bell and co. instance Talking Points Memo in the US,[4] a liberal news and comment site set up in 2000 by one entrepreneurial student, Josh Marshall, which now has a staff of up to thirty – but they will be much smaller than the relative behemoths with hundreds, even thousands of employees seeking to cover a vast waterfront of every kind of journalism. They write that though the consumption of news is likely to rise and new, and old, news providers will be clearer about what their audiences want, still, 'fewer of these sources will be "general interest"; even when an organization aims to produce an omnibus collection of news of the day, the readers, viewers and listeners will disassemble it and distribute the parts that interest them to their various networks. An increasing amount of news will arrive via these ad hoc networks than via audiences loyal to any particular publication.'

This book hasn't ignored the impact of the Net – on the contrary – but it has been mainly about what journalism's messages are, in the belief that it is the content of the messages which inform and move their readers, listeners and viewers. It's also the belief of the authors of 'Post Industrial Journalism': 'it is imperative', they write, 'that we collectively find new ways to do the kind of journalism needed to keep the United States from sliding into casual self-dealing and venality.' It's a curious, somewhat eighteenth-century, way of putting it, but it's a shared belief in the necessity of a deeply imperfect trade to a similarly imperfect, but recognizably democratic and civil, politics.

The fact that the Net and social media have provided those living in authoritarian states the tools with which to share messages defined by the rulers as subversive forces these rulers – apart from the outright terrorists among them, such as the ruling groups in North Korea and Eritrea – to both accept more leakage than their predecessors had to tolerate and to employ armies of censors and secret police to limit the flow.

The long slow death of newspapers is matched with the explosion of material on the Net, which has enormously increased the availability and scope of journalism, and, so far, has not diminished any part of it, except its income. You can get both more long-narrative journalism and more sex scandals, and can flip from one to another in seconds.

With that, the power and liberties of journalism have also been seen to grow. The huge leaks of the 2010s – the various WikiLeaks document dumps, those in 2016 and 2017 increasingly aimed at damaging the US Democrats and in March 2017, the CIA; the Snowden lift of some 1.5 million documents from the National Security Agency in 2013 and the Panama Papers leaks of 2016 – were not accompanied by arrests of journalists, though leakers were punished – in the case of Private Bradley/Chelsea Manning, savagely. (The sentence was commuted by Obama a few days before he left the presidency: Manning was freed on 17 May 2017, having served seven years.) Instead, the newspapers which ran the material were generally lauded by liberals, and grumblingly left alone by administrations and the security state. That does not mean that no damage was done by the breaches of the intelligence agencies; at a time when conventional warfare is carried on by means of cyber war, it's worth asking more sharply if the publication of this material is holding power to account, or breaching the defences of a free society.

I have made a marked distinction between democratic states and authoritarian states, because the amount of freedom that is on offer has the largest impact on a journalist's ability to do a proper job. But the considerable no man's land in between the two hosts all kinds of stabs at journalism, from which some examples have been plucked here. In that no man's land, the free activity of journalists is more or less sanctioned, and their results usually go unpunished by the state. But the pressure of the proprietors, as in India, happy to be called the world's largest democracy, and the deadly threat of criminal gangs, as in Mexico, a country of over 120 million people, inhibit journalism as much as the actions of states. In the post-Communist states – as in the Czech Republic – the high ideals that powered the revulsion against Communism have been brought down hard by the ambitions, manoeuvres and proclaimed silences of both the proprietorial and the governing classes. The Czech Republic remains, at the time of writing, relatively open; its partners in the Visegrád Group – Hungary, Poland and Slovakia – are not.

It's in the authoritarian states where there is the dreariest news. As this book was being written, the president/general secretary of China's Communist Party, Xi Jinping, has called for absolute loyalty from the Party media to the Party itself; the commentator Zhan Lifang said of Xi's tour of the TV studios and press newsrooms in February 2016: 'I think Xi is declaring his sovereignty over the state media to say who's really in charge.'[5]

In Russia, the relaxation of the last years of the Soviet Union under Mikhail Gorbachev in the late 1980s and the chaotic liberalizing of the Boris Yeltsin presidencies in the '90s have, in the 2000s and 2010s, been turned round decisively, back towards a largely controlled environment in which television, the mass medium, has been seized and fashioned into an organ of presidential flattery and anti-Western/nationalist propaganda. A few newspapers and websites remain to proclaim opposition, but the 'experiment' with a freer journalism is now over.

In the Middle East, the states which had undergone revolts generically known as the Arab Spring were noted for the mobilizing strength of social media and the more important critical voices spouting out of the new satellite channels on television. These have been abruptly shut down. In Egypt, the Arab world's largest and most important state, the coup against the rackety and putatively religious-authoritarian (elected) government of the Muslin Brotherhood has brought to power, once more, the military. Its leader, Field Marshal Abdel Fattah el-Sisi, now president, demanded and instantly got obedience from those papers and channels which had exulted in their brief springtime. Again, as this was written, the campaign by Turkish President Recep Tayyip Erdoğan against media which showed opposition has ratcheted up several notches, after an apparently serious coup in July 2016 aimed at overthrowing him.

At a talk on corruption early in 2017, I met Attahiru Jega, who teaches political science at Bayero University in Kano, Nigeria's second city. From 2010 to 2015 he was chairman of the National Electoral Commission, and oversaw two presidential elections which were regarded as fair and free. He is a strong voice for clean government and electoral reform, though a spell as head of the Commission left him with no illusions. A Nigerian journalist I knew, Sunday Daré, had with others started an investigative website, Sahara Reporters,[6] which attempted to follow up leads on corrupt practices reported to it by citizens. I asked Jega how the site was going. He said it was working well, and that Nigerian journalists in general were doing a much better job than in the past, exposing many instances of corruption. But he added: 'The problem is not with them. The problem is that when they investigate and reveal corruption, nothing happens. No one is charged. If you are protected, there is no retribution. And ordinary people expect that to be the case.' Freedom to publish is necessary, but not enough. The transmission belt between revelations of fraud, corruption and other criminality by members of the ruling class, which have a solid basis and action, must be acted upon by authorities. If not, journalism is powerless.

In a very imperfect trade, where most journalists in the world are probably at least a little corrupt and some very much so, the standards in journalistic practice that grew stronger – most importantly in the US in the latter half of the twentieth century – were a counterweight, an ideal, itself imperfect, for others who were serious enough about the job to sully it with accepting bribes or favours, or to accept with a shrug that the society and the politics that they were describing were themselves corrupt.

The man who became the American president in 2017 set about trashing the ideal, claiming it was built on tissues of lies, political bias and ignorance. He did so to bolster his own version of events, and to muddy every discussion about his presidency with charges, often baseless, until the casual observer – most citizens – would give up seeking to understand who was right, who wrong. It meant that the autocrats who set about reducing the small space available to real enquiry found a friend in the White House where they should have found a foe. They had common enemies. That this should be happening in America is hardly credible.

Journalism tries to make a sketch that makes sense of the world. It tries to say, and to show, that this happened. The relocking of the journalistic doors in large tracts of the world and the tacit encouragement this has received from the American leadership is presently journalism's worst feature, but it is not the end of the story. The story still has power.

Notes

Preface

1. B. Dooley, *The Social History of Skepticism*, Johns Hopkins University Press, 1999, p. 17.
2. P. Starr, *The Creation of the Media*, Basic Books, 2004, p. 146.
3. Ibid., p. 148.
4. http://towcenter.org/research/post-industrial-journalism-adapting-to-the-present-2.
5. J. Chalaby, 'Journalism as an Anglo-American Invention', *European Journalism of Communications*, 11 (1996), pp. 303–26, cited in P. Starr, op. cit., p. 147.
6. http://www.economist.com/news/china/21702069-region-and-america-will-now-anxiously-await-chinas-response-un-appointed-tribunal.
7. The elections for the Russian Duma, or parliament, in December 2011 were believed by many observers – some of whom were foreign observers, most of whom were Russian citizens using their mobile phones to record ballot stuffing and other infractions – to have been corrupt. United Russia, the parliamentary support group for President Vladimir Putin, took just under 50 per cent of the vote, and with that 53 per cent of the seats. (http://www.nytimes.com/2011/12/06/world/europe/russian-parliamentary-elections-criticized-by-west.html). The widespread realization of corruption prompted demonstrations in Moscow and other cities. In fact, even if the party had not had a majority in the Duma, at least two of the smaller parties – the Communists and the Liberal Democrats – would have voted with them on most issues, though of course at a price. In the presidential election the following March, Putin's majority of over 63 per cent was also strongly challenged (http://www.nytimes.com/2012/03/06/world/europe/observers-detail-flaws-in-russian-election.html): Golos, the election-monitoring NGO, recorded 3,000 complaints (https://www.washingtonpost.com/world/russians-voting-and-watching/2012/03/04/gIQA3j6CqR_story.html?utm_term=.2f142e7777a2). After a 'foreign agents law' was passed by the Duma

in 2013, severely hobbling NGOs that received foreign funds, Golos was the first to be named as a 'foreign agent' and later ceased its activity (https://www.hrw.org/russia-government-against-rights-groups-battle-chronicle).

8. http://hungarianfreepress.com/2016/07/28/poll-two-thirds-of-hungarians-think-fidesz-is-very-corrupt.

9. http://edition.cnn.com/2017/02/01/europe/french-investigation-penelope-fillon.

10. http://www.politico.eu/article/penelope-fillon-speaks-out-on-paid-post-for-her-husband-francois-fillon.

11. https://www.nytimes.com/2017/01/23/us/politics/donald-trump-congress-democrats.html.

12. http://www.politico.com/blogs/on-media/2017/01/embargo-new-york-times-wall-street-journal-editor-on-trump-and-the-media-233077.

13. M. Schudson, *The Power of News*, Harvard University Press, 1995, p. 30.

14. http://foreignpolicy.com/2016/06/26/the-collapse-of-the-liberal-world-order-european-union-brexit-donald-trump.

15. http://www.slate.com/blogs/the_slatest/2017/02/18/trump_calling_media_enemy_of_the_american_people_reminiscent_of_stalin_mao.html.

16. http://www.telegraph.co.uk/news/2017/03/07/donald-trump-probably-love-says-arnold-schwarzenegger.

17. https://www.ft.com/content/d6e87afe-dd6a-11e6-9d7c-be108f1c1dce#comments.

18. https://www.buzzfeed.com/jessicasimeone/trump-cancels-meeting-with-new-york-times?utm_term=.scBBMM3xy#.ufQQOO704.

19. https://www.nytimes.com/interactive/2016/01/28/upshot/donald-trump-twitter-insults.html?ref=todayspaper&_r=0.

20. http://www.voanews.com/a/trump-cpac-speech/3738517.html.

21. http://www.tabletmag.com/jewish-news-and-politics/226761/the-counterrevolution.

22. https://www.ft.com/content/d6e87afe-dd6a-11e6-9d7c-be108f1c1dce.

23. http://reutersinstitute.politics.ox.ac.uk/news/nine-ways-media-broke-news—-and-how-fix-it.

Part I

INTRODUCTION

1. http://www.themoscowtimes.com/business/article/billionaire-tycoon-prokhorov-to-sell-all-russian-assets/574178.html.

2. https://www.bloomberg.com/news/articles/2016-08-02/facing-kremlin-full-court-press-nets-owner-pivots-to-brooklyn; www.netsdaily.com/2017/4/21/15382192/prokhorov-has-yet-to-find-buyer-for-49-percent-stake-in-nets.

3. http://www.rferl.org/content/russia-prokhorov-rbc-media-holding-investigated/27728884.html.

4. http://reifman.ru/sovet-postsovet-tsenzura/vmesto-vstuplenija.

5. H. de Burgh, *The Chinese Journalist*, Routledge, 2006, p. 95.

6. H. Wang, *The Transformation of Investigative Journalism in China*, Rowman and Littlefield, 2016, p. 124.

7. https://www.theguardian.com/world/2016/feb/12/china-journalism-reporters-freedom-of-speech.

8. https://www.google.co.uk/#q=eritrea+press+freedom.

9. https://freedomhouse.org/report/freedom-press/2015/north-korea.

10. www.nybooks.com/articles/1995/06/22/ur-fascism.

11. E. Gellner, *Conditions of Liberty*, Hamish Hamilton, 1994, p. 26 et seq.

12. https://www.nytimes.com/2016/07/11/world/middleeast/saudi-arabia-islam-wah-habism-religious-police.html.

13. A. de Tocqueville, *Oeuvres Completes*, vol. 3, Paris, quoted in E. Gellner, *Muslim Society*, Cambridge University Press, 1995.

14. H. Wang, op. cit., p. 122.

15. www.reuters.com/artcle/us-safrica-election-idLSKCN1QT1DB.

16. https://www.theguardian.com/commentisfree/2012/jan/27/turkish-journalists-fight-intimidation.

17. E. Morozov, *The Net Delusion*, Penguin, 2011, pp. 85–112.

18. https://www.opendemocracy.net/arab-awakening/mina-fayek/social-media-is-still-powerful-in-egypt.

19. When looked up, 'blue bra woman' in Google to get the date, beside the reference to explanatory websites was a range of advertisements – from Simply Be, Topshop and Boux Avenue – for blue bras. They've gone now.

20. http://www.newyorker.com/magazine/2015/10/26/the-memory-keeper.

CHAPTER ONE

1. https://chinacopyrightandmedia.wordpress.com/2013/11/12/xi-jinpings-19-august-speech-revealed-translation.

2. H. Wang, op. cit., p. 85.

3. http://www.newyorker.com/magazine/2015/04/06/born-red.

4. D. Shambaugh, *China's Future*, Polity, 2016, pp. 2–3.

5. https://www.foreignaffairs.com/articles/china/2012-12-03/life-party.

6. https://next.ft.com/content/e6c12c24-df63-11e5-b072-006d8d362ba3.

7. http://www.nytimes.com/2016/05/03/world/asia/china-ren-zhiqiang.html.

8. https://www.nytimes.com/2016/02/23/world/asia/china-media-policy-xi-jinping.html.

9. http://www.nybooks.com/daily/2016/07/28/china-peoples-fury-south-china-sea-nationalism.

10. http://www.economist.com/news/leaders/21621803-communist-party-faces-its-toughest-challenge-tiananmen-time-it-must-make-wise.

11. https://www.foreignaffairs.com/articles/china/end-reform-china.

12. http://www.theatlantic.com/international/archive/2011/02/chinas-gdp-strategy-make-people-happy/71768.

13. http://www.newyorker.com/magazine/2011/07/04/the-han-dynasty.

14. www.economist.com/news/special-report/21701653-chinas-middle-class-larger.

15. http://www.nytimes.com/2011/11/07/world/asia/murong-xuecun-pushes-censorship-limits-in-china.html.

16. http://www.nytimes.com/2011/11/06/world/asia/murong-xuecuns-acceptance-speech-for-the-2010-peoples-literature-prize.html.

17. Y. Hua, *China in Ten Words*, trans. Alan H. Barr, Duckworth Overlook, 2011.

18. http://www.nybooks.com/articles/2014/12/04/chinas-brave-underground-journal.

19. https://www.cambridge.org/core/journals/china-quarterly/article/div-classtitlejiyi-remembrance-edited-by-diwu-beijing-and-shuhe-chongqing-bi-weekly-non-commercial-electronic-publication-distributed-via-the-internet-to-cultural-revolution-historians-worldwide-twelve-issues-by-mid-january-2009-each-issue-approximately-64-ppdiv/D2F50322B7F4687FCC89232523B1BFDF.

20. http://www.nybooks.com/articles/2014/12/18/chinas-brave-underground-journal.

21. http://www.nybooks.com/articles/2017/01/19/tan-hecheng-chinese-unspeakable/. Tan's book is now translated: T. Hecheng, *The Killing Wind: A Chinese County's Descent into Madness During the Cultural Revolution*, trans. Stacy Mosher and Guo Jian, Oxford University Press, 2016.

22. https://www.nytimes.com/2015/04/17/world/asia/china-journalist-gao-yu-gets-7-year-sentence.html?_r=0.

23. http://www.chinafile.com/document-9-chinafile-translation.

24. http://www.bbc.co.uk/news/world-asia-china-34929468.

25. http://www.economist.com/news/business/21589434-chinas-online-video-market-largest-and-most-innovative-world-it-also-most.

26. http://www.economist.com/news/special-report/21574628-internet-was-expected-help-democratise-china-instead-it-has-enabled.

27. https://reutersinstitute.politics.ox.ac.uk/sites/default/files/How_Chinese_journalists_use_Weibo_microblogging_for_investigative_reporting%281%29.pdf.

28. Ibid.

29. http://www.nybooks.com/daily/2013/07/10/censoring-news-before-happens-china.

30. www.papers.ssrn.com/sol/3/papers.cfm?abstract_id=2325101.

31. www.gking.harvard.edu/publications/how-censorship-china-allows-government-criticism.

32. www.foreignaffairs.com/articles/china/2015-06-16/china-soft-power-push.

33. https://advox.globalvoices.org/2013/01/07/china-sina-weibo-manager-discloses-internal-censorship-practices.

34. Li Wufeng, a career propaganda official, had reportedly jumped from the sixth floor of his office building. A source told the *South China Morning Post* that he had been questioned by Party 'discipline officers', but that source didn't know why. www.scmp.com/scmp/mobile/index.html#/article/1458062/desktop.

35. http://www.sixthtone.com/about-us.

36. http://www.sixthtone.com/news/poetry-festival-construction-workers.

37. Zhou, it has unfortunately become clear, had misunderstood: he thought the question

was directed to the 1968 Paris demonstrations, which happened only three years before he spoke. But the misunderstanding produced a world-copied answer, 'too delicious to invite correction', in the view of Chas Freeman, a US diplomat who witnessed the exchange, www.ft.com/cmsd/s/74916db6-938d-11e0-922e-00144feab49a.html.

38. H. Wang, op. cit., p. 44.
39. http://www.nytimes.com/2008/07/15/books/15kaku.html?mtrref=www.google.co.uk& login=email.
40. http://www.siweiluozi.net/2011_02_01_archive.html.
41. H. Wang, op. cit. p. 49.
42. http://www.nybooks.com/daily/2016/09/08/people-in-retreat-chinese-filmmaker-ai-xiaoming.
43. http://www.nytimes.com/2013/01/15/opinion/dim-hopes-for-a-free-press-in-china.html.
44. Ibid.
45. Ibid.

CHAPTER TWO

1. http://www.memri.org/report/en/print2445.htm.
2. http://www.telegraph.co.uk/news/worldnews/middleeast/saudiarabia/6436646/Saudi-female-journalist-to-get-lashes-for-show-discussing-sex.html.
3. http://news.bbc.co.uk/1/hi/world/africa/8147329.stm.
4. L. Wright, *The Looming Tower*, Penguin, 2006.
5. http://www.newyorker.com/magazine/2004/01/05/the-kingdom-of-silence.
6. http://www.economist.com/node/18399193.
7. http://www.academia.edu/4316716/The_Mission_of_Arab_Journalism_Creating_Change_in_a_Time_of_Turmoil.
8. http://www.meforum.org/604/telling-the-truth-about-the-palestinians.
9. Ibid.
10. http://www.jpost.com/Middle-East/Satirical-Palestinian-TV-show-elicits-anger-in-West-Bank.
11. http://www.jpost.com/Middle-East/Lawsuits-complaints-lead-PA-to-cut-satirical-TV-series-234138.
12. http://www.nytimes.com/2014/10/24/world/middleeast/lebanon-to-bar-syrian-refugees.html?_r=.
13. http://reutersinstitute.politics.ox.ac.uk/sites/default/files/Potential%20Change%20in%20Media%20Discourse%20on%20Sexuality%20in%20Lebanon.pdf.
14. J. Assange, *When Google Met WikiLeaks*, OR Books, 2014, Kindle Edition, loc. 142.
15. E. Schmidt and J. Cohen, *The New Digital Age*, Knopf, 2013, p. 9.
16. E. Morozov, op. cit., p. xii.
17. http://www.flockwatching.com/2011/09/21/human-rights-lecture-on-the-arab-spring-and-social-media-delivered-at-atlanta-tech-on-15-september-by-james-harkin.

18. http://reutersinstitute.politics.ox.ac.uk/sites/default/files/Good%20media%2C%20 bad%20politics%20New%20media%20and%20the%20Syrian%20conflict.pdf.

19. http://www.thedailybeast.com/articles/2014/04/06/a-woman-blogger-s-scoop-helped-save-tunisia-from-islamists.html.

20. Ibid.

21. http://www.theatlantic.com/technology/archive/2011/01/the-inside-story-of-how-facebook-responded-to-tunisian-hacks/70044.

22. http://www.economist.com/news/middle-east-and-africa/21617064-why-social-media-have-greater-impact-kingdom-elsewhere-virtual.

23. http://en.rsf.org/saudi-arabia-cyber-crime-law-used-again-to-01-07-2014,46554.html.

24. A. Hassan, *Media, Revolution and Politics in Egypt*, I. B. Tauris for the Reuters Institute, 2015, p. 75.

25. A. Ayalon, *The Press in the Arab Middle East*, Oxford University Press, 1995, p. 59.

26. M. Rodenbeck, *Cairo: The City Victorious*, Vintage, 2000, p. 216.

27. Ibid., p. 218.

28. wordpress.org/mideast/1205.cfm.

29. Rodenbeck, p. 218.

30. http://www.washingtonpost.com/world/middle_east/ahmed-fouad-negm-egypts-poet-of-the-people-dies-at-84/2013/12/03/ffe2df32-5c51-11e3-95c2-13623eb2b0e1_story.html.

31. See commentary on this and other texts in 'The Heikal Papers: A discourse on politics and the 1967 Arab–Israeli War with Egyptian President Gamal Abdel Nasser', Lieutenant Commander Youssef Aboul-Enein, US Navy, *Strategic Insights*, vol. 4, issue 4, April 2005; https://www.hsdl.org/?view&did=453717.

32. http://www.theaustralian.com.au/news/world/give-mohammed-morsi-a-chance-says-middle-east-sage/story-fnb640i6-1226422003346?nk=a941fe0496b4ca115f1b64833614 1f26.

33. 'L'Egypte racontee par Heikal', *Le Monde*, 3 March 2012; http://www.lemonde.fr/idees/article/2012/03/03/l-egypte-racontee-par-heikal_1651520_3232.html.

34. https://www.bloomberg.com/news/articles/2014-08-06/zombies-free-to-stalk-egypt-uncensored-as-sisi-critics-silenced.

35. http://www.aljazeera.com/news/middleeast/2014/10/egypt-declares-state-emergency-sinai-201410242283650878.html.

36. http://www.madamasr.com/sections/politics/egyptian-media-isnt-taking-prisoners-states-line-only-line.

37. http://www.nytimes.com/2014/10/16/world/middleeast/misstated-excerpt-of-a-times-article-offers-fresh-take-on-egyptian-president.html.

38. http://allafrica.com/stories/201610230180.html.

39. http://www.theguardian.com/world/2014/oct/12/sisi-regime-makes-satire-harder-egypt-cartoonists.

40. https://www.algemeiner.com/2013/07/22/al-jazeera-banned-from-egypt-government-press-conference-again.

41. www.theguardian.com/world/2014/jul/23/egyptian-judge-al-jazeera-devil.

42. www.theguardian.com/world/2014/nov/06/amal-clooney-egypt-journalist-mohamed-fahmy.

43. http://www.egyptindependent.com/news/another-media-host-taken-air-allegedly-over-army-criticism.

44. https://www.ft.com/content/bf73f5e8-0baa-11e6-9456-444ab5211a2f.

45. http://eprints.lse.ac.uk/59868.

46. http://www.foreignpolicy.com/files/war-college-paper.pdf.

47. www.actualitte.com/article/monde-edition/120-auteurs-journalistes-et-artistes.

48. http://www.newyorker.com/magazine/2017/01/02/egypts-failed-revolution.

49. https://www.foreignaffairs.com/articles/middle-east/egypt-s-nightmare.

50. www.the globalist.com/Egypt-al-sisi-under-pressure.

CHAPTER THREE

1. M. Schudson, op. cit., 1995, p. 220.

2. http://car.owu.edu/pdfs/1989-2-3.pdf.

3. http://www.achievement.org/autodoc/page/goroint-3.

4. A. Ostrovsky, *The Invention of Russia*, Atlantic Books, 2015. In the first part of this chapter, I draw heavily on Ostrovsky's insights.

5. http://www.telegraph.co.uk/news/obituaries/10950980/Eduard-Shevardnadze-obituary.html.

6. A. Ostrovsky, op. cit., pp. 99–101.

7. http://www.nytimes.com/1989/09/07/arts/hip-hot-and-hyper-soviet-tv-cuts-loose.html.

8. A. Ostrovsky, op. cit., p. 212.

9. http://www.nytimes.com/books/98/12/06/specials/remnick-lenin.html.

10. A. Ostrovsky, op. cit., p. 235.

11. http://www.ft.com/cms/s/2/a024f7ae-a7b1-11e4-be63-00144feab7de.html#axzz3TtDdFj00.

12. http://fpc.org.uk/fsblob/495.pdf.

13. https://next.ft.com/content/1d1f0f34-5e4e-11e1-8c87-00144feabdco.

14. http://news.bbc.co.uk/1/hi/world/europe/4481455.stm.

15. http://www.foreignaffairs.com/articles/141845/mary-elise-sarotte/a-broken-promise.

16. http://www.nytimes.com/2000/10/08/magazine/the-autumn-of-the-oligarchs.html.

17. http://www.lrb.co.uk/v29/no2/perry-anderson/russias-managed-democracy.

18. Ibid.

19. https://www.opendemocracy.net/od-russia/oleg-kashin/russian-matrix.

20. http://www.reuters.com/article/2012/08/28/us-russia-putin-perks-idUSBRE87R0D220120828.

21. K. Dawisha, *Putin's Kleptocracy: Who Owns Russia?*, Simon and Schuster, 2014.

22. A. Ledeneva, *Russia's Economy of Favours*, Cambridge University Press, 1998; *How Russia Really Works*, Cambridge University Press, 2006; *Can Russia Modernise?*, Cornell University Press, 2013.

23. K. Dawisha, op. cit. p. 11.

24. http://www.economist.com/blogs/easternapproaches/2014/04/russia.

25. http://www.theglobeandmail.com/news/world/a-former-kremlin-spin-doctor-rues-his-role-in-putins-rise/article533660.
26. http://www.theatlantic.com/international/archive/2014/11/hidden-author-putinism-russia-vladislav-surkov/382489.
27. http://www.nytimes.com/2011/11/05/world/europe/after-putin-and-medvedev-vladislav-surkov-is-russias-power-broker.html?_r=0.
28. http://www.dailymail.co.uk/news/article-2073178/Mikhail-Prokhorov-announces-plans-Vladimir-Putin-Russian-presidential-election.html.
29. https://www.opendemocracy.net/od-russia/richard-sakwa/surkov-dark-prince-of-kremlin.
30. http://www.nytimes.com/2011/11/05/world/europe/after-putin-and-medvedev-vladislav-surkov-is-russias-power-broker.html.
31. *Vedomosti*, 16 February 2010; https://wikileaks.org/gifiles/docs/54/5493458_good-article-.html.
32. www.commonweb.unif.ch/artsdean/pub/gestens/f/as/files/4760/25704_162118.pdf.
33. https://www.foreignaffairs.com/articles/russian-federation/2015-09-20/putins-philosopher.
34. http://www.nytimes.com/2016/09/21/opinion/how-a-russian-fascist-is-meddling-in-americas-election.html.
35. http://archive.spectator.co.uk/article/20th-november-1936/8/dictators-propaganda-by-aldous-huxley-the-mistake.
36. http://www.bbc.co.uk/news/uk-22569913.
37. J. Ellul, *Propaganda: The Formation of Men's Attitudes*, Vintage, 1973; quoted in P. Pomerantsev, *The Menace of Unreality*, the Institute of Modern Russia/The Interpreter, 2015.
38. https://www.facebook.com/SolidaritywithUkraine/posts/711627328951594.
39. http://www.newyorker.com/magazine/2014/03/03/patriot-games-2c.
40. http://www.bloomberg.com/bw/articles/2014-01-02/the-2014-winter-olympics-in-sochi-cost-51-billion.
41. http://uk.businessinsider.com/drugs-used-in-russian-doping-scandal-2016-6?r=US&IR=T.
42. A. Ostrovsky, op. cit., pp. 317–18.
43. S. M. Norris, *Blockbuster History in the New Russia: Movies, Memory, and Patriotism*, Indiana University Press, p. 274.
44. www.kinokultura.com/2006/12-campbell.shtml; quoted in S. M. Norris, op. cit., p. 283.
45. S. M. Norris, op. cit., p. 30.
46. http://www.nytimes.com/2015/01/28/world/europe/leviathan-arussian-movie-gets-applause-in-hollywood-but-scorn-at-home.html?_r=0.
47. http://www.ft.com/cms/s/2/a024f7ae-a7b1-11e4-be63-00144feab7de.html#axzz3Tz5r8hq6.
48. http://www.rferl.org/content/russia-media-kiselyov-propagandist/2519593.ht.
49. D. Skillen, *Freedom of Speech in Russia*, Routledge, 2016, pp. 69–71.
50. Ibid., p. 70.
51. Ibid., p. 69.

52. http://www.interpretermag.com/video-of-dmitry-kiselyovs-first-speech-at-ria-novosti%E2%80%8F.

53. http://www.theatlantic.com/international/archive/2014/09/russia-putin-revolutionizing-information-warfare/379880.

54. http://www.spiegel.de/international/world/spiegel-interview-russia-today-editor-in-chief-margarita-simonyan-a-916356.html.

55. https://www.dni.gov/files/documents/ICA_2017_01.pdf, highlighting her view that she was now a commander in a 'war'.

56. http://www.theguardian.com/media/2014/jul/18/mh17-russia-today-reporter-resigns-sara-firth-kremlin-malaysia.

57. http://www.newstatesman.com/world-affairs/world-affairs/2013/05/inside-russia-today-counterweight-mainstream-media-or-putins-mou.

58. K. Giles, 'Russia's "New" Tools for Confronting the West', Chatham House, March 2016, pp. 37–9.

59. www.theguardian.com/world/2007/mar/06/russia.lukeharding.

60. www.newyorker.com/magazine/2008/09/22/echo-in-the-dark.

61. M. Lipman, 'Media Manipulation and Political Control in Russia', Carnegie Moscow Center, February 2009.

62. www.reutersinstitute.politics.ox.ac.uk/publication/weeding-out-upstarts-kremlins-proxy-war.

63. All these books came out in new translations: *Zinky Boys*, renamed *Boys in Zinc*, is in a translation by Andrew Bromfield in Penguin (2017); *Chernobyl Prayer*, translated by Anna Gunin and Arch Tait, also in Penguin (2016); *Second-Hand Time*, published by Fitzcarraldo, is translated by Bela Shayevich. All are exceptionally well done.

64. http://freespeechdebate.com/en/media/interview-svetlana-alexievich.

CHAPTER FOUR

1. http://www.pen.org/defending-writers/eskinder-nega.

2. http://www.pen.org/nonfiction/letter-ethiopias-gulag.

3. https://www.imf.org/external/np/sec/pr/2015/pr15445.htm.

4. https://www.google.co.uk/search?noj=1&site=webhp&q=ethiopia+human+rights+US+state+department+2015&oq=ethiopia+human+rights+US+state+department+2015&gs_l=serp.3...99311.100638.0.101144.5.5.0.0.0.0.109.497.3j2.5.0....0...1c.1.64.serp..0.4.409.YLMIOPGUnicv.

5. https://freedomhouse.org/report/freedom-press/2016/ethiopia.

6. https://rsf.org/en/ethiopia.

7. https://www.opendemocracy.net/abiye-teklemariam-megenta/journalist-as-terrorist-ethiopian-story.

8. http://shorensteincenter.org/wp-content/uploads/2015/02/Turkish-Journalism-Yavuz-Baydar.pdf.

9. http://foreignpolicy.com/2014/09/22/either-with-us-or-against-us.

10. http://www.haaretz.com/news/middle-east/1.659931.

11. http://www.wsj.com/articles/SB10001424052970203917304574414503346981992.
12. http://www.economist.com/news/special-report/21689871-under-recep-tayyip-erdogan-and-his-ak-party-turkey-has-become-richer-and-more-confident.
13. http://www.bbc.co.uk/news/world-europe-34256762.
14. *Hürriyet*, 23 May 2015.
15. https://www.washingtonpost.com/opinions/ekrem-dumanli-turkeys-witch-hunt-against-the-media/2015/01/01/7544429a-8fad-11e4-ba53-a477d66580ed_story.html.
16. https://next.ft.com/content/417e5628-e225-11e5-8d9b-e88a2a889797.
17. america.aljazeera.com/opinions/2015/12/turkeys-long-history-of-attacks-on-the-press.html.
18. http://www.rethinkinstitute.org/wp-content/uploads/2014/11/Diminishing-Press-Freedom-in-Turkey-Turkey-Task-Force.pdf.
19. Quoted in Baydar, Shorenstein Center; http://shorensteincenter.org/wp-content/uploads/2015/02/Turkish-Journalism-Yavuz-Baydar.pdf.
20. http://www.spiegel.de/international/europe/spiegel-correspondent-forced-to-leave-turkey-a-1083144.html.
21. http://www.newyorker.com/news/news-desk/turkey-vs-twitter.
22. http://www.newyorker.com/news/news-desk/the-purge-begins-in-turkey.
23. http://www.newyorker.com/books/page-turner/the-silencing-of-writers-in-turkey.
24. http://www.newyorker.com/news/news-desk/the-end-of-democracy-in-turkey.
25. http://hsf.org.za/resource-centre/focus/issues-21-30/issue 24-fourth-quarter-2001/interview-with-rhoda-kadalie-human-rights-activist.
26. J. Winter, 'Serving a Fragmented Public', unpublished.
27. http://www.justice.gov.za/trc/report/finalreport/Volume%204.pdf.
28. http://afraf.oxfordjournals.org/content/107/429/611.abstract.
29. http://www.washingtonpost.com/wp-dyn/content/article/2006/10/23/AR2006102301311.html.
30. http://mg.co.za/article/2006-10-13-inside-the-sabc-blacklist-report.
31. http://mg.co.za/article/2006-10-27-the-astonishing-outburst-of-dali-mpofu.
32. http://mg.co.za/article/2012-10-28-zuma-avoids-zapiro-court-showdown-over-cartoon.
33. http://www.r2k.org.za/2011/08/02/sowetan-columnist-sacked.
34. http://sabctrc.saha.org.za/reports/volume4/chapter6/subsection3.htm.
35. Ibid.
36. J. Winter, op. cit.
37. http://www.hsrcpress.ac.za/product.php?productid=2092&freedownload=1; a chapter in *Changing the Fourth Estate: Essays on South African Journalism*, ed. A. Hadland, HSRC Press, 2005.
38. http://www.carnegiecouncil.org/publications/journal/18_3/Reflections%20on%20Journalism%20in%20the%20Transition%20to%20Democracy/5057.html
39. http://www.insidethegames.biz/index.php/articles/5234/thousands-welcome-semenya-home-to-south-africa.
40. http://www.hsrcpress.ac.za/product.php?productid=2092&freedownload=1.

41. https://www.africaleadership.net/ali-fellow-ferial-haffajee-gets-the-2015-international-press-freedom-award.
42. http://www.standpointmag.co.uk/dispatches-october-2016-rw-johnson-south-africa-jacob-zuma-anc-election.
43. http://www.corruptionwatch.org.za/why-is-corruption-getting-worse-in-south-africa.

PART II

INTRODUCTION

1. B. Kovach and T. Rosenstiel, *Elements of Journalism*, Three Rivers Press, 2007, p. 38.
2. B. J. Shapiro, *A Culture of Fact: England 1540–1720*, Cornell University Press, 2003, p. 3.
3. http://www.ina.fr/video/I04257844.
4. I. Hargreaves, *Journalism: Truth or Dare?*, Oxford University Press, 2003, p. 62.
5. 'Media, Knowledge, and Objectivity', lecture, 16 June 1993.
6. http://www.nytimes.com/2004/07/25/opinion/the-public-editor-is-the-new-york-times-a-liberal-newspaper.html?_r=0.
7. http://www.economist.com/news/europe/21708256-right-wing-german-media-brand-builds-following-politisch-inkorrekt.
8. B. Kovach and T. Rosenstiel, op. cit., p. 39.
9. S. Coleman, S. Anthony and D. E. Morrison, *Public Trust in the News*, Reuters Institute, 2009.
10. D. Zaret, *Origins of Democratic Culture*, Princeton University Press, 1999.
11. P. Starr, op. cit..
12. M. Schudson, op. cit., 1995, p. 99.
13. Ibid., p. 103.
14. http://www.wealthprofessional.ca/news/lionel- messi-arrested-for-tax-fraud-following-panama-papers-scandal-209970.aspx.
15. http://europe.newsweek.com/panama-papers-ukraines-president-defiant-despite-impeachment-push-443727?rm=eu.
16. http://www.politico.eu/article/panama-papers-defending-ukraine-president-petro-poroshenko-corruption-tax-finance-evasion.
17. http://www.bbc.co.uk/news/world-europe-35966412.
18. https://www.theguardian.com/news/2016/apr/04/panama-papers-david-cameron-father-tax-bahamas.
19. https://www.theguardian.com/news/2016/apr/03/panama-papers-money-hidden-offshore.
20. https://www.ted.com/talks/gerard_ryle_how_the_panama_papers_journalists_broke_the_biggest_leak_in_history?language=en.
21. https://www.theguardian.com/news/2016/apr/05/justice-department-panama-papers-mossack-fonseca-us-investigation.
22. C. Crouch, *The Knowledge Corrupters*, Polity, 2015; http://www.polity.co.uk/book.asp?ref=9780745669854#reviews.

23. P. Starr, op. cit., p. 395.
24. D. Van Reybrouck, *Against Elections*, Bodley Head, 2016, p. 54.
25. http://www.bbc.co.uk/radio4/reith2002.

CHAPTER FIVE

1. http://archive.financialexpress.com/news/the-foreign-handwriting/1000248.
2. https://qz.com/894886/trumps-media-policies-look-like-narendra-modis-successful-efforts-to-silence-the-press-in-india.
3. This figure strikes most foreigners as so high as to be exaggerated, but several studies come out with a figure roughly like that of Justice Katju's. A report by K. Nagaraj of the Madras Institute of Development Studies in March 2008 produced a figure of 166,304 farmers in the ten years from 1997 to 2006, that is, 45.5 daily. Nagaraj writes that this is certain to be an underestimation; www.macroscan.com/ani/mar08.pdf/Farmers_Suicides.pdf.
4. D. Gupta, *The Caged Phoenix*, Woodrow Wilson Center/Stanford University Press, 2009.
5. The passage on Condé Nast India is adapted from my piece 'A Week Inside India's Media Boom', *Financial Times* Weekend Review, 19 October 2012.
6. 'Pariah' itself is an eighteenth-century Tamil derivation from 'parai', a drum, the instrument then played by Untouchables.
7. http://indiatoday.intoday.in/story/narendra-modi-independence-day-speech-full-text-red-fort/1/377299.html.
8. P. Sainath, *Everyone Loves a Good Drought*, Penguin Books India, 2000.
9. S. Choudhary, *Let's Call him Vasu*, Penguin Books India, 2012.
10. https://www.youtube.com/watch?v=R3Bgas5HZI0.
11. A. Bhattacharya and M. Renganathan, *The Politics and Reception of Rabindranath Tagore's Drama: The Bard on the Stage*, Routledge, 2015, p. 87.
12. P. Mudliar, J. Donner and W. Thies, 'Emergent Practices Round CGNet Swara', *ICTD Journal*, 2012, vol. 9, no. 2.
13. The TAM ratings produced for the 170-million-plus households with TVs in India were challenged by NDTV in 2012 as being skewed and, because part owned by the WPP advertising corporation, influenced by the company's desire to keep advertising rates down. The government ordered the ratings replaced by the Broadcast Audience research Council (BARC), which, in September 2015, announced a new meter management company to produce more reliable results; https://technology.ihs.com/548353/indian-tv-ratings-companies-team-up-to-seek-improved-data.
14. http://indiatogether.org/humlog-women--2.
15. N. Sinha, 'Liberalisation and the Future of Public Service Broadcasting in India', *The Public*, vol. 3, 1996, p. 2.
16. S. Gupta: 'Post Liberalisation India: How Free is the Media', *Journal of South Asian Studies*, vol. 28, no. 2, August 2005.
17. A. Kapur, *India Becoming*, Riverhead Books, 2012.
18. Ibid., p. 9.

19. P. Roy, 'More News Is Good News', Reuters Memorial Lecture, 19 November 2012, Reuters Institute for the Study of Journalism – reutersinstitute.politics.ox.ac.uk.

20. D. Thussu, *News as Entertainment: The Rise of Global Infotainment*, Sage Publications, 2009, p. 101.

21. http://timesofindia.indiatimes.com/entertainment/hindi/movie-reviews/Rann/movie-review/5509463.cms.

22. P. Roy, op. cit.

23. R. Sardesai, *The Election that Changed India*, Viking, 2014.

24. Tejpal, one of the most highly rated of Indian journalists in his own country and abroad for his editorship of the investigative magazine *Tehelka*, was accused of sexually assaulting a young woman staff member in November 2013; the Supreme Court granted him bail. He strongly denies the charge: in 2016, his lawyers continued to challenge various aspects of the process; http://www.dnaindia.com/india/report-tarun-tejpal-moves-to-sc-against-goa-session-court-s-order-2052826.

25. https://www.youtube.com/watch?v=rF0NagK2-e0.

26. https://www.youtube.com/watch?v=xB_eWW5ttaM.

27. http://www.firstpost.com/politics/modi-will-never-be-pm-but-he-can-sell-tea-mani-shankar-aiyar-1345419.html.

28. http://www.ibtimes.com/indian-tea-party-narendra-modis-campaign-celebrate-popular-drink-his-humble-origins-1560987.

29. http://old.himalmag.com/component/content/article/5140-confessions-of-a-war-reporter.html.

30. http://www.outlookindia.com/magazine/story/covert-riots-and-media/214974.

31. http://www.newslaundry.com/2012/02/07/barkha-dutt-on-radiagate.

32. http://www.ndtv.com/opinion/the-cowardice-and-iniquity-of-what-arnab-goswami-has-called-for-1437493?trendingnow.

33. http://www.newslaundry.com/2012/02/07/can-you-take-it-barkha-dutt.

34. http://www.dnaindia.com/entertainment/report-most-of-my-critics-are-talentless-elderly-ladies-sagarika-ghose-1062473.

35. http://www.business-standard.com/article/pti-stories/dd-news-ahead-of-pvt-eng-news-channels-in-prime-time-115121300439_1.html.

36. http://www.bbc.co.uk/blogs/collegeofjournalism/entries/ae5fd09c-c333-48b5-9b35-06238d7f9e71.

37. http://www.caravanmagazine.in/reportage/bad-news?page=0%2C3&quicktabs_1=0&quicktabs_comment=0.

38. Ibid.

39. 'Reality Check', 2014; https://www.google.co.uk/?gws_rd=ssl#q=ernst+and+young+india+relatity+check.

40. http://blogs.wsj.com/indiarealtime/2011/05/20/raja-on-times-list-of-top-power-abuses/

41. http://www.transparency.org/whatwedo/publication/corruption_perceptions_index_2016.

42. http://www.gfintegrity.org/report/country-case-study-india/.

43. S. Subramanian, 'The Agitator', *New Yorker*, 2 September 2013; http://www.newyorker.com/magazine/2013/09/02/the-agitator-2.

44. 'Citizens Jain', *New Yorker*, 8 October 2012; https://www.google.co.uk/?gws_rd=ssl#q=citizens+jain+new+yorker.

45. www.blomberg.com/view/articles/2012-01-/india-s-top-newspapers-battle-for-readers-hearts-and-souls-choudhury.

46. V. Kohli-Khandekar, *The Indian Media Business*, 4th edition, Sage Publications, 2013.

47. http://reutersinstitute.politics.ox.ac.uk/sites/default/files/In%20need%20of%20a%20Leveson-%20Journalism%20in%20India%20in%20times%20of%20paid%20news%20and%20private%20treaties.pdf.

48. Ibid.

49. 'Has Narendra Modi Cleaned up India?', *Prospect Magazine*, June 2015.

50. http://www.outlookindia.com/article/News-You-Can-Abuse/263242.

51. http://presscouncil.nic.in/OldWebsite/Sub-CommitteeReport.pdf.

52. A. Giridharadas, 'Indian to the Core, and an Oligarch'; http://www.nytimes.com/2008/06/15/business/worldbusiness/15ambani.html?pagewanted=all.

53. In Giridharadas' profile, Mukesh had said that an Ambani network of spies and lobbyists in Delhi who collected intelligence about government and competitors had been overseen by Mukesh's younger brother Anil, who had worked with then split from him to form his own large company, Anil Dhirubhai Ambani Group, with a net worth (2014) of nearly $6 billion; when Anil had left, Mukesh said with a laugh, it had been 'de-merged'. Anil took out a $118.2 million suit against Mukesh, later dropped; http://www.dailymail.co.uk/news/article-1061745/Fifth-richest-man-world-sues-brother-sixth-richest-man-world-118m-libel-case.htm.

54. http://www.caravanmagazine.in/reportage/network-effect.

55. Ibid.

56. http://www.livemint.com/Companies/rqT2Oi8fwv4XVjJcHzlcVN/Inside-the-Network18-takeover.html.

57. https://article.wn.com/view-lemonde/2014/07/04/Rajdeep_Sardesais_parting_words_to_staff_Editorial_independe.

58. https://www.forbes.com/forbes/welcome/?toURL=https://www.forbes.com/sites/meghabahree/2014/05/30/reliance-takes-over-network18-is-this-the-death-of-media-independence/&refURL=https://www.google.co.uk/&referrer=https://www.google.co.uk.

59. Ibid.

60. http://www.caravanmagazine.in/reportage/the-tempest-prannoy-radhika-roy-ndtv.

61. http://www.firstpost.com/india/why-arnab-goswami-left-times-now-he-became-bigger-than-the-brand-a-thorn-for-the-jains-3087730.html.

62. V. Kohli-Khandekar, op. cit., p. 67.

63. http://www.trai.gov.in/sites/default/files/Recommendations_on_Media_Ownership.pdf

64. http://www.caravanmagazine.in/vantage/

the-big-five-the-media-companies-that-the-modi-government-must-scrutinise-to-fulfill-its-promise-of-ending-crony-capitalism

65. http://granta.com/introduction-india-another-way-of-seeing.

CHAPTER SIX

1. This chapter has been adapted from *Eserciti di Carta* (Paper Armies), by Ferdinando Giugliano and John Lloyd, Feltrinelli, 2013. Giuliagno is an economic commentator for Bloomberg and was the chief economic commentator of *La Repubblica*.

2. https://www.washingtonpost.com/news/worldviews/wp/2016/11/16/is-trump-a-berlusconi-let-a-berlusconi-expert-explain/?utm_term=.c7618c478208.

3. http://www.economist.com/node/13576329.

4. http://www.repubblica.it/2008/11/sezioni/spettacoli_e_cultura/saggio-giannini/saggio-giannini/saggio-giannini.html?refresh_ce.

5. http://www.abc.net.au/news/2003-05-30/editor-of-leading-italian-paper-resigns/1862256.

6. http://espresso.repubblica.it/attualita/2015/03/09/news/eugenio-scalfari-vi-racconto-come-e-nato-l-espresso-1.202937. (Disclosure: I wrote regularly for *La Repubblica* for a decade, to 2016).

7. P. Ginsborg, *Silvio Berlusconi: Television, Power, Patrimony*, Verso, 2004, p. 49.

8. Ibid., p. 34.

9. https://books.google.co.uk/books?id=jqH82GA1NWoC&pg=PA3&lpg=PA3&dq=enzo+f-orcella+1500+lettori&source=bl&ots=91Ty-BVj8m&sig=.-BoX1BkOK2IP7vCf7OTT6zLTj X8&hl=en&sa=X&ved=0ahUKEwj8jP752dvLAhXlNpoKHYV3ARJQ6AEIMDAC#v=onepa ge&q=enzo%20forcella%201500%20lettori&f=false.

10. http://www.newyorker.com/magazine/2011/04/11/booted.

11. http://www.theguardian.com/world/2003/jul/02/italy.eu.

12. P. Ginsborg, op. cit., p. 33.

13. http://web.mit.edu/allanmc/www/mcluhan.mediummessage.pdf.

14. A. Stille, *The Sack of Rome*, Penguin Press, 2006, p. 9.

15. http://www.rtdna.org/content/edward_r_murrow_s_1958_wires_lights_in_a_box_speech.

16. https://www.google.co.uk/#q=passigli+Everything+fits+in+nicely:+power+over+the+media+makes+it+possible+to+win+political+power&*.

17. http://www.corriere.it/editoriali/09_agosto_03/panebianco_pd_inchieste_giudiziarie_fe6d3260-7fec-11de-bb07-00144f02aabc.shtml?refresh_ce-cp.

18. http://www.newyorker.com/magazine/2008/11/03/girls-girls-girls-3.

19. http://www.telegraph.co.uk/news/worldnews/europe/italy/4339817/Silvio-Berlusconi-criticised-for-pretty-girl-rape-comment.html.

20. http://www.corriere.it/politica/09_agosto_28/feltri_attacco_boffo_avvenire_cei_3d76a938-93c4-11de-8445-00144f02aabc.shtml.

21. http://www.economist.com/news/europe/21635792-beppe-grillo-says-he-tired-and-his-movement-tired-his-autocratic-leadership-falling-star.

22. http://www.msn.com/en-ca/news/world/italian-populist-leader-suggests-juries-of-random-people-should-decide-what's-'fake-news'/ar-BBxTACD?li=AAggFp4.

23. G. Bocca, È la stampa, bellezza!, Feltrinelli, 2011.

24. A. Stille, op. cit.

CHAPTER SEVEN

1. http://www.columbia.edu/itc/journalism/j6075/edit/boor.html.

2. http://archives.newyorker.com/?i=2006-10-16#folio=130.

3. https://www.theguardian.com/media/2008/jun/13/pressandpublishing.media.

4. https://books.google.co.uk/books?id=q_zS3hsg42kC&pg=PT143&lpg=PT143&dq=MacK enzie+You+just+don't+understand+the+readers,+do+you,+eh?+He's+the+bloke+you+se e+in+the+pub,&source=bl&ots=eBsdHMvoV2&sig=Z92Nv3bXqFFGitEDmkt8SAICnwU &hl=en&sa=X&ved=0ahUKEwiYoqzwrPbSAhVkCsAKHXYIAQQQ6AEIIzAC#v=onepag e&q=MacKenzie%20You%20just%20don't%20understand%20the%20readers%2C%20 do%20you%2C%20eh%3F%20He's%20the%20bloke%20you%20see%20in%20the%20 pub%2C&f=false.

5. P. Morgan, The Insider, Ebury Press, 2005.

6. http://www.nytimes.com/2014/02/24/business/media/piers-morgan-and-cnn-plan-end-to-his-prime-time-show.html.

7. https://newrepublic.com/article/115507/how-piers-morgan-discovered-gun-control.

8. P. Morgan, Don't You Know Who I Am?, Ebury Press, 2008, p. 56.

9. www.tmz.com.

10. http://www.newyorker.com/magazine/2016/02/22/inside-harvey-levins-tmz.

11. Ibid.

12. http://www.dailymail.co.uk/debate/article-1251043/I-suspect-Gordon-Brown-regret-Piers-Morgan-show.html.

13. http://www.independent.co.uk/news/people/profiles/ian-hislop-provocateur-in-the-public-eye-2276884.html.

14. M. Engel, Tickle the Public: One Hundred Years of Popular Journalism, Gollancz, 1996, p. 10.

15. http://www.joe.ie/uncategorized/angela-merkel-depicted-as-a-nazi-on-cover-of-greek-newspaper/32301.

16. http://www.timesofisrael.com/greek-cartoon-depicts-german-finance-minister-as-nazi.

17. http://www.today-in-history.de/index.php?what=thmanu&manu_id=1463&tag=21&mo nat=5&year=1947&dayisset=1&lang=enhttp://nymag.com/daily/intelligencer/2.

18. H. Böll, The Lost Honour of Katharina Blum, Vintage Classics, 1993 (English translation).

19. A. McAfee, The Spoiler, Vintage, 2012.

20. The Diaries of a Fleet Street Fox, Constable, 2013.

21. https://next.ft.com/content/c87f9c1e-7a99-11e2-9c88-00144feabdco.

22. http://www.forbes.com/sites/marketshare/2013/05/24/the-30-most-popular-celebrity-gossip-sites-and-why-big-brands-love-them/#5f33b2065d7d.

23. http://www.lrb.co.uk/v35/n04/hilary-mantel/royal-bodies.

24. http://www.skysports.com/football/news/11095/8716388/david-beckham-talks-to-gary-neville-about-his-decision-to-retire.
25. http://webarchive.nationalarchives.gov.uk/20140122145147/http:/www.levesoninquiry.org.uk/about/the-report/.
26. http://link.springer.com/chapter/10.1057%2F9780230290679_2#page-1.
27. http://leveson.sayit.mysociety.org/hearing-6-february-2012/mr-paul-dacre.
28. http://www.pressgazette.co.uk/node/42394.
29. http://www.newyorker.com/magazine/2012/04/02/mail-supremacy.
30. http://www.bbc.co.uk/news/uk-politics-14192673.
31. http://onlinelibrary.wiley.com/doi/10.1111/1467-923X.12189/full.

CHAPTER EIGHT

1. http://webarchive.nationalarchives.gov.uk/20140122145147/http:/www.levesoninquiry.org.uk/wp-content/uploads/2012/07/Witness-Statement-of-Dr-Neil-Manson.pdf.
2. A. Hernández, *Narcoland*, Verso, 2013, p. 282.
3. http://lab.org.uk/mexico-journalists-risk-life-for-truth.
4. http://www.globalpost.com/dispatch/worldview/101026/mexico-drug-war-cartels-newspapers.
5. https://www.article19.org/join-the-debate.php/195/view.
6. A. Hernández, op. cit., p. 7.
7. http://www.theguardian.com/world/2010/dec/02/us-mexico-drugs-war-wikileaks.
8. http://www.insightcrime.org/brazil-organized-crime-news/brazil.
9. J. Keating, www.slate.com/blogs/the_world/2014/06/09/committee_to_protect_journalists_highlights_dangers_faced_by_brazilian_reporters.html.
10. https://cpj.org/reports/2014/05/hjalftime-for-brazilian-press-censoprship-violence-censorship-via-courts.php.
11. http://www.theguardian.com/media/greenslade/2015/may/21/brazilian-journalist-beheaded-during-mystery-investigation.
12. https://cpj.org/2015/05/second-journalist-killed-in-brazil-in-less-than-a-.php.
13. https://cpj.org.blog/2015/03/brazilian-bloggers-encounter-threats-online-and-of.php.
14. http://www.economist.com/news/americas/21636048-best-and-worst-times-latin-american-journalism-power-cursor.
15. http://www.marx2mao.com/PDFs/Lenin%20CW-Vol.%205-TC.pdf.
16. J. Jirák and B. Köpplová, 'The Reality Show Called Democratization: Transformation of the Czech Media After 1989'; http://www.globalmediajournal.collegium.edu.pl/artykuly/wiosna%202008/jirak-kopplova-czech-media.pdfhttp://.
17. www.theguardian.com/artanddesign/2015/jun/20/palaces-for-the-people-five-communist-buildings.
18. http://www.theglobeandmail.com/news/world/with-eloquence-and-authority-vaclav-havel-changed-europes-history/article4181665/.
19. http://www.nybooks.com/articles/archives/1990/jan/18/words-on-words/.
20. https://wikileaks.org/plusd/cables/10PRAGUE57_a.html.

21. J. Jirák and B. Köpplová, op. cit.
22. http://www.radio.cz/en/section/marketplace/ownership-changes-help-spark-new-media-flurry-in-czech-republic.
23. http://docplayer.net/24203464-The-rise-of-the-oligarchs-the-third-media-ownership-transformation-in-cee.html.
24. http://henryjacksonsociety.org/wp-content/uploads/2015/01/The-State-of-Democracy-After-25-Years.pdf.
25. http://foreignpolicy.com/2015/04/10/now-the-czechs-have-an-oligarch-problem-too-andrej-babis.
26. http://www.rferl.org/a/czech-tv-station-controversy-refugees-as-risk-reporting/27774568.html.
27. http://www.economist.com/news/europe/21707125-politics-central-and-eastern-europe-are-increasingly-driven-businesses-own-media.
28. http://www.worldpress.org/Europe/1098.cfm.
29. https://rsf.org/en/japan; the other main scale, by Freedom House, which ranks 197 states on a 0 (best) to 100 (worst) scale, gave a ranking of 42.
30. www.thediplomat.com/2014/12/japans-troubling-state-secrets-law-takes-effect.
31. www.fccj.or.jp/images/FCCJ-State-secrets-protest-eng.pdf.
32. http://www.japantimes.co.jp/opinion/2016/04/30/commentary/japans-meek-media-kowtows-government/#.V8WKiRQpLoc.
33. www.economist.com/news/asia/21693269-criticism-government-being-airbrushed.
34. www.nytimes.com/2015/05/21/opinion/the-threat-to-press-freedom-in-japan.
35. www.tofugu.com/japan/kisha-clubs-and-japanese-newspapers.
36. www.rsc.org/chemistryworld/2013/03/fukushima–nuclear-disaster-cancer-risk-increase.
37. http://www.pressnet.or.jp/english/about/guideline/.
38. https://cpj.org/blog/2011/05/following-disaster-free-press-association-of-japan.
39. www.freespeechdebate.com/en/discuss/an-impregnable-portress-of-information.
40. https://www.foreignaffairs.com/articles/israel/2016-06-08/end-old-israel?cid=nlc-fatoday-2016 0609&sp_mid=51570961&sp_rid=am9obi5sbG95ZEBmdC5jb20sS1&spMailingID=51570961&spUserID=NTIoMzQxNzkiODcS1&spJobID=941270830&spReportId=OTQxMjcwODMwS0.
41. http://bluewhitefuture.org/asher-susser-bw/.
42. http://www.haaretz.com/blogs/west-of-eden/.premium-1.606258.
43. A. Shavit, *My Promised Land*, Scribe Publications, 2013, p. xii.
44. http://www.timesofisrael.com/the-end-of-israeli-democracy.
45. http://www.haaretz.com/israel-news/.premium-1.721152.
46. http://www.timesofisrael.com/channel-10-ceo-new-board-chairman-did-insult-deri-shas.
47. http://www.timesofisrael.com/netanyahu-brought-about-iran-nuke-deal-says-ex-mossad-head-in-last-interview.
48. http://www.haaretz.com/opinion/.premium-1.605001.
49. http://www.haaretz.com/opinion/.premium-1.605294.

50. Y. Peri, *Telepopulism*, Stanford University Press, 2004, pp. 201–3.
51. https://www.theatlantic.com/international/archive/2014/11/how-the-media-makes-the-israel-story/383262.
52. http://goastreets.com/life-ap-bureau-chief-israel.
53. http://www.haaretz.com/think-tank-israel-faces-global-delegitimization-campaign-1.265967.
54. http://www.haaretz.com/israel--news/1.763704.

CHAPTER NINE

1. P. Starr, op. cit., pp. 3, 17.
2. http://www.bbc.co.uk/news/entertainment-arts-38854711.
3. P. Starr, op. cit., p. 17.
4. L. Menand, *The Metaphysical Club*, Flamingo–Harper Collins, 2002, p. 361.
5. M. Schudson, *Why Democracies Need an Unlovable Press*, Polity, 2008, p. 36.
6. G. Gozzini, *Storia del giornalismo*, Mondadori, 2011, p. 56.
7. https://www.law.cornell.edu/supremecourt/text/403/713.
8. https://www.youtube.com/watch?v=ERgbXRTC_K4.
9. 'Why Americans Hate the Media', *The Atlantic*, February 1996.
10. https://archive.org/stream/freeandresponsib029216mbp/freeandresponsib029216mbp_djvu.txt.
11. M. Dowd, 'As Time Goes Bye', *New York Times*, 9 March 2013.
12. http://inma.org/modules/join/wilkinson-feb2008-sna.pdf.
13. http://www.niemanlab.org/2015/01/newsonomichhhow-deep-is-the-newspaper-industrys-money-hole.
14. https://medium.com/@dicktofel/the-sky-is-falling-on-print-newspapers-faster-than-you-think-c84a2f9a9df4#.mk9d8j449.
15. http://www.niemanlab.org/2014/05/the-scariest-chart-in-mary-meekers-slide-deck-for-newspapers-has-gotten-a-little-scarier.
16. http://www.shirky.com/weblog/2009/03/newspapers-and-thinking-the-unthinkable.
17. http://shorensteincenter.org/wp-content/uploads/2012/03/last_call_carroll.pdf.
18. http://www.newrepublic.com/article/goodbye-the-age-newspapers-hello-new-era-corruption.
19. http://www.poynter.org/2013/mark-thompson-keeping-nate-silver-at-nyt-was-not-an-overwhelming-priority/222062.
20. http://fivethirtyeight.com/features/what-the-fox-knows.
21. 014/03/nate-silver-interview-fivethirtyeight-espn.html.
22. http://www.newrepublic.com/article/117068/nate-silvers-fivethirtyeight-emptiness-data-journalism.
23. http://www.huffingtonpost.com/2014/03/27/nate-silver-paul-krugman-attack_n_5041129.html.
24. http://www.vox.com/2015/2/9/8008365/advice-to-young-journalists.
25. http://www.newrepublic.com/article/j-school-confidential.

26. http://fusion.net/story/45832/to-all-the-young-journalists-asking-for-advice.

27. http://newsbusters.org/blogs/connor-williams/2014/08/08/msnbc-s-matthews-disses-colleague-ezra-klein-s-vox-not-interest-me-.

28. http://www.vox.com/2014/4/6/5556462/brain-dead-how-politics-makes-us-stupid.

29. http://www.politico.com/magazine/story/2015/02/vox-interview-barack-obama-115033.

30. http://www.theatlantic.com/magazine/archive/2008/11/why-i-blog/307060/?single_page=true.

31. http://dish.andrewsullivan.com/tag/the-end-of-the-dish.

32. https://www.youtube.com/watch?v=iLmkec_4Rfo.

33. https://www.youtube.com/watch?v=2BrZGDFCSCA.

34. http://www.forbes.com/sites/jeffbercovici/2013/09/18/shane-smith-vices-400-million-man-is-new-yorks-newest-media-mogul.

35. 18/vice-media-chief-said-to-pay-300000-for-dinner-for-30/?smid=tw-nytimesbusiness&_r=0&referrer=http://nymag.com/news/features/buzzfeed2013-4.

36. http://www.cjr.org/analysis/the_cult_of_vice.php.

37. https://www.youtube.com/watch?v=AUjHb4C7b94.

38. http://www.theatlantic.com/international/archive/2014/10/is-vice-documentary-on-ISIS-illegal/380991.

39. http://www.independent.co.uk/news/world/middle-east/inside-isis-the-first-western-journalist-ever-given-access-to-the-islamic-state-has-just-returned-9938438.html.

40. https://www.youtube.com/watch?v=3l1Mgxzlfzzs.

41. https://www.google.co.uk/#q=shane+smith+interviews+Barak+Obama+You+Tube.

42. http://knowyourmeme.com/memes/events/nike-id-sweatshop-e-mail-controversy.

43. http://nymag.com/news/features/buzzfeed-2013-4.

44. http://www.buzzfeed.com/bensmith/the-facebook-election#.yikr2nejZ4.

45. http://www.politico.com/blogs/on-media/2016/08/jeff-zucker-praises-corey-lewandowski-slams-vice-and-buzzfeed-226574.

46. http://www.cjr.org/the_feature/vice_freelancers.php.

47. Ibid.

48. http://www.politico.com/playbook/2015/11/politico-playbook-presented-by-jpmorgan-chase-co-365-days-to-election-how-fox-will-try-to-shame-cnbc-politicos-booming-europe-arm-expands-financial-services-vertical-bigger-london-bureau-top-hire-from-wsj-bday-john-harris-sarah-flores-211152.

49. http://www.vanityfair.com/news/2009/08/wolff200908.

50. http://www.poynter.org/2016/jill-abramsons-longform-journalism-venture-with-steve-brill-is-on-hold-for-now/403812.

51. http://beltmag.com/alt-racists.

52. https://daily.jstor.org/about.

CHAPTER TEN

1. D. Westen, *The Political Brain*, PublicAffairs, 2008. Westen's book was criticized sharply by David Brooks in the *New York Times*, who concluded that Westen's argument that

politics should appeal to emotions was wrong – 'It's not necessary to dumb things down to appeal to emotions. It's not necessary to understand some secret language that will key certain neuro-emotional firings. The best way to win votes – and this will be a shocker – is to offer people an accurate view of the world and a set of policies that seem likely to produce good results' (http://www.nytimes.com/2007/08/26/books/review/Brooks-t.html?_r=1&ref=books&oref=slogin). This criticism suffers after Trump's win.

2. http://uk.reuters.com/article/uk-usa-trump-scene-idUKKBN14V2MS.

3. http://www.newyorker.com/magazine/2016/02/22/did-social-media-produce-the-new-populism.

4. https://www.nytimes.com/2015/11/27/us/politics/donald-trump-says-his-mocking-of-new-york-times-reporter-was-misread.html.

5. https://www.nytimes.com/2017/01/08/arts/television/meryl-streep-golden-globes-speech.html.

6. http://www.politico.com/video/2017/01/conway-judge-trump-by-whats-in-his-heart-not-what-comes-out-of-his-mouth-061895.

7. http://web.archive.org/web/20141030135629/http://www.nytimes.com/2000/12/14/technology/14DOGG.html.

8. https://www.bloomberg.com/news/articles/2017-01-18/this-team-runs-mark-zuckerberg-s-facebook-page.

9. https://www.youtube.com/watch?v=eFQhw3VVToQ.

10. See, for example, M. Dice, *The Illuminati*, Resistance Manifesto, 2009, in which a centuries-old group is seen as controlling the world, responsible for widely diverse events. Dice writes that 'when one discovers, as in recent years, the growing credible information about these secret societies ... one sees a gaping hole in the legitimacy and accuracy of mainstream media and general knowledge'.

11. https://www.youtube.com/watch?v=2-Be9f7Ovgg.

12. https://www.youtube.com/watch?v=6w_-g4gdKpQ.

13. https://www.nytimes.com/2016/12/06/us/fake-news-partisan-republican-democrat.html.

14. http://edition.cnn.com/2016/09/11/health/hillary-clinton-health.

15. https://www.nytimes.com/2017/01/18/us/fake-news-hillary-clinton-cameron-harris.html.

16. https://www.washingtonpost.com/news/the-intersect/wp/2014/10/21/this-is-not-an-interview-with-banksy/?tid=a_inl&utm_term=.f44fef962a6e.

17. http://insider.foxnews.com/2017/01/17/tucker-carlson-slams-hoax-protester-group-dom-tullipso-demand-protests-manning.

18. https://www.washingtonpost.com/news/the-intersect/wp/2016/11/17/facebook-fake-news-writer-i-think-donald-trump-is-in-the-white-house-because-of-me/?utm_term=.86154a12d8c5.

19. https://www.buzzfeed.com/craigsilverman/how-macedonia-became-a-global-hub-for-pro-trump-misinfo?utm_term=.ghbNbbj9P#.eg66XXYjR.

20. https://www.nytimes.com/2016/11/25/world/europe/fake-news-donald-trump-hillary-clinton-georgia.html?_r=0.
21. http://www.newyorker.com/magazine/2016/11/28/obama-reckons-with-a-trump-presidency.
22. https://digiday.com/uk/facebooks-european-media-chief-addresses-fake-news-game-whack-mole/.
23. https://www.ft.com/content/2910a7a0-afd7-11e6-a37c-f4a01f1bofa1.
24. https://www.ft.com/content/37ea3ebc-a7cb-11e6-8b69-02899e8bd9d1.
25. https://www.nytimes.com/interactive/2017/business/media/trump-fake-news.html?_r=0.
26. http://time.com/4608555/hillary-clinton-popular-vote-final.
27. https://www.poynter.org/2017/did-fake-news-help-elect-trump-not-likely-according-to-new-research/445724.
28. http://www.telegraph.co.uk/news/2017/01/11/former-mi6-officer-produced-donald-trump-russian-dossier-terrified.
29. https://www.buzzfeed.com/kenbensinger/these-reports-allege-trump-has-deep-ties-to-russia?utm_term=.upKArr4po#.wpnQmmAE1.
30. https://www.ft.com/content/d6e87afe-dd6a-11e6-9d7c-be108f1c1dce.
31. http://www.oxfordpresents.com/ms/kelleher/edward-bernayss-torches-of-freedom.
32. J. Lloyd and L. Toogood, *Journalism and PR*, I. B. Tauris for the Reuters Institute, 2015, pp. 25–6. The passage on PR and political communication is adapted from this research.
33. Ibid., p. 22.
34. http://www.webershandwick.com/news/article/mediaco-drives-brand-publishing-interest.
35. http://www.prweek.com/article/1390297/weber-forms-innovation-council-bolster-mediaco.
36. https://www.theguardian.com/business/2016/apr/18/sir-martin-sorrell-pay-package-agm.
37. J. Lloyd and L. Toogood, op. cit., p. 35.
38. http://www.holmesreport.com/long-reads/article/2016-trend-forecast-corporate-reputation.
39. http://www.newyorker.com/magazine/2012/09/24/the-lie-factory.
40. http://www.washingtonpost.com/wp-srv/style/longterm/books/reviews/badboy.htm.
41. http://observer.com/2006/05/joe-kleins-turnip-day.
42. http://articles.latimes.com/2006/jul/13/local/me-cap13.
43. https://www.youtube.com/watch?v=UnW3xkHxIEQ.
44. http://www.salon.com/2016/02/15/bernies_man_behind_the_scenes_tad_devine_is_the_karl_rove_to_sanders_2016_populist_uprising.
45. https://www.nytimes.com/2014/03/11/us/politics/obamas-new-approach-takes-a-humorous-turn.html?_r=0.
46. http://www.slate.com/articles/news_and_politics/politics/2016/07/how_bernie_spent_his_millions_was_anything_but_revolutionary.html.

47. http://www.cosmopolitan.com/politics/news/a56404/who-is-hope-hicks-trump-press-secretary.
48. http://www.salon.com/2016/11/14/steve-bannon-runs-an-anti-semitic-website-is-a-misogynist-and-will-be-one-of-donald-trumps-senior-advisors.
49. http://www.hollywoodreporter.com/news/steve-bannon-trump-tower-interview-trumps-strategist-plots-new-political-movement-948747.
50. https://www.nytimes.com/video/us/politics/100000004886212/watch-live-trump-at-the-cia.html.
51. http://uk.businessinsider.com/jeremy-corbyn-relationship-with-the-media-2016-9.
52. http://www.newyorker.com/magazine/2016/02/22/did-social-media-produce-the-new-populism.

Part III

INTRODUCTION

1. B. Kovach and T. Rosenstiel, op. cit., p. 5.

CHAPTER ELEVEN

1. J. Ettema and T. Glasser, *Custodians of Conscience*, Columbia University Press, 1998.
2. http://www.independent.co.uk/news/people/news/french-actress-julie-gayet-wins-damages-from-closer-magazine-over-francois-hollande-affair-9219402.html.
3. https://www.whitehouse.gov/the-press-office/2016/03/28/remarks-president-2016-toner-prize-ceremony.
4. https://www.opendemocracy.net/ourbeeb/david-elstein/bbc-and-tories-is-it-war.
5. https://www.ft.com/content/2e21620c-7e2d-11e5-a1fe-567b37f80b64.
6. http://www.prospectmagazine.co.uk/opinions/selfhatredatthebbc.
7. http://biasedbbc.proboards.com/thread/1301.
8. https://www.google.co.uk/#q=Mance+FT+In+the+US++PBS+lost+the+best+rights+to+Sesame+Street+&*.
9. http://www.theglobeandmail.com/sports/hockey/hockey-night-in-canada-how-cbc-lost-it-all/article21072643/?page=all.
10. http://www.macleans.ca/news/canada/jian-ghomeshi-how-he-got-away-with-it/.
11. http://www.bbc.co.uk/bbctrust/dame_janet_smith.
12. http://www.dailymail.co.uk/news/article-3213746/Jeremy-Clarkson-receive-10m-new-Amazon-Former-Gear-host-tipped-receive-800-000-episode-stars-won-t-bad-either.html.
13. http://business.financialpost.com/fp-comment/cbc-not-the-publics-broadcaster-after-all.
14. https://next.ft.com/content/4625b188-e818-11e4-9960-00144feab7de.
15. http://www.theguardian.com/media/greenslade/2015/jun/22/press-freedom-under-threat-in-spain-says-ipi-delegate.
16. http://catalog.hathitrust.org/Record/006518564.

17. http://documents.irevues.inist.fr/bitstream/handle/2042/28328/2008_HS_161.pdf?sequence=1.

18. G. Muhlmann, *Journalism for Democracy*, Polity, 2010, p. 210.

19. http://www.challenges.fr/entreprise/20060613.CHA1211/3-questions-a-bernard-lallement-co-fondateur-de-liberation-libe-a-toujours-deteste-l-argent.html.

20. http://bruxelles.blogs.liberation.fr.

21. http://www.forbes.com/profile/patrick-drahi/.

22. J. Lloyd, *What the Media are Doing to our Politics*, Constable, 2004, pp. 39–40.

23. A. Jones, *Losing the News*, Oxford University Press, 2011, p. 49. This section is based on part of my book, *Journalism in an Age of Terror*, I. B. Tauris, 2017.

24. http://www.huffingtonpost.com/2013/11/20/bob-woodward-edward-snowden-guardian_n_4311354.html.

25. http://www.politico.com/story/2013/07/carl-bernstein-edward-snowden-comments-093697.

26. D. Ellsberg, 'NSA Leaker Snowden Made the Right call', *Washington Post*, 7 July 2013.

27. J. Assange, J. Appelbaum, A. Müller-Maguhn and J. Zimmermann, *Cypherpunks: Freedom and the Future of the Internet*, OR Books, 2013, Kindle Edition, loc. 1881.

28. A. O'Hagan, 'Ghosting', http://www.lrb.co.uk/v36/n05/andrew-ohagan/ghosting.

29. http://www.theguardian.com/world/2013/mar/01/bradley-manning-wikileaks-statement-full-text.

30. L. Harding, *The Snowden Files*, Guardian Faber Publishing, 2014, Kindle Edition, loc. 1295.

31. S. Turkle, *Life on the Screen: Identity in the Age of the Internet*, Weidenfeld and Nicholson, 1996, p. 263.

32. G. Greenwald, *No Place to Hide*, Penguin, 2015, Kindle Edition, loc. 1605.

33. *Washington Post*, 5 July 2014.

34. http://www.independent.co.uk/voices/comment/edward-snowden-s-secrets-may-be-dangerous-i-would-not-have-published-them-8877404.html.

35. http://www.theguardian.com/commentisfree/2013/oct/14/independent-epitaph-establishment-journalism.

36. G. Greenwald, op. cit., loc. 3319.

37. http://www.nytimes.com/2013/10/28/opinion/a-conversation-in-lieu-of-a-column.html.

38. A. O'Hagan, op. cit.

39. http://www.nytimes.com/2006/07/01/opinion/01keller.html?_r=0.

40. http://pressthink.org/2013/10/why-pierre-omidyar-decided-to-join-forces-with-glenn-greenwald-for-a-new-venture-in-news.

41. https://theintercept.com/2015/05/12/stephen-kim-ex-state-department-official-leak-case-released-prison.

CONCLUSION

1. M. McLuhan, *Understanding Media: The Extension of Man*, MIT Press Edition, 1994.

2. http://towcenter.org/research/post-industrial-journalism-adapting-to-the-present-2.

3. http://archive.pressthink.org/2006/06/27/ppl_frmr.html.
4. http://talkingpointsmemo.com.
5. http://www.theguardian.com/world/2016/feb/19/xi-jinping-tours-chinas-top-state-media-outlets-to-boost-loyalty.
6. http://saharareporters.com.

Bibliography

Theodore Adorno, *The Culture Industry*, Routledge, London, 2002

Fouad Ajami, *The Arab Predicament*, Cambridge UP, Cambridge, 1992

Anonymous, *The Diaries of a Fleet Street Fox*, Constable, London, 2013

Timothy Garton Ash, *Free Speech*, Yale UP, New Haven, 2016

Ken Auletta, *Backstory*, Penguin Press, New York, 2003

Honoré de Balzac, *Les Journalistes*, Arléa, Paris, 1998

Yochai Benkler, *The Wealth of Networks*, Yale UP, New Haven, 2005

Luca De Biase, *Cambiare Pagine*, RCS Libri, Milano, 2011

Philip Bobbitt, *The Shield of Achilles*, Allen Lane, London, 2002

Giorgio Boccaccio, *È la stampa, bellezza!*, Feltrinelli, Milano, 2011

Heinrich Böll, trans. Leila Vennewitz, *The Lost Honour of Katherina Blum*, Minerva, London, 1975

Daniel Boorstin, *The Image*, Pelican Books, London, 1963

Pierre Bourdieu, *Contre-feux*, Liber-Raisons d'Agir, Paris, 1998

Pierre Bourdieu, *Sur la télévision*, Raisons d'Agir, Paris, 1996

Kathleen Brady and Ida Tarbell, *Portrait of a Muckraker*, University of Pittsburgh Press, Pittsburgh, 1989

Leo Braudy, *The Frenzy of Renown*, Vintage, New York, 1997

Peter Burden, *News of the World?*, Eye Books, London, 2008

Hugo de Burgh, *The Chinese Journalist*, Routledge Curzon, London, 2003

Julia Cagé, *Sauver les médias*, Editions du Seuill, 2015

Manuel Castells, *Communication Power*, Oxford UP, Oxford, 2009

Shubranshu Choudhary, *Let's Call Him Vasu*, Penguin Books India, New Delhi, 2012

Nick Cohen, *You Can't Read This Book*, Fourth Estate, London, 2012

Michele Corradino, *È normale ... lo fanno tutti*, Chiarelettere, Milano, 2016

James Curran and Jean Seaton, *Power Without Responsibility*, Routledge, London, 2010

Sunday Daré, *Guerrilla Journalism*, Kraft, Ibadan, Nigeria, 2007

Nick Davies, *Flat Earth News*, Chatto and Windus, London, 2008

Brendan Dooley, *The Social History of Skepticism*, Johns Hopkins UP, Baltimore, 1999

Umberto Eco, *Turning the Clock Back*, Harvill Secker, London, 2007

Ruth Dudley Edwards, *Newspapermen*, Pimlico, London, 2004

Matthew Engel, *Tickle the Public*, Gollancz, London, 1996

James S. Ettema and Theodore L. Glaser, *Custodians of Conscience*, Columbia UP, New York, 1998

James Fallows, *Breaking the News*, Vintage, New York, 1997

Lara Fielden, *Regulating the Press*, Reuters Institute, Oxford, 2012

James S. Fishkin, *The Voice of the People*, Yale UP, New Haven, 1995

Jean-François Fogel and Bruno Patino, *Une presse sans Gutenberg*, Grasset, Paris, 2005

Chrystia Freeland, *Plutocrats*, Penguin Press, New York, 2012

Neil Gabler, *Life: The Movie*, Knopf, New York, 1998

Tim Gardam and David A. L. Levy, *The Price of Plurality*, Reuters Institute, Oxford, 2008.

Paul Ginsborg, *Silvio Berlusconi: Television, Power, Patrimony*, Verso, London, 2005

Anthony Glees and Philip H. J. Davies, *Spinning the Spies*, Social Affairs Unit, London, 2004

Misha Glenny, *McMafia*, Bodley Head, London, 2008

Stephen Glover, *The Penguin Book of Journalism*, Penguin Books, London, 1999

Giovanni Gozzini, *Storia del giornalismo*, Mondadori, Milano, 2011

Roy Greenslade, *Press Gang*, Macmillan, London, 2003

David Halberstam, *The Powers that Be*, University of Illinois Press, Urbana, 2000

Daniel C. Hallin and Paolo Mancini, *Comparing Media Systems*, Cambridge UP, Cambridge, 2004

James Hardin, *Alpha Dogs*, Atlantic Books, London, 2008

Ian Hargreaves, *Journalism: Truth or Dare?*, Oxford UP, Oxford, 2003

James Harkin, *Niche*, Abacus, London, 2012

Abdallah F. Hassan, *Media, Revolution and Politics in Egypt*, I. B. Tauris for Reuters Institute, London, 2015

Václav Havel, *Living in Truth*, Faber and Faber, London, 1986

Edward S. Herman and Robert W. McChesney, *The Global Media*, Cassell, London, 1999

Anabel Hernández, *Narcoland*, Verso, London, 2013

Richard Hoggart, *The Uses of Literacy*, Penguin Books, London, 1958

Richard Hoggart, *Mass Media in a Mass Society*, Continuum, London, 2004

Robin Jeffrey, *India's Newspaper Revolution*, Hurst, London, 2000

Alex S. Jones, *Losing the News*, Oxford UP, New York, 2009

Jeffrey P. Jones, *Entertaining Politics*, Rowman and Littlefield, Plymouth, 2010

John Keane, *The Media and Democracy*, Polity, Cambridge, 1991

Richard Keeble and John Mair (eds.), *The Phone Hacking Scandal*, Abramis, Bury St Edmunds, 2012

Joe Klein, *Politics Lost*, Broadway Books, New York, 2006

Venita Kohli Khandekar, *The Indian Media Business*, fourth edition, Sage, New Delhi, 2013

Bill Kovach and Tom Rosenstiel, *Elements of Journalism*, Three Rivers Press, New York, 2007

David Lane, *Berlusconi's Shadow*, Allen Lane, London, 2004

Walter Lippmann, *Liberty and the News*, Dover Publications, New York, 2010

Walter Lippmann, *Public Opinion*, Free Press, New York, 1997

John Lloyd, *What the Media are Doing to our Politics*, Constable, London, 2004

John Lloyd and Janice Winter (eds.), *Media Politics and the Public*, Ax:son Johnson Foundation, Stockholm, 2011

Joe McGinniss, *The Selling of the President*, André Deutsch, London, 1970

Joe McGinniss, *Fatal Vision*, Signet, New York, 1989

Marshall McLuhan, *Understanding Media*, Routledge, London, 2002

Janet Malcolm, *The Journalist and the Murderer*, Vintage, New York, 1990

Andrew Marr, *My Trade*, Macmillan, London, 2004

S. J. Masty, *The Muslim and the Microphone*, Social Affairs Unit, London, 2006

Noha Mellor, *Modern Arab Journalism*, American University, Cairo, 2007

Noha Mellor, *The Making of Arab News*, Rowman and Littlefield, Oxford, 2006

Louis Menand, *The Metaphysical Club*, Flamingo, London, 2001

Hugh Miles, *Al-Jazeera*, Abacus, London, 2006

Piers Morgan, *The Insider*, Ebury Press, London, 2005

Evgeny Morozov, *How Not to Liberate the World*, Allen Lane, London, 2011

David E. Morrison et al., *Media and Values*, Intellect, Bristol, 2007

Géraldine Muhlmann, trans. Jean Birrell, *Journalism for Democracy*, Polity, Cambridge, 2010

Géraldine Muhlmann, trans. Jean Birrell, *A Political History of Journalism*, Polity, Cambridge, 2008

Andrew Neil, *Full Disclosure*, Pan, London, 2006

Pippa Norris, *Public Sentinel*, The World Bank, Washington, 2010

Daniel Ockrent, *Public Editor*, Public Affairs, New York, 2006

Arkady Ostrovsky, *The Invention of Russia*, Atlantic Books, London, 2016

Vance Packard, *The Hidden Persuaders*, IG Publishing, New York, 2007

Bruce Page, *The Murdoch Archipelago*, Simon and Schuster, London, 2011

Philip Pan, *Out of Mao's Shadow*, Picador, London, 2008

Thomas E. Patterson, *Out of Order*, Vintage, New York, 1994

Yoram Peri, *Telepopulism*, Stanford UP, Redwood City, 2004

Lance Price, *Where Power Lies*, Simon and Schuster, London, 2010

Ben Rawlence, *Radio Congo*, Oneworld, London, 2013

Max Rodenbeck, *Cairo: the City Victorious*, Vintage, London, 2000

Nick Robinson, *Live from Downing Street*, Bantam Press, London, 2012

W. G. Runciman (ed.), *Hutton and Butler*, Oxford UP for the British Academy, Oxford, 2004

Giovanni Sartori, *Il Sultano*, Laterza, Roma, 2009

Donald Sassoon, *The Culture of the Europeans*, Harper Press, London, 2006

Jeffrey Scheuer, *The Big Picture*, Routledge, Oxford, 2008

Michael Schudson, *The Power of News*, Harvard UP, Cambridge, Mass., 1995

Michael Schudson, *Why Democracies Need an Unlovable Press*, Polity, Cambridge, 2008

Colin Seymour, *The Political Impact of Mass Media*, Sage, 1974

Ari Shavit, *My Promised Land*, Scribe, London, 2014

William Shawcross, *Murdoch*, Pan, London, 1993

Clay Shirky, *Here Comes Everybody*, Penguin, London, 2008

Daphne Skillen, *Freedom of Speech in Russia*, Routledge, London, 2017

Anthony Smith, *The Shadow in the Cave*, Allen and Unwin, London, 1973

Paul Starr, *The Creation of the Media*, Basic Books, New York, 2004

Sylvester Stein, *Who Killed Mr Drum?*, Corvo, London, 2003

Alexander Stille, *The Sack of Rome*, Penguin Press, New York, 2006

Paranjoy Guha Thakurta, *Media Ethics*, OUP, Oxford, 2012

John B. Thompson, *The Media and Modernity*, Polity, Cambridge, 1995

Mark Thompson, *Enough Said*, Bodley Head, London, 2016

Daya Thussu, *News as Entertainment*, Sage, London, 2009

Larry Tye, *The Father of Spin*, Holt, New York, 1998

A. Volkov et al. (eds.), *Pressa v Obshchestve*, Moscow School of Political Studies, Moscow, 2000

Stephen J. A. Ward, *The Invention of Journalism Ethics*, McGill-Queens UP, Montreal, 2004

David Welch, *Propaganda, Power and Persuasion*, The British Library, London, 2013

Drew Westen, *The Political Brain*, Public Affairs, New York, 2007

Arnold Wesker, *Journey into Journalism*, Writers and Readers Publishing Cooperative, London, 1977

Bernard Williams, *Truth and Truthfulness*, Princeton UP, Princeton, 2002

Michael J. Wolf, *The Entertainment Economy*, Penguin, London, 1999

Tom Wolfe, *The New Journalism*, Picador, London, 1990

Lawrence Wright, *The Looming Tower*, Penguin, London, 2006

Tim Wu, *The Master Switch*, Atlantic, New York, 2010

Index